PRAISE FOR

THE COUNTERFEIT COUNTESS

"The remarkable story of Janina Mehlberg almost didn't see the light of day. . . . The publication of *The Counterfeit Countess* is the result of the painstaking work of historical researchers and archivists who know the value of unearthing a narrative like this one, otherwise in danger of being forgotten. The result is a genuine contribution to scholarship that is also a memorable, inspiring tale of individual heroism."

—*The Wall Street Journal*

"A story of courage, compassion, and cunning so profound that it must be included with the greatest Holocaust literature. Janina Mehlberg is a heroine for the ages."

—Larry Loftis, *New York Times* bestselling author of *The Watchmaker's Daughter*

"Holocaust historians White and Sliwa masterfully piece together the previously untold story of a Jewish mathematician who, during the Nazi occupation of Poland, masqueraded as a countess while she helped free and feed thousands of Poles imprisoned at the Majdanek concentration camp."

—*Library Journal* (starred review)

"*The Counterfeit Countess* is a gripping tale of one woman's grit and courage in the face of unimaginable terror. That it is only available today, more than fifty years after Henry Mehlberg first attempted to get it published, is a reminder of how many Holocaust stories remain untold."

—Jewish Book Council

"The book is part adventure-war story, part inspirational tale of right winning over might, all of it thoroughly researched. It is all the more effective for being true and being told with vibrant energy so that Janina almost steps off the page."

—*New York Journal of Books*

"Powerful. . . . A heart-wrenching profile of resilience, ingenuity, and heroism."

—*Publishers Weekly*

"A fine delineation of personal heroism amid an era of utter human depravity."

—*Kirkus Reviews*

"This extensively documented account serves as powerful testimony."

—*Booklist*

"*The Counterfeit Countess* is an extraordinary testament to courage, resilience and humanity during the darkest months of the Holocaust. Beautifully crafted and meticulously researched by two of America's powerhouse World War II historians, this riveting story will ensure that the world never forgets the utterly remarkable Josephine Janina Mehlberg and an epic rescue mission that defied great evil. You will not put this book down until the very last word—it is a stunning piece of Holocaust history that will stick with you long after you're done."

—Debbie Cenziper, Pulitzer Prize–winning journalist and author of *Citizen 865: The Hunt for Hitler's Hidden Soldiers in America*

"A stunning masterpiece of a book about a previously overlooked hero of the war and the Holocaust. Never betraying any fear, 'Countess Suchodolska' performed seemingly impossible miracles again and again, routinely risking her life to save thousands of Polish prisoners in the Majdanek concentration camp. Elizabeth B. White and Joanna Sliwa have performed their own miracle by meticulously reconstructing her story and giving her the long-overdue recognition she so fully deserves."

—Andrew Nagorski, author of *Saving Freud: The Rescuers Who Brought Him to Freedom*

"Part biography, part adventure tale, *The Counterfeit Countess* is the astonishing history of 'Countess Janina Suchodolska,' a heroic Polish Jewish woman who rescued thousands of Catholic Poles during the Holocaust. Historians Elizabeth White and Joanna Sliwa turned sleuths as they painstakingly pieced together the story of her wartime activities from shards of information scattered across archives in Europe and North America. A riveting account of moral courage and an enduring commitment to save lives."

—Debórah Dwork, director, Center for the Study of the Holocaust, Genocide, and Crimes Against Humanity, The Graduate Center—City University of New York

"A truly extraordinary story, and all the more so for having nearly been lost to history."

—*The Jewish Chronicle*

"Profound and insightful, Mehlberg's life story makes for necessary reading."

—*Choice*

ALSO BY ELIZABETH B. WHITE

German Influence in the Argentine Army, 1900 to 1945

ALSO BY JOANNA SLIWA

Jewish Childhood in Kraków: A Microhistory of the Holocaust

THE COUNTERFEIT COUNTESS

The Jewish Woman Who Rescued Thousands of Poles During the Holocaust

ELIZABETH B. WHITE
AND JOANNA SLIWA

SIMON & SCHUSTER PAPERBACKS

New York Amsterdam/Antwerp London Toronto Sydney New Delhi

Simon & Schuster Paperbacks
An Imprint of Simon & Schuster, LLC
1230 Avenue of the Americas
New York, NY 10020

First Simon & Schuster trade paperback edition January 2025

SIMON & SCHUSTER PAPERBACKS and colophon are registered trademarks of Simon & Schuster, LLC

For information about special discounts for bulk purchases, please contact Simon & Schuster Special Sales at 1-866-506-1949 or business@simonandschuster.com.

The Simon & Schuster Speakers Bureau can bring authors to your live event. For more information or to book an event, contact the Simon & Schuster Speakers Bureau at 1-866-248-3049 or visit our website at www.simonspeakers.com.

Interior design by Ruth Lee-Mui
Maps by Paul J. Pugliese

Manufactured in the United States of America

1 3 5 7 9 10 8 6 4 2

Library of Congress Cataloging-in-Publication Data is available.

ISBN 978-1-9821-8912-9
ISBN 978-1-9821-8913-6 (pbk)
ISBN 978-1-9821-8914-3 (ebook)

CONTENTS

USAGE NOTES

Place Names

The names of the places where Janina lived in Eastern Galicia (today's Western Ukraine) changed in the course of the twentieth century, sometimes more than once. Just between 1939 and 1941, the name of today's Lviv changed from Lwów to Lvov to Lemberg. This book uses the place names that Janina knew and used. For places that have different names today, the current name is provided in parentheses the first time the place is mentioned.

Usage of "Poles"

Prewar Poland was a multiethnic state. The majority consisted of ethnic Poles who were Polish-speaking, predominantly Roman Catholic, and did not belong to another ethnic group. Like Janina, many members of Poland's ethnic minorities considered themselves loyal Poles, and during World War II many would risk and even sacrifice their lives for their nation. Polish citizens generally identified themselves and one another by their ethnicity. In this book, when the term "Pole" is not modified, it refers to a person of Polish ethnicity.

Baltic Sea
U.S.S.R.
GERMANY
GERMANY
U.S.S.R.
Treblinka
Warsaw
Sobibor
Radom
Lublin
Majdanek
GENERAL
GOVERNMENT
Zamość
VOLHYNIA
GERMANY
Bełżec
Auschwitz-
Birkenau
Kraków
Dębica
Lwów
Przemyśl
Żurawno
U.S.S.R.
PROTECTORATE
OF
BOHEMIA AND
MORAVIA
GALICIA
(added in August 1941)
SLOVAKIA
KINGDOM OF
HUNGARY
ROMANIA
Poland, During World War II
Borders of Poland on September 1, 1939
Line of Partition of Poland Between Germany and U.S.S.R. before June 22, 1941
0
100 miles
0
100 kilometers

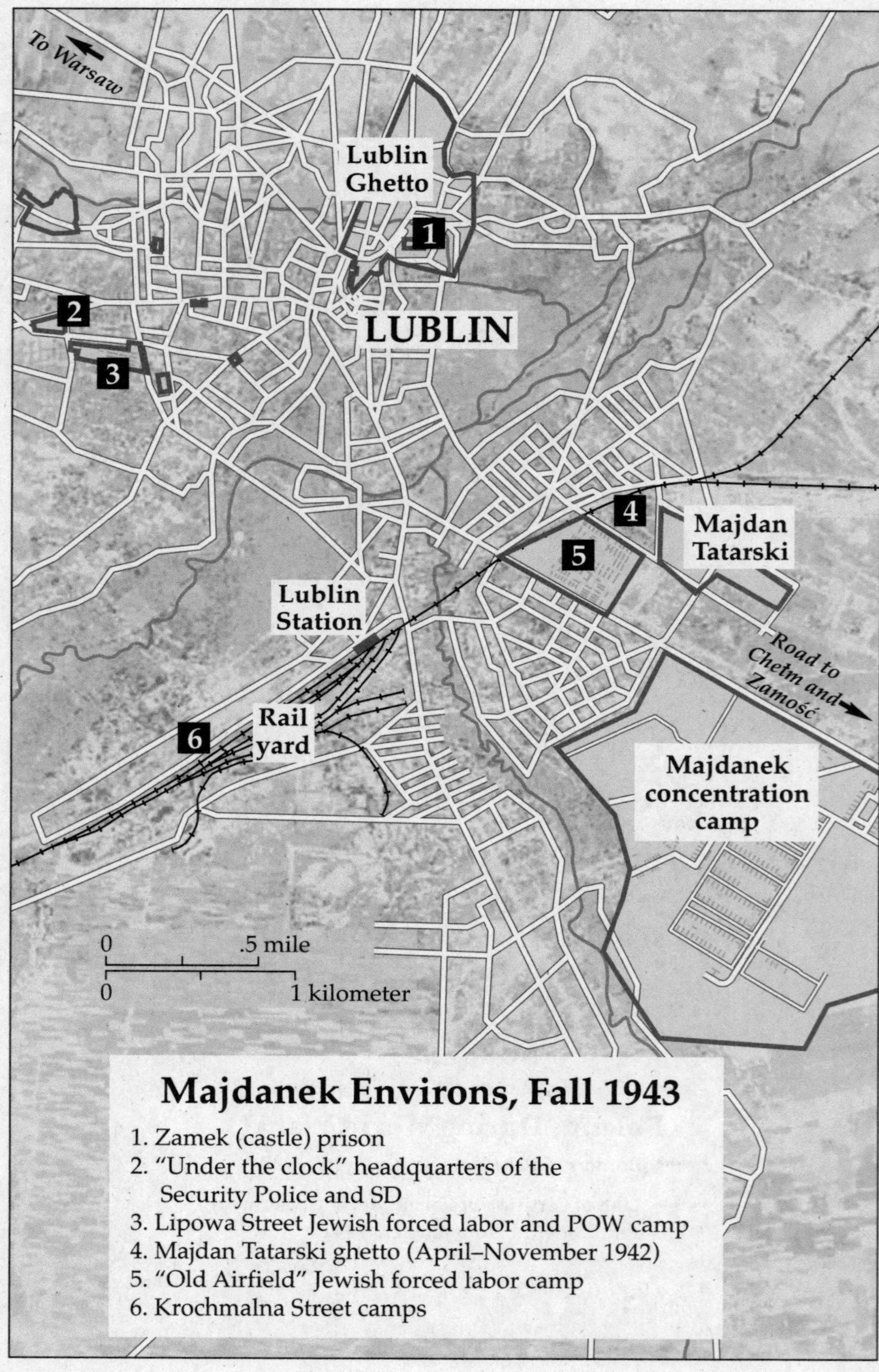

Majdanek Environs, Fall 1943

1. Zamek (castle) prison
2. "Under the clock" headquarters of the Security Police and SD
3. Lipowa Street Jewish forced labor and POW camp
4. Majdan Tatarski ghetto (April–November 1942)
5. "Old Airfield" Jewish forced labor camp
6. Krochmalna Street camps

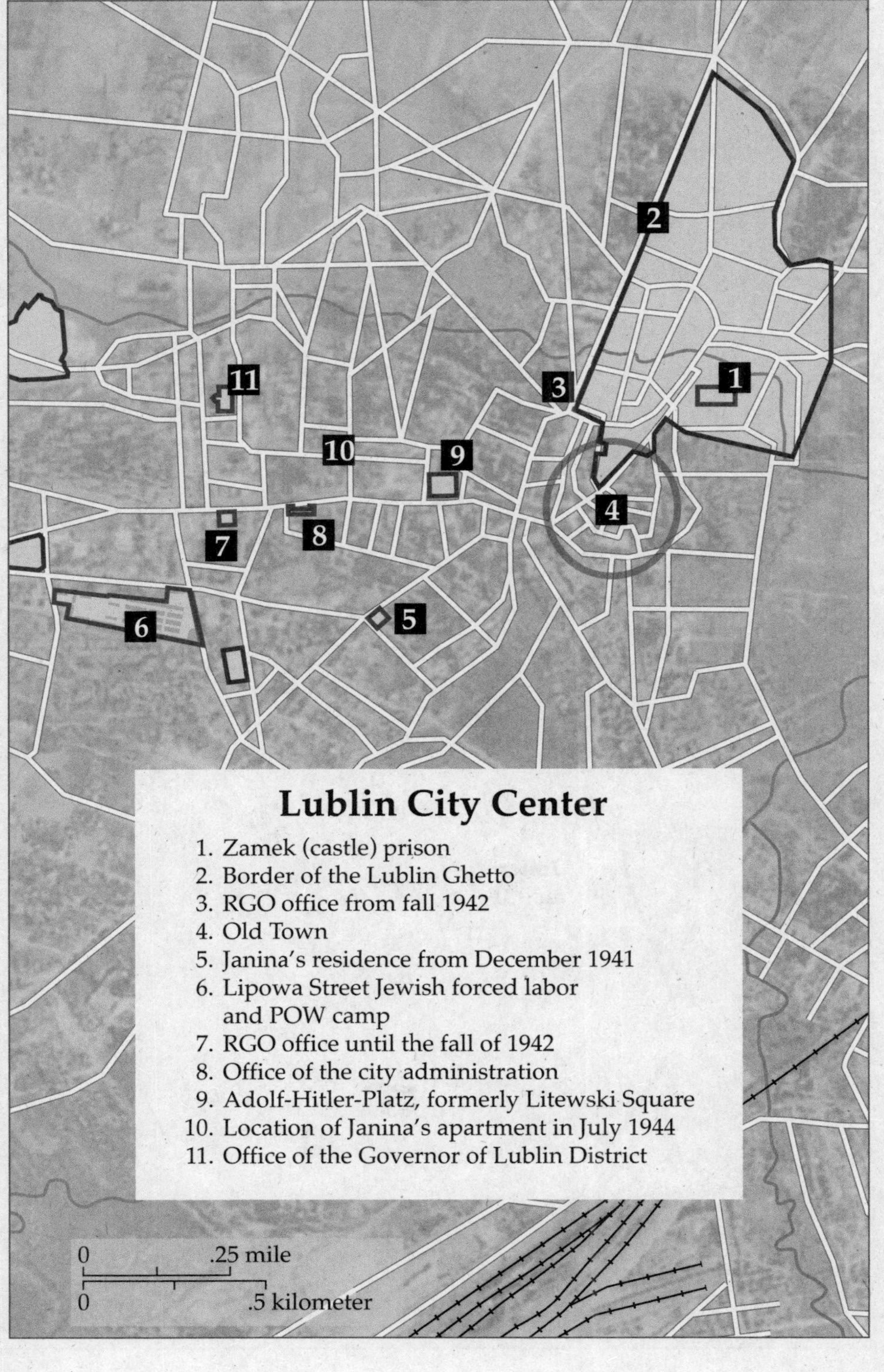
2
1
3
11
10
9
4
7
8
6
5
Lublin City Center
1. Zamek (castle) prison
2. Border of the Lublin Ghetto
3. RGO office from fall 1942
4. Old Town
5. Janina's residence from December 1941
6. Lipowa Street Jewish forced labor and POW camp
7. RGO office until the fall of 1942
8. Office of the city administration
9. Adolf-Hitler-Platz, formerly Litewski Square
10. Location of Janina's apartment in July 1944
11. Office of the Governor of Lublin District
0
.25 mile
0
.5 kilometer

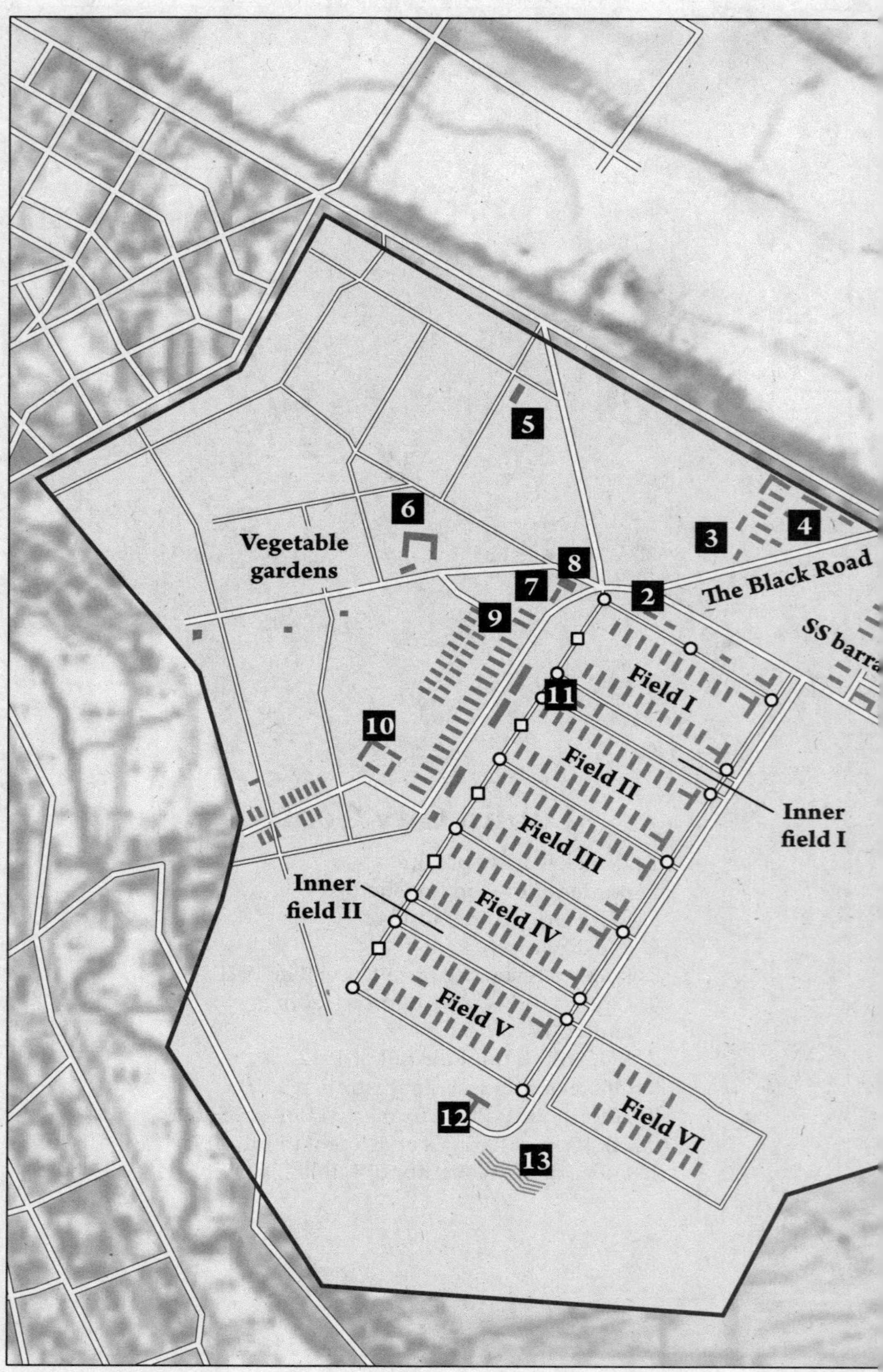
5
6
Vegetable gardens
8
7
9
2
3
4
The Black Road
SS barra
Field I
11
10
Field II
Inner field I
Field III
Inner field II
Field IV
Field V
12
13
Field VI

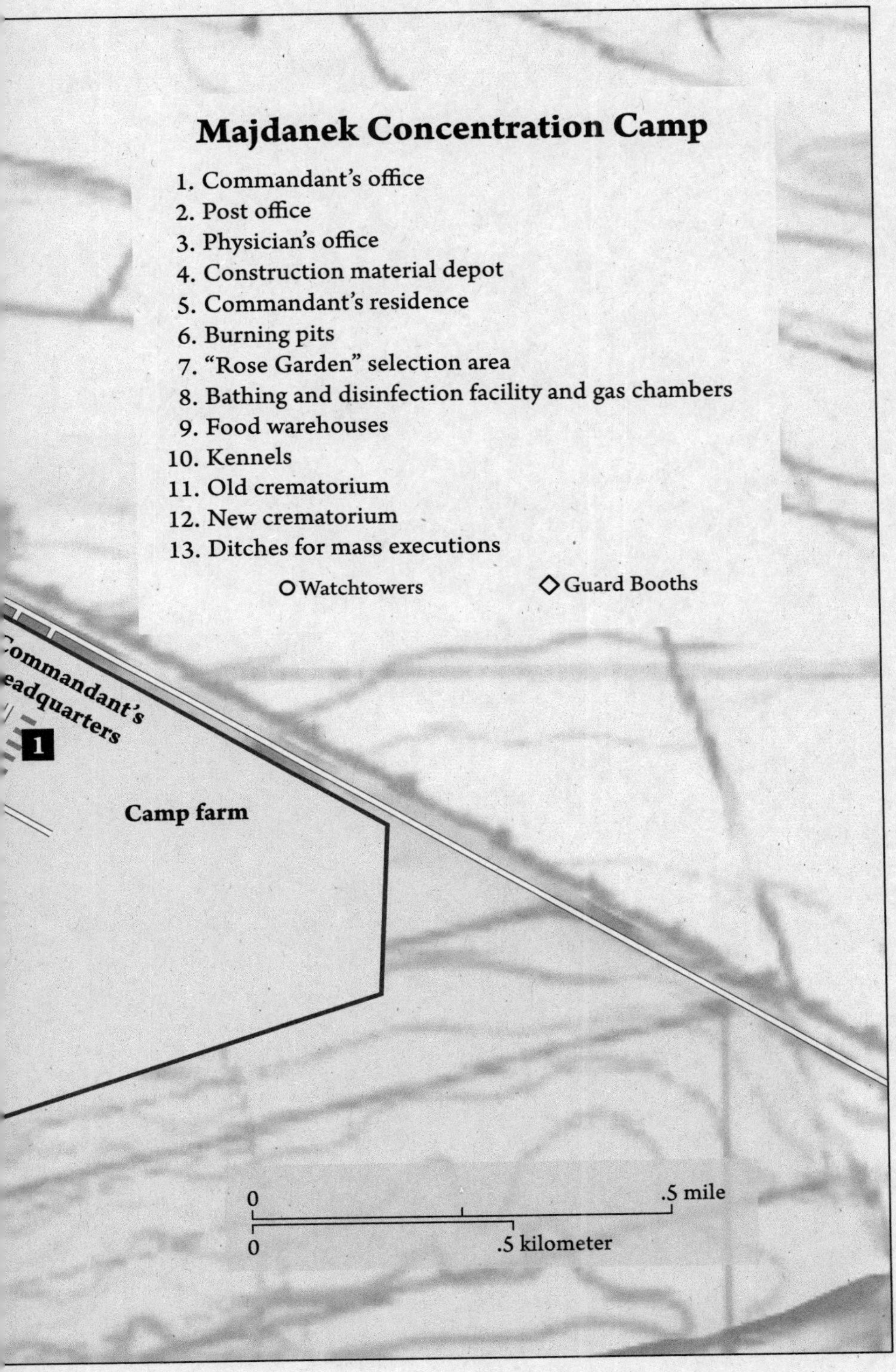

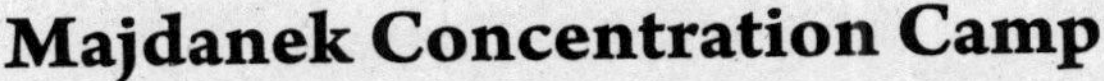

Majdanek Concentration Camp
1. Commandant's office
2. Post office
3. Physician's office
4. Construction material depot
5. Commandant's residence
6. Burning pits
7. "Rose Garden" selection area
8. Bathing and disinfection facility and gas chambers
9. Food warehouses
10. Kennels
11. Old crematorium
12. New crematorium
13. Ditches for mass executions
Watchtowers
Guard Booths
Commandant's
Headquarters
1
Camp farm
0
.5 mile
0
.5 kilometer

PROLOGUE

August 9, 1943
Lublin, Poland

Once again, the commandant of Majdanek concentration camp found Countess Suchodolska in his office, making yet another absurd demand.

SS-*Obersturmbannführer* Hermann Florstedt had served at several concentration camps in Germany, but Majdanek, he had found, bore little resemblance to them. Located in Lublin in German-occupied Poland, the camp was primitive and chaotic compared to the concentration camps in the Reich. Florstedt's assignment as the camp's commandant in 1942 had been a promotion, but also punishment for suspected corruption at Buchenwald. He had arrived at Majdanek to find a massive construction site with unpaved roads, no running water, contaminated wells, and open latrines that gave off an overpowering stench. Towering billows of smoke regularly belched from the camp's crematorium chimney, raining down the ashes of men, women, and children murdered in the gas chambers. Currently 23,000 prisoners were languishing in unimaginable filth. Infectious diseases were so rampant that even the SS guards sickened and died.

Majdanek did have one compensation in Florstedt's view: it was the repository of the personal belongings of many of the hundreds of thousands of Jews being murdered by the SS in German-occupied central Poland. SS warehouses in Lublin held mountains of clothes, shoes, furs, and leather goods, and boxes full of currency, jewelry, watches, wedding bands, and gold teeth. It was Florstedt's responsibility to ensure that Majdanek prisoners processed these goods so that the SS could fully profit from them. But who would notice if Florstedt and his most trusted men took some of the riches as recompense for their service in plundering and murdering Germany's racial enemies?

One of the vexations of Florstedt's work, however, was the meddling of Polish aid organizations that sought to provide food and medicines for Majdanek's Polish prisoners. The Polish Main Welfare Council and the Polish Red Cross were far more assertive than any similar organizations in the Reich. They had actually obtained permission to make weekly deliveries of bread and food products for the prisoners' kitchens, to supply the prisoners with packages of food and necessities, and to provide medicines for the camp infirmaries. And yet Countess Janina Suchodolska of the Polish Main Welfare Council continually pressed for more: to make more frequent deliveries of more food and more medicines. She even proposed delivering prepared soup for the prisoners. Such things would be out of the question in any other concentration camp. But when told no, the Countess simply made the rounds of higher SS and Nazi authorities until she finally persuaded one that her requests were somehow in German interests.

To make matters worse, the Countess used her visits to Majdanek to spy on the conditions there. Efforts to deter her had proved fruitless. The petite brunette aristocrat remained utterly unflappable in the face of shouts and threats from the SS. Recently, she had even alerted health officials to a typhus epidemic among the prisoners, forcing Florstedt to arrange some semblance of treatment for them.

Now she was pestering Florstedt about the thousands of Polish peasants in the camp. The SS had dumped them there in July after evicting them from their farms to make room for German settlers. Since the SS quickly culled the able-bodied adults for forced labor in the Reich, the peasants still in the camp were mostly children or elderly. After just a few weeks in the camp, these prisoners were already dying of dehydration, starvation, and diseases at a rate that was extreme even for Majdanek. Somehow, the Countess had persuaded German authorities to release the 3,600 Polish peasants still on

Majdanek's rolls, but only on condition that her organization provided all the necessary paperwork and found places for them to live. In just a couple of days, Countess Suchodolska and her coworkers managed to do both.

The Countess had arrived at the camp gate in the morning to receive the civilians. There she was informed, with no further explanation, that nearly half of them were no longer "available" for release. The remaining civilians had been assembled in the third of Majdanek's five prisoner compounds, about a kilometer from the gate where the Countess awaited them. The distance had proved too far for many to walk: the Countess had watched with increasing alarm as prisoners, trying in vain to hold each other up, stumbled, fell, and lay helpless in the dust. And so here she was in Florstedt's office, insisting that he allow trucks and ambulances to enter the camp and pick up the prisoners. Allowing Polish civilian transport inside a concentration camp was in complete violation of SS security regulations! But Florstedt knew there was no point in refusing—the Countess would just go over his head.

Within two hours, trucks, buses, and ambulances arrived, recruited by the Countess from businesses and organizations throughout the city.

In the end, 2,106 peasants were released from Majdanek in August 1943. More than 25 percent of them wound up in Lublin's two main hospitals, and nearly 200 died within days, over half of them children under age twelve. But some 1,900 survived, thanks to the efforts of Countess Suchodolska and her many colleagues.

Her efforts to help the prisoners of Majdanek did not end there. The Countess relentlessly pressed Nazi authorities for more concessions, and gradually they agreed to permit increased deliveries of food, medicines, and supplies. They even allowed her to bring in decorated Christmas trees so that the prisoners could celebrate the holiday. By February 1944, the Polish Main Welfare Council was supplying soup and bread five times a week for 4,000 Polish prisoners in Majdanek, in addition to other deliveries of food and medicine. The Countess herself usually brought the soup into the camp, under the close supervision of SS guards.

Throughout all her dealings with Nazi and SS officials, no one ever suspected that the indomitable Countess, so self-assured and aristocratic in her demeanor, was not a countess at all, nor was her name really Suchodolska. She was Janina Spinner Mehlberg, a brilliant mathematician, an officer in the underground Polish Home Army, and a Jew.

INTRODUCTION

In December 1989, historian Elizabeth "Barry" White received an unexpected package from a stranger. It contained a carbon copy on onionskin paper of an untitled, typewritten manuscript. The donor of the package, American History professor Arthur Funk of the University of Florida, explained that the manuscript was the memoir of Janina Mehlberg, a Polish Jew who survived the Holocaust by posing as the gentile Countess Janina Suchodolska in the city of Lublin. The memoir recounted how she had persuaded the SS to allow her to deliver food for thousands of prisoners in Majdanek (My-DAH-neck) concentration camp and how she used those deliveries to smuggle messages and supplies to resistance fighters imprisoned there.

Funk told Barry that, after the war, Janina (Yah-NEE-nah) Mehlberg immigrated to the United States. She died in 1969 in Chicago, where she was a professor of mathematics at Illinois Institute of Technology. After her death, her husband, the philosopher Henry Mehlberg, tried unsuccessfully to get her memoir published. Shortly before his death in 1979, he entrusted the memoir to Funk in the hope that the historian could publish it. Funk tried, but had been unable to interest any publisher in the memoir. He gave the manuscript copy to Barry because she had just delivered a paper on Majdanek at the American Historical Association convention, and so he hoped that she would find a way to make Janina Mehlberg's story known.

There was a Countess Janina Suchodolska in German-occupied Lublin during World War II, Barry knew. Postwar studies of the camp note that, as an official of the Polish Main Welfare Council, a relief organization, she personally made regular deliveries of food for prisoners at Majdanek and, as a member of the underground Polish Home Army, had worked to organize the resistance within the camp through smuggled correspondence. Many accounts of Majdanek by former prisoners mention the Countess, the brave and kind "lady with the sad smile" who brought them food, news of the war, decorated Christmas trees and Easter eggs, and Holy Communion wafers. Prisoners recalled how she never flinched when the SS screamed threats in her face, and they marveled at her success in winning astonishing concessions from Nazi officials, which they attributed to her knowledge of the German mentality. Some former prisoners credited her with providing not only the physical sustenance but also the hope that enabled them to survive. None of the studies or accounts, however, mentions that the Countess was using an alias, much less that she was a Jew.

Knowing the special circle of hell that was Majdanek, Barry read the manuscript with increasing astonishment—and skepticism. Lublin was the headquarters of the largest mass murder operation of the Holocaust, *Aktion* Reinhard. In connection with the operation, at least 63,000 Jews were murdered in Majdanek's gas chambers and shooting pits.[1] Thousands of non-Jewish Poles were imprisoned and died there as well. Yet, according to the memoir, a petite Jewish woman negotiated with top Nazi officials in Lu-blin, met frequently with SS officials at Majdanek, befriended Majdanek's SS guards, and regularly visited the camp's prisoner compounds. She continually and successfully pressed German authorities to permit her organization to provide ever greater quantities and types of relief for Majdanek's prisoners. It seemed from her account that she never accepted "no" as a final answer and always considered "yes" an invitation to ask for more. Even more incredibly, she used the deliveries as cover to smuggle correspondence and supplies to her fellow resistance members imprisoned in the camp, including tools to aid them in escaping. In addition to her work at Majdanek, she rescued Poles seized for forced labor in Germany and children taken from their families. The Gestapo threatened her, surveilled her, and sent spies to entrap her; on more than one occasion, she narrowly escaped arrest, torture, and death.

The gripping story told in the memoir seemed to Barry almost too fantastic to be true. On the other hand, the author had unusually detailed knowledge about Majdanek, its staff, and its prisoners that someone not personally involved with the camp was unlikely to possess. If the memoir was true, then it revealed a historically significant story that deserved to be made known. But if the memoir was true, why did Janina Mehlberg not come forward after the war to reveal her identity and take credit for her accomplishments? She only wrote the memoir in the 1960s, long after she had left Poland and become well established in the United States. If the memoir was untrue, why would Janina and Henry Mehlberg go to such lengths to perpetrate a hoax? Barry decided that she could not make any use of the memoir without first corroborating that Janina Mehlberg was Countess Suchodolska.

At that time, however, Barry had no way to verify the memoir. In 1989, the Internet was not yet generally available. Researching Janina Mehlberg's life then required poring over dusty files and peering at microfilm in Polish archives. Barry was then a new mother and working for the U.S. Department of Justice on investigations and prosecutions of Nazi criminals in the United States. She lacked the time and resources to conduct research in Poland, particularly as she did not know Polish. Since Funk also planned to give copies of the memoir to several archives, including the United States Holocaust Memorial Museum (USHMM), Barry hoped that some more qualified scholar would do the work necessary to verify the memoir and bring its story to light.

Years passed, then decades, with no indication that any scholar had examined the memoir. Funk died in 2007. The thought that she might be the only historian who knew about the memoir haunted Barry. What if its claims were true? Did she have a responsibility to ensure that they were verified and made known?

In 2017, working as a historian at the USHMM, Barry embarked on an effort to verify Mehlberg's claims and discovered a 1975 book review by a former Polish resistance member named in her memoir. Praising the contributions to the resistance at Majdanek of "Janina Suchodolska-Mehlberg," he mentioned that her memoir had yet to find a publisher.[2]

While this discovery persuaded Barry that Janina Mehlberg likely was Countess Suchodolska, she concluded that further proof of the memoir's claims was needed in order to publish it. Determined to recruit a historian with the necessary qualifications to corroborate the memoir and tell Janina Mehlberg's story, she sent the manuscript to Joanna Sliwa, who is an expert on the Holocaust in Poland. After reading the memoir, Joanna offered to partner with Barry to research Janina Mehlberg's life and tell her story to the world.

Through records, interviews, photographs, and contacts in nine countries on three continents, we have not only succeeded in verifying the details of her memoir but also have uncovered far more about Janina Mehlberg's remarkable accomplishments as Countess Suchodolska than the memoir recounts. The incident in the prologue to this book, for example, is not mentioned in the memoir but is based on the wartime documents of the Polish Main Welfare Council. The SS official she persuaded to order the release of the civilians in Majdanek was the manager of *Aktion* Reinhard, a man with the blood of more than 1.5 million Jews on his hands. In addition to her relief work at Majdanek, she provided food, shelter, and medical care for tens of thousands of Polish civilians evicted from their homes or abducted from their villages, establishing soup kitchens, hospitals, rest and aid stations, and orphanages for children separated from their families. She negotiated the release of thousands of Poles from transit and labor camps as well as from Majdanek.

We also discovered that, in the course of her life, Janina Mehlberg underwent several reinventions, altering her name and occupation—and becoming increasingly younger. As Pepi Spinner, born 1905, she obtained a doctorate in philosophy and logic at age twenty-two from the prestigious Jan Kazimierz University in Lwów, Poland. As Józefa Mehlberg, she worked as a math teacher and lecturer in Lwów from 1935 until 1941, when she and Henry fled to Lublin and obtained false identities. As Countess Janina Suchodolska, she became the secretary and eventually the deputy of the top official in Lublin District of the Polish Main Welfare Council. At the same time, as "Stefania," she served in the anticommunist Polish Home Army, the largest armed resistance group in German-occupied Poland. When Soviet forces drove the Germans out of Lublin in 1944 and installed a communist government, she became Dr. Janina Suchodolska, social worker, born in 1909. She served in postwar Poland as the deputy director of a welfare agency, tending to the neediest in her war-ravaged country. In 1950, she defected in West Berlin and immigrated to Canada as Josephine Janina Spinner Bednarski Mehlberg. Finally, in 1961, she became a U.S. citizen as Dr. Josephine Janina Spinner Mehlberg, born in 1915.

Although "Janina" was not her name until 1941, Janina Mehlberg retained it as part of her name for the rest of her life, and it is the name she used in her memoir. In a preface to the memoir that her husband, Henry, wrote after her death, he identified her as Janina Spinner Mehlberg. For these reasons, we decided to refer to her as Janina throughout this book.

When we set out to verify Janina's memoir, we planned that, if we succeeded, we would try to publish it along with text that would explain its historical references and the context of the events it recounts. This approach would preserve Janina's voice and perspective while helping readers to understand her story. The memoir starts at the beginning of World War II and ends in 1944, when Soviet forces captured and occupied Lublin. It is not a strictly chronological account, however, but a series of vignettes reflecting some aspects of her activities and experiences. It is written with the assumption that readers will be familiar with the people, places, and events to which it refers. On its own, the memoir cannot convey to most of today's readers a full appreciation of how remarkable Janina's story is. For example, today few people outside Poland have heard of Majdanek concentration camp. Yet in 1944, it became internationally notorious when its liberation by the Red Army provided the first physical evidence that the Nazi regime systematically gassed Jews. The camp was even featured in a film shown at the postwar trial of the major German war criminals in Nuremberg. Before the name Auschwitz became a synonym for the Holocaust, Majdanek was the international symbol of Nazi criminality.

After finding so much more about Janina's life and remarkable accomplishments than the memoir reveals, we decided to write a biography of Janina instead. By drawing heavily from Janina's memoir, we tell her story largely from her perspective, incorporating her thoughts and observations as she recounted them. The dialogue in this book is either drawn directly from the memoir or is based on conversations that the memoir describes. In the epilogue, we discuss how we corroborated Janina's memoir, her motives for writing it, and what it reveals about her character and the lessons she drew from her experiences. We end with Janina's voice by quoting the final passages of her memoir.

This book recounts the story of Janina's life within the context of the events that shaped her actions, integrating her experiences into the larger story of the terror and suffering that the Germans visited upon Poles both Jewish and non-Jewish during World War II. German-occupied Poland was ground zero of the Nazi "final solution" policy, the place where the majority of the Germans' Jewish victims died in ghettos, camps, killing centers, and shooting pits. Janina became Countess Suchodolska in order to escape their fate. Yet even as a supposedly "Aryan" Pole, Janina remained under threat from German policies of racist persecution and mass murder. Nazi ideology portrayed the Jews as the most dangerous of the Germans' "subhuman" enemies, but ethnic Poles ranked only slightly higher on the Nazi racist scale of human worth. Poland's German occupiers unleashed a campaign of systematic carnage that in less than six years claimed the lives of three million Jewish Poles and nearly two million non-Jewish Poles. The Germans also seized more than two million non-Jewish Poles to perform forced labor in the Reich, separating them from their families, and abducted tens of thousands of Polish children to transform them into Germans. The Polish Jewish jurist Raphael Lemkin[3] coined the word "genocide" in 1944 to describe the Germans' efforts to exterminate both Jewish and non-Jewish Poles.

Janina's story illustrates how Poles sought to resist the German occupation and to help one another survive. She was rescued by a non-Jewish family friend, Count Andrzej Skrzyński, who brought Janina and Henry to Lublin and provided them with identity papers as Count and Countess Suchodolski (Suchodolski is the form used for a man and, in English, for a couple). Jews living on false papers during the Holocaust in Poland tended to lie low and avoid going out in public as much as possible, lest they be recognized by a former acquaintance, betrayed by the trace of a Yiddish accent, or forced to show papers that would not stand up to scrutiny. But Janina could not bear to remain passive as so many of her compatriots suffered and died around her. With Skrzyński's backing, she enlisted in the Polish Home Army, the armed forces of the Polish Underground State. Of all the countries occupied by Nazi Germany, Poland had by far the most extensive underground resistance organization, and women played vital roles in it. In addition to serving as a courier and a spy, Janina helped to organize and worked with networks of mostly women who smuggled messages and supplies to imprisoned members of the resistance.

For decades after World War II, there was almost no scholarly or public interest in the experiences of Jewish women during the Holocaust or in the women who fought Nazi Germany through resistance and intelligence work. Funk told Barry that, in his effort to get Janina's memoir published, he sent it to an eminent Holocaust historian in the United States. While the historian found the memoir's story interesting, he concluded that the experiences of one woman Holocaust survivor did not make a compelling case for publication. At that time, the field of Holocaust studies was in its infancy, and historians were mostly focused on the actions and motivations of the perpetrators. That focus has since broadened, and Jewish women's responses to the Nazi genocide have become an important area of study. This century has also seen burgeoning public interest in stories about women who fought Nazi Germany and sought to rescue its victims. In telling Janina's story, we recount the feats of some of the other Polish heroines who risked their lives for their country and whose activities intersected with Janina's.

It was also through Count Skrzyński that Janina obtained a position with the Polish Main Welfare Council, known by its Polish initials, RGO. The Germans did not permit the RGO to tend to all Polish citizens, only to those whom the Germans considered racially Polish. In the district of Lublin, the RGO cared for hundreds of thousands of Poles expelled from their homes and communities, robbed of their property and livelihoods, subsisting on starvation rations, or consigned to prisons or concentration camps. It was able to provide so many with shelter, food, medicines, and clothing largely thanks to the generosity of the people of Lublin, most of whom were themselves suffering from privation and malnutrition as the intended consequence of German policies. Their contributions also made it possible for Janina to feed thousands of prisoners at Majdanek by delivering tons of bread and hundreds of gallons of soup on a nearly daily basis. At no other concentration camp did such a program exist.

World War II and the Holocaust have given rise to numerous inspiring stories about daring and selfless heroes who fought Nazism and rescued its victims. Some of the best known stories occurred in Poland. German industrialist Oskar Schindler has been deservedly celebrated in the book by Thomas Keneally and in Steven Spielberg's film *Schindler's List* for risking his life and exhausting his fortune to save the lives of some 1,200 of his Jewish workers. Warsaw zookeepers Jan and Antonina Żabiński, who hid nearly three hundred Jews and Polish resistance fighters on zoo grounds, are the heroes of the book by Diane Ackerman and film directed by Niki Caro *The Zookeeper's Wife*. There are even more books and dramatic treatments of the life of Irena Sendler, a Polish social worker who smuggled hundreds of Jewish children out of the Warsaw Ghetto and placed them in private homes and religious institutions. Books and films have recounted the astounding courage and feats of resistance of such Polish Jews as the Bielski brothers of the book by Nechama Tec and film directed by Edward Zwick *Defiance* and, more recently, the "ghetto girls" of Judy Batalion's *The Light of Days*.

Janina's story is unique. She was a Jew who rescued non-Jews in the midst of the largest murder operation of the Holocaust. She witnessed the beginning of *Aktion* Reinhard with the bloody deportation to the Bełżec killing center of nearly 30,000 Lublin Jews, and she was one of the first Poles to learn of its apocalyptic end with the mass shooting at Majdanek and two other camps of 42,000 Jews. As often as five days a week, she descended into the den of death at Majdanek, knowing that she would be gruesomely tortured and murdered if the SS discovered either her smuggling activities or her true identity. Over and over, she met with mass murderers to persuade them to help her rescue their victims, and she did so with astounding success: based on wartime records, we have documented that she negotiated the release from German captivity of at least 9,707 Poles, 4,431 of them from Majdanek. The deliveries of food and medicines that she organized likely saved thousands more prisoners from dying of starvation or disease. It is impossible to determine how many Polish lives would have been lost but for Janina's efforts, but the number surely has five figures.

Janina's memoir is both an account of her life during World War II and a meditation on human nature that seeks to draw some meaning from what she observed and experienced. She witnessed both the worst and the best of human capabilities. She saw that people who engaged in murderous cruelty could still commit acts of surprising kindness and even self-sacrifice, and that people who routinely risked their lives to save others could be self-serving or hateful. She recognized that some of her compatriots—including possibly some of those who worked with her, were aided by her, and lit candles and said prayers for her safety—would have denied her identity as a Pole if they had known she was also a Jew. But one of Janina's qualities that shines through in her account is her deep compassion for human frailties, and so her realistic assessment of human nature did not diminish her commitment to saving every life she could.

Janina was extraordinarily intelligent, keenly analytical, and remarkably quick-witted and innovative. Her specialty as a mathematician was probability, which served her well when her survival and success depended upon accurately calculating the tremendous risks she took every day. Ultimately, however, her actions were not guided by risk assessments, but by a simple mathematical principle: the value of one life is less than the value of multiple lives, and her life, if she survived without seeking to save others, would have no value.

Throughout her life, Janina refused to be defined or restricted by stereotypes: she was a woman in the almost entirely male field of mathematics; a patriot in a country that discriminated against her based on both her gender and Jewish identity; a Jew who risked her life to save non-Jewish Nazi victims during the Holocaust; and an anticommunist who served a communist government in order to provide aid to those in need. She saw herself simply as one human, bound to all other humans regardless of their misogyny, racism, or ideology, and she valued her own life only as it served other lives. Her story deserves to be told. The world needs her story.

ONE

BEFORE

When, near the end of her life, Dr. Josephine Janina Mehlberg put to paper the experiences and reflections she felt were worth preserving, she made no mention of her first thirty-four years. Nor did she record her work directing aid for millions of the homeless, destitute, and orphaned in post–World War II Poland, or even write a word about her later life as a math professor in the United States. Instead, the memories and lessons that prompted, even compelled her to write were from the period when World War II shattered her comfortable life as a Polish Jewish intellectual and she seemed destined for murder at the hands of Poland's Nazi occupiers. That was when she made a fateful choice: she would spend her remaining days not in fear and false hope of a meaningless survival, but in bold action to save as many others as she could before meeting a meaningful death. That was when she transformed into Countess Janina Suchodolska, a woman unknown to the many whose lives she saved, a woman haunted to the end of her days by the many she failed to rescue.

Janina was born Pepi Spinner on May 1, 1905, entering a life of rare privilege for a Polish Jewish girl.[1] Her father, Pinkas, was a wealthy estate owner, and she enjoyed a childhood of comfortable elegance.[2] The Spinners were well assimilated in local society and experienced little overt antisemitism. They mixed socially with the Polish nobles who owned the neighboring estates and whose children were Janina's playmates. Like their aristocratic friends, Janina and her older sisters, Chaja and Bluma, were taught at home by nannies and tutors who imparted to them the manners, skills, and knowledge expected of girls in Polish genteel society.

Janina's birthplace, the town of Żurawno (today Zhuravno), was in Eastern Galicia, a region that has had multiple rulers over the past millennium. Today it is part of Ukraine, but for centuries it was a Polish realm. In the late eighteenth century, Austria, Prussia, and Russia successively carved up the once mighty Commonwealth of Poland and Lithuania until they had swallowed it all. Austria helped itself to Galicia.[3]

All three powers tried to force their Polish subjects to assimilate. The Poles, however, refused to give up their identity, culture, and national aspirations, even after their uprisings were brutally suppressed. In 1867, as Austria struggled to hold its multinational empire together, it transformed into the constitutional monarchy of Austria-Hungary and granted some autonomy to other ethnic groups. Eastern Galicia, especially its capital, Lwów, became a center of Polish nationalism and culture.

Janina was fluent in German, the language of Austria, studied English and Russian, and could chat in Ukrainian with the peasants who worked her father's fields. She likely knew some Yiddish as well. Mostly, however, she spoke Polish and French with her Polish friends and aristocratic neighbors, and she absorbed their nationalist sentiments and veneration for Polish culture. This background of multilingual privilege provided her essential skills that she would draw on when, as an adult, her survival and freedom would depend upon her ability to be a convincing imposter.

When Janina was nine, World War I broke out and her happy childhood soon ended with loss and tragedy. Eastern Galicia was ravaged as a major battleground in the fight between the Russian Empire and the Central Powers of Austria-Hungary and Germany. In the first months of the war in 1914, Russian forces swept across Eastern Galicia and promptly confiscated all estates owned by Jews. The armies of the Central Powers drove the Russians out in 1915, but not before the retreating forces abducted hundreds of landowners and leading businessmen.[4] Among them was Janina's father. In 1918, her family received word that he had died.

The war rekindled the hope and determination of the Poles to win back their sovereignty, especially after the entry of the United States. The Fourteen Points program of President Woodrow Wilson called for an independent Polish state comprising all the lands where Poles were in the majority. Eastern Galicia, however, had a Ukrainian majority. As the Central Powers prepared to surrender in the fall of 1918, Eastern Galicia again became a battleground. Polish and Ukrainian forces fought each other as well as Bolshevik Russia's Red Army. In the grip of ultranationalist and ideological frenzy, soldiers on all sides slaughtered Jews. Well over 100,000 Jews were murdered in these post–World War I conflicts, and estimates range as high as 300,000, leading some historians to characterize the pogroms of that period as a prelude to the Holocaust.[5]

When the carnage finally ceased in 1921, Poland's eastern border enclosed large areas where Ukrainians, Belarusians, or Lithuanians were in the majority, including Eastern Galicia. Janina settled in Lwów with her mother, Tauba, and became a star student at her private girls' prep school, displaying a keen and curious intellect and a remarkable talent for mathematics. She was also ambitious and aspired to a career that would make full use of her intellectual gifts.

Lwów's Jan Kazimierz University accepted Janina to study under two of Europe's leading mathematicians: Stefan Banach and Hugo Steinhaus. Banach was then pioneering the field of functional analysis, but it was Steinhaus's work on probability theory and mathematical reasoning that particularly intrigued Janina. She obtained the equivalent of a master's degree in Exact Sciences, which qualified her to teach mathematics at the secondary level. But she aimed higher, to obtain a doctorate and teach at a university. Mathematics was not a welcoming field for women anywhere then, including Poland. Only five women obtained doctorates in mathematics in Poland before World War II, and only one of them in Lwów. Steinhaus, in particular, took a dim view of women in the highest level of his field.[6]

Janina was not one to let misogyny stand in the way of her goals. Jan Kazimierz University was also famous as the birthplace of the intellectual movement known as the Lwów-Warsaw School. Led by the charismatic philosopher Kazimierz Twardowski, it was a circle of mostly philosophers and mathematicians who viewed philosophy as a branch of science that was essential for understanding and advancing scientific and mathematical reasoning. Their intellectual meeting ground was the field of logic. Twardowski accepted women and Jews as his doctoral students and preferred graduate students with expertise in fields other than philosophy. By pursuing a doctorate in philosophy under Twardowski, Janina could advance her work in mathematics while also participating in the exciting explorations and discourse of his seminar. She applied to study under him, and he welcomed her as his student.[7]

Janina obtained a doctorate in philosophy in February 1928.[8] In her dissertation, titled "Mathematical Reasoning and Traditional Logic," she demonstrated that the principles of traditional logic alone are insufficient for mathematical reasoning, which must also draw on other sources of thought, particularly imagination and intuition. In the dark days to come, Janina would apply logic, imaginative innovation, and intuitive insight into human character to the task of resisting her nation's enemies and saving its citizens' lives.

Janina received an exciting opportunity to gain recognition for her work when the Polish Philosophical Society in Lwów invited her to present a lecture in May 1928. It was a bitter disappointment when a health crisis forced her to cancel. By the fall, she had recovered sufficiently to travel to Paris for a year of study at the Sorbonne. Then she returned to Lwów, where she found employment as a math teacher.

Sometime after her return, Janina crossed paths again with another Twardowski student, Henry (then Henryk) Mehlberg.[9] Just seven months older than Janina, he had obtained a master's degree in French in 1924 and a doctorate in philosophy in 1926 from Jan Kazimierz University, then spent two years studying in Austria, Germany, and at the Sorbonne. After he returned to Lwów in 1928, the only employment he could obtain was teaching French at a private preparatory school in the city of Lublin. He found the pay miserable and the city a boring backwater compared to Lwów.[10] With Twardowski's help, he obtained another position teaching languages in the city of Stanisławów (today Ivano-Frankivsk, Ukraine).[11]

When Henry reconnected with Janina, he found that the serious twenty-year-old he had known in his last year of graduate school had grown into a charming, lively, and stylish woman in her prime. She was now going by "Józefa" as her first name, which sounded more Polish and sophisticated than "Pepi." Henry thought her very pretty: petite and slim, with blue-green eyes and luxurious dark hair that framed a lovely face. He admired her combination of femininity with fierce intelligence. Henry tended to be intense and to dominate intellectual discussions, which sometimes caused his male colleagues to grumble. Janina, on the other hand, had no problem interrupting him or holding her own in their discourse, and she managed to do so with such gentle good humor that Henry did not take offense when they disagreed and could even be swayed by her opinion. Like him, Janina was well versed in many subjects outside her field, particularly European literature and history, and they engaged in wide-ranging conversations. Henry, enchanted, concluded that he had met his intellectual match. Janina appreciated the man capable of reaching such a conclusion.

In 1933, some calamity befell Janina that left her suffering deeply in body and spirit. Its precise nature is unclear, although it may have been connected with her mother's death that year. Henry supported Janina throughout the difficult time and their love for each other grew. The two married on August 6 in Henry's hometown, Kopyczyńce, before settling in Stanisławów. Henry hoped that in new surroundings and under his care Janina would recover. Her spirits did revive enough by the summer of 1934 for her to submit an article on mathematical pedagogy for a volume Twardowski was editing, but her physical health did not improve. In May 1935, with Twardowski's help, Henry was able to obtain treatment for Janina in a hospital in Lwów. After a two-week stay, her health and strength began to rebound.[12]

Janina and Henry had additional reason to rejoice in the summer of 1935: he had obtained a teaching position in Lwów and they were able to move back to their beloved city. Once again, they had Twardowski to thank. The professor had encouraged and critiqued Henry's writings on the philosophy of science and made sure that others in the Lwów-Warsaw School were aware of them. In 1934, the president of the Polish Philosophical Society in Lwów—former Twardowski student and renowned scholar Roman Ingarden—invited Henry to speak to the society about his theories.[13] The next year, he published (in French) his first essay on the causal theory of time. Even those who questioned his theory recognized the brilliance of his reasoning. The Lwów circle of the Lwów-Warsaw School wanted Henry among them and helped him find work in the city. Janina, too, obtained a position, teaching math at a girls' high school.[14]

After they moved to Lwów, Janina and Henry sat for studio photographs. Janina appears pale and thin in her photo, perhaps from the effects of her long illness, but exhibits her individual sense of style. She did not wear her hair in the short waves that were universally fashionable then, for she had never bobbed the long, thick locks that fell to her knees in gentle curls when she let it down. Instead, she wore her hair that day in a long chignon tied slightly to one side. For his photo, Henry struck the pose of a serious scholar, his blue eyes cast down in deep thought, his blond, wavy hair combed back from a high forehead and a hairline that was beginning to recede.[15]

The Mehlbergs settled into a comfortable life in Lwów. In addition to their teacher salaries, Janina received a yearly stipend from her father's estate, while Henry received some income as a titular partner in his father's distillery business in Kopyczyńce.[16] They rented a four-room apartment in a fashionable neighborhood near the university and furnished it to suit Janina's elegant taste.

But the atmosphere in the city had changed since their student days. The hopes and ideals that Poles had shared when they were fighting for their sovereignty faded and fragmented as they faced the challenges of self-government. Integrating three regions that for more than a century had operated with different legal, social, political, and economic systems and that had been ravaged by seven years of warfare proved difficult, divisive, and painfully slow. In the late 1920s, just as the economic situation finally began to improve, the Great Depression brought devastation.

Even more worrying was the political polarization that made the country increasingly difficult to govern. Poland had begun its independence as a parliamentary democracy that guaranteed the rights of the ethnic minorities who made up more than 30 percent of its population. But there were competing visions of who truly "belonged" to the Polish nation. The right-wing National Democrats believed that ethnic Poles should enjoy advantages that members of other Christian ethnic groups should only be able to acquire by assimilating, while Jewish Poles should be forced to leave the country altogether. Opposing this view was the hero of Poland's independence, Józef Piłsudski, a socialist who maintained that all residents of the Polish state should be full citizens. Fed up with the instability of Poland's multiparty system, Piłsudski overthrew the government in 1926, replacing it with a nonpartisan authoritarian regime.[17]

The economic misery of the Great Depression stoked ethnic hostilities and popular unrest. The Organization of Ukrainian Nationalists (OUN) embarked on a terror campaign against the Polish "occupiers," while the National Democrats and their fascist offshoot encouraged boycotts of Jewish businesses and even fomented pogroms. Much of the violence occurred in Eastern Galicia. In Janina's birthplace, Żurawno, perpetrators of a pogrom in April 1937 demolished Jewish shops and homes and beat Jewish residents.[18] At the beginning of January 1938, Jewish students at Jan Kazimierz University were forced to sit in the back of classrooms on what were called "ghetto benches"; many were beaten up, some were even murdered.[19]

The Polish regime responded to the growing unrest by becoming even more authoritarian, especially after Piłsudski's death in 1935. It also sought to co-opt the National Democrats' followers by adopting their rhetoric. It renounced the minority treaty that protected the rights of ethnic groups, exacted collective punishment on Ukrainians for OUN attacks, and called for the emigration of Poland's three million Jews.[20] Coupled with the bitter legacy of post–World War I ethnic violence, Poland's official repression of minorities fueled ethnic hatreds that were ripe for exploitation by its enemies.

Poland's most dangerous potential enemies were also its two largest neighbors: Germany to the west and the Soviet Union to the east. Both countries aspired to regain the swaths of territory they had lost to Poland in the aftermath of World War I. Despite Poland's best efforts to steer a neutral path between the two, its relations with them grew increasingly tense, especially after Adolf Hitler and his Nazi Party took power in Germany in 1933.

Hitler launched a campaign of territorial expansion in March 1938, when Germany annexed Austria. He then proceeded to wipe Czechoslovakia off the map by attaching the Czech lands to the Reich and establishing a self-governing satellite state in Slovakia. By April 1939, there was little doubt that Hitler had chosen Poland to be Nazi Germany's next victim. But Britain and France promised to come to Poland's aid if Germany attacked, and in the summer of 1939 they sought an alliance with the Soviet Union aimed at checking German aggression. Polish leaders thought that even Hitler would not be fool enough to risk a two-front war with Germany's three major European adversaries from World War I.

Then, on August 24, the world received stunning news: Nazi Germany and the Soviet Union, sworn ideological enemies, had signed a nonaggression pact, agreeing not to attack each other for ten years. Within two days, German troops were moving toward the Polish border.[21]

And yet, in 1939, Janina and Henry had reasons to be pleased with their status and optimistic about the future. Lwów's intellectual circles had welcomed them with open arms. Both were recognized members of the Lwów-Warsaw School, which had become one of Europe's leading philosophical circles. Janina was elected to the Polish Mathematical Society and published a critique in *The Journal of Symbolic Logic*.[22] Henry began work to obtain the habilitation, the postdoctoral certification that would qualify him to teach in a university. His published work was attracting notice and respect from philosophers both in Poland and abroad. He was regularly lecturing at the Philosophical Society and Jan Kazimierz University and was giving talks on the radio about Twardowski's philosophy. On at least one occasion, Janina joined him on air, to debate the question "Is Truth Relative?"[23]

Henry and Janina had a wide circle of friends, both Jewish and non-Jewish, who admired the couple's brilliance and enjoyed their warmth and kindness. Janina, generous and empathetic, was especially adept at forging friendships with people from many different backgrounds and walks of life.

Nothing about their lives prepared Janina and Henry for what was to come.

TWO

THE BEGINNING OF THE END

Shortly after dawn on September 1, 1939, the residents of Lwów heard the drone of German warplanes overhead, then felt the shattering blasts of bombs falling on their beautiful city. In shock and disbelief, Janina and Henry, like most others in the city, did not follow official instructions to retreat to the basement of their building, for they were confident that Poland's mighty air defenses would soon put a stop to the unpleasantness.

Two days later, however, with German bombers still dropping their payloads and Lwów's buildings crumbling, a rising sense of panic drove residents to their basements. Still, they took comfort from exciting news: France and Great Britain had declared war on Germany. Surely, Poles thought, Germany would soon be forced to withdraw its troops and concede defeat.

Then, a week into the war, the refugees began to arrive from the west, first in a trickle but soon in an unending river that filled the main roads as far as the eye could see. The trains had ceased running and only the wealthy had cars, so the refugees traveled mainly on foot, bicycles, or in conveyances drawn by horses or cattle. They arrived panicked and traumatized by the German blitzkrieg, having seen their homes and communities obliterated and hundreds of their fellow travelers killed on the way by bombs, shells, and strafing warplanes. With them came unsettling rumors: Polish forces were being routed; the government was fleeing the country.

Janina and Henry huddled in the stuffy basement of their building with the other residents. For long days and nights, they endured excruciating boredom broken by moments of terror as they listened to whistling bombs and screaming artillery shells and held their breath when their building shuddered from the impact of nearby explosions. Still, people clung hopefully to the assurances of Poland's leaders that the Polish Army was far superior to the German Wehrmacht and that the retreats of Polish forces were merely strategic.[1]

On September 17, as German forces were poised to take Lwów, news came that Soviet forces had crossed into Poland. For a fleeting moment, some Lwów residents grasped the hope that the Soviet Union had abandoned its nonaggression pact with Nazi Germany and was coming to Poland's rescue. In fact, the Soviets came to fulfill their part of the bargain with Nazi Germany. In a secret codicil to their pact, the Nazi and Soviet governments had agreed to divide Poland between them.

Janina and Henry had retreated to their basement as proud citizens of Poland. When the bombing and shelling finally ceased on September 22, they emerged as subjects of the Union of Soviet Socialist Republics. Per their secret agreement with the Germans, the Soviets occupied and annexed Poland's provinces east of the Bug River, including Eastern Galicia. The rest of Poland fell to Nazi Germany, which annexed Poland's western and northern provinces to the Third Reich. The remaining area, about one quarter the size of prewar Poland, became a German possession. Dubbed the General Government (*Generalgouvernement*), it was essentially a colony, ruthlessly ruled by a German administration for the benefit of its overlord. Just two decades after proudly declaring its sovereignty, the Polish nation again found itself without a state and occupied by enemies intent on eradicating not only its independence but also its identity.

On the heels of the Red Army, a wave of violence swept through Eastern Galicia. The occupying soldiers looted and raped at will. Incited by the Soviets to take up "scythes and axes" and destroy "Polish fascism," some Ukrainians complied with gusto. They looted estates and businesses and attacked their owners, sometimes murdering them. Most of the victims were ethnic Poles, followed by Jews. Believing that the land they seized would be theirs,

Ukrainian peasants welcomed the Red Army with bread and salt. The Soviets might preach about a workers' paradise without ethnic, religious, or social distinctions, but they understood the value of manipulating ethnic hostilities.[2]

In Lwów, renamed Lvov, Janina and Henry faced the prospect of homelessness. The Red Army confiscated thousands of homes and apartments of the city's mostly Polish and Jewish residents, or forced families to live in one room and serve the soldiers billeted in the rest of their abode.[3] Soon after the city was occupied, two Red Army officers arrived at Janina and Henry's door to determine how to dispose of their apartment's four rooms. Henry was not at home.

Greeting the officers in Russian, Janina graciously showed them around, hoping she could persuade them to let her and Henry remain in one of the rooms. The officers stared agape at the walls covered with shelves of books.

"Why do you own all these books?" one officer asked Janina.

"My husband and I are professors and needed to acquire them for our work," she replied.

The other officer, pointing to a book on the desk, noted that the author's name matched that on the apartment door.

"Are you related to the author?" he asked.

"He is my husband."

"So, your husband is not only a professor but a writer, and you teach as well."

Janina confirmed his conclusion. To her astonishment, the two officers then took their leave.

Under the Soviet regime, it turned out, teachers had a special status and could be allotted two rooms each.[4] Thus, Janina and Henry could remain in their apartment as before. The tenants in the apartment below, however, had to house four officers and their families.

But to keep their apartment, the Mehlbergs had to be approved for teaching positions. The Soviets strictly surveilled the personnel and curriculum at all schools to ensure the ideological purity of instruction. Ukrainian, Russian, and Yiddish replaced the Polish and Hebrew languages in primary and secondary schools. At Lwów's university, renamed Ivan Franko University after a nineteenth-century Ukrainian writer, the language of instruction was changed to Ukrainian, and many Polish and Jewish professors were dismissed. The philosophy department was expected to teach Marxist materialism, not the unorthodox views of the Lwów-Warsaw School.[5]

As the daughter of an estate owner, Janina qualified as a class enemy, while the Mehlbergs' activities in the Lwów-Warsaw School could have disqualified them from teaching. When they registered with authorities, Janina claimed that her father had been a simple bookkeeper on a Polish estate. She and Henry presented themselves as high school teachers, she of math and he of foreign languages. Neither field was ideologically suspect, and since Janina could teach in Ukrainian and Henry did not need it to teach French, they were approved to continue their work.

On October 22, Janina and Henry had to vote to "choose" what had already been decided for them: that Eastern Galicia would unite with the Ukrainian Soviet Socialist Republic. Every resident of Eastern Galicia was required to submit a ballot. Those who failed to come to a polling station were sought out and transported there, or the ballot box was brought to them. As she approached the ballot box, Janina, like all voters, had to show how she had filled her ballot.

The unsurprising election result was announced: 90.83 percent of Galicians voted for union with Ukraine.[6]

Hunger and want descended on Lwów. The Soviets confiscated most private enterprises and closed the banks, seizing all but a paltry sum in depositors' accounts. Even that amount became worthless when the ruble replaced Polish currency. The only legal way to acquire income was through wages, but there was massive unemployment thanks to the dislocations caused by the confiscations. There was an acute food shortage as well, and by the start of the unusually harsh winter of 1939–1940, no coal could be obtained for heating. Even the black market had little to offer, and its prices quickly spiraled beyond what workers' wages could afford. The search for food became an all-consuming quest. So little was available that the state-run stores simply listed the few goods they had for sale on their windows. People stood in line for hours, often overnight, in the dwindling hope that something would still be available when they finally reached the head of the queue.

The Mehlbergs had taken in a colleague of Henry's, and the two men shared in the search for food for their household. Bundled in all their warm clothing, they would set out in the dark hours before dawn, carrying knapsacks to hold whatever they could find. One early morning, they saw a store that was open, and in its windows were jars of liquid concentrate of ersatz tea. Excited at the prospect of surprising Janina with what had become a rare delicacy, the men bought two jars. The rest of their foray proved similarly successful, for they succeeded in buying a half pound of horsemeat after standing only six hours in line.

The two men returned to the apartment and, with conspiratorial grins, proposed to Janina that they warm up with a nice cup of hot tea. Then, in response to her look of puzzled surprise, they triumphantly opened their knapsacks to pull out the two jars, only to find that both had frozen and shattered while the men waited to buy the horsemeat. Trying to console them, Janina served up cups of ersatz lemon powder in hot water. In such trying times, ingenuity and imagination were necessary coping strategies.

People's constant food anxiety actually played into the hands of Soviet authorities. As a teacher, Janina had a front-row view of how the Soviets used food to indoctrinate children and students in Marxist ideology and turn them into active supporters of the Communist Party. Children received a hot meal daily at school and were organized into communist youth groups that met in beautiful confiscated homes and supplied sumptuous treats. Given the austerity they endured at home, children needed little encouragement to attend the meetings. At the universities as well, cafeterias supplied students and teachers with hot food. Numerous unions, committees, and professional associations were organized, and at each of their many meetings there were food counters with bread and sausages for sale. Janina noted that hungry stomachs tended to develop a strong appetite for political discussion.

But the Soviets relied much more on the stick than the carrot to ensure conformity and obedience to Marxist totalitarianism. Thousands of agents of the Soviet secret police, then known as the NKVD, descended upon Eastern Galicia to identify and determine the fate of all suspected enemies of the state. In February 1940, they carried out the first of four massive deportations of people categorized as threats to Soviet rule based upon their professions, class, or ethnicity. The victims included Polish landowners, civil servants, and police, landowning Ukrainian peasants, Jewish business owners, and the Polish and Jewish refugees from German-occupied Poland who refused to accept Soviet citizenship. Packed tightly into boxcars, the victims traveled with little food or water for days or sometimes weeks until they arrived at labor colonies in the tundra of Siberia or the steppe of Kazakhstan. According to the wartime Polish government in exile, 1.25 million Polish citizens were deported by the Soviets between February 1940 and June 1941, 400,000 of them from Eastern Galicia.[7]

Although forced to perform backbreaking labor, the deportees at least had a chance of surviving. In April 1940, the NKVD murdered 21,892 Polish Army officers, policemen, and members of Poland's intelligentsia in the Katyn Forest in western Russia and at four other sites.[8]

Certain that spies and traitors were everywhere plotting to overthrow Soviet rule, the NKVD and its informants relentlessly hunted for suspects. In Lwów, thousands disappeared into the four NKVD prisons to be tortured until they confessed and named others. The lucky prisoners were sentenced to eight years in a Siberian gulag; the rest received a bullet in the back of the neck.[9]

Like so many citizens of Lwów, Janina and Henry lived in constant dread that the NKVD would set its sights on them, perhaps as members of a suspect group or because of an allegation wrenched from an acquaintance desperate to escape torture. They listened nightly for the knock on the door signaling that their time had come.

Nevertheless, whether under German or Soviet occupation, Polish patriots like Janina and Henry maintained faith that their nation's subjugation was only temporary. After all, this was not the first time that Poland had been wiped off the map. The Poles found strength in the words of Poland's national anthem:

Poland is not yet lost
As long as we're alive.

Poland would rise again, Janina and Henry were sure. This was not the end.

THREE

TERROR COMES TO LWÓW

Shrieking in terror, young women were fleeing through the streets of Lwów. Those caught pleaded for their lives as their pursuers stripped and flogged them. Other rioters were dragging men out onto the streets and bludgeoning them. Hundreds were dying in the bloody frenzy. The victims were Jews, and their murderers were their neighbors. It was June 30, 1941, and German forces had just taken the city.

Since Nazi Germany's attack on the Soviet Union eight days earlier, Ukrainian nationalists had been preparing to vent their rage at their Soviet oppressors. The gruesome discovery of some 1,500 corpses of NKVD prisoners in Lwów's prisons added to their fury. Unable to get their hands on actual Soviet officials, Ukrainian militia groups settled upon Jews as scapegoats, even though many of the murdered prisoners were Jews. The slaughter continued for two days until German military officials finally stepped in and restored order on July 2. By that time, more than a thousand and possibly as many as 4,000 Jews had been murdered.[1]

Then a *Kommando* (detachment) arrived in the city from one of the SS *Einsatzgruppen*. These were the notorious task forces of the German Security Police and SD that enforced security behind the German front lines during military operations. The Security Police, consisting of the Gestapo and the Criminal Police, was a state agency, while the SD

(*Sicherheitsdienst*; Security Service) was the intelligence service of the SS (*Schutzstaffel*; Protection Squads), the armed security force of the Nazi Party, but the two were joined under one office at the start of World War II. One of the tasks of the *Einsatzgruppen* in the seized Soviet territories was to eliminate "Judeo-Bolshevism," the Nazi term for communism, through mass murder of communists, members of the intelligentsia, and above all, Jews.[2]

Janina and Henry did not witness the first Ukrainian rampages, as their neighborhood near the university was not predominantly Jewish. But two nights after the *Einsatzkommando* arrived in the city, its officials burst into the nearby homes of some two dozen prominent university professors, most of them Poles. The Germans arrested not only the professors but also family members and servants. By the end of the next day, nearly all were dead, shot in mass graves in the hills above the city.[3] Among the victims were three mathematicians whom Janina knew and respected.

Murders of Jews continued as well, although under the direction of the SS, the Ukrainian militia conducted them in a more orderly and targeted fashion. Between July 2 and 5, the militia rounded up thousands of male Jews and took them to an open-air sports arena, where they were brutally beaten and tortured. Most of the Jews were then marched to the woods outside the city, where, with the help of the Ukrainians, the SS shot them. The *Einsatzkommando* did not make an exact count of the victims but reported that they numbered between 2,500 and 3,000.[4]

The Wehrmacht, the German armed forces, established a military administration in Lwów, which the Germans renamed Lemberg. The city commandant placed ethnic Ukrainians in positions of power. Although Nazi ideology considered all Slavs, including Ukrainians, to be racially inferior, the Germans were as adept as the Soviets at exploiting ethnic divisions. The Wehrmacht had organized units of the OUN that marched into Eastern Galicia with German troops. With German encouragement, Ukrainian nationalists called on their ethnic brethren to seize villages and towns and take revenge against their enemies, especially Jews and Poles. Contrary to OUN expectations, however, Germany's Nazi leaders had no intention of granting sovereignty to the Ukrainians. After an OUN faction declared Ukrainian statehood in Lwów, its leaders soon found themselves guests of the SS in Sachsenhausen concentration camp.[5]

One of the military administration's first acts was to order all Jews between ages fourteen and sixty to register and wear armbands with the Star of David. For the SS and Ukrainian militia, the markings simplified the task of finding victims to murder.[6] Janina could only watch in sorrow as her friends in mixed marriages were forced by the armband requirement to choose between terrible options. Some non-Jewish partners divorced their Jewish spouses and took the children, in hopes of saving them. Some non-Jewish mothers even tried to claim that their children were illegitimate, since bastardy was better than having a Jewish father. Janina also had friends who had been practicing Christians all their life yet were classified as Jews by the Germans. They might have been able to hide their parentage from the Germans, but not from the Ukrainians. A professor of Polish literature well known to Janina and Henry was a devout Catholic whose Jewish parents were converted Christians and had baptized him at birth. After learning that he was required to wear the armband, he slit his wrists in his bathtub.

Janina and Henry donned the armband and experienced the full force of Nazi persecution. One of the first decrees banned Jewish ownership of radios. When Janina went to turn in hers at the designated place, she found a long line of other Jews lugging radios in the July heat. A few hours after she joined it, two armed Ukrainian militiamen guarding a small group of young men passed by. Suddenly, Janina was startled by a heartrending wail from an older Jewish woman standing near her in the line.

"That's my son! They are taking my son!"

Dropping her radio, the woman ran toward the men. One of the Ukrainians roughly shoved her away, but she continued to follow them, wailing for her son. The other militiaman grabbed her head in his hands and smashed it on the curb until she was dead. Then he kicked her body and rejoined the group. Janina could do nothing but keep her place in the line as it slowly shuffled past the bloody corpse. Such scenes had become common in the city.

On July 25, the Ukrainian militia embarked on a new, two-day pogrom. They targeted wealthy Jews, dragging them into the street, beating them, and then taking them off to be shot.[7] This time, they came to Janina and

Henry's neighborhood. Janina became aware of the danger when, drawn to her window by a commotion in the street below, she saw that a group of Ukrainian militia had dragged out the Jewish landlord of a neighboring building. The landlord was kneeling before one of the militiamen, whom Janina recognized as the building's janitor. As the landlord pleaded for his life, she heard the janitor snarl:

"No! Under the Bolsheviks you said I stole from you. Now it's my turn to send you to hell. I'm not going to lift a finger to save a rat like you!"

Janina was shocked. Often when the janitor was working outside the building, she would stop to chat, always remembering to ask about his children, who were clearly his pride and joy. When she learned one day that one of the children was seriously ill, she arranged medical treatment for the child. She could not fathom how the loving father and friendly neighbor she knew, who had shown no animosity toward her as a Jew, could so heartlessly consign another human being to a cruel death.

The next day, a truck pulled up in front of Janina and Henry's building and disgorged Ukrainian militia. Janina saw them enter the building and, assuming that they were looking for Jewish men, insisted that Henry hide while she pretended to be a visitor. When the knock came, Janina answered the door—and saw that the janitor was among the men. Somehow swallowing her fear, she stated that she was a houseguest of the Mehlbergs, who were not at home. Then the janitor spoke up.

"That's right, I remember seeing the Mehlbergs leave earlier."

The group moved on in search of other victims.

Janina closed the door and leaned against it, trying to process what had just happened. The man she knew to be responsible for the murder of at least one Jew had just saved the lives of two others, at considerable risk to his own. The two acts appeared incompatible, yet both were performed by the same person. Over the next three years, she would observe further instances of the human capacity to perform logically irreconcilable acts, and her observations would influence her calculations of risk as she daily put her own life on the line to save others.

By the time the pogrom ended on July 27, the Ukrainian militia had murdered some 1,000 victims in Lwów. The city commandant reacted the next day by imposing a two million ruble fine upon the city's Jews as punishment for "provoking" the Ukrainians.[8]

Things got even worse for Lwów's Jews on August 1, when Eastern Galicia became *Distrikt Galizien,* the fifth *Distrikt* or province of the General Government, the area of Nazi-occupied Poland that Germany did not annex in 1939. It was run by Nazi civilian administrators who ruthlessly exploited its resources and people and enriched themselves in the process. Some of the most corrupt and brutal veterans of Nazi rule in the General Government obtained leading positions in Galicia District, earning it the derisive nickname "Scandalicia" (*Skandalizien*). In fact, the district's first governor so far overstepped even Nazi standards for graft that he was recalled, tried, and executed in 1942.[9]

The new civilian administrators barred Jews from employment, schools, and public spaces. All Jews between ages fourteen and sixty became liable for forced labor. Civilian officials inspected Jewish residences, registered the furnishings, confiscated what was valuable, and evicted the inhabitants.[10] There was such a barrage of constantly changing regulations and decrees from different offices that Janina was never sure whether what she had done permissibly the day before had become prohibited overnight.

Lwów's new administration immediately levied an additional fine against the Jewish community. Janina and Henry did not have the cash to pay their part of the fine and so, like thousands of other Jews in the city, she went to St. Mary's Square in the city's Old Town to sell her two most valuable items, a ring and a custom fountain pen ornamented in 22-karat gold. The square was one of the most beautiful in the city, but now it seemed like something out of a fever dream. It was packed with people shoving and shouting in the stifling heat. Mixing among the desperate men and women seeking to sell their belongings were German soldiers, officers, and SS men with greedy grins. Some seemed to specialize in specific items, for Janina saw one hold up a hand with wedding rings to his fingertips, while another drew back the sleeve from his raised arm to show bracelets.

Janina recognized a friend in the crowd, the wife of a professor, who was trying to sell a bracelet, and the two women stood together. A German came over to inspect their items, asked Janina the price for hers, and then offered to buy them for half the amount she named. Civilians clustered around to watch. One of them spoke to Janina in German:

"Don't sell it to him. The pen alone is worth three times that much."

The German snorted in disgust and walked away. Whereupon an SS man simply snatched the pen from Janina's hand and sauntered off into the crowd. The civilian who had advised her not to sell tossed her a few złoty and quickly followed the SS man. That, Janina learned, was how business was done in St. Mary's Square.

Hunger became a constant companion for Janina and Henry. Their official rations provided less than 8 percent of the calories needed to survive, and they were only allowed to buy the few permitted foodstuffs—if they were even available—at a single market between the hours of 12:00 and 4:00 p.m. There they ran the risk that Germans or Ukrainians would attack and rob them or abduct them to perform grueling labor, from which many never returned.

Adding to the misery of daily life, typhus arrived in September with Ukrainian soldiers returning from German POW camps. Malnourished Jews living in crowded quarters proved especially vulnerable to the disease, which soon ran rampant in the city. This added to the Germans' determination to "solve the Jewish question" in Galicia. There were more than half a million Jews in the district, more than 100,000 of them within the city of Lwów. Nazi officials decided to cut the Jews off completely from the rest of the population by enclosing them in ghettos. Not all of them, though—first there would be a culling.[11]

Janina began to notice trucks full of Jews speeding toward Piaskowa Góra (Sandy Hill) in the city's heights in early October. And at night she would hear long bursts of gunfire coming from those heights. One day, she ran into a friend from her school days, a Pole, whose haggard appearance alarmed her. The distraught woman explained that she had fled from her home on Piaskowa Góra because it was just twenty yards from an execution site. Sleep continued to elude her, however, because the sounds of the gunshots and screams she had heard for so many nights never ceased echoing in her head.

The raids on Jews intensified, always for the announced intention of taking them for work. Sometimes that proved to be true, but the gunfire in the hills indicated that for many it was not. For Janina, like the other Jews of Lwów, every day involved a desperate calculation of the probability that venturing to the market, visiting a friend, or even staying at home would end either in abduction to perform agonizing labor or in death. There was no safe place for a Jew in Lwów.

People tried different strategies to avoid being taken. One day, Janina paid a visit to a young couple she knew from the university and was surprised to be greeted at the door by a gray-haired woman. After a double take, Janina recognized her friend. She had dyed her hair because she had to go stand in line to buy food at the market and feared that, as a healthy young woman, she would be taken for labor. Her strategy proved successful for several shopping forays, until the day she went out and never returned. The SS were seizing elderly women that day—and not to take them for labor.

Like the other Jews not yet taken, Janina kept a constant vigil for the trucks that carried SS men and Ukrainian auxiliaries. As she was watching out her apartment window early one morning, she saw a truck pull up and Ukrainian policemen enter the apartment building across the street, shouting that they had come to take the residents to work. A young, partially disabled Jewish clerk lived there with his pretty wife. The Ukrainians passed him over as unfit for work but seized his wife instead. The clerk reassured himself that his wife must have been taken for work, because the Ukrainians logically would have seized him if they were looking for victims to murder. At five the same evening, Janina watched as the clerk began standing outside the entrance to his building, waiting for his wife's return. At eight he was still there, leaning heavily on his cane. The next morning, he was still there, no longer waiting expectantly but crumpled in the doorway, sobbing. No one could get him to leave the entryway, so his neighbors finally notified his parents, who came and took him.

And then one night around 3:00 a.m., terror pounded on Janina and Henry's door. They tried to dress quickly as the pounding became louder. Shaking with fear, Janina opened the door. Ukrainian policemen barged past her and seized Henry.

"We're taking him for work," they announced.

Janina pleaded with them in Ukrainian, "He's a teacher, he's not much good for physical labor."

But they stomped out with Henry in tow, only partially dressed. Janina followed them, filled with despair and wanting only to share Henry's fate. But when she tried to follow them into the police station, one of the policemen pushed her away.

"What's your hurry," he sneered, "don't you know where they're taking him?"

This confirmation of her worst fear suddenly filled Janina with a reckless stubbornness. She stared into the policeman's eyes and did not move. Enraged, he screamed, "Get the hell out of here!" and cracked her in the face with his rifle butt.

A Wehrmacht officer entering the building witnessed the assault. He steadied Janina and advised her to leave, but she refused to budge. This seemed to impress him. Promising to find out what was happening to Henry if she left the station, he finally persuaded her to go stand in a doorway across the street. After half an hour, he returned.

"I took your husband out of the transport and am sending him to the Wehrmacht bakery for work. Now you can go home."

But, reeling and nauseous from the blow to her head, Janina continued to wait, not daring to trust the officer's assurances. Soon, she saw a truck depart with the other Jewish men collected at the station, and it headed toward Piaskowa Góra. Just then, she saw Henry emerge from the station's entry, escorted by two German soldiers. They turned and headed in the other direction, toward the Wehrmacht bakery. Another soldier came and told her that Henry would return at six that evening.

Still she stood in the doorway as the hours dragged by. At six, she cried out in relief as she spotted Henry walking toward her. And, amazingly, he was carrying a loaf of wheat bread, something they had not tasted in months. Back at their apartment, Janina tended to Henry's chest and arms, raw and blistered from his shirtless labor hauling hot loaves from the ovens. Yet, as they feasted on the loaf of bread, they were almost giddy with gratitude. The irony of their feelings was not lost on Janina, who remarked, "If a man has been beating you brutally for years, then suddenly stops and offers you a sip of water, he may seem to you the Lord of Mercy at that moment."

FOUR

TRANSFORMATION

Two small suitcases packed with only the bare necessities stood at the door, ready for Janina and Henry to grab them on their way out. It was December 7, 1941, and they knew they had to get out of Lwów. The city's nearly 120,000 Jews had received orders on November 8 to move into a ghetto by December 15. Reports of what was already happening there were horrifying, and not just because of the massive overcrowding and raging epidemics. To enter the ghetto, the Jews had to funnel through two gates under railroad bridges. As they filed in on foot, carrying the few possessions they were allowed to bring, German and Ukrainian police searched, robbed, and beat them. Men and women who seemed particularly poor or weak were seized and taken to the Security Police prison. Now it seemed that the prison must be full, for the police had blocked off the roads between it and the sand pits in the city's heights and dozens of trucks were speeding back and forth daily, traveling up with covered loads and returning empty. Gunfire constantly echoed from above.[1]

Even if they survived the gauntlet into the ghetto, Janina and Henry understood what awaited them there. News had reached Galicia's Jews that thousands of Jews were dying of starvation and diseases in the ghettos already established in German-occupied Poland. In Warsaw alone, the death rate was between 4,000 and 5,500 per month.[2] Janina and Henry lacked the kind of physical labor skills and connections that might get them a work card and, with it, the possibility of better rations, perhaps even an entire half of a room to live in, and most important, protection from mass shootings. For it was illogical to expect that the Germans would stop murdering Jews once they were all sealed into the ghetto, where finding victims would no longer require any effort. Janina and Henry were nothing if not logical. Going into the ghetto, they concluded, meant going to their deaths.

They had decided to join Henry's family in Kopyczyńce, where there was no ghetto yet, and Henry's father was sending a horse-drawn carriage to collect them. When it arrived, they opened their door and stopped short in surprise: an unexpected visitor stood there, about to knock. It was Count Andrzej Skrzyński (AHN-jay SKSHIN-skee), an old friend of Janina's family. He had taken the first civilian train allowed to cross into Galicia to seek out Janina and make her a proposition: she and Henry should travel back with him to Lublin. Skrzyński promised he could get them false papers, living quarters, and jobs.

Janina and Henry weighed the odds and concluded that the Count's proposal offered the best chance for long-term survival. But only if they could get to Lublin. Galician Jews could not travel outside the district without official permits, for which Janina and Henry did not qualify. That meant they must travel without wearing the Star of David armband or carrying papers that identified them as Jews, both offenses for which they would be shot if caught. Count Skrzyński was confident, however, that if they stuck with him during the journey, he could get them to Lublin.

On the morning of December 8, Janina and Henry gazed out the window and bid a silent farewell to their beloved city as their train departed the Lwów station. Janina remembered that the day was the Catholic holiday of the Feast of the Immaculate Conception, and she fondly recalled the processions, festivities, and fireworks of past years in the city. Lublin is about 130 miles northwest from Lwów, but when the railroads were built, Lwów was in Austria-Hungary while Lublin was part of the Russian Empire. The rail route between the two cities was circuitous and required several changes for which there were no set schedules, since civilian trains were regularly shunted aside for Wehrmacht transports that were speeding soldiers and supplies to the Eastern Front. The journey would take days.

The day was dark and frigid, and the passenger cars were unheated and unlit. Janina and her traveling companions jostled on the hard wooden benches for hour after long hour. The train would occasionally stop, and a German official would board with a flashlight to conduct a random check. Each time, Janina observed a young man who shrank back into the shadows, trying to hide a face pale with fear. She guessed that he, too, was a Jew.

After twenty-four hours, they had traveled little more than fifty miles to Przemyśl, where they had to change trains. Informed that they had to wait ten hours, Skrzyński and Henry went in search of food while Janina stayed in the cold, dark station with the two suitcases. After a while, she noticed bobbing lights slowly moving her way. Panic seized her. German police were examining all passengers and demanding to see their papers.

Janina was standing in a corner of the station and had no way to escape. How could she explain her lack of papers? Paralyzed with fear and despair, she could not think. Her luck, she concluded, had run out. A wave of relief washed over her that Henry and the Count would not be caught with her, followed by a wave of sorrow for their coming grief. As two policemen turned their lights on her and approached, she resolved to meet her fate with dignity.

"What do you have in these valises?" demanded one policeman.

Without replying, she bent to undo the latches, but her fingers fumbled with cold and nerves as she waited for the next demand: her papers. The other policeman shone his flashlight on her face, then said, "She doesn't look like a smuggler. Let's leave her alone." And they moved on to the next passenger. Janina slowly straightened and stood in a shivering daze for she knew not how long before Henry and the Count returned.

After a further day of travel, they arrived at Dębica—still 130 miles away from their destination—and faced another long wait for the next train. They were desperately tired, but German bombs had destroyed most of the city in 1939 and there were no hotels. Count Skrzyński found a railway worker who took them to a building with a number of bare cots. All but one were occupied by Polish travelers. The men insisted that Janina take the available cot with the Count's overcoat as a blanket, and they sought space to sleep on the floor.

They were startled from their sleep by harsh shouts of "*Raus, Alle!*" In the darkness, Janina could hear people groaning and a baby's wail. They all filed out, wondering whether they were about to be arrested, only to discover that the order came from a drunk German soldier seeking a place to sleep it off and unwilling to share space with "Polack swine." There was nothing to do but return to the station.

After three days and three nights, they arrived at Lublin. Hoping to slip out of the station quickly without encountering any police checks, the men went to retrieve the luggage while Janina sought a cab. She found one easily, then waited with increasing anxiety, straining for a sight of Henry and the Count, while the cab driver complained about losing other fares. Finally, nearly an hour later, she saw Count Skrzyński approach. He was alone.

"You and I are going home now," he said, taking her arm. "Henry was detained by some German police for something, and he'll come after us."

Janina broke away from him and ran back into the station. There she saw Henry being berated by a German official who was shouting that taking any baggage out of Galicia was strictly prohibited. Henry looked pale. At any moment, the official would demand to see his papers. Janina sprang into action.

"What do you want of my husband?" she demanded in German as she stepped in front of Henry and fixed the official with a haughty look.

Startled by her peremptory tone and apparent lack of fear, the official lost his swagger and replied in a lower voice, "He has broken a strict regulation on baggage."

"He could do no such thing," Janina retorted, "because when we left Lwów there was no such regulation!"

The official backed down and said lamely, "Anyway, he has to pay a fine."

If they agreed to the fine, Janina realized, they would have to show papers so it could be recorded.

"We are not going to pay any fine," she declared firmly, "because there was no regulation about this, and if you will put through a call to Lwów, you will hear it for yourself."

Now flustered and fuming, the official ordered them to get out, "and don't let me catch you another time!"

Careful not to give away their relief, Janina and Henry sauntered out of the station with their two bags. "Never has a harshly bellowed order sounded so sweet," Janina thought.

Decades later, she would reflect on the lesson she learned in this encounter and that she would use again and again to save lives in the years that followed it:

> *What do you do with your fear and trembling in a confrontation with a swaggering bully? You confine it to the small prison of the heart, letting none seep into the muscles of the eyes, hands, or legs; you quake within and show calm authority without—you pull off a hoax. You must not toady to them, you must not let them sniff blood. Composure and coolness toward them implied the backing of power, and in the face of power they might very well shrink.*

Three days earlier, Pepi Mehlberg had departed Lwów for Lublin. Countess Janina Suchodolska arrived there in her place.

FIVE

THE DYSTOPIAN UTOPIA

After the misery of their three-day journey, Janina and Henry were yearning for a bite to eat, a place to lay their heads, and a chance to thaw their frozen marrow. Their horse-drawn cab took them to 22 Narutowicza Street, where Count Skrzyński had arranged for them to stay. It was an elegant neoclassical building, with shops on the street level and four stories of residential space above lined with wrought iron balconies.[1] Passing under two grime-streaked caryatids that supported the arch over the entry drive, they rang the bell at an imposing set of carved wooden doors. A porter answered and led them through to the rear courtyard and the building's entry. As they followed him up an unlit staircase, Janina noted that the temperature inside seemed no warmer than outside.

The porter led them to a landing where an elderly lady was waiting and welcomed them warmly in French. The landlady was not at home, she explained, but she could take the Mehlbergs to the room that would serve in part as their living quarters. She led them to a vast, hall-like drawing room, with high ceilings and five huge French windows that opened to balconies. Janina thought it the perfect setting for a chamber music recital, with elegantly dressed ladies and gentlemen seated in gilded chairs. Now it was sparsely furnished and crisscrossed with lines of laundry. As Henry stowed their luggage in the corner that was to be theirs, Janina reached up to the lines to take down some linens, only to discover that they were frozen stiff. As she had feared, the room was freezing cold.

Just then, the landlady fluttered in, apologizing in French that she had not been present to greet their arrival. "But I never miss Vespers," she explained. She was Countess Władysława Strus, about seventy-three years old, petite, fine-boned, surprisingly agile, and with a face that radiated kindness. In addition to her Lublin home, her family had once owned large estates in Beresteczko and Hrubieszów, but the Germans had confiscated them. The lady who had first greeted Janina and Henry was Countess Władysława's sister, Madame Maria Czernecka, age seventy. She had been expelled from her husband's grand estate after the Germans arrested him. Since she had received no notice of his fate, she clung to the false hope that he was alive in the concentration camp that the Germans had established for Polish prisoners in Oświęcim in annexed Poland. The Germans called the camp Auschwitz.

Countess Władysława shared one room in her building with her sister and rented the others to tenants. When Count Skrzyński told her he was seeking living quarters for his wife's distant cousins, she readily offered part of her drawing room. Now the sisters clucked about the "nice young couple," endeavoring to make them feel welcome. Seeing the frozen linen in Janina's hands, Countess Władysława assured her that she needn't worry about the room's temperature.

"I had an iron stove brought in the minute I knew you were going to rent it, and I am going immediately to get some nice black coal, so we shall soon be as cozy as toast!"

Clutching her worn fur coat against her thin frame, the Countess bustled out of the room. The sight of a small stove in a corner did not reassure Janina. Her heart sank further when the Countess returned with "the nice black coal"—five lumps in a small dustpan. Clearly, the lady had no idea how much coal it would take to heat such a large room. Janina thought the scene could almost be a French comedy, were it not so cruelly real. The Countess proceeded to light the stove, getting coal dust on her hands and face. "Whatever would her butler in Beresteczko think if he saw her now?" Janina thought.

The stove was actually the sisters' cookstove. The Countess took charge of preparing the daily meal, a broth thickened with a bit of flour. She tended to it over the sickly flame with the same care as the roasts and stews that her servants had cooked for hours at Beresteczko, which raised rueful but affectionate smiles in Janina and Henry. If Janina suggested raising the flame, the Countess scolded her. "Janka, my dear," she said, using a diminutive form of Janina, "don't you know that the very best in any food is brought out by careful, watched over, very slow cooking?"

On Sundays, the Countess made pancakes of water and flour fried with bits of bacon and served with a tiny bit of jam. For weeks before her Saint's Day, however, the sisters would forgo the pancakes to save the flour, preparing to hold a real party for their friends. When the day arrived, they opened the dining table to seat twenty-four and covered it with a beautiful embroidered tablecloth, fine china, and flowers. From the pound of flour she had saved up, the Countess made shortbread cookies. Served on the lovely plates, with flowers between each place and ersatz tea in the delicate cups, they created a festive feeling in the guests. The Countess presided over the table like the lady of the manor she had once been. Her guests, including Janina and Henry, wore their Sunday best and spoke French in animated conversations. It brought back to Janina happy scenes from her childhood.

In addition to the little rent the Countess collected, the sisters lived off the wages of Madame Maria, who worked as a domestic for the Rylskis, members of the lower aristocracy. She went to and from work in dirty, worn bedroom slippers, saving her only pair of shoes for church. She performed numerous chores, including washing floors and carrying heavy baskets of coal, but she was given nothing to eat during her entire workday, because Madame Rylska complained that food was just too expensive. When Janina expressed outrage at this treatment, Madame Maria scoffed, "These are no hardships, my child. Hardship is what my poor husband must suffer in Auschwitz—if indeed he is still alive. What one does as a free man or woman, that should not be called hardship, unless we want to blaspheme against God's mercy!"

Whatever the temperature in their room, Janina and Henry always felt warmed by the tender kindness of the sisters. In time, they were able to return it by looking out for them and helping to support them.

Janina and Henry were now living in a part of Poland scarred and traumatized by more than two years of Nazi racist persecution. For Hitler, the conquest of Poland in 1939 was just one step toward fulfilling the mission that he believed Providence had assigned him: winning the *Lebensraum* destined for the German *Volk*. This vast "living space" would stretch from Germany to the eastern border of the European continent and would be settled by people of "German blood" from all over Europe. There they would produce the food, goods, and sons needed to ensure victory in the never-ending war for racial dominance. The fact that this future *Lebensraum* was already inhabited by tens of millions of Slavs as well as millions of Jews presented no moral or practical impediment, since Hitler considered both groups to be "subhuman." A minority of the Slavs would be retained to provide brute labor for their German masters; the rest, along with all the Jews, would in one way or another be made to disappear.[2]

German-occupied Poland became the laboratory where the measures for realizing the Nazi racist utopia were developed and tested. In September 1939, Hitler ordered that the western Polish provinces annexed to the Reich be made entirely German as quickly as possible by deporting their Jewish and Polish inhabitants eastward and replacing them with ethnic Germans imported from the territories occupied by the Soviet Union. All non-Jewish Poles were to be corralled in the occupied area east of the annexed territories, with the exception of one corner on the Soviet border. That area would become a "reservation" where all the Jews under Germany's control, both those in the Reich and in occupied Poland, would be forced to live. An enormous, unbreachable wall was to be erected along the reservation's western border to ensure that no Jews could return. This was to be a temporary arrangement, however, for eventually all of German-occupied Poland would be made entirely German.[3]

Hitler handed responsibility for realizing his vision to Heinrich Himmler, *Reichsführer* of the SS and Chief of the German Police.[4] He had at his disposal all the types of forces needed to impose the Nazi racist "new order" upon occupied Poland. His SS "race experts" would sort those genetically qualified to join the German racial community from those whose "blood" doomed them to servitude, ethnic cleansing, or mass murder. His concentration camps would permanently remove from society anyone seen as a potential threat to German rule, while his police forces along with his military formations, the Waffen SS, would sniff out, round up, and murder those considered too dangerous or unfit to be worthy of life.

To prevent the Poles from mounting any effective resistance to German rule, Hitler ordered the elimination of their leaders and educated classes. Following Germany's invasion of Poland, Himmler sent in his special task forces, the *Einsatzgruppen,* to track down 61,000 members of Poland's intelligentsia whose names had been collected by the SD before the war. The units summarily executed thousands of civilians, especially targeting Polish politicians, intellectuals, aristocrats, and even priests, teachers, doctors, and lawyers. By the end of 1939, these forces had shot some 40,000 Poles and 7,000 Polish Jews and sent tens of thousands more Polish civilians to the concentration camps in the Reich.[5] By the end of the war, the Germans would murder 25 percent of Poland's intelligentsia, including 15 percent of its schoolteachers and 18 percent of its Catholic priests. The losses were much higher for the professions in which Jews played a substantial role: Poland lost 45 percent of its doctors and dentists and 56 percent of its lawyers.[6]

Himmler wasted no time in launching the ethnic cleansing program to rid the Reich of Poles and Jews, an estimated six to eight million people. On October 30, 1939, he ordered that the first million be dumped into the General Government in the following four months. According to Himmler's plan, once all the Poles were deposited in the General Government, his race experts would screen them so that the few deemed "racially valuable" could be sent to the Reich to be assimilated. Annual screenings would follow of all Polish children between the ages of six and ten, and those selected would be sent off for assimilation as well. Once all their natural leaders had been murdered, the remaining "subhuman" Poles would lose their national and ethnic identities and become a reservoir of cheap, unskilled laborers.[7] Himmler proposed that the children of this underclass be schooled at most through the fourth grade, since Polish children would only need to be taught "simple counting up to 500 at most, writing one's name and . . . that it is divine law to obey the Germans. . . . I do not think that reading is necessary."[8]

As for the Jews, Himmler's race experts were developing proposals for getting rid of them all by shipping them somewhere outside of Europe. The French colony of Madagascar was the leading candidate, but others were also under consideration, such as Siberia above the Arctic Circle. Whichever remote, undeveloped, inhospitable destination was chosen, the expectation was that the four million people confined there under SS supervision would not long survive.[9]

For all his ambitions for the General Government, however, the reality was that Himmler was not in control there. Hitler assigned the task of ruling the General Government to Hans Frank, his personal lawyer and a committed Nazi since 1923. Frank's assignment was to govern the Polish territory just as Germany had once ruled over its African colonies: by seizing or exploiting everything of value, using the forced labor of its indigenous inhabitants, and eradicating all those who resisted. He answered only to Hitler and ruled by decree according to the *Führer*'s wishes.[10]

In the late fall of 1939, freight trains began arriving at stations in the General Government and disgorging thousands of men, women, and children forcibly deported from their homes in the annexed territories. Without warning, they had been rounded up at night by SS and police forces and forced to leave behind nearly all their possessions for the ethnic Germans who were to take over their homes, farms, and businesses. Just between December 1 and 17, 1939, the SS and police shipped 87,838 Poles and Jews to the General Government without giving prior notice to its officials. Frank protested vociferously that the resulting chaos was undermining his ability to exploit the region for Germany's benefit. In March, Himmler finally had to halt the deportations and agree that all future operations would be conducted in consultation with Frank and his officials.[11] This was just the opening round in a power struggle between the *Reichsführer* and the governor general that would continue for five years.

There was little disagreement between the two ideologically, however, especially when it came to rabid hatred of Poles and Jews. Frank yearned for the day when his realm would be *Judenfrei*—free of Jews—and populated by Germans, with a Polish minority as the servant class. The self-styled top legal mind of the Nazi Party, he abolished the Polish legal code but did not replace it with German law, since even its limited restraints on state power were more than he would brook in his realm. His non-German subjects could have no recourse against German excesses because nothing his officials did could qualify as an excess.[12]

Directly beneath Frank and answerable to him were the governors of the districts—Warsaw, Kraków, Radom, Lublin, and, from 1941, Galicia. Beneath the governors were the heads of the *Kreise*, local districts or counties. The applicants for these and other positions in Frank's administration tended to be minor civil servants, small businessmen, and Nazi Party officials seeking advancement that was unobtainable for them in the Reich because of their personal limitations, past failures, or criminal activities. They all had wide latitude to rule their individual fiefdoms as they pleased, provided they showed initiative in realizing Hitler's dreams of a racist new order. Competence and relevant experience were not requirements for positions in the General Government, only, as Frank explained, readiness to act as "warriors totally dedicated to the liquidation of the Poles."[13]

With no legal restraints upon its officials, theft and corruption became the hallmarks of the General Government administration. As the German head of the city of Lublin put it, "We have decided to behave, as officials, exactly the other way round than at home, that is, like bastards." Officials confiscated estates, factories, and businesses—especially those owned by Jews—and gave charge of them to relatives, cronies, or Germans who offered the right price. These "trustees" then brazenly embezzled the assets entrusted to them. Since it was official policy to eradicate every vestige of Polish culture, officials systematically plundered palaces, churches, and museums, destroyed national monuments and memorials, and closed libraries, looting or burning their works. In Kraków, the General Government's capital, Frank ensconced himself in the Wawel Royal Castle and confiscated a string of other palaces for his personal use, decorating them with all the finest trappings he could steal. His subordinates eagerly copied his example. German officials could enrich themselves by taking what they wanted or by demanding payment for not taking it. Bribery became the oil of the administrative machinery. For the right inducement, almost anything could be done; without it, almost nothing.[14]

Count Skrzyński, who served in the Polish resistance, helped Janina and Henry acquire identity documents that enabled them to pass as Poles. Henry became Count Piotr Suchodolski and Janina Countess Janina Stanisława Bednarska Suchodolska.[15] To obtain the documents, they first had to acquire birth certificates based upon the records of the churches where they were supposedly baptized, as well as a record of their wedding from a marriage registry. With these, they could register as residents of Lublin and obtain the all-important *Kennkarte*, the identity document that the Germans required all residents of the General Government to carry. But the Germans were well aware that many *Kennkarten* were forgeries or based on forgeries and so regularly changed the regulations, requiring extra stamps or adopting a new format for which the old *Kennkarten* had to be exchanged. With every change, Janina's and Henry's documents came under fresh scrutiny and, as the Gestapo expanded its investigations, increased risk of exposure.[16]

Shedding their Jewish identities only enabled Janina and Henry to exchange one form of persecution for another, somewhat less deadly, form. In the General Government, as well as in the Reich, a system of strict apartheid was imposed not only upon the Jews but also upon the "Poles," a term that for the Germans applied exclusively to persons of Polish ethnicity. Fraternization between Poles and Germans was strictly forbidden. Poles were barred from parks, gardens, museums, public swimming pools, and certain neighborhoods, as well as from all the better shops, restaurants, cafés, and most theaters and cinemas. They could only shop at certain hours, could only use designated areas of bus and train stations, and had to sit in the rear of public transport. University and secondary school education were banned for Poles. The Germans confiscated so many school buildings and shot or incarcerated so many teachers that Polish children lucky enough to attend elementary school could only do so for a few hours a week in unheated classrooms with seventy or more pupils.[17]

Food policy was one of the Germans' favorite tools for persecuting racial enemies. The General Government's economy was primarily agrarian, but much of the food it produced was sent to the Reich. In the fall of 1941, the official rations for Poles only supplied between 20 percent and 30 percent of the calories an adult needs to survive.[18] Instead of receiving rations directly, Polish Jews had to subsist on the tiny quantities of food their Jewish community was permitted to buy. In January 1941, the amount of flour authorized for the Lublin *Judenrat* (the Jewish council assigned to fulfill German demands and to provide for Lublin's Jewish residents) came to less than one pound per person—for the entire month.[19] Carbohydrates—mainly potatoes, beans, and bread—accounted for nearly all the calories in Poles' rations. The goal of Nazi policy was to weaken and decimate the Polish population so that it could not resist German rule or long-term Nazi plans to make most of the Poles and all of the Jews disappear from their native land.[20]

On top of starvation rations, General Government officials imposed a labor requirement upon Poles between the ages of fourteen and sixty and a forced labor requirement upon Jews twelve and older. Like the Jews, Poles could be seized at any time to perform heavy labor at construction or road-building sites or in labor camps. Unlike the Jews, they could be sent off to the Reich to work, a fate that had befallen more than half a million by the time Janina arrived in Lublin. At first, some Poles volunteered, believing German promises that they would experience better conditions and be better able to support their families back home. By now, however, Poles knew the truth: in Germany, they were given the worst jobs with the worst pay, could not change jobs, and had no recourse against employers who beat or raped them. Even before German Jews were ordered to don the yellow star, Polish laborers in the Reich had to wear a special badge marking them as Poles. When employers reported their Polish workers as lazy or disruptive, the Gestapo incarcerated them in "labor education camps" or even in concentration camps.[21]

Through Count Skrzyński, Henry obtained employment with Społem, the largest agricultural cooperative in Lublin District. He worked as an agricultural expert with a specialty in egg production. It was a job that allowed him to keep a low profile throughout the war.

Given Henry's long work hours, the task of obtaining groceries and supplies fell to Janina. The few stores that catered to Poles in Lublin could not be counted on to supply even the meager amount and types of food permitted under the ration system, and since these were insufficient for long-term survival, there was no choice but to seek provisions on the black market. Finding illicit vendors with the goods one needed and then bargaining to obtain them with cash or through barter was difficult and risky. As the war dragged on and shortages increased, people spent more and more of their time in the search for food and essential items. A popular Polish joke at that time summed up the situation:

> Two friends who had not seen each other for a long time met in the street:
>
> "What are you doing?"
> "I am working in the city hall."
> "And your wife, how is she?"
> "She is working in a paper store."
> "And your daughter?"
> "She is working in a plant."
> "How the hell do you live?"
> "Thank God, my son is unemployed."[22]

When she first wandered the streets of Lublin, Janina thought the city rather lovely, despite Henry's complaints about his earlier stay there. But everywhere she went, she found its beauty marred by the German occupiers. Litewski Square, lined with palaces of the local nobility and the Church of Saints Peter and Paul, had been renamed Adolf-Hitler-Platz. In its center, a huge map displayed the advance of Nazi control over Europe, and a loudspeaker, which the Poles dubbed "the Bellower," blared news of German victories and spewed antisemitic propaganda. The elegant shops and cafés of the broad boulevard Krakowskie Przedmieście bore signs barring entry to Poles. Walls were plastered with posters depicting Jews as dirty and lice-ridden and accusing them of everything from selling poisonous liquors to spreading typhus. Most appalling to Janina was the sight of the gaunt and sickly faces of the Polish children she encountered outside the crowded tenement buildings where their families were forced to live after the Germans took their homes.

Passing through the Gothic Kraków Gate, Janina entered the cobblestone streets of Lublin's Old Town. Its half-timbered houses with painted frescoes were crumbling yet still exuded charm. Heading toward the eighteenth-century Grodzka Gate, however, she found that the street was blocked and police were inspecting all who entered. A sign warned of the danger of typhus and identified the area beyond as the ghetto.[23]

The section of Lublin between Grodzka Gate and Zamek, the castle that loomed over the city, was the historic Jewish quarter, which dated back to at least the fifteenth century. Lublin's population of over 42,000 Jews had spread well beyond the quarter by 1939. In spring 1941, Lublin District Governor Ernst Zörner ordered that all Lublin city's Jewish residents be confined in a ghetto in one section of the Jewish quarter. In October 1941, Governor General Frank decreed that all Jews caught outside their assigned ghetto were to be arrested and shot, as well as any Poles discovered to have aided them. Entrance to the Lublin Ghetto was prohibited for all non-Jews except General Government officials on December 9, 1941, just before Janina and Henry arrived in the city.

By the start of 1942, more than 35,000 Jews were living in the ghetto, packed into synagogues, schools, warehouses, tenement buildings, and ancient wooden houses. With rare exceptions, there was no electricity or running water. It was no secret that starvation and typhus were rampant—as one SS official described it, the residents were "dropping like flies."[24] Hearing about conditions in the ghetto, Janina could not help but think with despair of her friends and colleagues who now suffered under similar conditions in Lwów.

Janina observed how German policies aimed to set Poland's different ethnic communities against one another. The Germans published antisemitic propaganda in the Polish language in order to inflame the Poles' prejudices against Jews. Lublin had a significant Ukrainian population and, as in Galicia, the Germans privileged it over Poles and Jews. Ukrainians received better rations, could educate their children through university, were allowed to frequent some establishments barred to Poles, and could even convert some Catholic churches to Greek Catholic or Orthodox. Poles with German ancestors could do even better by registering as *Volksdeutsche*, ethnic Germans. If accepted, they enjoyed the same rations and many of the same privileges as Reich Germans in the General Government. Some ethnic Germans welcomed the chance to join the supposedly superior Germans and support their new fatherland, including by looting and slaughtering Jews. But there were many Poles of German ancestry who had always considered themselves loyal Poles and resisted the temptation to obtain the privileges that Germans enjoyed, even though doing so branded them as suspected enemies.[25]

Not all Poles suffered equally under German policies, Janina discovered. The social order had turned topsy-turvy, with professors lucky to work as waiters and aristocratic ladies as maids. But some Poles fared considerably better, while a few even improved their standard of living, at least for a while. This was chiefly thanks to the black market. Like many other residents of the city, Janina's search for food took her into the countryside around Lublin to visit savvy farmers who had saved or hidden enough of their produce from German requisitioners to offer some for sale for cash or goods. She was surprised by the quantity and variety of luxury items she saw in the simple peasant households where she sought food. In one, there was a concert piano that no one could play; in others she saw record players that sat silent, given the lack of electricity. One day she visited a farmer who proudly showed her five radios and five sewing machines that he was saving as dowries for his daughters. Some of the peasant women she dealt with wore makeup and gave off the scent of expensive perfumes. Many of these goods came from Jews who had been forced to trade their most prized possessions in order to stave off starvation.

Madame Maria's employer, Madame Rylska, provided an example of how some people in the city managed to profit from Nazi persecution. Beneath her beauty and charm, Janina discerned, lay a rare talent for making money. Officially, Madame Rylska operated an elegant pastry shop and café, as well as a store selling baby carriages. Her main source of income, however, was smuggling, at which her son Olek proved particularly adept. One of their specialties was shoes, for which only Germans and *Volksdeutsche* received rations, but they also traded in the diamonds and gold that they acquired from Jews, their principal clients.

Janina understood that black marketeering and bribery were essential survival strategies in German-occupied Poland, and that they depended upon turning a profit and taking advantage of others' needs. Staying true to one's values could be a luxury few were willing to afford when Nazi policies set the price for doing so as survival for oneself or one's family. She observed this in one of Countess Władysława's tenants, a half-German young man who refused to register as *Volksdeutsch*. Janina admired how he shivered in his thin coat and ate boiled unpeeled potatoes like his other housemates. But then he married, a baby soon followed who turned sickly, and finally he traded in his Polish nationality for food and medicine to save his child.

It was not her place, Janina decided, to judge the choices others made to survive Nazi oppression. Had not she and Henry abandoned their families and friends for a chance to escape the Nazis' murderous plans? That knowledge would burden them both for the rest of their days.

SIX

ANNIHILATION

Of all the failed Nazis who found a second chance in occupied Poland, none was a greater fanatic or had a larger cloud over his head than Odilo Globocnik. An Austrian, he had served as the first Nazi head of Vienna after the *Anschluss* (annexation) in 1938. The appointment was an award for his service to the illegal Nazi movement in Austria, during which he had earned several prison sentences for treason and a reputation as a terrorist and assassin. But after just eight months in the Vienna post, he was dismissed for incompetence and threatened with arrest for allegedly enriching himself through bribery and embezzlement, especially of Jewish assets.

Luckily for Globocnik, he had made an important friend in Berlin: Heinrich Himmler. The pedantic *Reichsführer* SS, who had been plying Globocnik with his favorite works on racist theory, saw his pupil as a fanatically committed man of action who would stop at nothing to impose Nazi rule. That was a skill set Himmler knew he could use, and Poland's conquest offered the perfect opportunity to apply it. In November 1939, Himmler appointed Globocnik SS and Police Leader in Lublin District, with command over all the Waffen SS and police forces stationed there. The position effectively put Globocnik beyond the reach of the investigators who were pursuing him for his misdeeds in Vienna. It also ensured that he would be forever beholden to Himmler.[1]

As the SS and Police Leader in a General Government district, it was Globocnik's responsibility to terrorize the non-German population into unquestioning obedience to their German masters. His standard duties included incarcerating or murdering members of the Polish intelligentsia and applying disproportionate violence in response to any signs of resistance.[2]

In addition to his regular duties, however, Globocnik pursued several special assignments from his mentor and protector. Lublin was slated to serve two important purposes in Himmler's plan to achieve his racist utopia. First, it was to be the location of the reservation to which all the Jews under Germany's control, as well Roma (then called Gypsies) and other "undesirables," would be confined. But Himmler also believed that Lublin District had untapped human potential in the descendants of the Germans who had migrated into the region centuries before. Once identified and re-Germanized, this progeny would form the vanguard for Germanizing all of the General Government after Germany won the war. Creating the reservation and Germanizing the General Government became Globocnik's two most cherished goals.[3]

For the reservation, Globocnik chose a swampy region near the Bug River, where he planned to put 2.5 million Jews and Roma to work digging a giant antitank trench along the General Government's eastern border. Governor General Frank adamantly opposed the reservation plan, however. The General Government was already overburdened by the hundreds of thousands of Poles and Jews being expelled from the annexed territories, he complained. Globocnik suggested a simple solution to the problem of the expellees: if the Polish and Jewish communities of the General Government could not care for them, then they should be left to starve. This modest proposal did not meet with Frank's approval. In March 1940, he persuaded Hitler to call off the reservation plan.

Globocnik arrived in Lublin before most of the district's civilian administrators and immediately claimed complete control over the district's Jews, including their labor and assets. To make good on his power grab, he formed an auxiliary police force, called the *Selbstschutz* (self-defense), made up of ethnic German Poles who served as his private army. He deployed it to loot Jewish homes and businesses, rob Jews on the streets, and seize and abuse Jewish forced laborers. He also established camps where the *Selbstschutz* forced Jews to perform heavy labor on a variety of military and civilian projects in Lublin District. By the fall of 1940, 50,000 to 70,000 Jews were being forced to work in seventy-six camps in Lublin District. Thousands died from the primitive conditions or from being beaten or shot by their *Selbstschutz* guards.[4]

Jews were not the only victims of the *Selbstschutz*. Globocnik also deployed his private army in reprisal actions against Polish communities and in roundups of Poles for forced labor, during which his mercenaries robbed, raped, and murdered at will. Fed up with its excesses, civilian officials succeeded in forcing Globocnik to disband the *Selbstschutz* in fall 1940 and to give up all but one of his forced labor camps.

Janina discovered Globocnik's remaining camp, at 7 Lipowa Street, soon after she arrived in Lublin. Its prisoners included 2,500 Polish Jewish POWs.[5] Janina would sometimes watch as the SS guards escorted the camp's prisoners to labor sites in the city. The sight of the Jewish POWs in their Polish uniforms, marching in disciplined formation, their heads held high, filled her with pride. But her heart was also heavy with the knowledge that some non-Jewish Poles believed the national uniform was defiled when worn by a Jew.

While his reservation plans came to naught, Globocnik made good progress on the project he dubbed "Search for German Blood." When Himmler visited Lublin in October 1940, Globocnik enthralled him with proposals for Germanizing both the city of Lublin and the agriculturally rich Zamość region in southeastern Lublin District. The city would become a center of German culture and industry. In the Zamość region, the SS would expel the non-German peasants to establish idyllic villages populated by settlers chosen for their "German blood." Leading regimented lives governed by the SS, these happy settlers would produce the food and the offspring that Germany would need to wage its future wars. These plans had to remain on paper for the present, but Himmler ordered Globocnik to have them ready when the time was finally ripe to put them into action.[6]

That time already seemed to be approaching in the spring of 1941 as Germany prepared to attack the Soviet Union. German generals were certain that the Wehrmacht would defeat the Red Army in a matter of weeks. After the Soviet Union's inevitable collapse, it would finally be possible to realize Hitler's vision for the German *Lebensraum* in Eastern Europe. Following a meeting with Hitler in March, Frank triumphantly announced exciting news to his subordinates: "Where 12 million Poles live today will one day live four to five million Germans. The General Government must become as German a land as the Rhineland."[7]

At Hitler's direction, Wehrmacht leaders planned the Soviet campaign as a *Vernichtungskrieg*, a "war of annihilation" to be ruthlessly waged against the "Judeo-Bolshevik" enemy without regard to the rules of warfare. Military and civilian planners drew up occupation policies for the territories to be seized that would cause "umpteen million" civilians to die of starvation in just the first year. Himmler took charge of long-range planning for imposing the new racial order in the German *Lebensraum*. His *Generalplan Ost* (General Plan East) envisioned eliminating 30 to 45 million indigenous inhabitants by forcing them to starve or to migrate beyond the Urals. These victims would account for up to 85 percent of the Poles, 75 percent of the Belarusians, and 64 percent of the Ukrainians. The ten million Germanic settlers who would take their place would be led and controlled by the SS.[8]

Just four weeks into the Soviet campaign, victory against the Soviet Union already seemed at hand. Eager to put his plans in motion, Himmler met with Globocnik in Lublin on July 20, 1941, to give him several important assignments. The first was to begin the Germanization of the General Government by expelling non-Germans from the Zamość region and settling ethnic German colonists in their place. The second was to develop SS and police bases that would take the lead in pacifying and colonizing the territories farther east.

The third assignment Himmler gave Globocnik was to transform the city of Lublin into a military and industrial base that would provide the manpower, equipment, and supplies to support SS dominion in the "German East." The city would become a garrison for 60,000 SS and police forces and the site of a wide variety of SS-owned industries. To make way for the troops and industries, Globocnik planned to expel the city's Polish residents.

Lublin's transformation could not be achieved without an adequate labor supply, but for as long as the war lasted, Poles would be needed for labor in the Reich. Himmler fixed on two other sources for workers. One, at least for the time being, was Jews. Much to Globocnik's satisfaction, Himmler authorized him not only to expand the Lipowa Street Jewish forced labor camp but also to build a new one at a former airfield on the edge of the city. The other labor source would be Soviet prisoners of war. Himmler ordered construction of two huge concentration camps for Red Army prisoners, one in Lublin and the other in Birkenau, adjacent to Auschwitz. By March 1942, the planned capacity of the Lublin concentration camp expanded from 50,000 to 250,000.[9]

Eager as he was to attack his Germanization assignment, Globocnik first had a major logistical problem to solve: what to do with all the non-Germans living in the areas designated for German colonists. As usual, he hit upon a ruthlessly simple solution. If the two million Jews living in the General Government were killed, the Poles in the Germanized areas could be deposited in the ghettos. The conditions there would then simplify the task of getting rid of the Poles once they were no longer needed.[10]

That left the question of how to kill the Jews. This was a problem other Nazi and SS officials were wrestling with as well. Enthusiasm for sending the Jews to live elsewhere had waned as the war continued. On July 31, 1941, Hitler's deputy, Hermann Göring, formally authorized Reinhard Heydrich, the head of the Security Police and SD, to develop a plan for the "comprehensive solution" to the "Jewish question" in Europe, something Heydrich had long been working on. His *Einsatzgruppen* immediately proceeded to murder entire Jewish communities in territories seized from the Soviet Union. This approach had distinct drawbacks for the General Government, however. Shooting two million men, women, and children in an area the size of Belgium would inevitably attract international notice, might spark resistance, and would require manpower and resources needed for the war. And so Globocnik, ever the man of action, sought a way to annihilate the General Government's Jews that would be cheap, efficient, and easy to keep relatively secret.

Since the start of the war, Nazi Germany had developed a new mass killing technology for its "euthanasia" program to murder Germans with mental or physical disabilities. Institutionalized patients were sent to six special "sanatoriums," where they were asphyxiated with carbon monoxide in special gas chambers designed to look like showers. These facilities dispatched more than 70,000 victims before Hitler, in response to some grumbling among the Germans, ostensibly ended the program in August 1941 (although patients with disabilities would continue to be routinely murdered in sanatoriums and asylums until two months after Germany's defeat). The next month, Globocnik brought members of the technical staff that had developed the euthanasia gassing facilities to Lublin to advise him how to murder the Jews in the General Government with carbon monoxide.[11]

Globocnik met with Himmler on October 13, 1941, to present a plan for murdering the General Government's Jews. In isolated villages along the major rail lines, he would erect special compounds to which the SS would bring Jews in large transports and, within a few hours, asphyxiate them hundreds at a time with carbon monoxide in sealed chambers. These compounds would be cheap to build, as only the gassing barracks required any special materials; the only other buildings would be wooden warehouses for the goods looted from the victims and barracks for the small force needed to murder the victims. The carbon monoxide would be piped into the gassing barracks from the engine of a tank or large truck. Tall wooden fences around the compounds would hide the activities within from any outsiders who dared to come near.

To perform the hands-on labor of rounding up and murdering Jews, Globocnik planned to use a new private army he was recruiting from the Soviet POW camps. Designated by the location of their training base, the "Trawniki men" would become notorious for their brutality.[12]

Other SS officials developed variations of the euthanasia technology in the fall of 1941. Heydrich's technical experts produced gas vans, mobile transport into which carbon monoxide was pumped from cylinders or engine exhaust, killing the passengers while carrying them to their gravesite. At Auschwitz, SS officials successfully tested on Soviet POWs a different, readily available poison: hydrogen cyanide. Sold as Zyklon B, it was already in heavy use at concentration camps as a delousing agent.[13]

By the time Janina moved to Lublin in mid-December 1941, work was progressing on the first of Globocnik's killing centers, at Bełżec near the district's eastern border. At that same moment, Nazi Germany's Jewish policy was undergoing a momentous change, one that would expand the scope of Globocnik's murder operation beyond the borders of the General Government. After Hitler declared war on the United States on December 11, he announced to top Nazi Party officials that the time had come to fulfill the promise he had made in January 1939. In a speech broadcast around the world, he had then "prophesied" that if the "international Jewish financiers" of the world succeeded "once more" in fomenting a world war, "the result will be not the Bolshevizing of the earth, and thus the victory of Jewry, but the annihilation of the Jewish race in Europe!" He had meant the threat as a warning to Britain, France, and the United States not to interfere with Germany's conquest of Eastern Europe. Now that the war was truly global, however, he was determined to fulfill his prophesy.[14]

Reinhard Heydrich received the go-ahead for his "comprehensive" plan. On January 30, 1942, he assembled top German officials at a villa in Wannsee outside Berlin to assign them their tasks for achieving the "final solution of the Jewish question": the murder of all the Jews in Europe. To avoid unpleasant repercussions, the SS and police would ship the victims living outside Eastern Europe to occupied Polish and Soviet territories, where they would be dispatched with poison gas or bullets.[15]

Between March and late July 1942, Globocnik established three killing centers—Bełżec, Sobibor, and Treblinka—that daily murdered tens of thousands of Jews from all over Europe. In June, Globocnik named his mass murder program *Aktion* (Operation) Reinhard, in honor of Reinhard Heydrich, who had just died of wounds from an assassination attempt. In the twenty months of the operation, more than 1.5 million Jews and an unknown number of Roma were murdered in the three killing centers, and another 200,000 Jews were shot. *Aktion* Reinhard was the deadliest mass murder operation of the Holocaust—Auschwitz, with its 960,000 Jewish victims over nearly three years, ran a distant second.[16]

Aktion Reinhard's purpose was not just to murder Jews but to exploit them in every possible sense, right down to their hair and gold teeth.

Globocnik temporarily spared some *Aktion* Reinhard victims so he could force them to work in the SS enterprises he was developing in and around Lublin city. These enterprises were funded with the proceeds from looted Jewish valuables; operated with looted Jewish tools, materials, and machinery; and transformed Jewish personal possessions into goods for use by Germans. The huge prisoner of war camp complex being built on the outskirts of the city was to become a major site for these enterprises and for Jewish forced laborers. Its official name was *Kriegsgefangenlager* (Prisoner of War Camp) Lublin but, based on the camp's location in the Majdan Tatarski suburb, the locals dubbed it Majdanek.

Janina's first inkling that a new Nazi plan for Lublin's Jews was in the works came from Madame Maria, who relished imparting the gossip she heard at work. The café of her employers, the Rylskis, was near the Lipowa Street workshops, where their prewar Jewish tailor was forced to work. He would surreptitiously visit them on his return to the ghetto in the evening to alter clothes for them. He accepted food, which he took home to his daughter, but refused their money, explaining that when the time came, he hoped they would give him another form of payment. Then in February 1942, he came to them in anguish. The Germans had begun dividing the ghetto into two parts with barbed wire and now announced that the Jews had to apply for new identity cards. Jews who had jobs like his that the SS deemed important were to receive different cards from those who, like his daughter, did not. Rumors were flying that he and the other "privileged" workers would soon be moved into the smaller part of the ghetto.[17] The tailor felt sure that the Jews left in the larger ghetto section would be subjected to some new form of suffering and he feared that his daughter would not survive it. He begged the Rylskis to save her.

As March approached and the division of the ghetto neared completion, the tailor's visits became more frequent and his pleas more urgent. He even brought money to pay the Rylskis to save his daughter. But no amount of money could compensate for the risk he was asking them to take. The Germans had begun to execute Poles, sometimes including their family members, for trying to help Jews hide.

Much to everyone's astonishment, twenty-two-year-old Olek Rylski decided to save the tailor's daughter, whom he had never seen, and to do so by staging a sham wedding. He bribed a Polish family living next to the ghetto to take the girl in when she fled there one night. The next day, he moved her to a residence in another part of the city and secured an identity card for her from a Polish girl of the same age and physical description. The following morning, dressed in his best and accompanied by Father Santi, an Italian priest who had agreed to the scheme, he called upon his "bride," who looked lovely dressed in silk and tulle. They made an elaborate show of processing toward the town hall to register their marriage. Afterward, she moved into another place he had arranged for her and managed to survive the war passing as a Pole.

This story fascinated Janina. She had met Olek Rylski and taken him for an enthusiastic black marketeer who was utterly indifferent to the suffering from which he reaped his profits. He seemed, in fact, the type of Pole around whom Janina and Henry had to be most on their guard to avoid any suspicion of their Jewish identity. And yet he had risked his own life as well as the lives of his family to save a Jewish girl he did not know. Here was another example of people's ability to act against interest in ways that seemed out of character and irreconcilable with their previous actions. There were hidden variables at work in human nature, she concluded, that could defy logical inference.

The tailor returned once more to the Rylskis, brimming with happiness and gratitude for the safety of his child. They never saw him again.

Late on March 16, 1942, German police and Globocnik's Trawniki men surrounded Lublin's ghetto and then stormed in. Lublin residents outside the ghetto heard shouts in German, shrieks and cries, and intermittent bursts of gunfire. They glimpsed Jewish bodies lying in the ghetto streets in pools of blood. Poles living near a sand mine outside the city witnessed the shooting of the children from the ghetto orphanage. At night, people living along the route from the ghetto to the municipal slaughterhouse observed hundreds of Jewish men, women, and children shuffling by, clutching bags or suitcases containing the few items they were permitted to take with them. From the area behind the slaughterhouse, where there was a railroad siding, more gunfire could be heard. The Underground reported that the Jews, including the corpses of those shot, were packed into freight cars that sometimes sat on the siding for days before heading eastward.

Day after day, but especially at night, the shouts, shrieks, shots, and shuffling reverberated in Lublin. By April 14, some 28,000 residents of Lublin's ghetto had been murdered. More than a thousand were shot; the rest were gassed at the Bełżec killing center. The remaining 7,000 Jews were moved into a new ghetto in Majdan Tatarski. Three thousand were then selected and sent to Majdanek; all were shot. On April 20, 1942, Hitler's birthday, the liquidation of the Lublin Ghetto was complete.[18]

Lublin's ghetto was the target of *Aktion* Reinhard's inaugural operation. Its second target was the ghetto in Lwów.

The fate of the deported Jews was a hot topic of whispered discussions in Lublin. The Germans said that the Jews had been sent to perform labor "in the East," but people noted that many of the deportees were too old or young to work, while only able-bodied workers had been allowed to remain. Railway workers reported that the Jews were being taken to a small SS camp next to the village of Bełżec. Poles living in the vicinity described what they could witness from a distance: thousands of Jews were disappearing daily into the facility, which had only three small wooden barracks; no Jews were ever seen leaving; no food was being delivered, but carts piled with personal belongings regularly departed the camp for the rail station warehouse; a strong odor was emanating from the facility. By mid-April, word was spreading around the district: the Germans were murdering the Jews at the camp at Bełżec. Opinion was divided as to how, with the three chief guesses being electrocution, gas, or suffocation with a vacuum pump.[19]

The shocking realization that the Germans were murdering the Jews caused Poles to ask: "Will we be next?" They had good reason to wonder. After the prediction of a swift victory in the war failed to come true, Nazi leaders doubled down on their ruthless exploitation of the Polish population in 1942. They cut Poles' rations, increased the agricultural levies, and plundered Polish homes, farms, and businesses so that Germans on the home front would not have to experience shortages. Brutal raids became the order of the day. German forces swooped into villages, neighborhoods, and marketplaces to seize victims, or dragged them out of churches and off of trains and streetcars. The victims might be put to heavy labor on some local road building or construction project, sent to the Reich or to one of the hundreds of forced labor camps in the General Government, or they might be held as hostages, to be shot in reprisal for the next real or perceived act of resistance.[20] People were afraid to sleep in their beds and fled their homes at the merest hint of a raid. As one Pole wrote in his diary in March 1942, Poles were living with "the constant sensation of death, violence and injustice. The population is being terrorized. . . . The number of victims continually multiplies."[21]

Janina felt caught in a vise between horror and fear. The sounds of the Lublin Ghetto liquidation kept ringing in her ears, tormenting her with thoughts of her many loved ones in the Lwów Ghetto who were experiencing the same unspeakable fate. She was constantly conscious of the danger that she and Henry would be murdered as well. If Henry were seized in a raid, a physical examination would immediately expose him as a Jew, since he was circumcised, and they would both be murdered. But first would come the torture to discover who had helped them. Gruesome stories abounded in Lublin of the methods and implements that the Gestapo employed at Security Police headquarters. Janina worried that suspicion would fall on Count Skrzyński, or perhaps even Countess Władysława, if she and Henry were exposed as Jews. The constant tension she felt made it nearly impossible to sleep, and even breathing sometimes seemed to take effort.

One night, she started out of a fitful sleep to see circles of light dancing on the ceiling. Instantly she realized: flashlights! She ran to the window and carefully peeked out from a side of the curtain. German soldiers were going into the houses and apartment buildings along the street. Just two buildings away, she saw them bang on the door, rush in, and begin to drag men out to a waiting truck. In a panic, Janina ran to her landlady's room and woke the two sisters.

"Auntie Władzia, quickly, they're coming for Henry! Give me the key to the cellar so he can hide," Janina begged.

"I'll do no such thing, my child," Władzia exclaimed. "You're so upset that you can't think straight right now. If they take him from here, it's for labor or a concentration camp. But if they find him hiding in the basement, they will shoot him on the spot.

"Besides," she added more softly, "they are not going to take him. We have our special prayers for such occasions. Just go back to your room and wait and see."

Returning to their room in despair, Janina found Henry already dressed. She darted to the window. The truck was now right across the street. She watched as the Germans, brandishing bayonets, forced some men into it. The doors slammed. And then the truck drove off, taking the Germans as well.

Janina went back to the elderly ladies' room and found them both on their knees, praying fervently. Countess Władysława's face gleamed with tears and a strange peace. Janina told them the Germans had left, and after a few more minutes, they arose.

"Didn't I tell you that God hears our prayers?" Władzia asked. "Such prayers, anyway!"

Janina was not going to argue the point. She understood that the sisters' faith was what had enabled them to persevere through so many hardships. But Janina recognized that there would be other raids, and neither luck nor divine intervention could be counted on to spare Henry from being taken. No matter how she calculated the probabilities, the odds always pointed to the same result. Sooner or later, she and Henry would meet their fate: annihilation.

SEVEN

"BETTER TO DIE A SOLDIER"

Once Janina accepted that she would not survive the war, fear's grip on her began to loosen. The problem she needed to solve, she realized, was not how to survive, but how to live what remained of her life. The answer appeared obvious. She would devote herself to thwarting however she could the Nazi plans to destroy Poland and its people. For that struggle, she enjoyed one peculiar advantage: her false identity as a Polish countess. European class consciousness, even among the Nazis, bestowed an automatic deference on the nobility that she could exploit—as long as she could carry off the role of someone who took her privilege for granted.

So Janina went to Count Skrzyński and persuaded him to sponsor her membership in the Polish Home Army. It seemed best not to reveal her true identity. The Home Army, or AK (*Armia Krajowa*) as it was called, was the armed force of the Polish Underground State, the clandestine resistance organization that was active throughout occupied Poland and answered to the Polish government in exile in London. Recognized by the Allies, the government in exile was an uneasy alliance of prewar Polish political parties ranging from the right-wing, antisemitic National Democrats to the Polish Socialist Party. The members of the AK and the Polish Underground within Poland reflected the same range of attitudes toward Jews as did the parties in the government in exile. Jewish Poles did serve in the AK, but those who served openly as Jews were the rare exception, and some local AK commanders refused to admit Jews in their ranks. Skrzyński and Janina recognized that she was more likely to win the trust and acceptance of AK leaders as a Polish Christian aristocrat than as a Polish Jew.[1]

With Skrzyński vouching for her, Janina passed the vetting process to join the ranks of the AK. In a training cell consisting of a few other new recruits, all unknown to one another and using pseudonyms, she learned such skills as coding and how to spot and evade surveillance, as well as what to do and say if arrested. On the day of her induction, Janina took the oath of loyalty. Holding a crucifix, she swore:

> Before Almighty God and the Holy Virgin Mary, Queen of Poland, I take in my hands this Holy Cross, the sign of Suffering and Salvation, and swear loyalty to Poland, the Republic of Poland, to unyieldingly guard her honor and to fight for her liberation from slavery with all my strength—and unto death.[2]

Taking the oath and joining the fight against her nation's oppressor liberated Janina. "No more passive endurance of suffering and helpless fear," she thought. "Better work, risk, danger—better to die a soldier than a victim!"

The ultimate aim of the AK and the Underground State was to prepare a national uprising against the occupier. This was to occur when Nazi Germany was on the brink of defeat. The AK planned at that point to attack the German forces remaining in the country, drive them out, and then proclaim and defend sovereignty over Poland's prewar boundaries.[3] Collecting intelligence was an essential aspect of preparing for the uprising, and the AK relied heavily on women to spy on and transmit information about German plans and operations. Women tended to attract less scrutiny from the Germans than men, and they were less likely to be seized in raids, which made it easier for them to move about, observe German military movements and installations, and overhear conversations. Polish women who knew German and obtained clerical jobs in General Government offices were able to report on the contents of documents they handled and provide blank forms that the AK could use to forge orders or passes.[4]

The Lublin AK assigned Janina the code name "Stefania." One of her earliest assignments was as a courier, carrying information, orders, money, and other items between AK cells and commands. This was one of the most common tasks assigned to women not only in the AK but also in other clandestine resistance organizations. Janina often made her courier runs at night. Dressed in dark clothes and rubber-soled shoes, she slipped between buildings and kept to the shadows of alleyways. Periodically, she would stop to determine the direction of the gunfire that regularly echoed through the city, signaling that the police were either firing on another curfew-breaker, conducting a raid, or drunkenly proclaiming their mastery over the "Polack swine."

Sometimes, when Janina could not make a delivery immediately, she would entrust the packet to Countess Władysława. "Auntie Władzia" would take it without question, her eyes shining with pride, and she insisted that Janina not know where she had put it, so that suspicion would not fall on Janina if it were discovered. She also urged Janina not to hand her anything in her sister's presence or to confide in her sister. The warning was not needed, for Janina knew that Madame Maria, cheerful and gregarious, tended to babble about whatever she had heard or seen, oblivious to the potential consequences.

Another focus of AK activities was sending news and instructions to the Poles via clandestine publications and radio broadcasts. Count Skrzyński played a role in these efforts, and Janina joined him. Their assignment was to listen to foreign radio broadcasts, especially the BBC, take down their contents, translate them if in another language, and encode them. Like the Jews in the General Government, the Poles were ordered to turn in their radio sets, while members of ethnic groups permitted to have radios had to obtain a special license to use them.[5] Janina and Skrzyński's listening station was in the home of Mrs. Santi, mother of the Italian priest who had feigned to marry Olek Rylski and the Jewish tailor's daughter. As an Italian citizen, Mrs. Santi could own a radio, but Janina and Skrzyński did not use it for their clandestine work. Instead, they listened on the receiver of a Wehrmacht major who was billeted in Mrs. Santi's home and was often away in the evening. As they tuned and listened to his radio, Mrs. Santi would turn up the volume on hers while her daughter watched for anyone approaching the home. The daughter's warnings gave Janina and Skrzyński just enough time to slip out of the major's room. Anyone who entered the premises would find them with Mrs. Santi in her living room, attending to the German broadcast. The major's room also served as a meeting place for the members of the AK cell to which Janina and Skrzyński belonged.

In May 1942, Count Skrzyński accepted the position of the lead official in Lublin District of the Polish Main Welfare Council. Known by its initials, RGO (*Rada Główna Opiekuńcza*), it provided welfare services and relief to ethnic Poles and was the only Polish civil society organization permitted to exist and operate in the General Government. Skrzyński's was an almost impossibly challenging job in which he would be of immeasurable service to the people of Poland. It was also a job that would ultimately repay him with indignity and slander.

There had been an RGO in German-occupied Poland during World War I, and its founder, Count Adam Ronikier, proposed to reactivate it after the General Government was established. Since General Government officials took no interest in the welfare of the "alien" people they ruled, they welcomed the opportunity to offload responsibility for providing the neediest victims of German policies the bare essentials to support life. They were not about to allow a single Polish organization to provide services to all former Polish citizens, however. Instead, relief officials limited the RGO to aiding Poles and set up separate organizations to provide for Polish Jews and Ukrainians. To fund its operations, the RGO received a small portion of a special welfare tax imposed upon the Poles and could also seek donations, including from Polish diaspora organizations abroad, especially in the United States. These donations largely ceased after Germany declared war on the United States in December 1941. From then on, the RGO relied primarily upon donations in money and in kind from the malnourished and impoverished population of the General Government.[6]

The RGO's work was closely supervised by the General Government's Department of Population Matters and Welfare, known by its initials, BuF (*Bevölkerungswesen und Fürsorge*). Although part of the civil administration, it was established and led by some of the top race experts in the SS and was dedicated to realizing Himmler's vision of a racist new order in the General

Government. The section that directly oversaw the RGO also handled all "Jewish questions."[7]

Based in Kraków, the RGO organized a Polish care committee in each *Kreis* or county of the General Government's five districts. Each county committee organized branches within its *Kreis*. In Lublin District, the Polish Care Committee for the county of Lublin consisted of two committees, one for the county and one for the city of Lublin, that operated jointly, answering to the same board of directors and sharing offices and some personnel. Most of the people who organized and provided the care services were unpaid volunteers. Skrzyński's job was to oversee and coordinate the work of the committees and branches throughout Lublin District, report on their activities and needs to RGO headquarters, and conduct all communications on their behalf with district officials. His official title was Advisor to the Governor, meaning the German governor of Lublin District.

Skrzyński's immediate superior in the RGO was also his predecessor as advisor, Prince Henryk Woroniecki, who had moved to Kraków to serve as vice director of the RGO's central office. Woroniecki wanted to expand the RGO's operations in Lublin District and to develop it into an effective advocate for the Polish people. Before moving to Kraków, he had forced the head of the Lublin Polish Care Committee to resign because, in Woroniecki's view, he devoted far too little energy to the committee and far too much to his private business. Skrzyński would give no cause for such concerns.[8]

The title of advisor came with little support. Skrzyński used the office space of the Lublin Polish Care Committee and largely relied upon its staff. He needed an assistant to monitor the RGO's expenditures and distributions, submit the required reports to German authorities, and manage the various initiatives he was undertaking. It had to be someone with a good head for numbers, fluent German, and the tact and standing to interact effectively with both the RGO's overseers and its clients. He knew someone who not only met those requirements but whose noble title would be seen as an additional qualification by the many aristocrats who held leading positions in the RGO. But before she could take the job, Countess Suchodolska had to be vetted by the Lublin District BuF office, which among other things required proof of Aryan ancestry going back at least two generations. Somehow,

Janina passed muster. She was appointed Secretary to the Advisor, a position that combined the duties of personal assistant and office manager.[9]

Her new duties revealed to Janina the full measure of the misery that the Germans had visited upon the Polish population of Lublin District. Their needs were staggeringly great. The RGO was providing support and relief for tens of thousands of people in the district, many of them children. It ran soup kitchens, temporary shelters, and orphanages; provided support for the families of Polish POWs and forced laborers sent to the Reich; and supplied food, clothing, shelter, and medical care for the Poles expelled into the district from the annexed territories. The challenges Janina faced in her job could seem overwhelming, but the work was unquestionably meaningful. She embraced it with all her energy and determination.

The RGO had no institutional relationship either with the AK, the Home Army, or with the Underground State, and some RGO officials opposed any cooperation with them, justifiably fearing that they would be arrested and the RGO disbanded should the Germans discover that it was aiding resistance activities. Nevertheless, Skrzyński and Janina were far from the first or only members of the AK to obtain positions in the RGO. In fact, the AK actively sought to embed members in the care committees and may have played a role in obtaining Skrzyński and Janina's appointments. Having an RGO identity card was extremely useful to AK members because it entitled them to rations, exempted them from being seized for forced labor, and, most important, permitted them to travel about the counties and the district to provide RGO services. One perk of Janina's job was a special permit that allowed her to own and use a bicycle. Under the cover of their official duties, AK members working for the RGO acted as couriers, spies, and distributors of clandestine press.[10]

Janina came to play a key role in the AK's penetration of the RGO. It was her job to prepare and submit the identity cards of RGO employees for German approval, and she took advantage of this task to create cards for agents of the Underground. She was one of the few members of the AK who knew the identities of comrades working for the RGO.

Janina's position in the RGO exposed her to scrutiny from the Germans. The Security Police were deeply suspicious of the RGO, aware that its employees' duties and ability to travel could serve as cover for espionage and sabotage activities. The hostility was only deepened by RGO officials' many appeals to German civilian authorities to oppose reprisal actions by the SS and police and to secure the release of hostages and of Poles seized for forced labor. The Gestapo regularly surveilled and searched RGO employees and not infrequently arrested them. In fact, eleven RGO employees in Lublin District were arrested in the year before Janina took up her duties. Under the German occupation, 385 RGO employees would be executed for resistance activities, at least forty of them in Lublin District.[11]

Through the services it provided and its interventions with German authorities, the RGO mitigated the suffering of millions of Poles and rescued untold thousands who faced death from starvation, disease, exposure, or execution. Nevertheless, there were some Poles who viewed the RGO as collaborating with the Germans. General Government officials encouraged that perception, claiming that the RGO was evidence that they were working with and on behalf of the Poles. RGO officials were ordered to attend German-sponsored events and issue German-dictated announcements to the Polish population. Although the Polish government in exile granted Polish social organizations permission to cooperate with the German occupiers in work that aided Poles, there were some in the Underground who thought that RGO officials, especially RGO president Count Ronikier, went too far in accommodating the Germans. When Ronikier refused to participate in the fourth anniversary celebration of the General Government's founding in November 1943, however, he was arrested, and the RGO was threatened with disbandment. RGO officials had to tread a thin line between service to Poland and collaboration with its enemy.[12]

One initiative Skrzyński immediately sought to pursue as RGO advisor in Lublin was to provision the prisoners in the prison camp being built at Majdanek. Despite its official designation as a prisoner of war camp, it was in all but name a concentration camp, part of the system of camps in which the SS starved and worked to death political and racial enemies from all the countries under German control. Himmler did supply thousands of Soviet POWs in the fall of 1941 to build both Majdanek and Birkenau, the latter part of Auschwitz concentration camp. The POWs arrived at the two camps in what the SS termed a "catastrophic state," however, and proved incapable of labor.[13] The Wehrmacht captured 3.3 million Red Army soldiers by the end of 1941 and corralled them in open enclosures, providing almost no food or medical care, and transferring tens of thousands to the SS to be murdered. By February 1942, 2.2 million died. At Majdanek, almost 95 percent of the 2,000 Soviet POWs who arrived in October 1941 were dead three months later.[14]

In early 1942, Majdanek's prisoners included Polish peasants arrested for failing to meet the agricultural quota, Polish civilians seized as hostages, local Jews rounded up for forced labor, and prisoners of various nationalities transferred from concentration camps in the Reich. As the camp was established on land with no infrastructure, the SS had to hire local civilians with specialized construction skills. These workers returned to the city nightly with gruesome tales of what they had witnessed in the camp, of whippings and shootings and pits that had to be continually expanded to hold the ever-growing number of corpses.[15]

After his dreams of exploiting hundreds of thousands of Soviet POWs were dashed, Himmler fixed on a new purpose for Majdanek and Birkenau: they were to play vital roles in the "final solution." Majdanek was to serve principally as a site for Jews temporarily spared from the gas chambers of *Aktion* Reinhard's killing centers to work in SS enterprises, while Birkenau would perform the functions of both a Jewish forced labor camp and a killing center.

Lublin's residents first learned of Majdanek's new role in April 1942, when long trains of freight cars began arriving at the Lublin station from Slovakia. The wails and cries from inside the cars, begging for water or a breath of fresh air, identified the cargo as men, women, and children. Hundreds of men would descend from the trains, wearing the star on their clothing that marked them as Jews. Surrounded by shouting SS men and snarling guard dogs, they would be marched under curses and blows to Majdanek.[16]

By midsummer 1942, there were more than 10,000 male Jewish prisoners in Majdanek as well as over 500 Polish men. People in the Lublin area could see some of the prisoners on a daily basis as they were marched to worksites around the city. They were a frightening sight: filthy, skeletal figures in striped or painted rags, stumbling along in wooden clogs. As they returned at night, they would carry the corpses of the prisoners who had died or been killed at the worksite.[17]

In the fall of 1942, transports arriving in Lublin sometimes discharged all their passengers: Jewish men, women, and children. They disappeared into Majdanek. The next day, the clouds of smoke billowing from the chimney of the camp's crematorium and its nearby burn pits spread a noxious odor through Lublin. It became an open secret in the city that Jews were being murdered en masse at Majdanek.[18]

Skrzyński and Janina believed they might get permission to feed Majdanek prisoners because the RGO was able to provide food for Poles incarcerated in prisons in some parts of the General Government. The indomitable Countess Karolina Lanckorońska had almost single-handedly created the prison aid program. The daughter of a high-ranking Polish nobleman who served in the Austro-Hungarian Imperial Court, she had divided her childhood between a family palace in Vienna and another in Eastern Galicia. Her father's magnificent art collection inspired her to obtain a PhD in art history, and she became head of the art history department at Jan Kazimierz University in Lwów. When the Soviets occupied the city, she joined the Polish Underground, but then had to flee to the General Government, barely one step ahead of the NKVD. As a Red Cross nurse in Kraków, she learned that Poles were starving to death in General Government prisons. Outraged, she visited Count Ronikier to insist that the RGO provide food to the prisons and that she be put in charge of the effort. She met all three of the key qualifications for the position, she asserted: 1) she was a woman, so less likely to attract German suspicion; 2) she had no husband or children whose lives the Germans could threaten; 3) her German was flawless. The Countess was not a person one easily said no to. Ronikier accepted her proposal.[19]

Countess Lanckorońska discovered that in order to feed Polish prisoners, she had to obtain approval from the local German authorities in charge of each prison. And so, by train, bus, cart, sledge, and on foot, she traveled from prison to prison to negotiate permission for food deliveries. Civilian officials were generally amenable, but the Security Police viewed both her and her proposal with suspicion. In fact, the suspicion was justified, since the Countess regularly reported to her commanding officer in the AK all the information she was gathering about the number of prisoners and conditions in the prisons.

The Countess proved an effective negotiator. By autumn 1941, a growing number of prisons were receiving deliveries of food products or prepared meals from the local RGO care committees. She also negotiated permission for the Jewish social welfare organization to deliver food to Jewish prisoners. In addition, using her AK connections, she established local networks that smuggled food and clothes into the prisons. It was Lanckorońska who established the precedent for providing overt and clandestine aid to prisoners through the RGO that Janina was to follow in Lublin.

After Galicia became a General Government district in 1941, Countess Lanckorońska returned there to set up feeding operations in the district prisons and to oversee RGO activities in Stanisławów. There she incurred the wrath of the city's Gestapo chief, Hans Krüger. The Countess could be a formidable figure: tall, self-assured, decided in her opinions, unshakable in her values, and unafraid to speak her mind. Krüger considered her a traitor because, although her mother had been Prussian, she assured him that she was a Polish patriot. He was particularly infuriated by her persistent demands to learn the whereabouts of 250 members of Stanisławów's Polish intelligentsia whom he had ordered arrested. To silence her, Krüger had Lanckorońska arrested as well. Before consigning her to the execution squad, he boasted to her about his role in murdering not only the Stanisławów intelligentsia but also the university professors of Lwów.

Krüger did not get to execute Countess Lanckorońska, however. Through her relatives, she had contacts with the royal family of Italy, Nazi Germany's ally, and they intervened directly with Himmler on her behalf. Himmler ordered that she be transferred to Lwów and her case investigated there. In the Lwów prison, the Countess wrote a report detailing all that Krüger had revealed to her about the mass murder of Poland's intelligentsia. This placed Himmler in a dilemma: executing the Countess was politically inadvisable; releasing her was out of the question. So he consigned her to Ravensbrück, the women's concentration camp located fifty miles north of Berlin, where he expected the conditions would soon finish her off. Once again, Countess Lanckorońska defied expectations of her demise. She survived Ravensbrück—where she taught the prisoners art history—and outlived the *Reichsführer* SS by fifty-seven years.

In Lublin District, the RGO obtained permission to supply food products for the inmates of several prisons, the largest of which was in the Lublin castle. Lublin's Polish Care Committee also sought permission to supply food for prisoners at Majdanek in early 1942 but were met with refusal from the camp's commandant. Skrzyński intended to get a different answer.[20]

His first attempt failed. Karl Otto Koch was one of the "old-school" commandants, having served in the camp system almost from its beginning. In 1937, he became the first commandant of Buchenwald, then the largest concentration camp in Germany. Through embezzlement and extortion, he and his wife, Ilse—dubbed by the prisoners the "Beast of Buchenwald"—led a life so extravagantly lavish that the local SS and Police Leader arrested him for corruption. Himmler had Koch released and sent him and some of his staff members to Majdanek, where they would have a chance to redeem themselves.[21] Koch detested all concentration camp prisoners as dangerous enemies and viewed the "subhuman" Poles and Jews imprisoned at Majdanek with murderous contempt. No Polish civilian organization would be allowed to bring food to any camp he controlled.

The RGO tried paying civilian workers employed at Majdanek to smuggle food in for the prisoners. The cost proved prohibitive and the risk too great, for workers caught smuggling were beaten and imprisoned in the camp. By the time Janina began working for the RGO, it had abandoned this effort.

Janina did learn of one clandestine network that was successfully smuggling small amounts of food and medicines to the prisoners' infirmary in Majdanek. It had been established by the fearless thirty-five-year-old Saturnina Malm, who had been a volunteer social worker before the war. In January 1942, Malm began seeking to help a friend get messages to her husband, a physician imprisoned in the camp. Malm spent days scouting Majdanek's environs, getting as close as she could until the SS threatened to shoot her. Finally, she noticed that the camp's SS staff were bringing their laundry to a small house in a village near the camp. The laundress agreed to help Malm, and they recruited an SS guard to get a message to the prisoner physician, who was secretly treating the guard for a venereal disease. Malm succeeded in establishing regular contact with members of the Polish Underground imprisoned in the camp who worked in the infirmary. To provide the medicines and medical supplies they requested, she persuaded a Lublin physician to be the "finance minister" for her network. He collected funds from other Lublin physicians to buy the medicines, and Malm enlisted the aid of certain pharmacists to source and provide them.[22]

Through Malm's network, prisoners were able to inform the Underground about conditions in the camp. Prisoner physician Dr. Jan Nowak reported that Koch's approach to containing a typhus epidemic was to have 2,000 infected prisoners shot. In July 1942, word got out that eighty Soviet POWs had managed to escape one night, after which Koch ordered the slaughter of the forty remaining POWs.[23]

Koch could not prevent news of the escape from reaching Berlin. He claimed that the murdered POWs had been part of a massive, violent breakout that had overwhelmed the undisciplined guards. Himmler did not credit Koch's excuses. During a visit to Lublin shortly afterward, he fired Koch and had him placed under investigation for criminal negligence.

Janina could not stop thinking about Majdanek and the suffering of its prisoners, the vast majority of whom, she knew, were Jews. Everything she could learn about the camp, both through her own observations and Underground reports, filled her with horror. Finding ways to help not only the Poles but also all the victims imprisoned there, became her personal mission. She and Skrzyński hoped that they could persuade the new commandant to accept their proposal to deliver food to the camp. But, after a brief interlude under Ravensbrück commandant Max Koegel, Majdanek's command passed to Koch's protégé, Hermann Florstedt, who had served as deputy commandant at Buchenwald. According to SS gossip, Florstedt had also served Ilse Koch as one of her lovers. When Skrzyński and Janina tried to meet with him about feeding Majdanek prisoners, Florstedt's response was as emphatically negative as his mentor's.[24]

Janina had a mission, however, and refused to accept no as a final answer. She and Skrzyński were determined to continue pressing their request until somehow, eventually, they got to yes.

EIGHT

FROZEN CARGO

In the predawn hours of November 27, 1942, residents of the village of Skierbieszów in Lublin's Zamość County lurched out of sleep into a nightmare. SS and police forces were storming into their homes.

"You are being resettled," they were told. "Gather only what you can carry and report immediately in front of the church. SCHNELL!"

Less than two hours later, the Poles of Skierbieszów were carried off on open carts into the bitterly cold night and away from the homesteads where their families had lived for generations. Few would ever see those homes again.[1]

Other villages were hit that same day, and more and more in the days that followed. Janina learned of the resettlements as soon as they began from an Underground contact in Zamość. Shortly afterward, she began receiving panicked messages from the Zamość Polish Care Committee that many members of its branches had been seized in the raids. She and Skrzyński tried desperately to find out which villages had been resettled, where the expellees had been taken, and what was planned for them so that the RGO could intervene on their behalf. Janina had an additional task from the AK: find out which villages were slated for future resettlement so that the Underground could warn the residents and help them flee.

Janina reached out to both her official and her clandestine contacts within the district and local civilian administrations, but none could provide any information. The rivalry between Frank and Himmler extended to their underlings in the General Government, where the SS and police operated as a law unto themselves. SS and Police Leader Globocnik, in particular, had nothing but disdain for the governor of Lublin District, Ernst Zörner, and was not about to brook any interference in his pet project. On Globocnik's orders, civilian officials were excluded from all aspects of the resettlement operation.

In the weeks before the operation began, there had been a growing dread among the Poles of the Zamość region that the Germans would soon unleash a new terror upon them. Just a month earlier, the last ghettos in the county had been liquidated in brutal and bloody operations. Aware that they were being sent to their death, many of the Jews had sought to hide or flee. So for weeks after the roundups in the ghettos, massive manhunts ferreted out hundreds of Jews and slaughtered them, often in public view. The perpetrators were not just the Germans and the Trawniki men but also Polish policemen, firefighters, and even ordinary citizens. Some Poles watched aghast to see their brethren murder their Jewish neighbors; some even tried to save Jews. Few failed to grasp that the Germans might subject them to the same fate.[2] The commander of the AK warned his superiors in London that the moment all the ghettos had been cleared, "the Germans will begin to liquidate the Poles in the same fashion."[3] When the expulsions in Zamość began, many Poles assumed that the moment had arrived.

There was in fact a connection between the liquidation of the ghettos and the start of the resettlement operation. In July 1942, with Nazi leaders again confident of imminent victory over the Soviet Union, Himmler visited Globocnik in Lublin to accelerate the process of achieving the racist utopia. By the end of the year, he ordered, all the Jews in the General Government should be annihilated, except for a small minority who would be forced to work under SS supervision in closed labor camps or at Majdanek or Auschwitz. Once the ghettos were empty, Globocnik should begin Germanizing Lublin city and the Zamość region by expelling their Polish inhabitants and settling ethnic Germans in their place.[4]

Globocnik was overjoyed. "[N]ow all our most secret wishes will be fulfilled," he crowed to an SS colleague. He began the resettlement of Lublin at the start of October 1942, expelling the Polish residents of entire sections of the city as well as nearby villages. Many of the expellees turned to the Lublin Polish Care Committee for help, but even before the expulsions began it lacked the resources to provide for all those who already qualified for its aid. To make matters worse, some of its own workers were falling victim to the expulsions, including two who were placed in the new women's camp at Majdanek.

Then, on November 11, the Germans evicted Skrzyński, Janina, and the Lublin Polish Care Committee from their shared office space, which was located in the designated German district of the city. The RGO was allocated a formerly Jewish-owned building on Lubartowska Street, on the border of the former ghetto, but it required extensive renovations before Janina and her colleagues could work there. She and Skrzyński were still frantically scrambling to find shelter and supplies for the Lublin expellees when they learned of the expulsions in Zamość.[5]

Globocnik aimed to expel more than 33,000 Poles from the Zamość region and settle ethnic Germans onto their lands before the start of the spring planting season. His forces temporarily imprisoned the Polish victims in a former Soviet POW camp in the city of Zamość (renamed Himmlerstadt), where race experts conducted selections. The few children and adults deemed to be of German stock were to be drilled into good Germans. The remaining children between the ages of six months and fourteen years along with adults too elderly or disabled to work were slated to be dumped in vacant ghettos. Globocnik planned to send about 20 to 25 percent of the remaining youths and adults to Auschwitz, the rest to forced labor in the Reich or in the East.[6]

Globocnik's plans went awry from the start. As word of the expulsions spread, Poles fled into the region's forests. Globocnik's forces often arrived at a village slated for resettlement only to find it almost entirely deserted. The SS resettlement commission called in the officials of the RGO's Zamość care committee and forced them to issue a proclamation to the Poles in the region. It called on them to keep calm and remain in their villages, assuring them that only some Poles would be resettled and that no harm would come to them. But, the proclamation warned, the Germans would punish all those who fled. The SS also threatened to punish any attempt by the RGO to provide relief to the expellees.

The proclamation had no effect. By early December 1942, the RGO estimated that thousands of Poles had fled into the forests, while as many as 5,000 had been seized and placed in the Zamość camp. Rumors had come to the RGO about the selections in the camp and that families were being separated. Janina and Skrzyński assumed that the able-bodied adults would be sent for forced labor, but they tried in vain to learn what fate was planned for the rest.

The answer came in mid-December 1942. The RGO received notice that hundreds of families of Zamość expellees were to be resettled in vacant ghettos in Warsaw and Radom Districts. The local care committees urgently requested resources and advice from the RGO in Kraków, because the homes in those ghettos had been so thoroughly vandalized and looted that they were uninhabitable.

Before the month was out, transports from Zamość deposited more than 2,000 expellees in one county alone. They did not consist of families, however. Half of them were unaccompanied children, while most of the rest were elderly or disabled adults.

Globocnik's forces did not try to seize all the Poles in the resettled villages, mainly only those who owned land. Those left behind became virtual serfs, forbidden to leave their villages and forced to labor for the ethnic German settlers who took over the emptied homes and farms. The German masters whipped their workers, robbed their food stores, and demanded the clothes off their backs and the shoes off their feet.

By the end of December 1942, Globocnik's forces had snared almost 10,000 Poles, less than 30 percent of his goal.[7] About twice as many had fled, and those hiding in the forests were suffering terribly from lack of food and shelter in the midwinter conditions of deep snow and temperatures below 0°. Skrzyński and Janina could find no way to get aid into the region. The Count's protests to German authorities were ignored, his requests to send food and supplies to the Zamość camp went unanswered. The local care committees were no longer operating, as those members who had not been seized had fled. All Janina could do was to prepare the supplies and personnel so that the RGO could send them as soon as it received authorization to help the Poles in Zamość.

Increasingly, Poles in Zamość resolved not just to evade the Germans' resettlement plans but to fight back. Families fleeing into the forests took with them whatever they could of their produce and livestock and destroyed the rest, even burning their homes. In the forests, peasants formed or joined armed bands, some associated with the AK, that attacked the villages where ethnic Germans had been settled. In reprisal, SS and police forces burned villages that had not been resettled and slaughtered their Polish residents.

In Lublin and in Kraków, the RGO was ceaselessly protesting the resettlement action to General Government authorities. Shocked by the increase and ferocity of attacks by armed resistance groups, civilian officials grew more sympathetic to the RGO's pleas and began to suggest that the expulsions be halted. Globocnik ignored them. To him, the answer to resistance should always be ever more disproportionate violence.

The state of the expellees transported to Warsaw and Radom Districts evidenced the horrifying conditions in the transit camp at Zamość. When they were being expelled from their homes, Polish families were given so little time to collect their things—often just ten minutes—that some could not dress all their children in coats and shoes. In the camp, the adults and children selected as worthless for German purposes were separated from their families and penned in a compound surrounded by barbed wire. In the uninsulated wooden barracks, some without floors, barefoot and thinly clad children were consigned to the care of adults who were often unable to care for themselves. Exposure, severe malnutrition, lack of hygiene, and diseases quickly took their toll. By early January, dozens of children were dying daily.[8]

Conditions in the Zamość camp were little better for the youths and adults selected for forced labor. When hundreds of Zamość expellees arrived at Auschwitz in mid-December 1942, SS officials there complained that most were too starved and weak to perform labor. Per standard concentration camp practice, the SS had to "liquidate" those who could not work so that they would not burden the camp's resources. This complaint caused

SS resettlement officials to consider whether it would be better to ship all the expelled Polish children to Auschwitz to be murdered instead of sending them to the ghettos. Doing so would ensure that the children did not survive and pass on their "undesirable blood."[9]

Even worse than what they suffered in the Zamość camp was the agony the elderly and children expellees endured during transport to vacant ghettos. As they had when deporting the Jews, the Germans sealed the Zamość expellees into train cars and provided them with little or no food or water for their journey. The cattle and freight cars packed with expellees were often shunted aside to allow higher priority transports to pass, so it generally took days for the trains to reach their destination. When they arrived, members of the local population were there to greet them, organized by the RGO care committees. The Poles unloaded the expellees, provided hot meals for the ambulatory, rushed the weak or unconscious to local hospitals, and carried to the morgue the corpses of those who died in transit. It was not always possible to identify the dead, particularly the children. Such was the case with a six-month-old barefoot girl in a pink sweater and striped cap who died on a transport to Siedlce, about 130 miles from Zamość.[10]

The surviving expellees were entirely dependent upon the RGO care committees for shelter and the means to live. The RGO assisted some to go to relatives, recruited families to take in children, and arranged shelter for the rest. Care committee workers spent countless hours helping expellees register with authorities, access medical care, and apply for ration cards. Much of the food, clothing, and basic necessities that the care committees provided to the expellees was donated by Polish populations that were already suffering from severe shortages of all three.

Meanwhile, the able-bodied youths and adults shipped off to the Reich to perform brute labor lost all contact with their family members. Anguished letters poured into Janina's office from expellees pleading for news of their children and parents. Janina was desperate to help them, but helpless to do so.[11]

Finally, on February 9, 1943, the RGO received permission to care for the Poles in the Zamość camp.[12] Janina immediately dispatched to the camp the supplies and personnel she had readied for this moment. Among the workers were ten women members of the Underground experienced in running nurseries and kindergartens. Janina had recruited them and supplied them with RGO identity cards so that they could enter the camp. Their task was to register the hundreds of children and persuade their parents to transfer them to the RGO's custody. The workers promised that the RGO would send the children to relatives or provide shelter for them.

Janina had already arranged for a children's home to be established on Lublin's outskirts to house the children rescued from the Zamość camp. Many mothers, understanding the danger their children faced, readily consigned custody of them to the RGO, but some refused, desperately wanting to believe German assurances that they would be able to keep their children with them. Janina's women workers asked for guidance in dealing with these reluctant mothers.

Just at that time, Janina received a report from Underground contacts in Warsaw District about a Zamość transport found sitting silently on a railroad siding. When the doors were pried open, the frozen corpses of five hundred children were found inside. The Germans quickly resealed the wagon and directed its cargo to Sobibor to be incinerated in the killing center's burning pits.[13]

Utterly horrified, Janina was in no doubt about her next step. She responded to her workers in Zamość: ignore the mothers who refuse to consign custody of their children. By whatever means necessary, she directed, "take the children."

NINE

THE POLISH QUESTION

On the frigid morning of February 26, 1943, Janina set out with Prince Woroniecki and Count Skrzyński for a momentous appointment. Their mood was tense but optimistic as their car headed out of the city on the road leading to Zamość. About one kilometer out, Janina saw on her left, behind barbed wire, the giant warehouses of Globocnik's forced labor camp for Jews that was commonly called the Old Airfield camp because of its location. After another kilometer, she saw on her right the barbed wire that marked the boundary of Majdanek. Behind it in the distance, she could glimpse barbed wire fences and watchtowers surrounding an area that stretched nearly to the horizon. Within it, dark barracks hunkered in the dirty snow and a chimney spewed smoke that wafted over the road, its odor making Janina feel slightly nauseous.

Then the car pulled in at a gate guarded by armed SS men. Janina and her companions showed their papers and stated their business: an appointment with the commandant. They had come to present a plan for feeding Majdanek's prisoners. And this time, Janina knew, Florstedt could not refuse.

It was the turning tide of the war that led to German authorities' change of heart regarding RGO aid for Majdanek prisoners. Nazi Germany had been at the pinnacle of its power in early fall 1942, but since then British and

American forces had landed in North Africa, the Red Army had crushed German forces at Stalingrad, and Allied bombs were turning German cities into rubble. Germany needed more workers to replace the men it was shipping to the crumbling fronts, and it needed more food imports to prevent shortages from sapping morale at home. Nazi leaders looked to the General Government for both.

This led Governor General Frank to suggest a reconsideration of German policy toward the Poles in December 1942. As he sagely observed to his subordinates, "one cannot simultaneously annihilate the Poles and count on Polish labor power." The General Government would accomplish all that it was called upon to do for the German war effort, he asserted, but first the fundamental question needed to be answered: "Should . . . we starve the Poles to death, or feed them?"[1]

Heinrich Himmler was mulling a similar question with regard to the 110,000 prisoners in his concentration camps. Germany needed workers, and he had a captive workforce. He dreamed of turning his camps into major industrial sites where prisoners would produce matériel for arms industries that would pay the SS for the forced labor. The principal impediment to this plan was that the whole point of the concentration camps was to destroy the prisoners, not develop them into productive workers. He would be able to offer German industry far more laborers if only 80,000 prisoners hadn't died in the last half of 1942, nearly 90 percent from starvation, exhaustion, disease, or injury. This number only included registered camp prisoners, not the Jews who were murdered on arrival at Auschwitz and Majdanek. If Himmler was going to extract maximum profit from his concentration camps, then he needed not only to acquire more prisoners but also to find ways to keep them alive and able to work—preferably ways that did not require additional expenditures by the SS.[2]

So in late October 1942, Himmler decreed that families and private persons could send monthly packages of food and clothing to individual concentration camp prisoners. This was soon followed by directives to the concentration camp commandants and doctors to lower the mortality rate among their prisoners. Instead of annihilating prisoners through labor, the camps were now to be reservoirs of forced laborers that served the economic interests of the SS.[3]

This change in policy did not enable Janina and Skrzyński to get permission to feed Majdanek's prisoners, however. Even though Majdanek was part of the concentration camp system, it still carried the official designation of a prisoner of war camp. Moreover, it was primarily a camp for Jews, who accounted for nearly 90 percent of the camp's prisoners at the end of 1942. In fact, Globocnik considered it one of "his" *Aktion* Reinhard camps and demanded that its commandants cater to his demands. Although thousands of Polish hostages and peasants were also imprisoned in Majdanek during 1942 as collective punishment for resistance to German rule, they were considered temporary detainees who were supposed to be released after a few weeks, provided they survived that long.[4] Since Majdanek was not a concentration camp with Polish political prisoners, Florstedt could reject RGO claims that it had standing to feed Majdanek prisoners.

But in February 1943, Majdanek's prisoner population became more diverse. In his quest for prisoner laborers, Himmler directed that able-bodied Polish inmates in General Government prisons be transferred to his concentration camps, particularly Majdanek and Auschwitz. He also ordered mass roundups of unemployed able-bodied Poles and anyone suspected of participating in the resistance, all to be placed in Majdanek, Auschwitz, or the camps in the Reich. Majdanek and Auschwitz were also to take in men, women, and children seized in anti-partisan operations in territories captured from the Soviet Union. Himmler even directed that a special camp for Soviet children be established within Majdanek's women's compound. Except for the few selected for Germanization, these children would be trained to labor for the rest of their lives in the workshops of the concentration camp system.[5]

Following Himmler's directives, in early 1943 the Security Police shipped to Majdanek several thousand Poles gathered from General Government prisons or seized in raids. By early February, Poles outnumbered the Jews among the camp's inmates. Reflecting its new status as a camp for Polish political prisoners, Majdanek was designated a concentration camp on February 16, 1943. Its official name was Waffen SS *Konzentrationslager* Lublin.[6]

At the same time, the RGO was taking advantage of Frank's increased interest in preserving the lives of his Polish subjects, at least until the end of the war. With the civilian administration's support, on February 9, 1943, the RGO finally obtained blanket permission from the Security Police and SD in the General Government to deliver food, clothes, and necessities for Polish inmates in all the prisons. Since Majdanek's Polish political prisoners were under the jurisdiction of the Gestapo, which was part of the Security Police, Skrzyński and Janina realized that the RGO now had a basis for claiming the right to feed those prisoners. There was no time to lose, for they had learned that Polish prisoners were dying in Majdanek after just a few weeks of captivity there. It was even rumored that Polish prisoners no longer able to work were being murdered in the camp's gas chambers along with Jews.[7]

To obtain authorization to feed Majdanek prisoners, Skrzyński and Janina had to navigate the bureaucratic maze of the General Government's administration. Skrzyński generally brought Janina with him when he met with General Government officials so that she could take notes, provide information that supported his requests, and communicate the instructions received at the meetings to the care committees. There may have been a psychological advantage to bringing her as well. German officials generally displayed their contempt for their Polish visitors by refusing to extend them common courtesies, such as standing to receive them or inviting them to sit. Yet class consciousness was so ingrained even in SS officers that they tended to rise instinctively when presented to a German-speaking noblewoman. This then confronted the official with a dilemma. Sitting while the lady stood might feel uncomfortable, which left the options of either standing throughout the meeting—perhaps facing away to display disdain—or inviting the lady to sit, in which case the men present would sit as well. Once this point of order was resolved, the meetings generally followed a pattern: Skrzyński would state the reason for his intervention; the official would then harangue them about the lazy, uncivilized Poles and their failure to appreciate the justness and magnanimity of German rule; finally, they would get down to business.

When Skrzyński and Janina renewed their quest to feed Majdanek prisoners, their first visit was to the BuF department for Lublin District, the civilian agency whose permission was needed for any RGO initiative. In 1942, the Lublin BuF had been reluctant even to allow the RGO to raise public donations. Now that Frank was pushing a somewhat conciliatory policy toward the Poles, however, the BuF was obliged to be more open to Skrzyński's requests. When Skrzyński and Janina presented their proposal to organize a relief operation for Majdanek prisoners together with the Polish Red Cross, the BuF consented.[8]

Skrzyński and Janina's next stop was at the Gestapo office in Lublin. It was housed in a corner building with a distinctive curved façade and a clock high above the entry that had become the symbol of terror to Lublin's residents. It was well known that "under the clock" dark and airless basement cells were stuffed with bloody, mangled prisoners awaiting their next turn at interrogation by the Gestapo's torture specialists. Janina and Skrzyński's visit was brief, for the official they met immediately cut them off. If the RGO wanted to feed Majdanek's prisoners, it would have to get permission from the chief of the Security Police and SD for all of Lublin District, SS-*Hauptsturmführer* (Captain) Hellmut Müller. For that meeting, Skrzyński brought in more firepower: Prince Woroniecki, the RGO's vice director in Kraków.

Skzyński's strategy worked: Woroniecki won Müller's permission for the RGO and the Polish Red Cross to provide food, medicines, and supplies for the Polish prisoners under Security Police jurisdiction at Majdanek. When Florstedt received Müller's notice to this effect, he had no choice but to make some concessions to the RGO delegation.

In any event, now that he was under strict instructions to reduce prisoner mortality, Florstedt saw the value in accepting the RGO proposals. He agreed that the RGO and the Polish Red Cross in Lublin could organize the delivery to Polish prisoners of packages containing food and necessities sent by the prisoners' relatives. Each package, weighing no more than 2 kilograms (4.4 pounds), had to be properly addressed to a specific prisoner at the camp, and relatives could pay the RGO's Lublin Polish Care Committee or the Polish Red Cross to prepare the packages in their name. In addition, he authorized the Lublin Polish Care Committee to make a weekly delivery to Majdanek consisting of one kilogram of bread for each Polish prisoner as well as beans, potatoes, and vegetables to be added to the prisoners' soup. The care committee could also deliver blankets and straw for the Polish prisoners' mattresses, while both the RGO and the Polish Red Cross could supply medicines requested by the camp doctor. Woroniecki won another concession that was nearly as important to the Polish prisoners and their families as the food and package deliveries: the right for Polish prisoners to send one letter or two postcards a month.

On the return from Majdanek, Janina shared her two companions' joy over the concessions Woroniecki had won, but she was anxious to get to work. Although the Lublin Polish Care Committee and the Polish Red Cross in Lublin would be supplying the packages and food, the Germans specified that Skrzyński's office had overall responsibility for the delivery of aid to Majdanek. Skrzyński immediately entrusted the details of the operation to Janina. As soon as she got back to her office, she had to send notice to all the RGO care committees about soliciting packages for Majdanek prisoners and publish an appeal for donations in money and kind. She also planned to solicit donations personally from Lublin businesses and organizations and to enlist the help of her Underground contacts. Now that she could finally pursue the mission she had set herself, she would make sure that it did not fail for lack of resources.

As Janina expected, her colleagues at the Lublin Polish Care Committee and the Polish Red Cross sprang into action the moment they received the go-ahead to supply aid to Majdanek. The Red Cross was in charge of receiving and delivering packages from prisoners' relatives, including those that relatives paid the Lublin Polish Care Committee to prepare. By mid-March 1943, the two organizations were providing an average of 1,700 packages to Majdanek per week.

In addition, the Lublin Polish Care Committee had to obtain the blankets and straw for the prisoners' beds, collect the ingredients to be added to the prisoners' soup, and bake more than six tons of bread for delivery every week—one kilogram for each of the 6,000 Polish prisoners who according to Majdanek authorities were being held in the camp. Obtaining and preparing the food was the responsibility of Antonina Łopatyńska, the head of the Lublin Care Committee's Nutrition and Care Department. Although she did not speak German, she had a special knack for extracting allocations of strictly rationed goods from German officials, cowing the clerks by sternly lecturing them through an interpreter on international law pertaining to the treatment of populations in occupied territories.[9]

For Janina, the permission to feed the prisoners at Majdanek was a rare cause for hope in the midst of the massive suffering that, despite their ceaseless and exhausting efforts, she and her RGO colleagues could do so little to alleviate. If only they could arrange for enough packages to be sent to Majdanek, then, combined with the bread and soup ingredients the Lublin Polish Care Committee was providing, it would be possible to substantially increase the Polish prisoners' chances for survival. What is more, Janina knew that each of Majdanek's compounds housed not only Poles but also prisoners from other national and ethnic groups, including Jews. Since the kitchen in each compound fed all the prisoners from the same cauldrons, the products that the RGO provided for those kitchens would enrich the soup that was fed to all of the camp's prisoners. Although the RGO was barred from providing aid to non-Polish prisoners, Janina envisioned eventually supplying sufficient quantities of products to stave off starvation for all of Majdanek's prisoners, not just the Poles.

Problems ensued immediately, however. Both Janina's office and the Polish Red Cross were inundated with pleas from people desperate to learn whether their loved one was a prisoner in Majdanek. Some had received notice months earlier that the person they sought was consigned to Majdanek, but they had learned nothing more since; some had only heard rumors that their relative had been sent there. But Florstedt and Müller refused to provide a list of Polish prisoners in Majdanek or even to identify the prisoners who had died.

Moreover, it quickly became evident that few of the thousands of packages being sent to confirmed prisoners at Majdanek were actually reaching them intact. Each package was accompanied by a preprinted postcard that the recipient was supposed to return to acknowledge receipt. But prisoners' families were complaining to Janina that they were not receiving the cards, or that the signatures on the cards they did receive were forged. She learned that the camp SS inspected every package and seized many of the contents before sending them on to the "kapos"—concentration camp prisoner functionaries—in the prisoner compounds, who looted them as well. When a package actually got through to a prisoner, it generally contained nothing but moldy bread.

Problems also arose with the director of the Lublin Polish Care Committee, Tadeusz Dąbrowski, and the head of the Polish Red Cross in Lublin, Ludwik Christians. Because the care committee did not have its own transport, it relied upon the Polish Red Cross to deliver not only the packages but also all the other goods it provided for Majdanek prisoners. In the first three weeks of March 1943, the care committee sent to Majdanek via the Polish Red Cross nearly twenty tons of bread in three shipments. There had been no deliveries of the products that were to enrich the prisoners' soup, however. The estimate for the monthly cost of those products came to a staggering sum, and food prices were continually rising. Dąbrowski decided it would be best to delay delivering the products for soup until the care committee had one or two months' supply on hand. Christians had an additional concern about providing the products to Majdanek: they would be consumed by all the camp's prisoners, not just the Poles. That, of course, was exactly Janina's intention. As a prewar politician, Christians had represented the radical wing of the antisemitic National Democrats. He firmly believed that the mission of the Polish Red Cross should be to aid ethnic Poles, and only ethnic Poles.

Skrzyński brought in Woroniecki to settle the matter. In late March, the Prince met separately with Christians and Dąbrowski to hear them out, and he rejected the arguments of each. Regardless of who consumed the products provided by the care committee, he lectured, providing the products for the Polish prisoners was "our great and absolute duty." There was no time to lose, for the Germans might revoke permission for the Majdanek food deliveries at any moment. Lest there be any doubt about his instructions, the Prince put them in writing: "Begin the feeding action immediately."

It appeared that Janina's mission to feed all the prisoners at Majdanek might succeed after all.

TEN

MAJDANEK

If Hermann Florstedt entertained any hope that his assignment as Majdanek's commandant bode well for his career, his first day at the camp in November 1942 must have quickly dispelled it. The rumors of rampant corruption at Buchenwald when he served there as Koch's deputy had cast a pall over his reputation, so his posting to Majdanek was less a vote of confidence than a last chance at redemption. His instructions were clear: clean up the mess Koch had left behind, establish order and discipline, and develop Majdanek into a center of industrial enterprises where prisoners produced goods for the SS. His first tour of the camp made it equally clear that his chances for success were exceedingly slim.

Florstedt had served at Sachsenhausen as well as Buchenwald, but Majdanek bore little resemblance to those two concentration camps in the heart of the "Old Reich."[1] It was, instead, a primitive outpost of German rule in a hostile territory. When he arrived there, Florstedt found a vast, chaotic construction site on an expanse of open land that was four times larger than Buchenwald.[2] There were no paved roads or pathways, and the autumn rains had turned the sandy soil into mud so deep it sucked even the boots off the feet of the SS men. At one point, the SS drew up blueprints for the camp to hold 150,000 prisoners and the factories they would work in, but—as with many of Himmler's ambitious plans—the continuing war forced the project to be curtailed. Until Germany's victory, when there would be no lack of construction materials and transport, Majdanek was slated to have a capacity of 25,000 prisoners and an industrial area with sixty-four workshops and warehouses. Theoretically, it already had sufficient barracks to house 25,000 prisoners in November 1942, though many lacked windows, doors, and furniture. But only six buildings had been erected in the industrial area, and the barracks for the guards and the camp administration were still under construction.[3]

What had been constructed appeared improvised and shoddy. The "protective custody camp"—the SS term for the area of a concentration camp where prisoners were detained—covered more than seventy-five acres and consisted of five rectangular compounds called "fields" and two narrower "inter-fields," all adjacent and surrounded by a double barbed wire fence and watchtowers. Unlike the sturdy prisoner barracks at Buchenwald, which had quarters for dining and sleeping as well as lavatories, the barracks at Majdanek were uninsulated wooden buildings with no internal divisions and no running water. In some compounds, the barracks were actually horse stables with barn doors, dirt floors, and only an opening under the eaves to let in light. The tar paper that covered the barrack roofs quickly curled and flaked into the swirling wind.

Alongside the barracks were the latrines: cement troughs in the ground crossed lengthwise by boards on which the prisoners perched to relieve themselves in the open. Afterward, they could not clean themselves, since the compounds had no running water or bathing facilities, and the SS rarely allowed the prisoners to fetch buckets of well water for washing. In any event, health authorities had condemned the water in the camp's three wells as contaminated with E. coli and ammonia. There were bathing and disinfection barracks just outside the protective custody camp, but they were largely reserved for newly arriving prisoners.

Because of the food shortages in the General Government, the prisoners' diet at Majdanek made the sparse meals at Buchenwald seem sumptuous. Starving prisoners drinking contaminated water, unable to bathe, and continually plagued by lice and fleas created the perfect conditions for epidemics of dysentery, scabies, tuberculosis, typhoid, and the dreaded typhus that sickened and killed even the SS guards. The three barracks in Field I that served as the "hospital" were overflowing with sick and injured patients who could expect little treatment other than a brief reprieve from hard labor. Once prisoners appeared incapable of returning to work, however, they were left to die or were murdered. There were over 8,000 prisoners in Majdanek when Florstedt arrived, but more than three times that many had been registered at the camp in the previous eight months. In November 1942 alone, 2,999 died. Smoke poured constantly from the chimney of the crematorium located between Fields I and II. The two oil-fired ovens, which could burn at most one hundred bodies in twelve hours, could barely keep pace with demand. The stench in the camp compounds from open latrines, thousands of unwashed bodies, and burning corpses was so overpowering that Florstedt determined to visit the protective custody camp as rarely as possible. When he did, it was always in his car and with a lit cigar clenched firmly in his teeth.

Thousands more victims were dying at Majdanek than the official death statistics indicated. Between March and September 1942, Majdanek's role in *Aktion* Reinhard had been to work to death the Jewish men temporarily spared from the gas chambers of the killing centers in order to labor in SS enterprises. By October 1942, however, Majdanek had two operational gas chambers and began serving as a small-scale killing center as well. Jewish men, women, and children arrived by the hundreds from the last ghettos and labor camps that Globocnik's forces were clearing in Lublin District, including Majdan Tatarski and Zamość. The pace of arrivals picked up when gassing operations ceased at Bełżec in November. Newly arrived Jews rated unfit for work and all the children and elderly were immediately gassed or, when their number exceeded the camp's gassing capacity, shot in the Krępiec woods, where the victims' corpses were burned. *Aktion* Reinhard's year-end report on the number of Jews it had "resettled" in 1942 tallied the victims of four sites: Bełżec, Sobibor, Treblinka, and Majdanek. Of the operation's 1,274,166 victims, Majdanek accounted for 24,733.[4]

Keeping operations at Majdanek completely secret was nearly impossible, Florstedt found. There were no walls around the camp, just barbed wire fencing. Buildings on a hill at the edge of Lublin looked down into the camp, and houses in a neighboring village were close enough to have a view of Field V. There was no fence at all around much of the camp's southern perimeter, including where it abutted the part of the village of Dziesiąta that the SS had not razed and added to Majdanek. By day, the only thing separating the remaining villagers from the prisoners laboring in the camp's vegetable gardens was the line of sentries who guarded the area. At night, the villagers went onto the camp's grounds to fetch water from their only well.

Florstedt did not even have trained SS Death's Head guards to enforce security and discipline. Some of the officers and NCOs were experienced concentration camp hands, but the rest of the SS men were either older reservists or, increasingly, ethnic Germans from Croatia, Hungary, or Romania recruited to serve as cannon fodder for the Waffen SS. The recruits sent to Majdanek had been rated too weak or inept to serve at the front without first being whipped into shape at a concentration camp. They tended to be semiliterate and to speak in dialects Florstedt could barely understand.[5] The SS could not even cobble together enough of these cohorts to meet Majdanek's requirements, and so a battalion of Lithuanian auxiliary police served at the camp as well, few of whom spoke any German. They did share the Germans' contempt for Poles and Jews, however, and were notorious among the prisoners for being trigger-happy. In addition, to assist in the mass murder process at Majdanek, Globocnik assigned some of the Trawniki men who provided the manpower for *Aktion* Reinhard. These brutish guards, mostly Ukrainians, ignored regulations and went drinking and whoring in Lublin after curfew, then sullenly endured the lashes they received as punishment.[6] Florstedt found that resentment and discontent were rife among Majdanek's guard forces.

Florstedt's security challenges multiplied in early 1943 with the arrival of thousands of Polish political prisoners. Among these men and women were trained members of the Underground, and their co-conspirators on the outside, including Janina, immediately sought to contact and assist them. Some resistance members in Lublin secured jobs as civilian construction specialists in the camp so that they could scout for colleagues, smuggle food and medicines to them, and relay messages. Two Underground cells of women hid packages at night in several sites in the camp's vegetable gardens and then retrieved the messages that prisoners left there. One cell, based in Dziesiąta, also provided lodging for prisoners' family members and bribed the sentries to look the other way while the visitors spoke to prisoners laboring in the camp fields.[7] No matter how much Florstedt threatened to punish guards who had dealings with prisoners or civilians, there were some who could not resist the temptation to augment their meager wages and boring diet when offered the right amount of money or bacon.[8]

Although Florstedt granted the RGO permission to provide packages and food for the prisoners, he suspected it was planning to use the deliveries to support and expand the resistance within the camp. That was, in fact, Janina's assignment. As information came in to her about the location of Underground members in the camp, she saw to it that they were sent packages from "family members" in the resistance. Through the AK, she worked with several groups of women to obtain the ingredients and assemble the packages, among them the network that Saturnina Malm had established to provide medicine and food to the camp infirmary. Another group was headed by the baker Antonina Grygowa, a woman of modest means renowned in Lublin for her generosity to anyone in need. Together with her two daughters, she ran a bakery that produced bread for the Lublin Care Committee's soup kitchens during the day. At night, they baked more bread to add to the packages they provided for prisoners at both Majdanek and Zamek, the prison in Lublin's castle.

A problem soon arose with the bread in the RGO packages: it was turning moldy before the prisoners received it. The cause, Janina determined, was that in an effort to increase the prisoners' caloric intake, the Lublin Polish Care Committee was sending slices of bread with fat spread upon them. She conferred with Łopatyńska and Grygowa to come up with a solution. Sending the fat in a separate container was not an option, because it would be stolen before the prisoner received the package. After some experimentation, Grygowa devised a recipe for rolls baked with extra shortening that did not mold quickly. Since fats were strictly rationed, Łopatyńska had to work her magic with German officials to get the extra shortening for the bakers.

Once the delivery of food products for the prisoners' soup finally began in April 1943, Janina could visit Majdanek to collect receipts for the food and supplies from the RGO and to discuss future deliveries. She often rode there on the horse-drawn Red Cross truck with its driver, Ludwik Jurek, who was also an AK member. At Majdanek, she could get no farther than the commandant's headquarters, next to the main road and largely out of view of the protective custody camp. Somehow, she vowed to herself, she would eventually win access to places within the camp where she could directly observe and maybe even interact with the prisoners. In the meantime, she made sure on all her visits to chat up the SS guards at the checkpoint and the clerks in the headquarters. For many of those she interacted with, the kindly attentions from the distinguished lady with perfect German provided a welcome break from their tedious routine.

On a visit to Majdanek in early May 1943, Janina saw a sight that filled her with horror: a giant plume of thick, black smoke rising from an area west of the protective custody camp. She knew that the last inhabitants of the Warsaw Ghetto, despite heroic resistance, were being sent by the thousands to Majdanek. The smell of burnt hair and roasting flesh emanating from the plume left her in no doubt as to its source.

Relatives of Polish prisoners in Majdanek pleaded for the RGO's help in getting their loved ones released. In May, through interventions with the Security Police, Skrzyński was actually managing to win the freedom of dozens of Poles seized in street raids or held as hostages. Upon their release, these prisoners were taken to the office of the care committee and RGO in Lublin to be fed and given medical treatment, clothes, and money for the journey home.

Janina made a point of debriefing the released prisoners about their experiences and observations at Majdanek. What she heard exceeded her darkest imaginings. They told her that the prisoners' daily diet consisted of a bitter swill called coffee, soup made from rotten vegetables and weeds, and one eighth of a loaf of bread, with a tiny bit of marmalade and horsemeat sausage twice a week. Since they had no dishes assigned to them, they ate the soup sitting on the ground out of unwashed bowls that were used by several prisoners during the same meal, and the marmalade was delivered into their filthy hands. They talked of how prisoners driven mad with hunger would snarl and fight like animals over a bit of stale bread. They spoke of bodies covered with lice, scabies sores, mud, and feces from chronic dysentery, and of going for a month or more without bathing or even a change of clothes. And they described heavy artillery wagons with chest-high wheels, filled with skeletal corpses that daily traveled from the prisoner compounds to the crematorium, pulled and pushed along the deeply rutted camp road by twenty starving prisoners under constant whipping from kapos and SS men.

Janina also learned about the Jews newly arriving at Majdanek. Men, women, and children waited on bare ground sometimes for days without food or water in the "rose garden," the prisoners' term for a barbed wire enclosure next to the bathing facility. After finally undergoing a brief examination by camp officials, some were directed to the building with showers and disinfection tubs, while the rest, mostly children and people over forty, were forced to strip and then rushed to the gas chambers to be murdered. Usually, the SS conducted the gassings at night, while tractor engines were running to drown out the victims' screams. But now so many Jews were arriving that the SS were gassing them during the daytime as well. Every night, the protective custody camp was filled with the wails of Jews mourning the loss of their children, parents, wives, and husbands.

Prisoners released from the women's camp in Field V informed Janina that 2,000 Belarusian women and children seized in anti-partisan raids had been placed in the camp since March. The older children were held separate from their mothers in barracks surrounded by barbed wire. Since their arrival, typhus had broken out and was now raging in the compound.[9] The prisoners spoke with awe of a Polish physician, Dr. Stefania Perzanowska, who had persuaded the SS to let her set up an infirmary barrack and was providing medical treatment for prisoners. Since there were few other medical professionals among the women prisoners, she had established a nurse training program for volunteers. But she had little more than a stethoscope and some thermometers to work with and almost nothing in the way of medications, disinfectant, gauze, or bandages. There were so many typhus patients in the women's compound, Janina learned, that it had become impossible to quarantine them.[10] From former male prisoners, Janina heard that typhus was now spreading in the other prisoner compounds as well.

This information inspired Janina with an idea. So far, she had been unable to get a meeting with Majdanek's chief doctor, even though Florstedt had authorized the RGO to consult with the camp physician about supplying medicines for the Polish prisoners. Now she decided to use the new typhus epidemic in the camp to get the doctor's attention. In mid-May, she obtained a meeting with the German medical superintendent of Lublin District. Appealing to him for help was a risky gambit, but she calculated that he might agree, if not out of human decency, then out of self-interest.

As usual, she was left to wait until well after the appointed time before being ushered in to see the superintendent. He was standing when she entered, looking out a window, and he did not address her. She decided to dispense with the usual introduction.

"There is a typhus epidemic in Majdanek," she announced. "Our committee seeks permission to provide inoculations."

The doctor reacted predictably, spewing invectives against meddling Polish organizations that demanded rights, helped traitors, and coddled criminals. She waited until his harangue ended.

"I came to you because you are a physician, though now it seems I might as well have gone to the SS. But I came to you because you supposedly once swore an oath to relieve sickness and suffering, and I thought a doctor would surely help."

He turned from the window to face the petite woman who had just addressed him with such calm effrontery. Then he invited her to sit down.

"I'll think about it," he said in a different tone, "but how would you get it there?"

"We could send it to you," she replied, "and you could deliver it to the Majdanek authorities."

He began to pace his office while she explained what she had learned, that there were hundreds of typhus patients in the infirmaries and many more, including children, who were sharing bunks with prisoners who were not yet infected.

He interrupted her. "I'll go to the camp and see for myself what can be done. But," he threatened, "if any of you start spreading horror stories, you know what will happen to you!"

He then went to the telephone, first to call the district doctor, who hadn't heard anything about the situation. Then he called the head of the BuF department, who denied the whole thing. Nevertheless, the superintendent arranged a group tour of the camp hospital for the next day and invited Janina to accompany him. Janina readily accepted this opportunity to go inside the protective custody camp.

By the time of the inspection, Janina had received word that the infirmary barracks were being cleaned and aired and prisoners moved. Janina met the superintendent's group at the commandant's headquarters and then was transported with them to the men's "hospital" in Field I. As their car turned onto the road that ran by the prisoner compounds, Janina glimpsed to her right a building complex under a large wood awning that partially shielded what it covered from view. Based on drawings of the camp smuggled out by resistance members, she realized that the gas chambers were located somewhere under the covering.

At the first entry, they turned past a wooden guard booth and through a gate between two barbed wire fences. She was startled by the sight of flower beds riotous with colorful May blooms. On each side of the compound, a row of ten long wooden barracks stretched back some three hundred yards. She could see little of the rest of the protective custody camp, other than the chimney rising from the next compound on her right. It was impossible not to see and smell the smoke wafting from it or from an area some two hundred yards away, but no one remarked upon it.

The infirmary barracks that they visited seemed very basic but not overcrowded, and they could see that the patients were receiving treatment from prisoners who were well-qualified physicians. The SS orderlies acknowledged that there was some typhus but maintained it was well under control. The physician prisoners, looking ashamed and fearful, kept silent. In the course of the tour, however, one let slip that while the quarantine barrack had two hundred beds, four hundred prisoners had been diagnosed with typhus just the day before.

The medical superintendent recognized that typhus was becoming epidemic at Majdanek again and that it might spread to Lublin and to German soldiers. He told Janina that he would speak with the commandant and instructed her to come to his office the next day. She arrived promptly the next morning and, after a weary wait, received welcome news: she had an appointment to see a Dr. Blancke in Majdanek that very day.

SS *Hauptsturmführer* Dr. Max Blancke had been exceedingly busy at Majdanek ever since his arrival from Natzweiler concentration camp in April 1943. Much of his time was immediately taken up with eyeballing the prisoners in each compound in order to determine which ones were incapable of work and unlikely to recover. Those he selected were placed in a *Gammelblock*, a barrack surrounded by barbed wire where prisoners were left without food or water, lying in their excrement on the dirt floor until they died or were finally taken out to be murdered. Because of the typhus in the women's camp, he had developed a method of selecting prisoners without getting too near them: he had them walk by him with bare legs and feet and sentenced to death those showing edema and sores. In addition, since the transports of Jews began arriving from Warsaw in late April, he had been working long hours day and night in the "rose garden" choosing victims for the gas chambers. Even though Blancke sent thousands to their deaths, Majdanek's population of registered prisoners had grown from 11,000 when he arrived to almost 25,000 by mid-May, more than two thirds of them Jews. He had no time or desire to meet with a woman from some Polish charity, but he could not ignore the medical superintendent's order.

When Janina arrived at Majdanek, two SS men escorted her to a white, two-story house located halfway between the road and the protective custody camp and left her to wait under guard. Eventually, a rather young, attractive man arrived and motioned her to enter an office.

"What do you want to see me about?" Blancke barked impatiently.

"As if he doesn't know," Janina thought, but she patiently explained the purpose of the RGO, Florstedt's agreement that it could provide medicines to the camp, and the medical superintendent's instruction that she meet with the camp doctor. Blancke continued to feign ignorance. When she mentioned the typhus epidemic, however, he exploded.

"There is NO typhus epidemic in this camp!" he thundered. "And as for your other concerns, I am not in the least interested in the welfare of Poles!"

Blancke's fury alarmed Janina, and she wondered whether he could have her arrested. Stilling her nerves, she said, "I have come to offer, on behalf of my organization, a shipment of serum against typhus for all the inmates of Majdanek. We have been delivering food parcels for the prisoners, authorized by Gestapo headquarters." She placed a tiny stress on the words "authorized" and "Gestapo." "We also take some care of prisoners when they are released, and having heard that there were typhus cases at Majdanek, we thought we would like to protect the camp's inmates."

"Doesn't your committee have any better causes than to help these scoundrels?" Blancke demanded. "What's the matter with you charity ladies? Don't you think that if serum were necessary, I, the chief physician here, would see to it that we got it? Anyway, the typhus cases are all quarantined, and the other inmates have no contact with them!"

Janina lowered her eyes and kept silent. Blancke's bullying was not going to deter her. If he refused the serum, she would just go back to the superintendent.

That thought apparently occurred to Blancke as well. After a pause, he said in a milder tone, "Of course, if your committee happens to have the serum, it wouldn't be bad to give it to the prisoners, preventatively, just as prophylaxis, you understand."

"That seems a good idea," she responded.

"Even with the greatest care in quarantining," he went on, "lice can travel from barrack to barrack, so maybe it's as well to inoculate them all and be done with it."

Blancke authorized Janina to send 4,000 vials of serum to Majdanek. She realized this was not enough even for all the Poles in the camp, but she considered this just the first step in the campaign she intended to wage to provide medicines to Majdanek. She persuaded Blancke to meet with the Lublin Polish Care Committee's physician, Dr. Tadeusz Krzyszkowski, to discuss the prisoners' medical needs. The result of their conference was a list of medicines that the Lublin Polish Care Committee and the Polish Red Cross scrambled to fill.

But every step forward toward saving Majdanek's prisoners met with reverses. By the end of May, the Polish Red Cross estimated that only

20 percent of the packages it was delivering were getting to the addressees. Camp authorities now maintained that there were only 3,000 Polish prisoners in the camp, far fewer than the actual number. Consequently, the quantity of bread and food products that the Lublin Care Committee was authorized to supply was too little to make a difference in the diet even of the Poles, much less of the many thousands of other prisoners. Camp officials had started making difficulties even about these deliveries. And Florstedt reneged on his promise in February to allow Polish prisoners to write to their families. Mail had to be censored, and Florstedt had no desire to deploy staff to the task.

To break through the intransigence of Majdanek officials, Skrzyński appealed to Security Police Chief Müller, who instructed Florstedt to meet with the Count. When he arrived at the commandant's office on May 25, however, Skrzyński found not Florstedt but the chief of Majdanek's administration department, Heinrich Worster. The commandant had much more important matters to attend to, Worster explained. Nevertheless, he assured Skrzyński that the RGO could continue supplying bread and food products and could also provide certain medicines, especially vaccines. The food deliveries were to occur each Saturday before noon. In addition, the RGO could supply mattress straw twice a month, and Worster requested immediate delivery of as many blankets as possible. Worster even promised that Polish prisoners would be permitted to send a postcard to a relative and to receive correspondence in return. When Skrzyński pressed him about informing families when their loved ones died in Majdanek, however, Worster refused. He also insisted that the RGO could only supply food for 3,000 prisoners.

Following Skrzyński's conferences with Müller and Worster, Polish prisoners were assigned to work in the camp post office and the rate of package delivery began to improve. Camp authorities also distributed preprinted postcards to the Polish prisoners, along with strict instructions for filling them out. Even this limited ability to communicate with their families improved the prisoners' chances for survival, because it enabled the families to write back and send packages. For the prisoners, the emotional sustenance provided by the correspondence was as precious as the physical sustenance in the packages.[11]

Blancke's acceptance of typhus serum from the RGO was only for appearance's sake, for vaccinating less than 20 percent of Majdanek's prisoners could not possibly stop the disease from spreading among the unvaccinated. The camp's SS leaders were more intent on covering up the epidemic than controlling it. At the beginning of 1943, the Inspectorate of Concentration Camps had placed the camp under a two-month quarantine, during which even the SS were not permitted to leave, a situation that was ripe for mutiny. No one wanted a repeat of that experience. Not long after the medical superintendent's inspection, however, Florstedt received notice that a commission was coming from Berlin to check out a report that typhus was again becoming rampant in the camp. He made it clear to his subordinates that the commission was not to find evidence of the disease in the camp infirmaries.

When Dr. Perzanowska received the order not to report any cases of typhus, there were hundreds of typhus patients isolated in two barracks of the women's camp in Field V. She had no idea what she was supposed to do with them. Then Erich Muhsfeldt, the chief of the crematorium, paid her a visit. His job involved not just disposing of prisoners' corpses but also murdering prisoners selected for death who were not gassed. During his drunken binges he would sometimes barge into the women's infirmary, fire his pistol wildly, and accuse Perzanowska of committing sabotage by shielding malingerers. On this day, accompanied by a medical orderly, he watched as Perzanowska treated patients. Seeing a Jewish woman with the telltale rash, he asked Perzanowska whether the patient had typhus. When she nodded in the affirmative, he and the orderly took the woman into a storeroom and shut the door. After a few minutes, Muhsfeldt emerged and told Perzanowska to look inside. The patient lay dead. Muhsfeldt then screamed at her, "No more typhus in the women's hospital! Understood?"

Perzanowska and her staff spent all that night altering the records of the patients in the two isolation barracks, assigning them a variety of diagnoses. A few days later, Dr. Blancke rushed the group of medical inspectors from Berlin through the women's wards. As Dr. Perzanowska stated the fictitious diagnoses, the inspectors did not bother to look at the patients, who bore the visible signs of their true affliction. At the end, the commission leader addressed her:

"No typhus in the camp?"

"No typhus at all, sir," she replied.[12]

Haunted by the stories she was hearing from the released prisoners, Janina became obsessed with finding more ways to help Majdanek prisoners not just to survive, but to want to survive. "We must do more!" she said again and again to her colleagues and to herself, even crying out the words in her sleep. She conceived a plan for delivering prepared soup to the camp, but her colleagues in the Lublin Polish Care Committee and the Polish Red Cross scoffed at the idea. The Germans would never allow it, they insisted, and even if they did, the logistical challenges of preparing and delivering vats of soup for thousands of prisoners were insurmountable.

With more packages passing through SS inspection at Majdanek, Janina's Underground network began smuggling small messages in the parcels they were preparing, hiding them in a bread roll or at the bottom of a marmalade container. Janina wanted to let her comrades in the camp know that they were not forgotten, that there were many people on the outside who were taking great risks to help them, and so they must not give up hope. Many of them had been completely cut off from the world since long before their arrival in Majdanek and had undergone excruciating torture by the Gestapo. Some, she knew, had finally broken, and now they were suffering in a hell of shame in the camp, scorned by the other prisoners. Janina wanted to reach them as well, to let them know that their comrades on the outside saw them as martyrs, not traitors, deserving of honor, not shame. She arranged to send them messages of appreciation in parcels or passed news of a German defeat or partisan attack to them via comrades who were civilian workers in the camp.

For Janina, the sight and smell of the smoke over Majdanek felt like a constant reproach for her failure to help those who had been reduced to ashes. She had to devise more ways to help those still living. As long as they suffered, she could find no peace.

ELEVEN

JANINA'S LISTS

On July 6, 1943, Majdanek prisoners toiling in the sweltering heat near the main road noticed a billowing cloud of dust advancing from the direction of Zamość. It was not like the dust storms that had been swirling through the camp during the summer drought, coating everyone and everything with a fine, gray grit. This cloud kept over the road, steadily extending from over the horizon. Soon, the prisoners saw its cause: hundreds of exhausted, sweaty, grimy peasants lugging bags of belongings. Most seemed to be women, children, or elderly.[1]

These were the victims of Globocnik's latest operation to pacify and Germanize southern and southeastern Lublin District. It combined an anti-partisan campaign code-named "Wehrwolf" (a combination of the *Wehr* of the Wehrmacht with the word for werewolf, *Werwolf*) with a resumption of the resettlement program that had been suspended in March for the planting season. In late June, German army units along with Waffen SS and police forces set up a dragnet around villages in Zamość and two neighboring counties and proceeded to arrest all the Polish men between the ages of fifteen and forty-five, shooting any who put up resistance. While planes spotted from above, troops methodically combed the fields to find those who sought to flee. A few days later, Globocnik's forces returned to seize the men's families. In retaliation for partisan attacks and resistance to their methods, the Germans destroyed some villages entirely with bombs and fire and murdered all the inhabitants, including children, by shooting them or burning them alive.

Globocnik had the seized civilians placed in three transit camps in the region. After all the men underwent interrogation for ties to the Underground, the SS resettlement commission intended to conduct the usual sorting of the useful from the useless. Globocnik's plan for the latter was to house them in a former POW camp where they would be forced to perform light labor for however long they lived.[2]

Although Globocnik sealed the area and cut off telecommunications, word quickly reached Skrzyński and Janina of the attacks and the filling transit camps. Skrzyński immediately sought to travel to the region to investigate conditions and organize the care committees' response, but the SS and police forces refused to honor his travel authorization from civilian officials. On July 1, Skrzyński persuaded Security Police Chief Müller to issue him a police pass to travel in the affected counties. He spent most of the rest of the month there, regularly reporting to district civilian authorities and the RGO in Kraków about German atrocities and the disastrous effects of the resettlement operation.[3]

Janina was highly skeptical of the German resettlement authorities' promise that, unlike the winter resettlement operation, this time they would not separate Polish children from their families. A plea for help she received from a grandmother in Zamość confirmed her suspicion. The woman's four granddaughters were being held in a transit camp despite the fact that the Germans had shot their father and their mother's whereabouts were unknown.

Janina resolved to learn all she could about the children in the transit camps and to track them as they were placed on outgoing transports so that they could eventually be returned to their families. Reactivating her committee of child care workers from the previous resettlement operation, she dispatched them to the rail stations by the transit camps, where the RGO was allowed to provide some food and necessities to the expellees as they boarded the deportation trains. Janina assigned her workers, mostly members of the

Underground, to report back the number of children on the transports, the date and place when each transport departed, and whatever information about the transports' destination they were able to wheedle out of officials and railway workers. The women particularly looked for unaccompanied children and occasionally succeeded in slipping a few out of the transports.[4]

By early July, the transit camps were so overcrowded that the SS resettlement commission decided to send some of the expellees to Majdanek. In two days, nearly 6,000 Poles arrived at the camp, many of them forced to walk the fifty miles from Zamość. The escort guards shot those who fell behind as encouragement for the others to keep going. By the end of July, the commission had sent some 9,000 Polish expellees to Majdanek.[5]

The camp, already at its theoretical capacity, was completely unprepared for this influx of prisoners. Barracks intended for 250 prisoners held 1,500 or more, with multiple people to each bed and others sleeping cheek by jowl on the floor. All, including the children, had to stay outdoors during the day under the broiling sun and stand for excruciating hours during the roll calls before dawn and at dusk. They relieved themselves in the open latrines and had no way to wash their bodies or clothes, or their infants' diapers. Their suffering became immeasurably worse when Florstedt cut off the water to the protective custody camp and ordered the execution of anyone caught using water to drink or wash. Although Majdanek had finally been connected to Lublin's sewer system, the severe summer drought had caused the municipal waterworks to fail. The only liquid the prisoners received was the "coffee" given out in the morning and the disgusting soup that was passed around in unwashed bowls and, like everything else in the camp, was gritty with dust. The sight of prisoners hauling sloshing buckets of well water for the camp's flower beds only added to their torment.

Conditions at Majdanek were especially devastating for the children. Starvation and dehydration swiftly hollowed out their already malnourished bodies. They sickened from measles and mumps as well as the typhus that inevitably swept through the expellees. And they daily witnessed traumatizing scenes of vicious beatings and of naked corpses piled in wheelbarrows, arms and legs twitching like macabre puppets on the bumpy journey to the crematorium. More and more children died as each day passed.[6]

With Skrzyński away investigating conditions in the region of the Wehrwolf operation, Janina took charge of all interventions with German authorities concerning Majdanek. Camp officials did not regard the Zamość expellees as concentration camp prisoners and so did not include them in the tally of Poles the RGO was authorized to provide for. Janina did manage to negotiate some increase in food, but it was not enough to make any significant difference in the prisoners' nutrition. Any joy she felt at being allowed to provide 250 liters of milk for the children evaporated when she learned that most of it was siphoned off by the SS and kapos. Her only real achievement was to arrange the transfer to Lublin's children's hospital of 153 desperately ill Polish children in Majdanek. Their extreme emaciation shocked Janina and made her even more desperate to rescue those still in the camp.[7]

Meanwhile, on July 3, Janina learned that transport trains were depositing whole families of starving expellees in the transit camp near the Lublin city train station at 6 and 31 Krochmalna Street. Immediately after arriving, they were being taken to be deloused at a facility outside the camp. Poles living nearby had spontaneously set up a soup kitchen and were bribing the guards to allow them to feed the expellees as they passed by. Seeing an opportunity to rescue more children, Janina and a few of her AK colleagues joined the feeding effort. As they served food to throngs of expellees awaiting delousing, the women offered to take children to be cared for, and they succeeded in whisking some away. Once trains began departing from Krochmalna to the Reich carrying entire families, however, fewer parents were willing to give up their children. Janina decided that the risk involved in taking the children now outweighed the potential reward.

Janina made the neighborhood soup kitchen an official RGO operation, and her call for the local population to donate food for the expellees met with instant success. Since she could not get permission to distribute food inside the Krochmalna camp, she had carts set up outside its gates for receiving and distributing the donations. The commotion this caused induced the Krochmalna commandant, the ethnic German Zdzisław Musielski, to relent. He gave Janina three passes for Lublin Polish Care Committee workers to distribute prepared soup, food items that expellees could take with them on their journey to the Reich, and milk and rolls for the camp infirmary. The Polish Red Cross also provided bread, preserves, and milk. Janina often used one of the passes herself so that, while distributing food to the expellees, she could question them. She then passed on any useful information she gleaned to the Underground.[8]

Meanwhile, armed with Skrzyński's reports, the RGO's leaders in Kraków were petitioning for the resettlement operation to stop and its victims to be released. When RGO president Count Ronikier went to see Frank on July 23, he was astonished by the gracious reception he received. The governor general professed that he, too, opposed resettlement and pacification operations, and he promised to stop them. What's more, Frank granted the RGO significant new funding for its work and announced that the General Government would soon institute new policies to improve conditions for the Poles. The change would include an increase in rations for Poles who showed themselves to be loyal and productive subjects. Henceforth, Frank declared magnanimously, "no working person will have to starve *anymore*" in the General Government (emphasis added). It soon turned out that, thanks to *Aktion* Wehrwolf, the power dynamics in the General Government were shifting in a direction that would provide the RGO far more leeway for rescuing Polish victims of Nazi persecution.[9]

Earlier in the year, Frank's proposals for a somewhat kinder and gentler policy toward the Poles had found no support from Himmler or Hitler. Before *Aktion* Wehrwolf began, Frank pleaded with Hitler to put off the Germanization of the General Government until after the war and to stop the slaughter of women, children, and the elderly in reprisal actions. He complained that these tactics were only causing chaos in the countryside and threatening the harvest while driving the Poles into the arms of the Bolsheviks. Himmler insisted, however, that Globocnik would somehow manage to Germanize and pacify the region without harming the General Government's economy or security. As a sop to Frank, Himmler promised that once *Aktion* Wehrwolf achieved its goals, he would transfer Globocnik out of the General Government. Hitler backed Himmler, who authorized Globocnik to proceed with his campaign. Within days of its start, Frank's worst predictions began to come true.

By the time of his meeting with Count Ronikier, however, Frank had acquired an influential ally in his efforts to rein in the power of the SS and police in the General Government: the new governor of Lublin District. Globocnik's close relationship with Himmler had empowered him to ignore most of former governor Zörner's orders and decrees. But Governor Richard Wendler was Himmler's brother-in-law and even dearer to the *Reichsführer* SS than Globocnik. Wendler reacted with fury to the effects of Globocnik's operation, which Skrzyński was documenting in his letters of protest to the governor. The partisans were growing stronger by the day and were attacking the new ethnic German settlements so frequently that the settlers were abandoning their farms and refusing to return. Since the Polish peasants were either being seized by Globocnik's forces or were fleeing them, there was no one left to tend the fields, so the prospects for the harvest appeared dim. Even the SS general in charge of anti-partisan warfare conceded that Globocnik's tactics had failed. In a July 27 letter to "Dear Heinrich," Wendler informed Himmler that Globocnik had created a "spectacular fiasco" in Lublin District. The governor urged his brother-in-law to "install Globocnik in his new assignment as soon as possible and get him out of here."[10]

Himmler agreed to send a new SS and Police Leader to replace Globocnik in Lublin District by mid-August. In the meantime, on July 31, Globocnik had to concede that Wendler's civilian authorities would take control of prisoners in the transit camps who were not suspected of participating in the resistance. The District Labor Office would take custody of those selected for labor, while the RGO would take over the expellees rated as unfit for work.[11]

Globocnik did not immediately leave Lublin, however, in part because he still had some tasks connected with *Aktion* Reinhard. There was also some question about his next post. Himmler wanted to promote Globocnik to a Higher SS and Police Leader, but the number of positions was declining with the Germans' retreat on the Eastern Front. After Italy surrendered to the Allies in September 1943 and Germany occupied the northern half of the country, a new position opened up in Globocnik's hometown, Trieste. There, Globocnik proceeded with his usual gusto to slaughter civilians and ship Jews to their death.[12]

Globocnik's dismissal had immediate consequences for Janina's work. On August 2, she accompanied Skrzyński to meet with Wendler regarding a list of demands that the Count had submitted two days earlier. The governor acceded to nearly all of them. He assured them that there would be no more resettlement raids and that collective punishment in reprisal for partisan attacks would cease. While Wendler did not have the authority to close the transit camps, he had arranged permission for the RGO to take charge of the camp inmates who were ill, as well as all orphans and unaccompanied minors. The released expellees were forbidden to return to their villages, but the RGO could settle them elsewhere in the district. The SS and Police Leader would authorize RGO personnel to enter the five transit camps, including the one in Majdanek, and would instruct the commandant of each camp to provide information about all the Polish expellees who had been interned there. The governor further promised that local officials would cooperate with the RGO and issue passes to its workers so that they could perform their duties. Finally, the governor declared that, other than the people seized in pacification actions to be sent to the Reich, not one more person would be forcibly deported out of his district. He invited Skrzyński to contact him directly regarding any major issues he encountered and to continue keeping him fully informed about events in the region.[13]

Stunned by the sudden reversal in resettlement policy, Skrzyński and Janina left Wendler's office determined to make good on his concessions before the policy could change again. Their first step was to see Security Police Chief Müller, who arranged for them to meet that same afternoon with Globocnik's chief of staff about access to the transit camps. Janina recognized the significance of this appointment. Despite Wendler's promises and assurances, it was not he, but the SS and police who controlled the fate of the expellees. If she and Skrzyński could win the support of the SS and Police Leader's chief of staff, then their ability to aid the expellees would be assured. What Janina did not know was that she was about to confer with a mass murderer of her people.

SS *Sturmbannführer* (Major) Hermann Höfle was, like his boss, an Austrian, and had also done prison time before the *Anschluss* for illegal Nazi activities. After joining Globocnik's staff in 1940, he became the SS and Police

Leader's advisor for Jewish Affairs (*Judenreferent*) and, in 1942, the manager of *Aktion* Reinhard. His main responsibility was to handle the logistics of moving the operation's victims from their homes or from ghettos to the killing centers and forced labor camps. He established transit ghettos where Jews from Poland and beyond were concentrated and selected for labor or death. He coordinated the ghetto clearance operations with local police and civilian authorities and deployed units of Trawniki men to carry them out. Not content to manage operations from his desk in Lublin, he supervised many of the operations in person. His elevation to Globocnik's chief of staff was recognition for his managerial skills in organizing the murder of over 1.5 million Jews in just seventeen months. At the time Skrzyński and Janina visited him, Höfle was preparing to clear the Białystok Ghetto of its last 30,000 inhabitants.[14]

The meeting went well. Höfle promised that the RGO could obtain lists with the names of detainees in the transit camps who could be released to the Polish care committees. He also invited Skrzyński to contact him personally on any matters involving police orders. The memorandum on their meeting does not note whether Höfle stood to greet Countess Suchodolska.[15]

The next day, just after Skrzyński set out on another tour of the Zamość region, a summons arrived for him from Höfle. Janina showed up in Skrzyński's stead at the appointed time the next morning. She explained Skrzyński's absence and suggested that Höfle meet the next day with Count Stanisław Łoś, who was in charge of resettling the expellees after their release. But Höfle was seeking immediate action, and he recognized that Janina was, like himself, the person who acted behind the scenes in her organization to get its work done. Since Globocnik had accepted Wendler's demand that civilian authorities take control of the expellees, the SS and police now wanted to close the transit camps as quickly as possible. Höfle informed Janina that the RGO was to take custody of all the women and children and all the men rated unfit for work who were still in the camps. He instructed her to contact the commandants of the transit camps "immediately" to determine the number of detainees to be released.[16]

Janina rushed back to her office and sent instructions to RGO officials in the Zamość region to contact the commandants of the three transit camps there. Then she set out for Majdanek. She was confident that Musielski would provide the numbers for Krochmalna but suspected that Florstedt would raise difficulties. Since Janina had authorization from Höfle, Florstedt was obliged at least to meet with her. She explained to the commandant that she was to obtain the number of women, children, and disabled expellees in Majdanek who were to be released, and she told him of Governor Wendler's promise that the RGO would be allowed to send workers into the transit camps to provide care for the expellees. Florstedt dismissed both demands as irrelevant for him. The expellees in Majdanek were not listed in the camp's registry because they were under the jurisdiction of the SS resettlement commission. If Janina wanted to have them released, she would have to get their names elsewhere and provide them to Florstedt along with an official order transferring each one to the RGO's custody. As for the governor's promise, Majdanek might be serving as a transit camp for expellees, but it was still a concentration camp, he informed her, and the only way he would allow RGO workers to enter it would be as prisoners.[17]

Janina was annoyed but not discouraged. Florstedt could make things difficult, but he could not prevent the release of the expellees in Majdanek, and she intended to make that happen as quickly as possible. She would just have to get their names from the resettlement commission, and with Höfle's backing, she knew she would succeed.

The next morning, August 5, the BuF held a conference at its office that was attended by Höfle, Janina, and Łoś and Dąbrowski of the Lublin Polish Care Committee. They all agreed on a plan to settle the expellees released from the transit camps in Lublin and Puławy counties. Janina made a plea for the immediate release of the expellees in Majdanek and presented information about their rising mortality rate in the camp. The resettlement commission would provide her the information and authorizations she needed, Höfle assured her.

After the conference ended but before Janina left the BuF, an official of the resettlement commission strutted into the office. To Janina's surprise, he flatly rejected her request for information about the expellees to be released from Majdanek. With a dismissive glance at the BuF chief, he asserted that no matter what assurances the RGO had received from civilian officials, he had the final say on the fate of the expellees. There would be no releases from Majdanek until the commission had finished examining the children, since it was certain that some had German blood and so should be united with their racial brethren in the Reich.

Janina felt almost amused by this puffed-up SS sergeant who thought he could thwart her mission. She informed him that it was SS and Police Leader Globocnik (said with slight emphasis) who ordered the release of expellees from Majdanek, and his chief of staff had just this hour assured her of full compliance from the resettlement commission. At her suggestion, the BuF chief offered to put the commission official through to Höfle so that he could explain why he was refusing to comply.

The official's tone changed. There were 3,600 Polish expellees eligible for release in Majdanek, he told Janina, but he lacked the personnel to prepare all the necessary paperwork for freeing them in the near future. Janina quickly assured him that the RGO would happily relieve him of the paperwork burden. They then agreed that the RGO would receive the names immediately and the expellees would be released in stages starting on August 9.

Janina also pressed for permission to establish an aid station in Lublin where the released expellees would receive food and vaccinations against contagious diseases before journeying to their new residences. This the resettlement official refused, insisting that those freed proceed immediately to their place of resettlement before the residents of Lublin could observe their condition and make contact with them. In the end, though, Janina won on this point as well, for a short time later the resettlement official visited her office in a more conciliatory mood. He approved the aid station and agreed that Janina could bring a Red Cross doctor and a few orderlies to Majdanek to deal with expellees who required immediate hospitalization. The resettlement official assured Janina that one car would be sufficient transport for that purpose.

A massive mobilization effort ensued to prepare for the release of the expellees in Majdanek. The Lublin Polish Care Committee established a rest station in a church on Betonowa Street near the train station where it and the Polish Red Cross would feed hundreds of people a day, provide them parcels for their journey, and administer medical care and vaccines.

The care committee also recruited escorts to take the expellees to the communities where they were to settle and obtained the tickets and passes for the journeys. The local care committee branches prepared to house, feed, and clothe the new arrivals, register them with authorities, and help them obtain work and ration cards. Individuals, organizations, and businesses volunteered help and donated money, food, clothing, diapers, and medicines. Janina was easily able to recruit typists in the city to help the care committee's clerks prepare release certificates for 3,600 people and the lists of those to be released on specific dates.

On August 9, 1943, Janina and a Polish Red Cross physician arrived at the Majdanek guardhouse at the gate to the "Black Road" that led to the protective custody camp. This was the point where she was to receive custody of the eight hundred expellees on the list she had submitted the day before. But when the SS resettlement commission official handed her back the list at the guardhouse, her heart sank: half the names were crossed off. The only reason he would give for the change was that those persons were "no longer available."

Then Janina waited, staring at the point where the Black Road dipped down to the right and disappeared around the corner between Field I and the bathing facility with the gas chambers. She had been informed that the expellees to be released that day would depart on foot from Field III. The August sun was blazing and her eyes stung from the dusty air. Finally, they began to appear on the road, thin, gray figures progressing slowly up the slope toward her. Some were walking, some were staggering, many were struggling to carry children or to hold up sick or elderly relatives. More and more fell or simply gave up and were now lying on the dust-covered stones of the recently paved road. Looking closely at the stones, it was possible to find some that bore Hebrew letters. Previously, they had marked the gravestones of Lublin's Jewish cemeteries.

When the people who reached the transfer point saw the SS resettlement official, they were afraid to speak to Janina and hesitated to follow her instructions because they did not trust that they were really being freed. Eventually, some told Janina in anguish of relatives who were supposed to accompany them but were too weak to walk out of Field III or had collapsed soon after leaving it.

The moment that Janina and all Lublin had anticipated with such hope had turned into a disaster. Janina realized that many of the expellees who managed to get to the transfer point would not be able to walk two kilometers farther to the rest station on Betonowa Street. The one ambulance the Red Cross had sent could not possibly ferry all the people who clearly required hospitalization. And what was to be done about all the people who could not reach the transfer point? Of one thing she was certain: they could not be left in the camp, not even for one more day. She pleaded with the SS resettlement official to allow transport into the protective custody camp to bring out the expellees from Field III. Such permission could only come from Majdanek's commandant, he informed her.

Janina dashed to camp headquarters and marched straight into the commandant's office, demanding to speak with Florstedt. When he appeared, she matter-of-factly informed him that she needed to use his telephone to call for transport that would bring the expellees unable to walk from Field III to the rest station. She would then need passes for herself, the Red Cross physician, and the transport drivers to go to Field III to collect the expellees. Enraged by the Countess's brazenness, Florstedt was on the verge of ordering her out of his office, but then he reconsidered. He realized that, if he refused the Countess, she would eventually get her way by appealing to Höfle. The commandant was counting on Globocnik to recommend him for promotion and had no desire to incur the wrath of his chief of staff.[18] Florstedt instructed his staff to put through Janina's telephone calls and to issue her passes for six people to enter the protective custody camp.

Janina called the Red Cross, the volunteer fire department, the Społem agricultural cooperative, the Kucharski soap factory, Sochacki Company, and estate owner Count Smorczewski. Within two hours, horse-drawn trucks, ambulances, and wagons were pulling up to the gate of Field III. Janina and the Red Cross physician were waiting there and entered the compound to find a scene of ghastly chaos. Based on the physician's hasty triage, Janina instructed the drivers which expellees to take to the rest station or hospital. Janina willed herself to focus entirely on the task at hand lest she be overwhelmed by the sight, sound, and smell of the starving, sick, and dying all around her. Only that night, after everything was done, did the images flood into her mind that would haunt her for years to come. Especially of the children, skin-covered skeletons who stared blankly out of sunken eyes, too weak even to cry.

Janina received custody of just 399 people that day. So that the other transfers would proceed more smoothly, she persuaded the SS resettlement official not to be present, promising to provide him a full report. On each of the following four days, the transfer of custody began with Janina receiving the list of people to be released, on which hundreds of names were crossed off.[19] Polish transports then proceeded to Field III to collect those too feeble to walk. Once the transfer was completed, Janina handed back the list and made her report.

In all, Janina received custody of 2,106 expellees out of the 3,600 whose release she had requested. The Red Cross physician sent 394 of them immediately to Lublin's hospitals. At the rest station, Red Cross personnel vaccinated expellees in the hope of protecting them from typhus and preventing them from spreading it, but little could be done about the lice that visibly crawled on their skin and in their hair. Some of the released expellees, desperate to stay with their families, hid their symptoms. Within a few days of their release, another 140 were sent to Lublin hospitals from nearby villages. Of the 534 expellees released from Majdanek who were treated in Lublin hospitals, 183 died, most from typhus, including 101 children aged twelve or younger. An unknown number of the released expellees died in their new communities, as did some of their neighbors, felled by the spreading typhus epidemic.

Janina took little comfort in the fact that her efforts had served to free more than 2,000 people from Majdanek, most of them women and children. What had happened to the nearly 1,500 whose names had been crossed off her lists? Janina again appealed to Höfle, who asked the resettlement commission for an accounting. It was just a clerical error, the commission replied. It presented a tally purporting to show that all the rest of the 8,566 expellees it had sent to Majdanek had been selected for labor, except for 186 who had died in the camp. Janina immediately recognized that the commission's tally left 54 people unaccounted for. She suspected that they had died after the commission gave her the names of the expellees to be released.[20]

While she was seeking the releases from Majdanek, Janina also hounded the Lublin Labor Office about the expellees in the Krochmalna Street transit camp, which the Labor Office controlled. Thousands of expellees continued to arrive at Krochmalna as the transit camps in the Zamość region shut down. Janina informed the Labor Office of Governor Wendler's personal promise that no more expellees would be sent to the Reich against their will. Therefore, she insisted, the Labor Office was obliged to provide the RGO a list of all the Polish expellees who were in the camp and to grant the Lublin Polish Care Committee's workers unfettered access to them to help them find homes and jobs. When the Labor Office balked at fulfilling these obligations, Janina appealed to the offices of the governor and the SS and Police Leader. Soon afterward, the Krochmalna Street transit camp released three hundred sick expellees to the Lublin Care Committee and issued it ten passes for its workers to speak with the remaining expellees in the camp.

Even though it could no longer send the expellees to the Reich against their will, the Labor Office could still assign the able-bodied to work involuntarily at labor sites within the General Government where they faced abuse, deprivation, and unsafe conditions. Only a valid labor card could exempt a Pole from such assignment, and so Janina sought to get as many labor cards as possible for Krochmalna's able-bodied detainees. She and her colleagues with access to the camp questioned detainees about their professions and past work experience and compiled lists that Janina sent to large employers such as Społem, the forestry department, the school superintendent, and the various chambers for agriculture, artisans, and medicine. The employers then sent representatives to the camp to claim specific detainees as their workers.

In the second half of August, there were so many expellees in Krochmalna that it was taking the Lublin Polish Care Committee up to six hours a day to distribute food to them all. Generally, the new arrivals had already been selected for labor, but the epidemics spreading in the crowded conditions quickly caused hundreds to be rated as unfit. By the end of the month, Janina had obtained the release into RGO care of 1,022 Poles from Krochmalna. Hundreds were admitted to Lublin's overflowing hospitals. In the infectious disease wards, two adults or three children had to be assigned to each bed.[21]

In all, Janina managed to secure the release into RGO care of 3,128 expellees taken captive by the Germans during the resettlement operation in the summer of 1943. That number represented less than 10 percent of the 36,389 people the SS resettlement commission reported seizing. The commission sent 29,214 to forced labor, mostly in the Reich. Altogether, between November 1942 and August 1943, the Germans seized or drove 100,000 Poles from three hundred villages in the Zamość region and replaced them with 14,000 settlers deemed to have German blood.[22]

Even after confirming that the transports from the transit camps were carrying children together with their relatives, Janina continued to gather information about the children being sent out of the district. She was able to get copies of transport lists from a woman working in the district labor office. Janina also directed women working for RGO branches at border stations to keep watch for the transports and report back about which ones left the General Government and in what direction. Her fears for the children were confirmed when she began to receive letters from frantic parents reporting that their children had been taken from them once they had crossed over into the Reich. After the war, Janina would provide Polish investigators a list of children between the ages of two and fourteen who had been taken in the resettlement operation and sent to the Reich on twenty-nine transports between July 7 and August 25, 1943. Janina believed that many of the children wound up in the special camps where abducted children were drilled into little Germans and beaten if they cried for their families or spoke in their native language. The total number of children on the list came to 4,454.[23]

TWELVE

RESCUE

By the end of August 1943, Lublin's main cemetery contained row upon row of freshly dug graves, each containing the body of a Zamość expellee whose release from Majdanek or Krochmalna had come too late. So many children died that the city ran out of coffins for them, and so some had been buried in bags.[1]

The plight of the deportees released from Majdanek made a deep impression upon the people of Lublin and strengthened the resolve of many to resist the German occupiers. The AK networks that Janina worked with to aid Majdanek prisoners were expanding as a consequence. They were now under the direction of Irena Antoszewska of the Central Underground Care (*Centralna Opieka Podziemia*), known as OPUS, the organization within the AK that aided imprisoned members and sought to organize resistance cells in the prisons and camps. The manager of a restaurant, Antoszewska served Germans in the front of the premises while her AK colleagues assembled packages in the back. She obtained the food for the packages by soliciting donations from estate owners in the countryside and collecting products that AK units looted from German supplies. Janina gave her a pass as an official supplier of the RGO so that she could justify to German inspectors why she was transporting large quantities of food from the countryside into the city.[2]

The OPUS relief network included Saturnina Malm, who was producing packages for Majdanek prisoners at night in her tenement building with the help of family and colleagues. They had to mail the packages, because Ludwik Christians, as head of the Lublin Polish Red Cross, forbade his organization to accept them for delivery. He feared that Majdanek officials would bar the Red Cross from delivering any packages if they discovered that some came from people who were not relatives of prisoners.[3] To avoid suspicion, each member of Malm's group carried the packages out in intervals, using the building's three exits, and delivered them to workers at the post office who could be trusted not to reveal the packages' true origin. Malm was also corresponding regularly with prisoners in Majdanek via AK colleagues working as electricians in the camp. They used a small house near the Old Airfield forced labor camp for Jews as a letter drop.

The risks Malm was taking were enormous, yet in late August 1943 she took on perhaps her greatest risk of all. As she was carrying correspondence to the letter drop, she came upon a large group of Jewish women under SS guard who were being force-marched from the Old Airfield camp's railroad siding to Majdanek. They were among the 11,000 Jews sent to Majdanek in August and September from the Białystok ghetto. Malm quickly walked away from the road to avoid the SS, then felt a sudden tug at her elbow. Turning, she saw a terrified fourteen-year-old girl with a pleading look in her eyes who had somehow slipped away from the group unseen. In a split-second decision, Malm took the girl in hand and ducked out of sight with her. Malm's husband, Mikołaj, helped her get the girl to their building, where they hid her in an attic. Regarding the tremendous danger his wife had placed them in, Mikołaj Malm said simply, "What will be, will be . . ."

The girl was Sara Roth, the only survivor of her family. She might have passed as a non-Jewish Pole, but she spoke little Polish and her Yiddish accent marked her as a Jew as soon as she opened her mouth. Malm gave her books in Polish to study in the attic during the day and then took her out behind the building in the evening to give her air and teach her how to pronounce the words she was reading. Sara was a quick study and before long could speak and write Polish fluently. With the help of an orphanage director, Malm was able to get Sara documents with the identity of a deceased Polish girl. Sara survived the rest of the war as Jadwiga Naremska.[4]

Janina's work for the RGO had come to feel like bailing water on a sinking ship. The Lublin Polish Care Committee lacked sufficient resources to support all the expellees released from Majdanek and Krochmalna whom it had settled in Lublin County. Meanwhile, Krochmalna continued to fill with thousands of Poles seized in anti-partisan operations, and the Labor Office was now insisting on immediately releasing all those rated unfit for labor to the care committee before it had a chance to find them places to live. The rest station on Betonowa Street was so crowded that people were having to stand throughout the night. Skrzyński and Janina had been trying for over a year to get approval for the care committee to set up a night shelter in Lublin, but they could get no response from city officials. In addition, Lublin's hospitals were so overcrowded that they were releasing the care committee's charges before they had fully recuperated, and the only place the committee had to put them was in a school. There were no beds in the building, so the patients slept on the floor. But now the school year was about to begin, and the city administration had ordered the committee to vacate the premises.[5]

Janina's efforts to aid Majdanek prisoners were also foundering. While Polish prisoners were receiving more packages, they were no longer allowed to write to their families except for returning the card acknowledging receipt of a package. The camp's authorities were also curtailing the RGO's delivery of bread and products for soup. And yet, the SS and police were stepping up their raids in Lublin County, seizing Poles off the streets and out of public transit and sending them to Majdanek. Hostage taking was also on the rise. The Order Police, the uniformed branch of the German police, ran a special camp for hostages in part of Majdanek's Field IV, and its population swelled to nearly a thousand by early September. They were primarily Poles seized as collective punishment for communities that failed to meet the agricultural quota or in order to deter assistance to partisans. By regulation, hostages were supposed to be men between the ages of seventeen and forty. Only one man in a family was to be held as a hostage, and hostages were to be released after four weeks. In reality, whole families were sometimes detained as hostages, and the length of detention at Majdanek was more likely to be four months than four weeks. Although the hostages were not forced to work in the camp, starvation and disease still took their toll, and the majority of hostages died before release or shortly afterward.[6]

Still, Janina drew hope from the new power dynamic in Lublin District and resolved to take advantage of it while it lasted. Unlike Globocnik, the new SS and Police Leader, Jakob Sporrenberg, seemed inclined to cooperate with civilian authorities and to respect Governor Wendler's decrees. Given the governor's role in freeing the Zamość expellees, Janina decided to seek his aid in securing other releases and in forcing civilian officials to address the pressing needs of the Lublin Polish Care Committee. Skrzyński was now spending most of his time in the eastern and southern counties of Lublin District, so Janina was handling the work that was based in Lublin County, including most communications with German authorities there.[7] She lacked the status to approach the governor's office directly, however. So she called in Prince Woroniecki from Kraków.

Woroniecki contacted Wendler, who ordered the chief of his administration, Ernst Schlüter, to ascertain the RGO's concerns and determine what could be done to address them. When Woroniecki and Janina met with Schlüter on September 2, the Prince turned the meeting over to her. Impressed by the Countess's presentation regarding Polish civilians at Majdanek, Schlüter immediately contacted the camp administration about releasing all hostages detained there against the regulations, as well as all persons seized in raids who were not suspected of illegal acts. That same day, Majdanek released three hundred hostages. Then, in a triumph for Janina, Schlüter asked her to return the following week to discuss the situation of the expellees who were being settled in Lublin County. As they walked out of the meeting, Woroniecki congratulated Janina on its outcome. She now had a direct line to the governor's office, and she intended to make the most of it.

At the start of her meeting with Schlüter on September 8, Janina informed him that, despite his instructions to Majdanek authorities, many hundreds of Poles were still being held there as hostages or as victims of raids. Her statement had its intended effect, for Schlüter immediately called

Majdanek, this time with even better results: 1,400 Poles were released from the camp that day and 400 the next. At Janina's request, Schlüter also instructed Majdanek officials to return the belongings of the expellees who had been released and to give the belongings of those who had died to the Lublin Polish Care Committee.

Then Janina presented facts and figures about the needs of the expellees, about the hundreds who had died and the hundreds who were still overwhelming Lublin's hospitals. She informed Schlüter that the Labor Office was dumping the Poles at Krochmalna rated unfit for work onto the Lublin Polish Care Committee without any provision for housing or feeding them. In light of this situation, she requested his support in persuading civilian authorities to allocate space and furnishings to the care committee so that it could establish a shelter and a convalescent hospital. As in all her dealings with German officials, Janina framed her requests as matters that the Germans would care about—for example, as prophylactic health measures rather than humanitarian assistance to Poles—and emphasized how it was in the Germans' own interests to grant them.

Schlüter found Countess Suchodolska to be most persuasive and sympathetic. He promised that he would order the Building Office to allocate space for a night shelter and that he would look into the possibility of establishing a convalescent home. Then he made another phone call, this one to the chief of the Labor Office, whom he ordered to come to an arrangement with the Countess that would ensure proper care for the Poles in Krochmalna who were unfit for work.

Finally, Janina brought up the difficulties she was encountering in getting the special IDs and train passes that the care committees' personnel required to perform their work. Schlüter invited Janina to submit a list of the care committee personnel who needed the IDs and passes and promised that he would personally issue them. Janina made sure that many of the people on that list were her colleagues in the Underground.

Immediately after the meeting, the chief of the Labor Office contacted Janina, and within two days they had worked out an agreement regarding Poles in Krochmalna who were rated unfit for labor. They would remain in the camp until the Lublin Polish Care Committee arranged shelter for them, during which time the care committee would have complete access to them at any time and could take them out of the camp temporarily for medical treatment and appointments with officials. Until their release, they would be fed by the camp with support from the care committee. Having learned her lesson during the release of the expellees from Majdanek, Janina also negotiated for transportation for the deportees once they were released from Krochmalna.[8]

Janina's appeal to Schlüter for space to establish a convalescent home also succeeded. On September 15, the district administration allocated to the Lublin Polish Care Committee part of a building that it could use to house expellees released from the hospital but still too weak to travel to their new homes. The Polish Red Cross provided the personnel and administered the facility under the supervision of care committee medical officers.[9]

As the settlement of the released expellees from the Zamość region progressed, a new emergency confronted Skrzyński and Janina. Polish refugees were fleeing into Lublin District from the multiethnic former Polish territory of Volhynia (Wołyń), which was just to the east of the district and outside the General Government's borders. The region had become a battle zone. In response to increasing attacks from Polish, Ukrainian, and Soviet-backed partisans, the Germans were conducting pacification operations with their usual brutality. Simultaneously, inspired by the changing tide of the war on the Eastern Front, Ukrainian nationalists were conducting their own ethnic cleansing campaign against the Poles so that Ukraine could claim sovereignty over the region at the war's end. Units of the Ukrainian Insurgent Army (UPA) were destroying Polish villages and massacring their residents by the thousands in order to drive all other Poles out of the region. Polish partisans were attacking Ukrainian villages in retaliation.[10]

The Security Police were rounding up the refugees and placing them in transit camps along with Poles seized in pacification operations. Once the usual selection of the able-bodied for work in the Reich was completed, the question remained of what to do with those not fit for labor. The Security Police decreed that they should return to Volhynia, but the RGO denounced that policy as tantamount to sentencing the refugees to death. The Security

Police then proposed to place them in concentration camps. After urgent lobbying efforts by the RGO, the General Government administration in Kraków finally settled the matter. None of the Volhynian refugees would be sent to work in the Reich against their will, and only those suspected of ties with the resistance would remain under Security Police jurisdiction. All the rest were to be cared for by the RGO, which would be responsible for settling them within the General Government.[11]

Janina soon learned that, German promises to the contrary, Poles from Volhynia were still being sent to the Reich against their will. In Volhynia, the Germans encouraged frantic Polish civilians who had seen their homes burned and their loved ones slaughtered to sign up for transports that would take them to safety in the General Government, where they would be cared for by the RGO. Instead, healthy young adults who signed up for the transports discovered that they had been registered as volunteers for labor in the Reich. In addition, the Germans continued to conduct raids to seize laborers in Volhynia, and as a result many transports carried people who had not volunteered to go the General Government.[12] Determined to prevent as many as she could from becoming forced laborers in Germany, Janina devised a multifaceted rescue operation.

The RGO's vastly expanded responsibilities in Lublin District required it to recruit more personnel. Thanks to Janina, many of the new hires were members of the Underground. She assigned some of them to provide food and emergency supplies to the refugees when their transports crossed into Lublin District from Volhynia. When Janina received official notice of an incoming rail transport, she alerted the local care committee to set up a care station at the crossing point. The care station workers handed packages of food, clothes, and diapers to the refugees, many of whom had fled with just the clothes on their backs. The committees also set up field kitchens to serve soup to the refugees and guards during longer stopovers. While providing these services, Janina's Underground employees interviewed the refugees to determine whether any were being transported against their will. The same was done by the care committee members working in the temporary transit camps. The information was passed to Janina.

Sometimes Janina could use her official contacts to rescue Volhynians seized for labor. At others, she had to resort to clandestine means. Her Underground employees used various strategies to help individual refugees slip away from a transport or transit camp. These included bribing guards, smuggling people out on the carts that carried vats of soup, or supplying workmen's clothes so they could blend in with other workers as they left the camp. Far more daring and dangerous was the strategy used to rescue groups of involuntary refugees. Railway workers in the Underground would attach an empty car to the rear of a transport train and direct the passengers to be rescued to transfer to it. Then, at that station or the next, the car was uncoupled. When the train left, the car remained, and members of the Underground helped the passengers escape, often to join AK units in the area.[13]

Her Volhynian rescue operation soon put Janina in grave peril. As a result of her official interventions, the Germans realized that she was receiving specific information about Poles from Volhynia who had been designated for forced labor in the Reich. They also did not fail to notice that some of those persons were disappearing en route. Janina received a threatening letter from Governor Wendler. His officials had informed him that care committees under Janina's supervision were obstructing the orderly evacuation of people from the Eastern territory and persuading volunteers not to go on to Germany but to escape from the transports. He was therefore making her personally responsible for every act of sabotage and escape. He ordered her to send a copy of his letter immediately to all the Polish care committees in Lublin District along with her own instructions to confine their assistance to Volhynian refugees strictly to distributing food and clothes. Any other activity, the letter threatened, would be considered sabotage and subject every member of the committee to arrest.

Wendler's threats frightened Janina. Continuing her rescue efforts would endanger not only herself and her workers but potentially also the RGO's entire program of aiding the refugees. Abandoning her efforts and allowing Poles to be abducted to the Reich was not an option, however. She decided to comply with the letter of Wendler's orders but not with their spirit. She sent Wendler's letter to the care committees along with her own directive to refrain from any activity other than the provision of food and clothes. The dispatch of both the letter and the instructions was logged in her records and the copies were placed in the files of her office and of the committees. She made one exception, however. She did not send the letter and directive to the care committee of the city of Lublin, because she knew its leaders were meek enough to obey them. Then, she sent couriers to all the other care committees in Lublin District with instructions to ignore the letters and carry on as before. Henceforth, however, she decided that only members of the Underground would perform illegal activities so as not to endanger ordinary committee workers. And so, the escapes continued and the fugitives, supplied with false identity cards, disappeared.

The destination of many of the Volhynian transports was the Krochmalna Street transit camp. The Lublin Polish Care Committee had responsibility for registering the refugees in the camp and provided physicians to ascertain the health status of all the detainees. The director of the care committee's aid to Krochmalna, Józefa Olbrycht, was also Janina's partner in the Volhynian rescue operation. Olbrycht instructed the AK members working under her in the camp to suggest to healthy detainees that they report certain symptoms to the physicians hired by the care committee. Consequently, a surprisingly large proportion of the young adults in the camp were being diagnosed with illnesses that precluded their assignment to forced labor.[14]

Officials of the BuF resented that Janina had circumvented their authority to get the support of Wendler's office for RGO initiatives. Her activities with the Volhynian refugees only deepened their anger and distrust. This was especially true of the director of the BuF office of Lublin city. Irmgard Villnow despised Poles in general and Countess Suchodolska in particular, whom she viewed as meddling in matters that came under Villnow's jurisdiction. One evening in October 1943, Villnow raided the offices of Janina and the Lublin Care Committee on Lubartowska Street. Somehow, she knew to go directly to Olbrycht's desk, where she found a list of Volhynian refugees who had been interviewed in the temporary transit camps. She absconded with the list and the correspondence log of the care committee for Lublin city.

The next morning, the head of the district BuF office ordered Janina, Christians, and Stanisław Kalinowski, counselor to the city care committee, to appear in his office at noon sharp. Seeing Villnow there, Janina knew she was in trouble, for she had learned of Villnow's raid on the care committee offices from the building's porter, fellow AK member Józef Wendrucha.

"Why are you sabotaging the orders of the German authorities and why have you not circularized our letter to all the care committees in the district?" Villnow demanded.

"But I *did* send that letter," Janina protested. "You need only check all the logs for proof that I did!"

Then Villnow, confident that she was about to destroy Janina, triumphantly produced the log of the Lublin city care committee as evidence that Janina had not sent it the letter. Next, Villnow presented the list she had taken from Olbrycht's desk and demonstrated that it contained names of people who had crossed into Lublin District from Volhynia but had not been registered at Krochmalna. She accused Janina of arranging for the unregistered persons to escape and insisted that she must have had the help of the Lublin Polish Care Committee and the Polish Red Cross.

The district BuF chief, Fritsche, began to shout at the three of them that they had committed treason and would be turned over to the Gestapo for prosecution. He continued with a tirade about German casualties and charged that "It is people like you three who are responsible for the bombardment of German cities!"

The two men were even more frightened than Janina. She had told them nothing about the Volhynian rescue operation, even though Christians also worked for the Underground. They both turned on her, demanding to know whether there was in fact an "Operation Volhynia" and insisting that if there were, then only she could be held responsible for it. "My colleagues, collaborating to get a confession from me!" Janina thought in dismay. But she managed to appear outwardly calm while she frantically searched for a plausible explanation.

"Yes," she responded evenly, "I direct the operation to assist Volhynians, but I do so in complete accordance with German regulations. The list that Frau Villnow found in our office is from September, before the Lublin Polish Care Committee was required to register the refugees, and some of those on the list undoubtedly departed before the registration was conducted.

Furthermore, not all the refugees who receive RGO care at the border are sent to Krochmalna. Obviously, the Lublin Care Committee could not register refugees who were no longer at the camp, much less those who never passed through it."

Then, with a touch of indignation and a slightly raised voice, Janina repeated that there was ample proof that she had circulated the German letter to every county care committee in the district.[15]

"Why not to the Lublin city committee?" her colleagues demanded.

"Frau Villnow has insisted that since she is the supervisor of the city care committee, I am not to give it orders. I therefore assumed that she would send the letter and an accompanying directive to the city committee. I followed the order I received exactly by sending the governor's letter to the county committees along with my own directive that the governor's orders be obeyed. If I was supposed to send it to the city committee as well, then the most I can be accused of is negligence, but no more so than Frau Villnow."

Fritsche, who had picked up the telephone receiver to call the Gestapo, put it back in its cradle. He ordered everyone but Janina to leave his office, as he had instructions for her that did not concern them. Once the others left, he continued in a mild tone.

"Well, we all forget things sometimes. Why not send out your recommendations when you get back to your office?"

"I certainly shall," Janina replied, "but Frau Villnow must do so, too, so that mine will follow hers."

Janina then expressed with apparent sincerity her appreciation for all the Germans were doing to save Poles in Volhynia from being murdered by Bolshevik and Ukrainian bandits. She regretted that the Poles sometimes misunderstood their German rescuers' intentions.

Upon leaving Fritsche's office, Janina found her two colleagues waiting for her, looking pale and shaken. Both attorneys, they congratulated her for conducting her defense "like the best lawyer."

"I had to," Janina replied dryly, "when my two would-be counselors, one the president of the Bar Association, were ready to sell me to the enemy!" She thought of the many other occasions she had experienced during the war when a woman had kept her head while the men around her lost theirs.

That evening, Wendrucha called on her at home. He asked her to go into the courtyard behind her building, where she found some young men who had escaped from a transport from Cumań (Tsuman) in Volhynia. There were about 450 persons on the transport, they explained, mostly young, strong single men and women. They had been told that they were being brought to the General Government to be given over to the RGO, but after they arrived at the Lublin station, they learned that they were about to be sent to Germany.

Janina was determined to help them but, considering Wendler's letter and her narrow escape that morning, decided to go through official channels. Realizing her odds of success would be stronger if no one were missing from the transport, she asked the young men to return to it.

"I give you my word as a Polish woman," she assured them, "that you will be freed along with all the others."

They accepted her word and returned.

After a sleepless night of worry that she would not be able to keep her word, Janina went to see the Labor Office official responsible for Krochmalna. Despite the Nazi Party badge he always proudly displayed on his lapel, Herr Geissler had often proved to be accommodating. Upon entering his office, Janina immediately demanded to know why an entire transport of people who had not volunteered for work in Germany was about to depart for the Reich. Forgetting to maintain her usual composed demeanor, she complained in a raised voice, "These people were told they were to be handed over to our committee. I talked to them at the station and have promised to take them under our care. If you won't release them, I'll go to Kraków and intervene with your top authority. After all, the decree against forced labor for Volhynians came from the governor general himself!"

She counted on Geissler's failure to recognize that technically she did not have authority to intervene for the persons in the transport, because they came from outside the General Government. She had ceased to be surprised at how little many German officials knew about the regulations they were supposed to enforce, probably because they had no background in government administration. Geissler, for example, had been a pharmacist in Germany before becoming an important official in Poland.

Angered by Janina's tone, Geissler ordered her to return to her office. An hour later, she received a call from her assistant, Janina Wójcikowa, who was working at Krochmalna. She reported that all the freight cars had been emptied and the whole Cumań transport was there in the camp. Then Geissler called Janina and ordered her to remain in her office to receive a visit from pertinent officials who would explain the situation to her. Uneasy about these "pertinent officials" and their "explanation," Janina decided she should have someone she trusted nearby and so called Wójcikowa back to the office. Hours passed, and when it was time for the office to close, Geissler called again, telling her to stay there. Wendrucha decided to remain at his post so that he could see who came for Janina.

Wójcikowa paced the floor nervously, worried that the longer the delay, the less likely Janina's visitors were coming merely to make explanations. Back and forth to the window she paced; then, while looking out it, she suddenly gasped.

"A car with two Gestapo officers—just at our building—just getting out of the car. My God, did you *have* to interfere?"

"I'm sorry," Janina replied quietly, "I *had* to, after those men went back to the transport because I promised to free them all."

So they waited for the steps in the hall. They seemed to take so long coming. Wendrucha slipped out and down the back stairs, then returned in a flash with the news that the officers had gone into the next building and had merely parked the car outside theirs!

Night fell and still they waited. They turned out all the lights except in Janina's office, and Wójcikowa sat in the dark room next to it, leaving the door open so she could see who came and hear what was said. Finally, two cars stopped outside the building and three men emerged, one of them Geissler. When they reached Janina's office, they found her busily writing a memo and referring to a file.

"Working late?" Geissler asked.

"Didn't you ask me to wait for you?" she replied with a shrug. "No use wasting time, there's plenty of work here." She knew better than to show anxiety to German officials.

"You're coming with us to the camp now," Geissler said.

"Fine," Janina answered. As they left, she directed a furtive glance toward the next room.

Geissler took Janina in his car while the two men traveled in the other. They arrived at Krochmalna, where Commandant Musielski was waiting to receive them. Geissler told him of Janina's claim that the people in the Cumań transport had not volunteered for labor in the Reich, which Musielski denied. Apparently, the people had been frightened into agreeing that they had volunteered. Janina asked that she be allowed to talk with them. Since Musielski knew Polish, Geissler agreed.

So the announcement went over the megaphone that all from Cumań should come to the yard because the RGO was there. Once they had assembled, Janina addressed them.

"I know that you were taken by force, and I promise you, on the honor of the RGO, that nothing will happen to you if you tell the truth. Did you, or did you not apply to work for the Germans?"

Her urgent question was answered by silence. She repeated it, and after another short silence, a few people came forward and anxiously stated, "They said that in the General Government they would hand us over to the RGO. That's why we went to register with them."

Janina turned to Geissler. "So that's the way it was, you see."

Taking Janina to the camp office, Geissler declared he would hand over all the families to RGO care, but only the sick ones among the single youths.

Stubbornly, Janina asserted, "If you don't give them all to me, I'll go to Kraków about it. Every single one."

He yielded, but only if she would take them immediately. She suspected he thought that would be impossible, but she agreed, certain that she could get Społem's transport manager, Piotr Kosiba, to send trucks, as he had when the expellees were released from Majdanek.

As she exited the camp to arrange the transportation, Janina encountered Wójcikowa, who was wiping tears from her eyes. She had followed

Janina in a cab and burst out crying with relief when she saw that the two cars were going to Krochmalna, not to the Gestapo.

Społem promised to send sufficient trucks by 1:00 a.m. Janina returned to the Volhynians and told them to be ready to leave with the committee that night. "I told you, we keep our promises!" They wept with relief, and she trembled at the thought of how close she had come to breaking her promise. The RGO later settled the group in a village fourteen miles from Lublin.

Despite her success in freeing the transport, Janina was thoroughly upset with herself. She realized that, in her worry and exhaustion, her intuition had failed her, causing her to misread Geissler. Her tone and behavior with him had escalated the situation into a confrontation that might easily have led to her arrest. It was good that she had learned how to prevent fear from paralyzing her, but she had also been trained that intelligence agents must sharply observe the enemy's moves, discern their promise and their threat, and tailor their own actions in response. She must never make assumptions about the future based on past success, for no two situations were alike and every action involved a unique set of risks. She must calculate those risks as precisely as possible to determine the probability of success and then weigh whether what was to be gained was worth the price of failure. Especially now, when she was on the verge of achieving her mission to feed all of Majdanek's prisoners.

THIRTEEN

SOUP WITH A SIDE OF HOPE

In mid-September 1943, Hermann Florstedt thought he had actually pulled it off. In the ten months since he became Majdanek's commandant, he had overseen the completion of most of the planned construction projects. The camp had new workshops and warehouses that employed prisoners in a variety of jobs, including producing furniture and uniforms for the SS and repairing hundreds of thousands of shoes reaped from *Aktion* Reinhard. A new crematorium with five coke-burning ovens was rising behind the protective custody camp. At last, the prisoner compounds had been connected to the municipal sewer system, and the prisoner barracks were gradually acquiring lavatories with running water. Globocnik had given him a glowing recommendation, asserting that Florstedt had been "extraordinarily valuable" to him and praising his success in remedying the "intolerable conditions" at Majdanek.[1]

Florstedt's crowning moment had come on September 7, when he attended a conference with top SS officials in Berlin. There he learned that all of Globocnik's forced labor camps for Jews were about to become subcamps of Majdanek. Florstedt was to command at least eleven camps in the General Government with well over 50,000 prisoners, the vast majority of them Jews. Along with this change would come his promotion to SS-*Standartenführer* (Colonel).[2]

But it was not to be. One of the "intolerable conditions" Florstedt had failed to remedy was the high mortality rate among Majdanek's registered prisoners, who did not include Jews sent there to be killed on arrival. An SS study presented to Himmler in September revealed that Majdanek was the only concentration camp where the mortality rate rose in August, to 7.67 percent for men and 4.41 percent for women. A male prisoner was ten times more likely to die at Majdanek than at Dachau. Auschwitz had the second highest mortality rate: 3.61 percent for its registered women prisoners.[3]

Even more worrisome to Florstedt was the revived SS investigation of Koch, his mentor at Buchenwald and Majdanek's first commandant. The SS investigators were now looking into corruption at both camps. Before they visited Majdanek in mid-1943, Florstedt had the prisoners murdered who worked in the *Effektenkammer*, the warehouses where all the belongings of incoming Jews and prisoners were sorted and searched for valuables. Florstedt's minions overlooked one of the prisoners, however, who was in the infirmary and survived to testify. The investigators learned that Koch and members of his staff routinely filched jewelry, money, and luxury items from the *Effektenkammer* and that the practice had continued under Florstedt. During the transports to Majdanek of thousands of Jews in spring 1943, the investigators heard, Florstedt held regular scavenger hunts in the "rose garden" following selections. Turning over the dirt with spades, he and his top henchmen found jewelry, gems, and gold currency buried there by the waiting Jews to hide them from the SS. Stealing the loot from the victims was not a crime, but pocketing it was.[4]

Koch and his wife, Ilse, were arrested on August 24, 1943. One month later, Florstedt was recalled to Germany for questioning, then officially arrested on October 20. Koch was tried, sentenced to death, and executed on April 15, 1945. Florstedt was still in prison in March 1945, but his fate after that remains a mystery.[5]

In Florstedt's absence, the routine for delivering packages and food products for Majdanek prisoners changed. The camp SS finally agreed that it would be more efficient if, instead of leaving everything at the camp headquarters, Jurek, the Red Cross driver, took the packages directly to the post office, which was next to the protective custody camp, and delivered the bread and the products for soup to the food warehouses, which were across from the entry to Field I. Unbeknownst to Christians, Jurek was now picking up the packages being prepared by OPUS, the AK prisoner aid organization, and delivering them with the packages from the Red Cross and the Lublin Polish Care Committee. The increasing number of packages from all three sources required a change to twice-weekly deliveries, on Tuesdays and Fridays, in addition to the delivery of RGO bread and soup products on Saturdays. During his deliveries, Jurek communicated covertly with the prisoners working in the post office and at the warehouses. He also smuggled messages with such regularity that the prisoners nicknamed him "the postman."[6]

When Janina accompanied Jurek on the Saturday deliveries, she could only get as far as the gate to the protective custody camp, where she turned in the record of the delivery and received the receipt. While she waited for Jurek to return, she would try to converse with the SS men who pulled duty there and so get to know which ones were friendly or at least willing to accept "gifts." Some would have nothing to do with her, but two of the regulars, the Polish ethnic Germans Alfred Bajerke and Alfred Hoffmann, proved quite approachable. She had also developed a good rapport with another Polish ethnic German who worked in the camp headquarters, SS Sergeant Wilhelm Karl Petrak.[7]

Janina was now able to witness some of the cruelty and suffering at Majdanek that she had heard about from released prisoners. From her post at the camp gate, she observed prisoner work squads going to and from labor outside Majdanek. They marched in rows under the guard of armed SS men and dog handlers and to the shouts and blows of kapos. The Jewish prisoners mostly wore the striped concentration camp uniform, but many of the non-Jews wore ill-fitting civilian clothes painted with the letters "KL" (for *Konzentrationslager*) in red. Seeing their gaunt and wounded frames, Janina wondered how they could possibly perform hard manual labor for eleven hours a day or more, six days a week.

One day, she watched a returning labor squad as it filed through the gate. They were required to stand at military attention as they waited to pass through, but one elderly prisoner was visibly drooping. Suddenly, an SS guard emerged from the sentry box and, in full view of Janina, kicked the prisoner and hit him so hard in the face with a truncheon that blood went flying. Taking evident pleasure in Janina's horrified expression, the guard sneered at her, "They don't know what discipline is. That's why we finish them off in less than twenty days!" Then he returned to the sentry box and took a swig from a bottle.

The guard may have hoped to frighten Janina, but, four years into the war, she had seen too much violence to be so easily shaken. It only strengthened her resolve to fight back by saving as many lives as she could.

When she learned of Florstedt's absence, Janina saw a potential opening for overcoming his officials' obstruction of the RGO's assistance to Majdanek prisoners. She persuaded Petrak to help her bring the matter of prisoner correspondence to the attention of the acting commandant, Martin Melzer, who was the commander of Majdanek's SS Death's Head Guard Battalion. Her approach succeeded: Melzer authorized her to make regular deliveries of postcards for distribution to the prisoners.

Janina personally brought 6,000 postcards to Majdanek, rejoicing that the Polish prisoners would finally be in contact with their families. Then she had her first run-in with the commander of the protective custody camp, SS Lieutenant Anton Thumann. His very name struck fear in the hearts of the SS guards as well as the prisoners, for he was a foul-tempered drunk who took sadistic pleasure in torturing prisoners with his whip, truncheon, and vicious dog, Boris. Thumann's motto was that prisoners who survived longer than three months at Majdanek were thieves and vermin that deserved to be exterminated. Florstedt had given him free rein in running the protective custody camp, and he did not see why that should cease under an interim commandant who had never run a concentration camp. When Janina tried to deliver the postcards, Thumann refused to accept them.[8]

Thumann probably assumed that the matter was closed, but he was about to learn that no issue with Countess Suchodolska was finally resolved until it was resolved to her satisfaction. She appealed to Melzer, and in the end, Thumann was obliged to take the cards from her. Accepting them was not the same as agreeing to distribute them, however. OPUS soon received a smuggled message reporting that the prisoners were still not allowed to write to their families.

Another smuggled message at the end of September 1943 reported that typhus was on the rise again in the camp, and tuberculosis was spreading as well. Although many more packages were reaching the prisoners, much of their contents continued to be plundered by the SS and kapos. Starvation was amplifying the toll of the epidemics, and mortality in the infirmaries had risen 50 percent.[9]

This was crushing news. It seemed to Janina that she had accomplished almost nothing in the seven months that she had been overseeing the aid program at Majdanek. It was time to escalate matters, she resolved. She would appeal to Lublin District authorities about Majdanek officials' failure to uphold the agreements regarding prisoners' correspondence and the delivery of packages, food, and medicines to the camp. This time, she planned to press for even more than what had previously been agreed. She had not given up on her plan for providing prepared soup to Majdanek prisoners. The epidemics at Majdanek, she realized, provided her a basis to argue that providing nourishing soup for at least the sick prisoners was in the Germans' interest. She consulted Łopatyńska, head of the Lublin Polish Care Committee's Nutrition and Care Department, who conceived a plan for how the care committee could prepare the soup in its kitchens in addition to all the other food it was serving to the needy. Figuring out how to deliver it would be up to Janina.[10]

So Janina paid another visit to the district medical superintendent. He did not question her report of epidemics at Majdanek and saw the sense in her proposal to provide not only typhus serum to the camp but also a special diet for sick prisoners. At his direction, she went to see Blancke.

Janina's meeting with Majdanek's chief physician followed the usual pattern. Blancke called Janina a nuisance, reminded her that Majdanek was a concentration camp, not a sanatorium, and then accepted her offer of typhus serum. When she proposed providing soup for the sick prisoners, though, he scoffed. For that she would need the commandant's permission, which Blancke clearly doubted she would get. To her surprise, however, Blancke authorized her to speak with a prisoner physician, Dr. Nowak, regarding the camp infirmaries' needs for medicines and supplies.

The news that Janina was going to speak with a prisoner named Dr. Nowak caused some excitement among her OPUS colleagues, because Malm had been corresponding for more than a year with a Dr. Jan Nowak, a member of the Underground imprisoned at Majdanek. Jan Nowak is a common Polish name, however, and there was at least one other Dr. Nowak at Majdanek. In the hope of determining whether the doctor she spoke with was Malm's correspondent, Janina tore a two-złoty note in half and had one of the pieces smuggled to him.

On the day of her appointment to speak with Dr. Nowak, Janina received strict instructions at camp headquarters: no physical contact with prisoners was permitted, and she must confine the conversation strictly to the purpose of her visit. Then she was driven to the guard booth just outside Field V, where the men's infirmary had recently moved. She immediately noticed a pathetically thin but bright-eyed Jewish boy about ten or twelve years old standing by the compound gate. His green armband identified him as one of the "runners," usually Jewish boys put to work as couriers in the men's fields. Between their courier runs they had to stand all day in every kind of weather in a small area between the barbed wire fences next to the gate. After Janina showed her pass to the SS guard, he ordered the boy to fetch Dr. Nowak.

Janina chatted pleasantly with the guard while she waited. In time, the boy reappeared with a prisoner who gave his name, Nowak, and his prisoner number. Janina nodded to him, smiling warmly, then looked at the boy with a raised eyebrow. "Izio," he whispered, which in Polish may be a diminutive for Izaak, Izrael, or Izydor. As Janina turned back to Nowak, she felt something brush her coat and then saw Izio scamper back to his post. As she and the doctor spoke, she casually reached inside her coat pocket and felt a torn bill, the other half of the two-złoty note.

In addition to enlisting the aid of the district medical superintendent, Janina sent an appeal to the new Security Police chief, Karl Pütz. She informed him that Majdanek officials were failing to comply with the directives of his predecessor, Müller, authorizing the RGO to feed Majdanek's Polish prisoners and permitting the prisoners to write to their families.[11] Not long after she submitted her appeal, Janina received a summons from Majdanek's interim commandant to meet with him at the camp on October 15.

Janina assumed that Melzer had heard from Pütz, but she did not know what instructions the latter had given. Her repeated interventions about conditions at Majdanek had made it clear that she was somehow receiving information that the Germans considered to be top secret. Every time she went to Majdanek, Janina was keenly aware that the SS might not allow her to leave because of suspicion that she was connected to the Underground or, even worse, that she was not who she claimed to be. So before setting out for Majdanek on October 15, she gave her keys as usual to Wójcikowa along with instructions on what to do should she not return. She also generally took an RGO employee with her to Majdanek who could report back if she were arrested. On this day, she took the office interpreter, who in fact was a priest from Poznań who had taken refuge in Lublin after being released from Dachau. Sensitive to what Father Juliusz Winiewski had suffered there, Janina had him wait for her in a cab outside the Majdanek headquarters gate.

Relatively speaking, the meeting began almost cordially. Melzer directed Janina to sit and present her business. Starting with the issue she thought most likely to meet with success, she informed Melzer that his order authorizing the prisoners to send postcards to their families was being ignored. Melzer called Thumann and the SS official in charge of the post office into the meeting. In no uncertain terms, the commandant ordered that the postcards Janina had brought be distributed immediately to the Polish prisoners along with an announcement that they were permitted to write to their families twice a month. He instructed Janina to bring a new set of cards to the camp in three weeks.

Janina moved on to her next issue: the packages being delivered by the Red Cross were not arriving to the addressees intact. The postal director protested that this was not his fault. His office was fulfilling its duty by forwarding all parcels to the compounds in which the addressees were held. This answer did not satisfy Melzer, who ordered the postal director to ensure that packages reached their addressees. Finally, Janina presented her offer to provide prepared soup for the patients in the prisoner infirmaries, framing it not as a new request but as conforming to the spirit of what had already been granted. Melzer's manner immediately turned brusque.

"This is a concentration camp," he lectured her, "and the only camp that permits outsiders to feed the prisoners. To grant further privileges here would be an injustice to the prisoners in the other camps, and justice, order, and discipline are the principles that guide *all* actions by the SS. The inmates here constitute an element hostile to German authority, rebels and bandits who would be sentenced to death by any court! Yet here, they are being held in protective custody, which you must surely recognize is better than prison. And whenever prisoners are found to be innocent, they are immediately released. You do know this, do you not?"

"No," Janina replied, "I am unfamiliar with the details of concentration camp administration. I only know that the inmates here are not free and that, since this concentration camp is in the General Government, my institution is obligated to provide for the Polish prisoners, just as it does for the inmates of prisons. I am simply proposing to feed the sick with an additional item, which hardly seems like an excessive privilege, and surely it is in the interests of SS authorities. After all, the district medical superintendent has endorsed the proposal."

Melzer ordered her to go wait in the reception area. After a long while, she saw Blancke enter the commandant's office. Then there was another long wait, during which she became increasingly gloomier about her prospects for success. The guard on duty even remarked that the commandant might have forgotten about her. Finally, she was called back in.

Melzer's first question revived Janina's hope: "How do you propose to deliver the soup?"

"The Lublin Polish Care Committee can make the soup in its twenty-four kitchens and transport it here on trucks," she replied. "If the trucks take the soup directly to the compounds with infirmaries, then the camp routine will not be disturbed."

Melzer handed Janina a document that he instructed her to read and sign. It was a formal agreement setting out the conditions for the RGO to deliver soup twice a week for 830 sick Polish prisoners, as well as other food products recommended by the Lublin Care Committee's physician. The agreement specified that Janina bore sole responsibility for the deliveries, which were to be made by her in person or by one other whom she could designate. She was to provide a list of the contents of each delivery to the guard at the camp gate, the commandant's office, and to Blancke or his staff.

Janina signed, trying not to look triumphant. "When shall the soup deliveries occur?"

Blancke answered, "On Tuesdays and Thursdays, starting next week."

"May I consult an infirmary physician about the kinds of soup to bring and other products and medicines that the patients need?"

Blancke nodded.

After Janina signed the agreement, Melzer interrogated her about her background, residence, activities, her husband and his job at Społem, and her affiliations. Then he released her with a warning: "One can always gain entrance here, but the exits may not be quite so obvious."

Elated, Janina returned to the cab and found the driver and Father Winiewski in astonished relief. After so many hours, they assumed that Janina had been arrested. Yet they had waited, the priest praying the Rosary. The cab driver knew Janina well and always picked her up when he saw her if he didn't have a fare. He would not take her money, saying, "An oldster like me, I don't need it anymore. But when I stand before St. Peter, I can tell him I always helped you on your errands of mercy, and he will like that." Now he swore that he would go to confession that evening and say thanks that the Countess had been spared.

Janina's colleagues could scarcely believe the news. She notified Woroniecki, who promised to wire her money from Kraków. Then she and Łopatyńska set to work on their plan. They would be delivering 1,250 liters of soup a week, plus special bread and other products approved by Blancke. Łopatyńska found sufficient volunteers among her kitchen staff to prepare the soup at night, but they needed extra kettles or vats to transport it. Janina thought of milk cans, which could hold 25 liters, and she called around to estates near the city hoping she could collect a total of fifty. They all arrived the next day. Since Jurek delivered packages to Majdanek on Tuesdays, Janina had to find other transport for the soup. As usual, Kosiba of Społem readily offered to provide the necessary trucks and drivers.

The next day, Saturday, Janina rode with Jurek to Majdanek to make the weekly delivery of bread and food products from the Lublin Polish Care Committee. In the headquarters office, Petrak issued her a pass to speak with Dr. Nowak after checking with Blancke. There was a heavy frost, and a bitingly cold wind raked Majdanek's plain. As an RGO official, Janina was permitted to have a fur coat, but she preferred to shiver rather than wear it around Majdanek's freezing prisoners. She rode with Jurek and an SS guard to Field V, where she found Izio on the porch of the guard booth. Before he ran to fetch Dr. Nowak, he whispered to her, "Today's guard isn't a beast. He even let me into his booth to warm up a while and gave me some tea, but he always looks around first to make sure no one sees."

That day's guard, a Tyrolean, welcomed Janina into the booth and proved especially talkative. Then Dr. Nowak arrived at the gate, and she exchanged a wordless greeting with him as he flatly stated his name and prisoner number. Janina was writing in her notebook the food and medicines needed in the infirmary when, suddenly, they heard the Tyrolean hiss, "Thumann's coming!"

Before they could turn, Thumann was upon them in a rage. "I will lock you in!" he bellowed to the guard and set to beating Dr. Nowak on the head with his truncheon.

"And you!" he screamed in Janina's face. "Do you think that this is a sanatorium? You will bring nothing here, and I'll see to it at headquarters!"

He turned on his heel and stomped off. Dr. Nowak, bloodied, disappeared. Izio looked ashen, and the guard muttered, "What a beast." When Janina returned to Jurek, who had observed the confrontation, he crossed himself and thanked the Holy Virgin for protecting the Countess this time.

On October 19 at 11:00 a.m., Janina set out from Lubartowska Street atop one of the Społem trucks laden with cans of soup and baskets of bread, while colleagues smiled and waved from the windows.[12] They arrived at Majdanek precisely at the appointed time. The guard at the gate to the protective custody camp had received no notice about the delivery, so they had to wait as he sent word to camp headquarters. After nearly an hour, a medical orderly entered the guardhouse with a woman in a striped prisoner uniform. The woman announced her name: "Perzanowska."

Janina started and felt tears come to her eyes. This was Dr. Stefania Perzanowska! Janina had heard so much from released women prisoners about Perzanowska's inspiring leadership and how she had single-handedly created an infirmary in the women's camp where prisoners received expert and tender care. And now Janina was meeting her, a true heroine. Perzanowska's appearance alarmed Janina, however. It was not just that the doctor was painfully thin but that she seemed drained of any color, listless and apathetic. But when Janina smiled warmly at her and gave her own name, a light seemed to kindle in the doctor's eyes.

Blancke had informed Perzanowska the day before that she was to take receipt of a special delivery for the women's infirmary the next day. He warned her not to engage in any conversation beyond the minimum necessary to conduct the transaction. That morning, wanting to make a good impression when she received whatever was in the delivery, Perzanowska had put on the least filthy of her uniforms and kerchiefs and resolved to try to smile, if she could only remember how. It was almost a year since she had been arrested in Radom for Underground activities. After fifteen brutal interrogation sessions, the Gestapo gave up trying to extract information from her and dumped her in Majdanek in January 1943. Since then, the camp's daily routine of unbearable suffering and unrelenting violence had steadily ground her down and drained her spirit. She tried to appear confident and caring to the desperately ill and dying women she could do so little to help, but in fact she felt almost devoid of human feeling, enclosed in a hard, cold shell of indifference.

As she approached the guardhouse, Perzanowska saw the trucks laden with cans and baskets and realized with a shock that this was the delivery she was to receive. Then she entered and saw a slender, handsome brunette with thick dark braids piled on her head like a crown. "Suchodolska of the RGO" Perzanowska heard the woman say. Somehow, her voice, her smile, her look of deep concern, and the warmth of her empathy penetrated Perzanowska's shell and made her feel human again.

The doctor stared in wonder at the woman as she read out the list of the food in the delivery and explained that the same delivery would be made twice a week and could include additional food and medicines as approved by the camp doctor. Here was someone, Perzanowska marveled, from that other world—"outside the wire"—that had come to seem a universe away. What efforts had been made, what risks taken to bring this largesse to the doomed? Perzanowska turned to the medical orderly and asked, "May I express the thanks of the prisoners to Madame?"

The SS duty officer, having become bored as Janina read the list, was attending to other things. The medical orderly indicated to the women that they should step outside. They did so, then Perzanowska, fighting back tears, struggled to find the words to thank Janina. "You don't know what it means to me to speak with you, a free woman. Everyone in Field I will be so grateful when I tell them what you have done, and so envious when they hear that I met with you!"

Janina looked at the orderly. "Will you allow me to shake hands with the prisoner?" She showed him her palms. "You see I have nothing in my hands, I will not give her anything, just shake her hand." The orderly looked around, saw no guard was watching, and said gruffly, "Shake hands, if you must, but make it fast!" Janina, tears on her cheeks and trembling, took Perzanowska's hand, squeezed it, and said, "Tell the others in the compound that this handshake is for all of them, from all of us who are still free!"

Suddenly, SS guards spilled out of the guardhouse and sentry box screaming at Janina to finish and leave. Perzanowska watched in awe as Janina did not even flinch but calmly informed them in proper German that she was authorized to speak with the doctor about the needs of the infirmary, to learn the number of patients needing special diets, and to write down what was needed. Furthermore, as there were different kinds of soups and breads in the delivery, she needed to show the doctor where they were placed in the truck. So Janina and Perzanowska climbed onto one of the trucks, and as Janina announced which can had what kind of soup and explained what was in the baskets, she asked Perzanowska under her breath in Polish whether she wished to send a message to anyone. Perzanowska, feeling the guards' eyes on her, gave a slight nod. Then Janina, notebook in hand, told the orderly that she had to take down the information of the persons who received the delivery. The oblivious orderly stated his name, while Perzanowska muttered an address in Lublin and a brief message to be sent there.

Finally, some SS men got in the trucks and drove them off to the protective custody camp. The officer of the day informed Janina that she was to pick up the cans outside the gate at 1:00 p.m. the next day. Then Janina watched as Perzanowska walked slowly back down the road to hell. It was a vision that would haunt her for days.

But Perzanowska was actually smiling. "There were brave people on the outside who were taking risks to help the helpless victims of Majdanek!" she thought with amazement. And she diagnosed the cause of the sensation that had just come upon her: hope.

When Janina returned with the next delivery, she met Perzanowska and a prisoner named Bargielski from Field V, whose prisoner number, 15, marked him as one of the "old-timers" in the camp. They were accompanied by an SS officer and a woman in the uniform of an SS *Aufseherin*, the term for a woman guard in the concentration camp system. She smiled graciously at Janina and held out her hand, apologizing that her gloves—which were immaculate—were too tight to remove. After Janina reported the contents of the delivery, the woman exclaimed:

"The soup is sure to be delicious, Polish women being such good cooks. I'm glad the patients will be so well nourished. Why, even the staff don't get such nutritious soup!"

Before she replied to this outlandish statement from the obviously well-fed *Aufseherin,* Janina saw Perzanowska brush her fingers to her lips. Janina said nothing.

The woman was Else Ehrich, commander of the women's concentration camp at Majdanek, known for her military bearing and the methodical way she daily beat prisoners bloody with a riding crop she tucked in her boot. During the roll calls in the women's camp, she sought out prisoners who appeared unable to work and sent them to be murdered in the gas chambers or crematorium. She also participated in the selections of newly arrived Jewish families, seizing children from their mothers and slinging them by their feet into the trucks that took them to be gassed. Once, when Perzanowska asked for milk for the Belarusian infants in the camp, Ehrich slapped her hard across the face and screamed, "This is not a sanatorium, this is an extermination camp!"[13]

Once that day's delivery was complete, Janina went to the headquarters office to turn in the list of contents. When she took off her coat, a note fell out of the pocket. Quickly snatching and concealing it, she felt her heart lurch. Had the *Aufseherin* slipped it in to compromise her? When she returned to her office, she found it was a note from Bargielski. "Ovomaltine and calcium preparations badly needed for the TB cases. Can't ask camp doctors because very sick are immediately sent to the crematorium. Please bring in next delivery—very urgent!" She had no idea how Bargielski had managed to get the note in her pocket under the eyes of the SS.

Janina consulted her OPUS colleagues about getting the products to Bargielski. They decided to fix false bottoms to some of the milk cans. The next day, a tinsmith sent by the AK completed the job. Then Janina had to figure out how to let Bargielski know where to find the goods. Even if Bargielski were the one sent to receive the delivery, she dared not try to tell him, because the duty officer on Tuesdays was often Hoffmann, who knew Polish.

On Tuesday, Janina made her first smuggling foray to Majdanek. Hoffmann was on duty and invited her into the guardhouse. "That committee of yours must care a lot about these prisoners," he said. "The Polish Red Cross sends some kid here, but your committee sends you in person." Janina was impressed that he knew the difference between the RGO and the Polish Red Cross, because most people attributed the RGO's activities to the latter.

Looking a little embarrassed, Hoffmann continued. "There's a poor devil of a woman working in the laundry, very sick, needs a bit of milk. I could pay for it, but I can't leave to get it. Would you be able to get some for her?"

Hoffmann's request could be a trap, Janina recognized, but her intuition told her otherwise. Weighing the probabilities, she decided that the chance to win his goodwill was worth the risk, particularly considering the contraband she was attempting to deliver that day. She gave the SS man a sympathetic look and replied, "If it means so much to you, of course I'll bring some milk for her. One of my colleagues used to own an estate and is still able to get milk there without a ration coupon."

Then Perzanowska and Bargielski arrived. As Hoffmann looked on, Janina pointed to one of the trucks and addressed Perzanowska: "There are the cans for your field, and I must say you women are much better dishwashers than the men—you scour the bottoms of the cans properly." "As to you," turning to Bargielski, "please be careful not to leave soup in the can, and pay better attention to cleaning the bottoms!" The prisoner, looking repentant, responded, "Considering what the committee is doing for us, we promise to see that everything is thoroughly cleaned."

Janina's relief that Bargielski evidently understood her message was countered by fear that Hoffmann had grasped it as well. Would the promise of milk buy his silence? She spent all night imagining she heard footsteps approaching that would soon be followed by a knock on the door and a journey to the Zamek prison. But she survived the night and the next day rushed to check the cans after they were retrieved. The smuggled products were missing, and in the bottom of one can she found a note: "All is in order. God bless your committee. Please continue. We know that the Countess can do everything. We can, too."

The SS had become accustomed to her deliveries, Hoffmann would soon be in her debt, and she had a way to smuggle messages and contraband into the camp. Time for her next step, Janina decided: to get past the camp gate and obtain access to the prisoner compounds. She called on Petrak in the headquarters office and requested a pass.

"You have permission to bring in the food," he said, "you don't need anything *more*. It depends on the man on guard, but if you have trouble with him, we'll do something. I hear that the prisoners are better off and your committee is working very well."

She left puzzled. Did Petrak mean that her permission to deliver the food did not specify where she was to leave it? She decided to test that.

On the next delivery day, with Ovomaltine, calcium, and tiny packages of butter tucked in the bottoms of the cans, Janina found Hoffmann on guard. "Wouldn't it be less complicated," she asked him innocently, "if we just drove up to the gates of the fields and deposited the cans there? After you check everything, of course." Then she handed him the milk for his girlfriend in the laundry.

Hoffmann thanked her but said she would have to get a pass from headquarters to go to the compounds. "Would you put in a call to Sergeant Petrak for me, then?" she asked. Her mention of Petrak seemed to make an impression on Hoffmann, and he called the headquarters office to arrange for Janina to see the sergeant. Petrak, evidently satisfied that Hoffmann would raise no objections, issued Janina a pass to the protective custody camp.

Janina returned to Hoffmann, who made a cursory inspection of the trucks, assigned an SS man to ride with her, and waved her on. And so, Janina passed through the gate with the trucks and their contraband. The risk she was taking was enormous, she knew, but it was outweighed by the greater opportunities she now had to help Majdanek's prisoners.

At Field I, neither the guard at the gate nor the *Aufseherin* on duty questioned the change in procedure for the delivery. Perzanowska looked at Janina with surprise and awe. The doctor had grown bolder in her interactions with Janina, and the two were developing their own language, based on gestures, facial expressions, quickly whispered Polish words, and the inflection of their official exchanges in German. After the contents of the truck had been unloaded, Janina instructed Perzanowska and the *Aufseherin* that the empty cans be placed outside the compound gate for retrieval the next day. "And," Janina said, turning to Perzanowska, "don't forget to scrub the bottoms." Looking steadily at Janina, Perzanowska nodded with a hint of a smile. Janina was certain the doctor understood her meaning.

The next stop was at Field III, which had a typhus infirmary. Since the compound was under quarantine, Janina could not interact with any of its prisoners. Then she proceeded to Field V, where the delivery went smoothly. Bright-eyed Izio beamed at Janina from his space between the wires. She smiled back, thinking of the plans she was already making for him. The Tyrolean had guard duty again in the booth and seemed pleased to have a chance for another chat with the Countess. He even told her how and where she should stand so that the guard in the tower could not observe her interactions with the prisoners.

On her next delivery, Janina brought along her assistant, young, vivacious, and astute Hanka Huskowska. As Janina anticipated, the SS men and male kapos were so eager to get Hanka's attention that they failed to keep theirs trained on Janina's activities.[14] She even managed to say a few encouraging words to Izio. That night, she knew, Izio was going to receive a precious gift. Janina had learned that his mother was working in the women's infirmary and had succeeded in getting a message from her to Izio, which was hidden in one of the soup cans in that day's delivery.

Riding back to the office, Janina felt almost happy. So much had changed in just a few weeks. Prisoners were now writing to their families, and consequently the number of packages continued to increase. They were arriving to the addressees intact as well, because a prisoner committee had been assigned to distribute the packages in each of the compounds that housed Poles. The typhus serum had been delivered and administered. Already, messages smuggled out of the camp were reporting that conditions had improved.[15]

It was not nearly enough, of course, but now she was confident that she could do much more. Since the SS weren't checking the actual quantities of the deliveries, she would steadily increase them. She would deliver other items to sustain and support the prisoners as well. Among the messages she was inserting in the soup cans were reports about the Germans' accelerating retreat in the East and the steady advance of British and American forces up the boot of Italy. Together with the increased food and medicines they were receiving, the knowledge that the Germans were losing the war and that the people of Lublin were going to such lengths to help them would provide the prisoners the strength and the hope that they needed to survive. And not just the Polish prisoners. Somehow, she would get enough food into the camp to feed all the prisoners at Majdanek, including Izio, his mother, and the thousands of other Jews in the camp. Her determination to achieve this goal had never lagged, but now she had logical reasons to hope for success.

It was Tuesday, November 2, 1943.

FOURTEEN

HARVEST OF DEATH

When Janina returned to her office, she found Father Santi waiting to report some troubling news. The SS at the Lipowa Street forced labor camp for Polish Jewish POWs had ordered the noncommissioned officers to change from their uniforms to civilian clothes, which some were refusing to do. Since the Germans' demand seemed to Janina to violate international law, she reported the news to her AK commander, a Polish Army colonel with the code name Łodzia.

During the night, Janina heard sporadic gunfire but did not consider it to be out of the ordinary. The next morning, however, she received an alarming report: all of the more than 2,000 prisoners of the Lipowa Street camp had been marched out under heavy SS escort in the direction of the train station and Majdanek, and some had been shot along the way. Janina checked with her contacts at the station: no prisoners had arrived there, and no transport trains were scheduled. It seemed most likely, then, that the prisoners had been marched to the Old Airfield Jewish forced labor camp just outside the city or a little farther on to Majdanek. Colonel Łodzia ordered Janina to investigate.

At the office, Janina found her assistant Hanka waiting for her in distress. Her family lived on an estate close to Majdanek, and since dawn that morning they had been hearing regular salvos of gunfire reverberating from the camp.[1]

Janina decided to go with the truck driver who was picking up the soup cans at Majdanek that day. As they passed the Old Airfield camp, she looked for activity there. She would normally see Jewish prisoners about the grounds, but today the camp appeared to be deserted. When they drew nearer to Majdanek, they found the road was closed, and armed sentries ordered them to turn back.

Janina had the driver pull over before they passed the Old Airfield camp. In the cold rain, she made her way to a house near the road and asked the woman who answered her knock whether she had observed anything unusual at the camp. The woman told Janina of being wakened before dawn that morning by a commotion on the road. Peering out her window, she had watched as thousands of figures passed by in the twilight while Germans shouted orders and dogs barked. They were heading in the direction of Majdanek.

Clearly, Janina thought, the prisoners from both the Lipowa Street and the Old Airfield forced labor camps had been taken to Majdanek. She knew the camp to be already near capacity and wondered how it could take in thousands more prisoners. Hanka's report of gunfire that morning suggested a horrifying answer: the SS were shooting some prisoners to make room for the rest.

Back at her office, Janina called Melzer's adjutant at Majdanek. He informed her curtly that Majdanek had a new commandant and he was far too busy to pay attention to her business. Janina explained that, since the Lublin Polish Care Committee had not been able to retrieve its soup cans that day, she wanted to confirm that the next day's delivery could occur as scheduled. No, it would not be possible to enter the camp on Thursday, either, the adjutant replied. Then he added with a chuckle, "There'll be too much food for the prisoners tomorrow, anyway."

Janina called back to Majdanek and asked to be put through to the office that granted entry passes. As she anticipated, Petrak answered the phone, but he did not identify himself. When would the RGO be able to make its next delivery? she asked. Call back tomorrow about making the delivery on Friday, he advised her.

Janina had orders from her commanding officer to find out what was happening, and she was determined to obey them. On Thursday, she visited Hanka and they borrowed her family's horse and buggy, saying they had business in Zamość. Finding the road blocked on either side of Majdanek, they took back roads through the fields and got to the border of the Majdanek farm. As they observed the camp, they saw black smoke begin to rise in the vicinity of the new crematorium. It was not coming out of the crematorium's tall chimney, however.

Back in Lublin, panicked rumors were circulating. The sound of gunfire coming from Majdanek had lasted all day on Wednesday. Some people who lived on a rise above the camp reported that from their rooftops they could see hundreds of armed SS and clouds of gun smoke behind the protective custody camp and catch glimpses of groups of naked people exiting the rear of Field V in the direction of the gunfire. And for two days, civilian workers had been barred from the camp. Thinking of the black smoke she had just witnessed rising behind the protective custody camp and remembering the adjutant's comment about "too much food," Janina shared the general fear that the SS had murdered all the prisoners at Majdanek. When she called about making the soup delivery on Friday, however, Petrak told her that the trucks would be allowed to enter.

Janina reported this news to Colonel Łodzia. It might be a trap, he pointed out, but they agreed it was worth the risk in order to confirm that Majdanek's prisoners still lived. There would be no contraband in the delivery, however.

On Friday, Hanka insisted on accompanying Janina to Majdanek. Before the camp came into view, they saw plumes of thick, black smoke rising from it. At the guardhouse, the friendly Tyrolean SS guard was assigned to be their escort. He climbed up on their truck looking glum and uncharacteristically said nothing as they drove to the protective custody camp.

They found Dr. Perzanowska waiting at Field I. Her face was ghastly pale and terror stared from her red-rimmed eyes.

"I'm surprised they let you in," the doctor whispered. "We are going through torture. Yesterday, and the day before. If they'd just finish us up, like the Jews, if they would only make it quick!"

Janina tried to suppress the nauseating horror that was rising in her.

Perzanowska was clearly in shock, she concluded, and so maybe the doctor's words did not really mean what Janina feared they did. She tried to show Perzanowska what was in the truck, hoping to rouse her, but the doctor paid no interest. "It's the end, anyway, for all of us," she said, as if in a trance.

"Do you need any medicines for your patients?" Janina urged.

"We need nothing anymore. We won't need anything." After a pause, the doctor looked at Janina. "I am glad that you could come today, that we could still see each other." Then she turned and walked back into the compound.

At Field III, Janina usually saw Jewish as well as Polish prisoners waiting behind the gate to take in the cans and baskets, but today she noticed that there were only Poles. The same was true at Field V, and the prisoners who unloaded the truck all looked despondent. Even the SS and kapos in the compound seemed sullen, despite Hanka's presence. Izio was not at his usual post.

"Where are the others?" she asked Bargielski.

"Gone," he answered.

"And Izio?"

"They are all gone." Then he added, "The days and the nights are horrible."

After the truck had been unloaded, Bargielski addressed her in a formal tone. "I would like to take leave of you, and may God protect all of us." Then he walked away.

Hanka pulled Janina toward her and whispered, "I can't stand it any longer! They all seem to know something terrible that's going to happen to them."

As they rode back to the guardhouse, the Tyrolean suddenly spoke quietly, "All the Jews are dead." He paused, then added, "What are they doing? Don't they know what human beings are?" Before dismounting the truck at the guardhouse, he looked at Janina and said, "May God protect you, lady."

Despondent, Janina and Hanka rode back to Lubartowska Street in silence. The truck was laden with the empty soup cans from Tuesday's delivery, and Janina had them checked. In the bottom of one, they found a long letter. It reported that over thirty-six hours, Majdanek's Jewish prisoners as well as the prisoners of the Lipowa Street and Old Airfield camps had been murdered. The authors of the letter felt certain that, because Germany was losing the war, the SS planned to exterminate all the prisoners so that no witness to their atrocities would survive. Although the letter's authors doubted they would see Janina again, they had to write down what had happened to keep from going mad. If she did receive the letter, they warned, she should not come to the camp again.[2]

The massacre had begun before dawn on November 3, the authors wrote. They heard the sound of gunfire, then music began to play from truck-mounted loudspeakers that had been brought into the camp. Waltzes, marches, and tangos blared, and in between each number came the sound of shots and screams. At morning roll call, the Jewish prisoners were ordered to gather, then they were steadily herded to Field V. An SS man told the authors that the Jews were being "finished off" and described what was happening. The Jews had to undress in a barracks at the back of Field V. In groups of ten, they were forced to run naked through an opening in the barbed wire and between a gauntlet of SS men that led to three 100-meter-long ditches lying in zigzags near the crematorium. For several days preceding the massacre, three hundred Jews had been forced to dig those ditches, supposedly for protection in air attacks. Now, each group of ten Jews, some made up of women and children, had to enter one of the ditches and lie on the ground or on the bleeding, twitching bodies of those who had gone before. Members of police and Waffen SS units assigned to the operation then shot the victims with machine pistols. It was rumored that some members of the camp SS participated in the shooting as well, none more enthusiastically than Thumann. Throughout the day following the massacre, Thumann directed a hunt in all the prisoner compounds to find Jews who had hidden and drag them to the ditches to be murdered.

The slaughter of an estimated 18,000 Jews at Majdanek on November 3, 1943, was just one scene in the bloody final act of *Aktion* Reinhard. To Himmler, 1943 had seen an alarming increase in violent resistance from Jews in Poland who were no longer in any doubt as to the fate the Germans planned for them. It had taken the SS nearly a month to put down the Warsaw ghetto uprising in the spring, at a cost of more than one hundred SS casualties. On August 2, prisoners at the Treblinka killing center set fire to it, and one hundred of them succeeded in escaping. The SS also met violent resistance from Jews in the Białystok and Vilna (Lithuanian: Vilnius) ghettos. The last straw for Himmler occurred on October 14, when more than three hundred Jews broke out of the Sobibor killing center, killing eleven of the SS staff and two Trawniki guards in the process.[3] *Aktion* Reinhard had practically completed its task of "resettling" the Jews of the General Government to mass graves and burn pits, and those who had been temporarily spared for labor now presented an unacceptable risk. So Himmler ordered the liquidation of the operation's camps and prisoners.

SS and Police Leader Sporrenberg received the assignment. He assembled a force of 2,000 to 3,000 men from the SS and police that murdered at least 42,000 Jews on November 3 and 4, 1943. It was the largest German mass shooting operation of the Holocaust. Sporrenberg gave it a celebratory code name: *Aktion Erntefest*, Operation Harvest Festival.

FIFTEEN

CHRISTMAS AT MAJDANEK

On Tuesday, November 9, 1943, Janina returned to Majdanek, to the place where, just a week earlier, she had entertained such hopes for a Jewish boy whose ashes now rose in the noxious black smoke that was smothering Lublin. She willed herself not to think about that. This was not the time for fear and anguish. She was no longer Pepi Spinner Mehlberg, whose own ashes ought to be mixed with those of her family and friends in Bełżec or in the bags of fertilizer that Majdanek sold to local farmers. She was Countess Janina Suchodolska now, and she had a mission. Now, more than ever, she would see it through.

As she visited the compounds, Janina could see that the prisoners' panic of Friday had dissipated. Some AK members among the prisoners had replaced the Jews who had worked in the camp's offices. From the records they could access, the prisoners concluded that the slaughter of the Jews was not the prelude to evacuating Majdanek and murdering its remaining prisoners. In fact, it was said that the new commandant took some interest in improving conditions for the prisoners. There had been a noticeable decrease in arbitrary beatings, and bedridden prisoners were no longer required to report for the morning and evening roll call.[1]

The prisoners' equanimity disturbed Janina. No longer fearing they were about to be slaughtered, they seemed almost sanguine about the murder of their fellow prisoners and impervious to the smoke and the stench of thousands of rotting corpses that engulfed the camp. It would take weeks to dispose of all the bodies, and every time Janina saw the smoke as she approached Majdanek, her inner Countess had to reassert herself over the Pepi who yearned to howl her grief.

She had a mission to accomplish, and the rumors about the new commandant inspired her with an idea for expanding her deliveries—and her access—to Majdanek's prisoners. She immediately sought a meeting with the commandant, which Petrak arranged without any trouble.

When SS *Sturmbannführer* Martin Weiss first learned of his appointment to be commandant of Majdanek, he was told that he would be taking over an extensive system of camps that provided laborers for the growing SS industrial complex in the General Government. He arrived in Lublin just in time to witness the collapse of the SS industries on November 3 as most of their laborers were murdered. Weiss had been chosen for the Majdanek post based on his experience and accomplishments. A Nazi "Old Fighter," he had served in the concentration camp system since its birth in 1933 and rose to the position of commandant at Neuengamme in 1940. In 1942, he took command of the original SS concentration camp, Dachau, and in one year managed to decrease its monthly prisoner mortality rate to the lowest of all the concentration camps, 0.23 percent. Even though he lost more than 85 percent of his anticipated workforce in *Aktion Erntefest*, Weiss was still expected to preserve the labor capacity of the remaining prisoners.[2]

Janina found Weiss to be, if not cordial, at least somewhat interested in what she had to say. She started by introducing the functions of the RGO within the General Government and especially its duty to provide for Polish prisoners. In fulfillment of that duty, her organization was delivering soup and bread to the Majdanek infirmaries for the sick prisoners, as well as bread and food products for the rest of the prisoners. Currently, she informed him, the deliveries for the sick prisoners occurred on different days from the deliveries for the others, and her organization was also having to retrieve the soup cans between food delivery days. She explained that it would be much more efficient and less expensive for her organization if it could bake and deliver the bread for all the prisoners on the same days that it delivered soup. In fact, she concluded magnanimously, her organization now had the capacity to prepare the soup three times a week and would be willing to provide it if a more efficient delivery schedule could be worked out.

Weiss appeared to accept Janina's representation of the RGO feeding program at Majdanek as simply the way things were done in the General Government. He questioned her proposal, however. Majdanek was a concentration camp, a precisely organized and tightly run maximum security facility, he lectured her. Its purpose was to isolate dangerous criminals and enemies, not to accommodate the wishes of some social welfare organization. The current delivery schedule was dictated by the necessity of minimizing disruptions to the camp regime. The meal times for the infirmaries were different than for the rest of the prisoner compounds. Moreover, if the bread were delivered on the same days as the soup, then prisoners would have to be diverted from their weekday labor assignments in order to fetch it from the food warehouses.

Janina acknowledged Weiss's concerns but insisted that if the Lublin Polish Care Committee simply delivered the bread directly to the compounds, as it did the soup, then the baskets could be taken in at the convenience of the SS and there would be no need to divert prisoners from their labor. She said this as though it were normal for a civilian organization to be accessing the prisoner compounds. As long as Weiss accepted this, then her proposal for delivering the bread would seem perfectly logical.

Weiss agreed to Janina's entire proposal. The Lublin Care Committee could supply soup and food for the sick prisoners three times a week and make its weekly delivery of bread for the other prisoners directly to the compounds on one of the soup delivery days.[3] As she returned to her office, Janina allowed herself a moment to gloat. The baskets for the bread loaves and the heavy two-ply paper bags for bread rolls provided more opportunities for smuggling contraband in addition to the false bottoms of the soup cans. With access to each of the prisoner compounds, she could not only increase communications between prisoners and the outside world but also between prisoners in the different fields, making it easier to organize the resistance within the camp. Based on her reading of Weiss at the meeting, she felt confident that she could win more concessions from him. Commandant

Weiss did not yet realize, Janina thought, that when she asked for a finger, she meant to get the whole hand.

Now that Janina was authorized to expand the feeding program at Majdanek, she had to find more funds and products. She put out a public call for donations and contacted businesses, unions, social organizations, landowners, and farming cooperatives. Once again, the people of Lublin impressed her with their generosity. The nuns of the Ursuline convent provided hundreds of liters of cream soup per week for tubercular prisoners or other patients with special dietary needs. Teams of upper-class women volunteered to peel and chop vegetables and scrub the giant kettles that Łopatyńska had built into the Lublin Polish Care Committee's kitchens. Kosiba agreed to provide two more Społem trucks for each of the delivery days. Wagons and trucks arrived daily at the care committee's storerooms to drop off large quantities of food. Janina simply signed the receipts and did not ask after the origin of the goods or the legitimacy of the donors.

Społem's warehouses stored the food for the Germans in Lublin as well as the rationed products for Poles. Janina was in regular contact with its general manager, who sometimes complained to her about the challenges of his job, particularly the continual problem of loss and breakage. If he mentioned that 3,000 kilograms of sugar had just gone missing from a particular warehouse, Janina would notify the Lublin Polish Care Committee to send a rental truck to that warehouse to pick up the "missing" sugar.

No one in the camp SS raised any objections when Janina began delivering baskets of bread to each of the prisoner compounds in Majdanek, even when she made the bread deliveries on every day that she brought soup for the infirmaries. Nor did the SS show any interest in the quantities she was delivering or ask why deliveries often included additional items, such as apples and onions. She steadily increased the quantity of soup and rolls, so that there would be enough to feed all the Poles in the compounds with infirmaries. Because she could now speak with a physician in Fields I and V up to three times a week, she was fielding more requests for medicines, which she supplied either openly, with Blancke's approval, or clandestinely in the bottom of soup cans or in the bags of rolls, which also concealed hundreds of individual portions of butter.

In addition to medications, the prisoner physicians asked Janina to procure a new X-ray machine to replace their broken one, as well as a pneumothorax device for treating TB patients. X-ray machines were expensive and not made in Poland, but Janina assigned the task of locating one to an RGO physician. After just a few days, he reported that some doctors in Lublin were willing to supply one. Since it would be impossible to smuggle the machine into Majdanek and to hide its use, Janina decided to seek Blancke's approval for it to be provided to the camp. She did not mention the pneumothorax device, however, because the prisoner physicians were anxious not to draw Blancke's attention to the growing number of prisoners with TB, lest he isolate them in a barrack and leave them to die without treatment. Blancke accepted the offer of the X-ray machine.

Janina had not consulted with the Polish Red Cross leadership about the change in the RGO feeding program at Majdanek, although Jurek was assisting in the soup delivery. When Christians learned of the new deliveries, he demanded a meeting with Skrzyński and Lublin Polish Care Committee chairman Dąbrowski to discuss the situation. Since Christians was in both open and clandestine contact with the prisoner physicians at Majdanek, he was receiving some of the same requests for medications as Janina, so he had legitimate concerns about duplication of efforts. He also had his usual concerns about the RGO using resources meant for Poles to feed the prisoners of other nationalities being held at Majdanek.[4]

At their November 16 meeting, Skrzyński sought to placate Christians without actually agreeing to any changes in the RGO's assistance to Majdanek prisoners. The Count acknowledged the overall responsibility of the Polish Red Cross for medical and hygienic assistance to Majdanek's infirmaries. The RGO stood ready to support the Red Cross in its efforts, he assured Christians. For example, the RGO had just obtained permission for a new X-ray machine from the camp physician and was sourcing one that the Red Cross could deliver to the camp. The Lublin Polish Care Committee would still provide food products for weekly delivery to Majdanek by the Red Cross, but it would also continue its own deliveries to the camp of soup, bread, and other types of food, as well as medicines. Since the food was being apportioned appropriately in each prisoner compound by a committee of its Polish prisoners, Christians need not worry that non-Polish prisoners would receive it. Skrzyński promised that his office would henceforth consult with the Polish Red Cross beforehand about interventions with German authorities regarding aid to Majdanek and would notify it promptly regarding the outcome of RGO interventions.[5]

In order to deconflict the provision of medical assistance to Majdanek, the Polish Red Cross and the RGO asked Weiss to allow a committee of prisoner physicians to meet regularly with representatives of both organizations regarding the supply needs of the camp infirmaries. Weiss not only consented but also authorized the committee to meet with the organizations' representatives in the office of the Polish Red Cross in Lublin. Before each meeting, the Red Cross arranged for relatives of the committee members to be present on its premises that day. It then persuaded the committee's SS escorts to allow contact between the physicians and their family members by offering the escorts a lavish feast and entertainment.[6]

Janina was always under SS guard when she visited the protective custody camp, but now her visits had become such an accepted part of the camp's routine that she felt it was safer to observe her surroundings more openly and even move around. One day while she watched a truck being unloaded at Field IV, she saw a teenaged prisoner speaking to another youth in Polish. As he was telling a story with obvious relish, she moved closer to hear what he was saying.

"He went out that morning with his gang to break stones on the road. A bunch of Jews, the gang was. And awfully slow. So he took the hammers from the two slowest ones, made them lie down, and started banging on their heads with their hammers as they should have been doing to the stones! Nearly finished them off too, but the SS stopped him so there wouldn't be corpses in the work area. And then," he concluded, "you should have seen them work—like beavers!"

Janina glared at the boy, her first instinct to judge him a born psychopath. Then she considered once again the terrible choices that the German occupiers forced Poles to make in order to survive, choices that hardened many and drained them of their empathy. How much worse it was here in Majdanek, where survival for more than a few weeks required luck, cunning, and ruthless devotion to self-interest. Her glare turned to a look of pity. What child would not become warped under such circumstances?

The same was true for many of the SS men, she realized, for most of the guards she was getting to know were ethnic Germans who had not volunteered to serve at a concentration camp. Still, under the constant indoctrination, harassment, and threat of punishment from their superiors, they had acclimated to their role as brutal persecutors of the prisoners. They were not devoid of humanity, however, as Hoffmann and the Tyrolean guard had proved. Even some of the experienced camp SS whose routine brutality toward the prisoners she had observed would sometimes help her by looking away when she passed a package to a prisoner or by warning her when Thumann was expected to make his rounds. Human connection could sometimes evoke kindness even from the habitually cruel. That knowledge guided how she pursued her mission at Majdanek and factored into her calculation of the risks she undertook.

Via the false bottoms of the soup cans and the baskets and bread bags, a regular correspondence developed between Underground members in the camp and those on the outside. Prisoners sent out the names of others who were not members of the Underground but were not receiving packages. Janina forwarded those messages to the AK's OPUS aid organization, which then "adopted" those prisoners and sent them packages as well.[7]

Janina tried to ensure that only AK members employed by the Lublin Polish Care Committee were involved in secreting the messages and contraband she was smuggling into Majdanek and retrieving what the prisoners sent out. Her assistant Hanka was not in the AK, for she had sworn to her mother not to join any resistance organization after her father was taken hostage and killed. Hanka quickly figured out that the Majdanek deliveries were being used for smuggling, however, and she begged Janina to allow her to participate in the operation. Hanka had proved so valuable to Janina that she agreed, and she designated Hanka to be her replacement on days when Janina could not accompany the deliveries.

In November 1943, the Lublin Polish Care Committee provided 20,000 kilograms (44,000 lbs.) of bread, 15,700 liters (over 4,000 gallons) of soup, and various other foods to Majdanek. The quantities seemed enormous, and yet Janina knew all too well that they were not enough. This fact was driven home to her one snowy day as she was riding into the camp with a soup delivery. The trucks always wobbled on the stones of the "Black Road," but today hers was skidding as well. As it entered a curve, she realized that it was falling over, so she leapt from the seat and tumbled in the snow. She got gingerly to her feet, feeling pain in her side but finding that nothing seemed broken. Then she saw with horror that the contraband items she had been carrying in a small bag had scattered in the snow. Prisoners working nearby ran to the overturned truck, and when the first one neared her, she pointed at the items, signaling for help. He quickly organized retrieval of the items as the SS guard struggled with the horses, which were being choked by their harness. After righting the wagon and replacing the empty cans, the prisoners fell upon the spilled soup, scooping up the vegetables and drinking the soup-soaked snow. When Janina passed the same spot as she exited the camp, she saw that the ground was bare and there was no trace of the soup. She was moved that the prisoners all helped her before they started on the soup, but the incident impressed her with the urgent need to do still more for them.

So she visited Weiss to request another finger and came away with much of the hand. The commandant agreed that Polish prisoners could receive an unlimited number of packages and that family members could send prisoners clothing as well. He increased the frequency with which families could write to prisoners to three times a month. He even agreed that the camp would respond to inquiries about specific prisoners from their families and from the RGO if they provided precise data about the prisoners. Still Janina pushed for more: to provide soup for all the Polish prisoners in Majdanek, not just those in the infirmaries. That was not up to him, Weiss told her, she would need to get the consent of the chief of the Security Police and SD of Lublin District. Which Janina did. Consequently, in December 1943, the Lublin Care Committee began providing all of Majdanek's Polish prisoners soup, rolls, compote, and other food products three days a week.[8]

Shortly before Christmas, Janina finally obtained the pneumothorax device that Majdanek's prisoner physicians had requested. Her next challenge was to figure out how to deliver it, for it was far too large to fit in a bread basket or the bottom of a soup can. It would have to be incorporated into a truck in some way that would elude SS inspection. Her AK colleagues constructed a wooden case for it that fit under the floor of the driver's seat of one of the delivery trucks. This left the problem of how, once the truck got to Field V, the device could be unloaded without the SS seeing it. Through their secret communications with Janina, Bargielski and Dr. Nowak proposed a plan.

Now that the Lublin Polish Care Committee was providing meals for all the Polish prisoners, it had to send two trucks for every prisoner compound. The day before she planned to deliver the pneumothorax device, Janina informed camp authorities that one of the care committee's soup kitchens needed repairs and so she would send just one truck to Field V the next day. When she brought the delivery, Janina was riding on that truck. Hiding her nervousness, she bantered as usual with the duty officer while the SS inspected it. It passed, and she rode on to Field V, where Bargielski and Nowak awaited her. Feigning surprise that there was only one truck, Bargielski announced that there was no point in diverting prisoners from their labor to unload it when it could just go directly to the kitchen. This was part of the plan, for the truck driver knew he was to drive into the compound, had been trained to remove the device from the truck, and had willingly agreed to undertake the risk. But suddenly, Bargielski told the truck driver to get down so that he could drive the truck instead. Then he jumped on and drove off.

Janina cast a glance at the guard in the tower and held her breath. He had swung his machine gun around and was watching Bargielski driving the truck. Apparently concluding that Bargielski would not dare to do such a thing without orders, the guard did not fire.

Janina fretted. Would Bargielski know how to remove the case from the truck? Would he damage the device or mix up the parts so that Dr. Nowak would not be able to reassemble it with the coded instructions he had received? Would he be caught? And she questioned the wisdom of the enterprise, whether saving some tubercular prisoners was worth endangering the whole operation at Majdanek. Had she calculated the risks correctly?

Bargielski returned with the truck. Janina rode on it back to Lubartowska

Street, where the driver retrieved the case and handed it to her. Inside it was a package with a card that read "With thanks and Christmas wishes from the prisoners of Field V." Janina cried out in wonder when she opened it. The package contained a beautiful Nativity scene made with pieces of cardboard, matches, bits of bread, strips of colored paper from packages, and snips of cotton from the hospital. It contained the manger, the infant Christ and Mary, a tiny Christmas tree, and where the scene usually depicts shepherds or the Magi, three prisoners made of cotton wool, dressed in concentration camp uniforms. There were even tiny bulbs to light the whole scene. Janina wondered at the ingenuity, labor, and love that had gone into making this fantastic gift in utter secrecy inside a concentration camp. In the midst of their suffering, its creators still felt the need and found the strength to give something back to those who cared about them. Janina kept the gift for some years among her most prized possessions as evidence of the perseverance of humanity and creativity even in conditions designed to crush the human spirit.

Before receiving the gift, Janina had already been thinking about doing something special for Majdanek prisoners for Christmas. She consulted with her colleagues at the Lublin Polish Care Committee, suggesting that the committee might send in some delicacies in the double-bottomed cans.

"What about trees?" one asked in jest. "Surely you plan to smuggle in some of those."

Janina thought it over. "I'll ask the commandant," she replied.

Weiss had become quite accustomed to Janina's visits. She could never tell whether he regarded her as a nuisance that he had to put up with or as the ally she claimed to be in the effort to keep his prisoners alive. As usual, he listened impassively to her latest pitch. Christmas Eve would fall on a Friday, which was not a delivery day for the care committee. She proposed that the committee send in an extra delivery on that day of packaged and prepared food that the prisoners could have to celebrate Christmas the next day. Weiss consented. Then she brought up the question of the trees.

"Christmas trees," Weiss said. Janina thought she detected a slight tone of surprise—perhaps even amusement?—in his response.

"Yes. We happen to have enough from a generous donor to provide one tree for each of the prisoners' barracks."

"There could be no question of lighting them," Weiss admonished.

"Of course," Janina replied. And Weiss consented.

When the RGO brought the next soup delivery, Perzanowska noticed that Countess Suchodolska seemed genuinely cheerful. She always greeted the doctor with a warm smile, but today it lacked its usual hint of sadness. In the snatches of conversation they held while conducting their official business, the Countess said, "I've been to the commandant. He's allowing me to come to you on Christmas Eve. I will come at noon."[9]

Janina was sure the people of Lublin would provide the Christmas treats she planned to deliver to Majdanek, but she was overwhelmed by their actual response. All the candy and pastry shops offered sweets, farmers donated foods, stationery stores agreed to supply tree trimmings, and Społem found an unusual amount of breakage in eggs and jam jars. As the items poured in, willing hands came forward to cook special hams, bacon, and sausages, and to bake babkas, macaroons, cookies, poppy seed cakes, and strudels. Together, employees and volunteers of both the Lublin Polish Care Committee and the Polish Red Cross worked day and night to assemble the delicacies in packages for 5,500 prisoners. Instead of the usual soup, the Christmas Eve delivery would bring borscht with meat pierogi, dried mushroom stew, cabbage rolls with rice, and the traditional Polish Christmas dessert, egg noodles with poppy seeds and sugar. Children in the care committee's shelters made decorations that were hung on the large trees for the barracks, while additional, smaller trees were added to the delivery for the prisoners to decorate themselves. Finally, the delivery would include wafers for the Polish Christian tradition of breaking wafers with loved ones on Christmas Eve, as well as Holy Communion wafers that priests imprisoned in the camp would distribute in secret nighttime ceremonies.[10]

At noon on Christmas Eve, Dr. Perzanowska stood at the guard booth outside Field I and thought she must be dreaming. One huge platform truck after another passed by, loaded with cans and barrels and piled high with evergreen trees. When the trucks for Field I arrived, she inhaled the trees' scent deeply. It was the smell of freedom, she thought, and tears began to roll down her cheeks. Then Countess Suchodolska approached, obviously very moved as well. She persuaded the guard to allow her to break a wafer with Perzanowska. While they shared the wafer, gazing into each other's tear-stained faces, Perzanowska felt that they had consecrated an unbreakable bond between the prisoners and their compatriots in freedom. Never again would she feel abandoned in the concentration camp, for she knew that there were many outside it who held her in their hearts.

Janina also got the guard's permission to shake hands with the prisoners who were unloading the truck. As she did, she expressed to each the Christmas greetings of the RGO and Lublin Polish Care Committee. Hanka, who had accompanied Janina to Majdanek, shared a wafer with one of the other prisoners. There were more tears, and even laughter as the women unloading the trucks wrapped their arms around the fragrant trees.

Suddenly, Janina heard several prisoners gasp and the guard snap to attention. A car had pulled up to the guard booth, and out of it stepped Weiss. Janina had heard that the commandant hardly ever visited the protective custody camp, and never for more than a few minutes. She had not seen him on any of the previous soup deliveries. But now he approached the unloaded barrels and ordered a prisoner to open one. It contained the noodles. Janina's joy evaporated and her heart became a heavy lump. Besides the packages and trees, she did not have permission to deliver anything other than the usual soup and bread. She racked her brain for an explanation.

"What do you have here?" Weiss demanded, pointing at the noodles.

"We had to change the menu. The soup we usually bring spoils in a day, and since we're not allowed to come on Christmas, we substituted noodles."

"Do the other prisoners get the same thing?" he inquired.

"Yes, Herr *Kommandant*, except for the hospital patients. For them, Dr. Blancke ordered a special diet," Janina lied. Blancke took no interest in the diet of sick prisoners, but she hoped that mentioning his name would help make her explanation sound plausible. Her stratagem apparently worked, for Weiss lost interest and returned to his car, which headed back toward camp headquarters.

At each prisoner compound she visited, Janina persuaded the guard to allow her and Hanka to break a wafer with a prisoner and to shake hands with the prisoners unloading the trucks. Not a few of the male prisoners cried, and she even saw the Tyrolean SS man wipe away a tear. One of the older, experienced SS officers was heard to mutter, "Man, at home in Germany, this would never happen."[11]

From Majdanek that day, Janina went to the Krochmalna Street transit camp, bringing a similar feast of borscht and noodles as well as articles of clothing. There, she participated in a celebration together with the district medical superintendent and an official from the labor office. As Janina distributed the wafers to the detainees, occasionally sharing one, they pressed upon her their tearful gratitude. Then they all joined in singing Christmas carols.

Janina also obtained permission to deliver extra parcels and food to Majdanek on New Year's Eve, although they were not as sumptuous as the Christmas Eve delivery. In the days following the holidays, she received a smuggled letter from a committee of Polish prisoners in each compound describing how they had celebrated Christmas Eve by decorating their trees, dining together, breaking the wafers, singing carols, and even putting on skits. The holiday committee from Field I sent their description of the celebration in verse. Janina was pleased to learn that many Polish prisoners had shared the bounty from their packages with non-Poles, especially in the women's camp and the camp infirmaries.

That Christmas at Majdanek became an indelible memory for the Polish prisoners who experienced it and survived the war. Even decades later, it would remain for many of them one of the most meaningful experiences of their lives. The indifference and selfishness that had possessed them in their struggle to survive dissipated, at least for a time, as they came together to feast, sing, and pray. Gazing at the huge Christmas tree in each barrack, sparkling with its handmade decorations, prisoners felt a deep, spiritual connection to their Polish culture and traditions, and to the compatriots who had provided them with this symbol of hope and token of love. That night, the sound of Polish voices carried from compound to compound at Majdanek. They were singing "God Save Poland."

SIXTEEN

CAT AND MOUSE

On a sub-0° day in early January 1944, a ghastly parade coursed slowly along the streets from Lublin's freight station to Majdanek. Hundreds of skeletons dressed in flimsy striped uniforms lurched through the snow in their wooden clogs, struggling to hold themselves upright in the unrelenting wind. Every few yards, a body fell, so the parade left a two-kilometer string of corpses in its wake. Three months earlier, these skeletons had been mostly young, healthy men from nearly every country that Germany occupied. Then, they had been forced to labor in the tunnels of the Buchenwald subcamp Dora, where the Germans planned to manufacture a new class of strategic missiles. Now, injuries, starvation, and disease had rendered these men worthless to the SS, which had packed them into unheated boxcars and sent them on the long journey to Majdanek without food or water. At the freight station, prisoners incapable of walking and the corpses of those who died en route were stacked on top of one another in trucks that delivered them to the camp.

This was just one of the transports that brought some 8,000 desperately ill and disabled prisoners to Majdanek in the first three months of 1944. Since the SS industries in Lublin were shut down following Operation Harvest Festival, Majdanek had lost its purpose as a reservoir of labor for the SS. In December 1943, it was designated a "convalescent camp," in reality, a place where prisoners deemed useless were sent from other camps to die. Their maladies included end-stage TB, intestinal infections, kidney failure, shattered bones, and blindness brought on by the conditions of their forced labor. The men of this transport from Dora, many of them French, were placed in barracks in Field IV and left there without any medical treatment to subsist on the meager camp diet. After three weeks, those still alive were moved to the lice- and flea-infested barracks of the men's infirmary. After three months, of the 250 young Frenchmen in the transport, only eight still survived.[1]

Soon after the Dora transport arrived, Janina received a coded message from Henryk Szcześniewski, an AK member imprisoned in Field III. The compound had received 1,500 prisoners from the sick transports who were desperately ill with dysentery, and one third of them had already died. He urged Janina to get medication to the compound as quickly as possible.

Janina immediately sent Lublin Polish Care Committee employees out to scour the city and nearby towns for antidysentery drugs, and by the next morning they had accumulated 1,000 doses. However, since there was no longer an infirmary in Field III, she could not obtain official authorization to deliver it there. Anxious to get the medicine to the compounds before that afternoon's soup delivery, she called Petrak and claimed that, because of a shortage of trucks, she needed to deliver the soup in two transports. He agreed to issue her two passes to the protective custody camp that day. Janina's AK colleagues in the care committee storehouse quickly loaded two trucks, secreting the drugs in the false bottoms of the soup cans, and she took them to Field III. Szcześniewski organized the administration of the drugs.[2]

Some days later, Szcześniewski sent word that five hundred of the patients were still alive and appeared to be recovering. Janina did not know whether to be pleased or appalled. She was determined to get more drugs to the sick prisoners in Fields III and IV, but smuggling was too risky given the types and quantities of medicines that were needed. So she paid a visit to Blancke.

She found Majdanek's chief physician packing up his office. He was being transferred to the new Plaszow concentration camp in Kraków. In the course of their many interactions over the previous months, Blancke's rudeness toward Janina had moderated to grudging respect. But as she presented her proposal to deliver medication to Fields III and IV, he cut her off.

"You have done enough. Too much, in fact. And you should be grateful that you are still at liberty."

"How much does he know?" Janina wondered, and that old intruder, fear, crept into her heart. She had realized going in that her explanation for how she knew about the sick prisoners in Fields III and IV was not very plausible. Had she fatally miscalculated in making this proposal?

"I am a physician, not a policeman," Blancke continued. "Leave well enough alone and stop making requests. I am not going to say anything to the commandant about your request but, personally, I believe that from now on you should be barred from the camp."

Then, with a look of special intensity, he concluded, "I think you understand what I mean. You have done more than enough!"

Janina's fear slipped away. She felt almost touched. Here was an SS officer who had sent thousands of Jewish and Polish prisoners to their deaths. Yet, although he evidently knew that she was conducting clandestine operations at Majdanek, he had essentially spared her life by not reporting her. Even a monstrous criminal could retain vestiges of humanity.

By 1944, the giant map in Adolf-Hitler-Platz in Lublin had been removed and the "Bellower" had ceased broadcasting. Instead of celebrating their latest military victories, the Germans were pasting up posters in the city announcing all the people who had just been sentenced to death for resisting German rule or shot as hostages in reprisal for partisan attacks. Governor General Frank had changed his policy toward his "foreign" subjects yet again. Furious that, despite his magnanimity, Polish partisan attacks were escalating, he abandoned his objections to reprisal actions and in October 1943 ordered the death penalty for every Pole who disobeyed any German order or in any way hampered the German "rebuilding effort" in the General Government. As usual, Frank's policy had the opposite of its intended effect. If a Pole could be murdered by the Germans just for living in the wrong place or failing to follow an impossible rule, what did the

Poles have to lose by actively resisting them? One Underground member calculated his odds of survival as follows: there were 30,000,000 Poles, and 3,000 were being seized every day; the likelihood that he would be seized on any given day was thus one in 10,000. Consequently, there was no point in worrying.[3]

Thousands of Poles made the same calculation and flocked to join the many, disparate armed organizations operating in the General Government. Attacks were occurring every day, in every district, and executions and reprisals increased accordingly. In January 1944, Janina received a report from Majdanek prisoners that new trenches had been dug next to the crematorium and loudspeakers placed on its roof. Soon afterward, buses began traveling up the new road that ran along the back of the prisoner compounds directly to the crematorium. The SS withdrew the prisoners working in the area whenever the buses arrived, but a few were able to hide in places in Field V from which they could observe. Prisoners, their hands bound with wire, were pulled from the buses in groups of two to five. The SS forced the men, women, and sometimes children to run through the snow into a trench and shot them with automatic rifles. Most of the victims were from the Zamek prison in Lublin, others had been seized in pacification operations. The buses continued arriving with regularity, usually multiple buses on the same day, bringing hundreds to their death. At the same time, a steady stream of prisoners was flowing into and out of the hostage camp in Field IV. When a hostage heard the SS call his name, he rejoiced at the prospect of being released, but his joy turned to terror when, after leaving the compound, he was marched not to the right, toward freedom, but to the left, to the slaughterhouse of the crematorium.[4]

In 1943, the typical punishment for a civilian caught smuggling items into Majdanek was incarceration in the camp for several weeks, which some did not survive.[5] Now, smuggling was a capital offense. Still, Janina was not about to pass up the opportunity her expanded deliveries to Majdanek offered for organizing the camp resistance. Every week, she was bringing 21,000 kilograms of bread, 5,400 liters of soup, and 6,600 rolls, along with other products, in three deliveries. The number of cans, bags, and baskets on each delivery was so large that the SS could not spare the time to inspect them all closely. Janina calculated that the odds of the SS discovering the false bottoms of the cans or the particular bag or basket that contained messages or contraband were low enough to justify the risk to herself and to the feeding program.

Prisoners serving in the AK organized cells in each of Majdanek's compounds and appointed at least one member to the prisoner committee that received the RGO deliveries. Every time she went to the camp, Janina was able to communicate with an AK comrade in each of the compounds. In Field V, her contact was Dr. Henryk Wieliczański. Before the war, he had been Izaak Halperin. Neither he nor Janina ever learned that the other was a Jew.[6]

Between Janina's verbal communications and the correspondence she was smuggling, the Majdanek AK cells were in regular contact with one another and able to establish an overall command for the camp based in Field V. It sent out weekly reports about the conditions in the camp and the personnel, strength, and plans of the SS. Dr. Romuald Sztaba reported information about V-1 missile production that he collected by interviewing the prisoners in the Dora transports. Janina also provided the AK intelligence information that she gleaned from her chats with SS guards and officials at the camp.[7]

The Gestapo at Majdanek knew that there were organized resistance operations in the camp and was constantly seeking to sniff them out. Through torture, threats, and inducements, it turned some Poles into spies and infiltrated them into the compounds. Janina received warnings from prisoners and from her AK commander to be on her guard. She was hardly blind to the risk she was undertaking, which was far greater than they realized, and she never entered the camp without a touch of paranoia. Was that prisoner working at the food warehouse just a little too eager to help her? She had a nagging suspicion of her AK contact in Field IV, Nowakowski. That compound had been the hardest to organize, because Poles were in the minority there, and most of them had been arrested for criminal rather than political offenses. One day, in light of rumors of a denunciation in the camp, Janina included no contraband in the delivery. At Field IV, an SS officer awaited the delivery and proceeded to inspect every can, bag, and basket. After he found nothing, he seemed to throw a glance at Nowakowski. Perhaps Janina imagined it, but she could never be sure.[8]

One day, Hanka confessed her fear that her aunt was going to betray Janina. The woman believed that Countess Suchodolska's activities at Majdanek were a cover for resistance work, and she accused her niece of breaking her promise not to join the Underground. Hanka argued heatedly with her, denying that the Countess was involved in any illegal activity. She was proud to work with the Countess and to be in her confidence, Hanka told her aunt, and in any case she would willingly risk her life for the Countess because hers was more valuable to Poland. Her aunt was garrulous and liked to boast of knowing secrets and so might bring suspicion on Janina, Hanka warned. Janina thought it best to pass Hanka's warning to Colonel Łodzia. Soon afterward, the aunt received a letter warning that if her loose talk led to anyone's arrest, she would be tried by a secret tribunal of the Underground.

As Janina was working in her office early one morning, a visitor entered and asked to speak with Count Skrzyński. The Count was not due to arrive for some time, Janina told the visitor, who appeared to be an estate owner. He said that he would wait. He did not sit, however, but paced about the room. Janina noticed that he was casting oblique glances at the reports and RGO identity cards lying on her desk. Then he asked her about the map and chart on the wall on which she kept track of the RGO's activities throughout the district. But as she explained them, he kept his eyes on her rather than what she was showing. She began to grow uneasy.

Wójcikowa, Janina's assistant, entered the office. "What shall I do about the gentleman's dog? It's becoming quite restless," she said.

A dog. Only Germans went around with dogs. But the visitor explained that he had brought the dog to the city to take it to the veterinarian. Since it was getting late, he asked to have a telephone call put through. Janina wrote down the number he gave her and immediately recognized it.

Looking the visitor in the eye, she said, "This is the number of the Security Police main office."

The man then identified himself as an officer of the SD and demanded to inspect the building.

Before they left her office, the SD official suggested that Janina bring her coat, since the building was cold and she was coughing. Seeing Janina go out with her coat over her shoulders, Wójcikowa immediately assumed that Countess Suchodolska was being arrested. Wendrucha, the building porter, had warned Wójcikowa when she arrived for work that "some Gestapo fellow is in the Countess's office." Janina calmly explained that the SD official had come to inspect the building, and she asked Mrs. Olbrycht, who ran the aid program at Krochmalna, to show him the storeroom. After finding nothing of interest, the official entered the office of the Lublin Polish Care Committee's secretary, Father Behnke, a young priest who dressed in lay clothing, as the RGO was forbidden to employ clergy.[9] The official demanded to know Behnke's name, birth date, address, and work duties, and then asked, "Have you been in the army?" This put Behnke in a quandary, because admitting he had not served would raise the question of why.

"No," Behnke answered nervously.

"Why not?"

"I was too young," he stammered, but the official quickly calculated that Behnke had been just the right age for the draft in 1939.

Janina stepped in to rescue the young man. "He didn't pass the physical. Category C, maybe even O. He doesn't want to talk about it with young girls around the office."

The official looked suspiciously at Janina. "How come you know so much about military classifications?"

The priest tried to help her out with "Oh, the Countess knows everything, even army ratings!"

But wary, the official said to Janina, "You must have had dealings with the army. Or was your husband perhaps an officer?"

"No," Janina responded. With sudden inspiration, she added sadly, "He is in another one of those excusable classes."

The SD official interrogated a few more employees and finally left. Janina concluded that the point of his visit had been to intimidate her and her colleagues. There could be no doubt now that they had come under the suspicion of German security officials. Janina's AK commander ordered her to obtain an extra identity card in case she had to flee. Tucking up her hair so that it looked short, she had a new photo taken and affixed to an identity card with the name Jadwiga Wojarowsan.

Despite the SD official's visit, Janina took on even more risks in her work at Majdanek. At Perzanowska's request, she began smuggling books into the camp, separating them into sections that she hid in the bread baskets. She brought in works by celebrated Polish writers as well as medical texts for Perzanowska. And to keep prisoners abreast of the progress of the war, she ensured that they received the Underground's daily radio digest, the *Biuletyn Informacyjny*. Sometimes the AK instructed her to make contact with a particular prisoner in one of the compounds. She would whisper the prisoner's name to the AK representative there, who then arranged for the prisoner to be present for the next delivery. With a nod of the head, Janina's comrade would indicate the prisoner, to whom Janina would pass a message or small parcel. Occasionally, Janina even arranged for family members of prisoners to see their loved one by bringing them on a delivery run and passing them off as RGO workers.[10]

As more and more sick transports arrived, Majdanek's weekly death tally shot up into the hundreds. The infirmary in Field V was overwhelmed with 3,600 patients, 1,000 of them Poles. There were thousands of Poles among the sick transport prisoners in Fields III and IV as well. Janina was supplying soup for them, and adding more fats and nutrients than the Germans allowed. At Perzanowska's request, she sent sauerkraut to Field I to combat scurvy in more than seven hundred sick prisoners sent from Ravensbrück.[11] In Field III, the Polish prisoners gave their soup to non-Polish prisoners in the sick transports, thanks to Janina's AK contact, Stanisław Zelent, who headed the food distribution committee for the compound. Zelent also requested packages for specific non-Poles in the compound. This was not happening in Fields IV and V, however, where so many of the Poles were themselves at death's door and desperately needed all the food they could get.[12]

Standing outside Field V with Hanka during one delivery, Janina observed a cart being pushed and pulled by prisoners as it passed in the direction of the crematorium. With a shock, she realized it was full of corpses.

But sitting on top was a living skeleton, his ribs and collarbone clearly visible through waxy yellow skin. Dark, burning eyes sunk deep in their sockets stared in horror and despair. Janina nearly cried out, but Hanka grabbed her hand and squeezed it. They must not draw the attention of the SS to what they had seen and understood.

This experience deepened Janina's obsession with finding ways to do more for the prisoners. She began pleading with Weiss to permit soup delivery five days a week. "It would really be the same overall amount," she lied, "but it's very hard on us to cook and deliver such quantities at a time." After obtaining approval from the Security Police, Weiss assented to the added deliveries.

Beginning in February 1944, Janina and/or Hanka delivered food to Majdanek every Tuesday through Saturday. Officially, the weekly quantity of the deliveries came to 7,250 liters of soup, 9,000 butter rolls, 4,000 kilograms of cabbage, plus bread, milk, butter, compote, cacao, and smoked meat, adding 935 calories to the daily diet of Polish prisoners. Janina calculated the caloric value of the actual deliveries to be 1,200 calories per day per Polish prisoner. Between the RGO deliveries and the packages they were receiving, Polish prisoners were faring far better than ever at Majdanek and were visibly healthier and stronger than the other prisoners.[13]

The feeding program at Majdanek was a relatively minor aspect of Janina's and the RGO's activities in Lublin District. In February 1944, the RGO was supporting 120,842 adults and 51,721 children in the district. It estimated that another 100,000 people qualified for its care. The Lublin Polish Care Committee was providing food for 3,000 prisoners at Zamek as well as the detainees passing through the Krochmalna Street transit camp. Refugees were arriving at Krochmalna not only from Volhynia but also from neighboring counties in Lublin District to which ethnic fighting had spread. Others in the camp had been seized in pacification operations or roundups for labor. There were so many sick and injured in the transit camp that Janina finally persuaded the Labor Office to establish a hospital there and even to provide beds, blankets, and straw mattresses. She also obtained the release of 787 Volhynian refugees between February 1 and mid-March, for whom the RGO provided shelter and support. During the same period,

832 victims of pacification operations were able to return to their homes from Krochmalna, thanks to the efforts of Skrzyński and Janina.[14]

Janina and the Lublin Polish Care Committee were able to meet the demands of five deliveries a week to Majdanek in part because the Polish government in exile was supporting the feeding program with substantial funds. This attracted the envy of Christians, who complained to the government in exile that the RGO was using its funds to feed not just Polish prisoners but also the prisoners of other nationalities at Majdanek. The Polish Red Cross should take over the program, he insisted, because it could be trusted not to misuse the funds.

The government in exile sent a representative to question Janina about Christians's claim. Exasperated, she freely admitted that her goal was to feed everyone in the camp, regardless of nationality. The only proof of eligibility she required was need and suffering. There were no limits to what she would willingly do to help the prisoners, but she had no heart for turf battles. If the Polish Red Cross were deemed more capable of running the feeding program at Majdanek, she would raise no objection, but she would no longer have any part in it. The government in exile put the question of who should run the feeding program to the AK command in the camp. It polled the prisoners and sent their response in a coded message: they wanted the RGO to continue feeding them.

RGO headquarters sent Janina a letter of commendation for her tireless service to aid Majdanek prisoners, but she found the whole affair disheartening. She collaborated closely with Polish Red Cross workers in providing both licit and illicit assistance to Majdanek, and Christians himself had taken great risks in the same effort. He sent reports to the Underground about Majdanek and even collected clandestine photos of the camp. Yet he seemed intent on destroying the collaboration between his organization and the RGO, apparently just so he could take sole credit for the Majdanek relief program.

Janina was equally discouraged by rivalries among the people she was trying to aid. The Polish political prisoners in Majdanek in 1944 represented nearly every resistance organization in Poland, and they organized corresponding cells within the camp. The organizations arranged for their members to receive packages, and most contributed to the RGO food deliveries as well. But the animosities between the various organizations were shared by their comrades within the camp. Janina found the evidence of their discord in soup cans that were returned from Majdanek still full of soured soup, because the prisoners could not agree how to distribute it.[15]

In late February, Janina frequently had the sense that she was being watched. Since the visit of the SD official, Wójcikowa had taken to accompanying Janina to and from work. As they started out for the office one morning, Janina noticed that a young man whom she had recently seen several times outside her building was walking some distance behind them. She ducked into a shop, pretending that she was looking for some article. When she and Wójcikowa exited, Janina saw the man across the street. When they passed the Kraków Gate, she felt that he was close behind them. Wójcikowa stopped to read a new poster on the wall listing the victims of the latest mass execution, all of them from her and Janina's neighborhood.

"How terrible!" Wójcikowa lamented.

"Can't be helped," Janina replied. "If they are guilty, what else is there to do but shoot them?"

Wójcikowa looked at her aghast. After they got to the office, Janina explained the reason for her remark.

"Oh!" Wójcikowa exclaimed. "I've seen that young man outside your building before and just assumed that he lived there."

Janina stopped seeing friends or anyone else she could avoid, fearing that the Gestapo would suspect them as her accomplices if she were arrested. The janitor of her building told her that a man had quizzed him about her comings and goings. She took to carrying the counterfeit identity card that she had received from the AK at all times, secreted on her body.

One morning in early March, Janina heard footsteps behind her as she turned into the carriageway beneath the Lublin Polish Care Committee's building. In the courtyard, Społem trucks were being loaded with bread. The drivers lifted their caps to her, as always, but the finger of one man as he did so seemed to point across the way. As she climbed the creaky steps to her office, she heard other steps below and realized that something was about to happen.

Janina rushed into her office, calling for Olbrycht and Hanka. She gave the counterfeit identity card to Olbrycht and asked her to warn Henry not to come home if Janina were arrested. As she finished, Wendrucha burst in.

"A suspicious-looking fellow just walked up, went out on a rear balcony, and is watching over the back entrance!"

Then things happened fast. Wendrucha and Olbrycht hustled Janina into a storeroom, and Wendrucha ran off. After a few minutes, he returned and pushed her into the next room, where the bread was stored. He directed her to crawl into a sack, then threw some loaves in after her. Suddenly, Janina was airborne as Wendrucha and two drivers tossed her into a truck. The engine started and Wendrucha called, "Go to the people's kitchen and get the soup."

The truck traveled some distance before stopping with a lurch. Janina heard a ripping sound and later learned that the driver was changing the license plates. The truck set out again, with Janina jostling uncomfortably among the sacks in the back. When it finally stopped and she was unpacked, she found herself before the home of the driver. He rushed back with the truck while Janina, feeling stiff and warped, was put to bed and made to drink hot tea. Less than an hour later, the driver returned in a cab to inform her that there had been no attempt to arrest her and it was safe to return to the office.

Upon her return, Hanka and Olbrycht greeted her with tears of relief and recounted what had transpired during Janina's "abduction." Just after Wendrucha and Olbrycht had put Janina in the storeroom, a gentleman and lady entered the office and asked to see the general manager of the RGO. Wendrucha showed them to the office of Stanisław Sikora, the manager of the Lublin Polish Care Committee. The lady asked Sikora that she be sneaked into Majdanek on one of the food delivery trucks, explaining that she had a sister there, and it was rumored she would soon be transported to another camp. If the RGO could not take the lady to see her sister, would it at least take a letter to the unfortunate woman with photos of her poor children? The gentleman said he would make the effort worthwhile and offered Sikora a considerable sum.

Sikora was a stickler for the rules and regulations and unaware of Janina's smuggling activities at Majdanek, so the couple's request and attempt to bribe him struck him as outrageous. "Are you out of your minds to ask us to destroy all our work for one favor?" he demanded, and then dismissed them.

The couple next sought out Janina's office, where they found only Hanka. The lady pleaded her case with great feeling, but Hanka, rather more politely than Sikora, informed her that what she requested was impossible.

"If only the Countess Suchodolska were here, I'm sure she would do it for us. She has the heart of a real Polish woman!" the lady lamented.

But Hanka asked them not to interrupt her work further. The man left, but the lady stayed on to kiss Hanka's hands, sobbing and imploring her to take the things into the camp. As Hanka got up to leave the room, the lady asked, "Won't you at least tell me when the Countess is coming? Has she been here this morning?" Hanka replied coolly that she had just come in and did not know the whereabouts of the Countess. Finally, the lady left.

Hanka had grasped the situation at once. She was sure that the couple had been sent by the Gestapo to trap Janina into doing something for which she would be arrested when she arrived at Majdanek. It seemed the Gestapo were still seeking confirmation of their suspicions before making such a high-profile arrest.

Despite the danger, Janina resolved to go with the food delivery to Majdanek that day. Not to appear might look suspicious. She ordered all contraband removed from the trucks and gave detailed instructions about the many matters that others would have to handle if she were arrested. She also destroyed the counterfeit identity card. Her disappearance now would implicate too many others, she realized.

Janina and Hanka, riding on the lead delivery truck, arrived at the gate to Majdanek's protective custody camp just as a sleek sedan was departing. Hanka tugged Janina's sleeve and threw a glance at the passing car. Inside it, Janina saw an elegantly dressed couple. She looked back at Hanka, who nodded and said quietly, "The same people."

Now on friendly terms with all the SS who manned the guardhouse, Janina asked the duty officer about the couple who had just left.

"Them?" he replied. "Just some folks who had an appointment with Thumann."

Janina continued chatting with him and learned that, until about an hour earlier, extra SS had been put on guard at the gate. She realized that, if the couple had won her consent to their request, the SS would have conducted a thorough inspection of the trucks that day and arrested her when they discovered her illicit cargo.

Janina had escaped the trap, but it caught Wendrucha instead. A few mornings later, Janina found Wendrucha's wife waiting for her at the office. A torrent of words poured out of the distraught woman. "They" had taken Wendrucha. Two of them had knocked on the door at midnight and, when she answered, pointed their guns at her and barged inside. They ordered Wendrucha to dress while they searched the home, ransacking drawers, looking behind pictures, rousting the children and turning over their beds. Finally, they pushed Wendrucha into a car and drove off.

The woman's news shook Janina to her core. Wendrucha, one of her closest accomplices in the AK, was likely at that moment being tortured by the Gestapo. She immediately sent an official inquiry to German authorities seeking information about the RGO employee who had been taken into Security Police custody the night before.

The next day there was still no response to Janina's inquiry, but the Polish custodian of the Zamek prison appeared unexpectedly to deliver a coded message from Wendrucha. "I know nothing. They beat me, asking about some woman. But I know nothing of her. I only want my three children to be cared for. I believe the Countess will provide for them. I believe that one has to choose those who can be most useful. I, a soldier, was fated to die in battle. Good-bye to all. No time to mention names. Please remember the orphans."

The risk he was taking so frightened the custodian that he was practically in a state of collapse and had to be revived. Fortunately, Janina had appropriate medication on hand, because it was not uncommon for people to come to the RGO office in extreme distress.

A few days later, Janina received another coded message from Wendrucha.

His torturers were accusing him of purposely taking the couple to the wrong office in order to buy time so that he could help Janina escape.

Finally, a response arrived to Janina's official inquiry. Wendrucha was dead. The cause of death: heart attack. Janina pulled every string she could to retrieve Wendrucha's body, which she viewed together with Father Santi. All the fingers on both of Wendrucha's hands were horribly broken.

Grief and guilt weighed heavy in Janina's heart. If she had not taken some prisoners' relatives into the camp to see their loved ones, the Gestapo would not have set that trap for her. And if she had heard the lady's pleas for help, she might have given in. She had let sentimentality overrule logic, and this was the consequence. Wendrucha had saved her life and lost his own as a result. All Janina could do was to give a job to Wendrucha's wife and provide financial assistance for his three children for some years after the war.[16]

SEVENTEEN

THE PLOT

Three weeks before Easter 1944, Janina arranged to meet with Majdanek's commandant to propose a holiday celebration for the prisoners. As usual, she brought an RGO employee with her, this time another priest in lay clothing, Father Michalski. When they arrived at the camp headquarters, the commandant's aide told them that Weiss was on his way and allowed them to wait in his office with the door open, just across from the aide's desk. As Janina made a show of unbundling herself from her coat and scarf, she glanced at a memo lying on Weiss's desk. The heading read "Re: Camp Evacuation."

"So this is it," she thought. With the Red Army advancing across Eastern Galicia, there had been speculation for weeks that the SS would abandon Majdanek. Now the order had come. At least, according to what little she was able to read, the plan appeared to be to transport the prisoners to other camps, not to shoot them.

Weiss appeared and approved Janina's proposal to provide traditional holiday treats for Majdanek's prisoners on the day before Easter.[1] "Just some eggs and sweets," she assured him, which, compared to bringing in decorated trees at Christmas, seemed practically business as usual. By this point, Weiss had decided that it generally wasn't worth his time to argue with the Countess, since she would just keep returning with the same request or would take it to the chief of the Security Police. She had a way of making her proposals sound so logical that it almost seemed irrational to refuse them.

As soon as her meeting ended, Janina rushed back to her office to send word of the evacuation to the Underground and to the AK command in Majdanek. The news of their impending evacuation dashed the hopes of Majdanek prisoners that they would soon be liberated by the advancing Soviet forces. But some speculated that the transports might offer the opportunity for escape. The AK cells in every prisoner compound sent a request to District Command that armed units attack and liberate at least one of the transport trains before it crossed out of the General Government into the Reich.

The AK District Command agreed in principle to the prisoners' demand and sent a request for approval and support troops to the AK high command. In the meantime, it ordered Janina, in collaboration with prisoners working in the camp administration, to collect precise information about the times and routes of the transport trains, which prisoners would be on each train, and the strength, arms, and disposition of the SS escort.[2] Janina wondered whether it was really possible to attack a train carrying more than 1,000 prisoners—some doubtless sick or injured—and liberate them without many being killed. But she was not going to question orders, despite the enormous personal risk involved. She understood how desperately her comrades in the camp yearned to be free. If the cost of achieving that at least for some of them was her own life, it was a bargain she was willing to make.

Once the news of Majdanek's evacuation became public, Janina met with Weiss to discuss the future of the RGO feeding program for the camp. As the prisoners were sent off, she pointed out, she would need to know how many Poles remained so that the food deliveries could be adjusted accordingly. She also asked permission to distribute food packages to the departing prisoners and to augment the rations they would receive for the journey. Weiss agreed that a day or two before each transport, Janina would receive information about the number of Poles it included. For each of them, the Lublin Polish Care Committee could supply one kilogram of bread, 0.5 kilogram of rolls, and 20 decagrams (7 ounces) each of bacon, sugar, and honey.[3]

A plan was beginning to take shape. AK members working in the camp registry were to obtain the evacuation transport lists and, through bribes and "clerical errors," ensure that one of the transports would contain a large contingent of their comrades. That transport would be the target for liberation. When Janina received word of the impending transport from Majdanek headquarters, she would notify her colleague Maria, who operated a secret radio transmitter in the Lublin Polish Care Committee's soup kitchen at the city train station. It would be Maria's job to discover the timetable and route of the train through her contacts at the station. Colonel Łodzia would then arrange for armed units to be deployed for the attack along with trucks to disperse the prisoners out of the attack area. Some of the resistance members on the transport would have to know the plan in advance so that they could spring into action and direct the other prisoners when the attack began. Janina would have to supply them with weapons that they could secrete on their bodies as well as precise instructions and hand-drawn maps showing where transport waited for them once they escaped the train.[4]

There were so many moving parts to this plan, so many ways it could go wrong or be discovered by the Germans, particularly given that Janina was already under Security Police suspicion and surveillance. For once, Janina tried not to calculate the probabilities and just kept focused on the task at hand. But the constant work and vigilance were wearing her down. She now weighed only eighty-six pounds.

All hope for liberating a transport seemed lost when, on the night of March 28, Majdanek was placed under total lockdown following the escape of nine prisoners. While working in the camp's vegetable gardens, the prisoners managed to pry open a sewer grate unseen and then slithered a few hundred yards through human waste to freedom. The lockdown was to last until the camp was evacuated, during which time no civilian workers would be allowed to enter, none of the SS could leave, and the prisoners were all confined to their compounds. The AK cells had no way to communicate with the outside world or even with one another.[5]

Not ready to give up on the plan to free her comrades, Janina decided to take a gamble. The next day, she arrived at Majdanek with trucks hauling the regular delivery of hundreds of gallons of soup and several tons of bread.

When the duty officer refused her entry, she adamantly refused to leave and insisted that he contact Weiss. It was out of the question, she declared, that in a time of such desperate food shortages, the commandant would allow all this food to go to waste. A call was put through to headquarters, and Janina got her pass to the protective custody camp.[6]

The deliveries restored communication with the AK command in Majdanek, which sent Janina a message via an empty soup can reporting what it had learned about the upcoming transports. There would be two on April 2, one to Bergen-Belsen and one to Natzweiler, with some AK members on the latter. Two more transports, both to the Gross-Rosen concentration camp in eastern Germany, would likely depart on April 4 and 5, taking most of the remaining Polish male prisoners. The AK members working in the prisoner registry were arranging for the majority of the AK members designated for Gross-Rosen to go on the second transport. The AK command urged that this transport be liberated.[7]

Janina immediately sent this information to Maria and to "Elżbieta," the head of "Sahara," the AK intelligence operation responsible for Majdanek. The AK District Command needed to know the route of the train as soon as possible in order to plan the attack, while Elżbieta had to provide Janina with the weapons and supplies for the prisoners who would lead the escape from the train in time for Janina to deliver them. She worried that the decision to allow the RGO deliveries would soon be reversed.

When Janina arrived at Majdanek with the food delivery on Friday, March 31, she was handed a notice that 730 Polish prisoners would be transported from the camp on Sunday, April 2. The extra rations supplied by the RGO for the departing prisoners should be delivered with the Saturday food delivery. Janina was pleased. The notice confirmed both that the AK command's information was accurate and that she would be allowed to make at least one more delivery. As she approached Field III, however, she found Thumann waiting for her. That was always a bad sign. Janina steeled herself for whatever was to come.

"Move on!" he ordered. "This compound is for transport prisoners. They don't need your food."

"But the transport isn't leaving for two days," Janina pointed out.

"How do you know that?" he demanded. There was a look of triumph in his eyes, and he stepped forward as if to seize Janina. He thought he finally had proof that Countess Suchodolska was a spy.

"Headquarters notified me this morning. I'm to bring packages and extra rations for all the transport prisoners tomorrow," Janina replied pleasantly.

Thumann stopped and scowled. "You'll bring nothing to this compound."

"But Commandant Weiss specifically authorized the packages for departing prisoners. Let's just check with him, shall we?"

Weiss overruled Thumann, who now had further reason for his enmity toward the Countess.[8]

Maria reported that the transports to Gross-Rosen would travel south from Lublin, through a forested area, before turning west. Via Elżbieta, Janina received packets of razor blades and flasks of liquor, some of it spiked with drugs. These were for the prisoners who would lead the breakout from the Gross-Rosen transport. Majdanek's guards were notorious for drunkenness, so the prisoners expected that they could easily ply the transport guards with the drugged liquor. Then the prisoners were to attack the intoxicated guards with the razors once the assault from outside units began. Having learned from Thumann that the prisoners selected for transports were being gathered in Field III, Janina had the items secreted in the soup cans to be delivered to that compound on Saturday, April 1.

As usual, Janina's first stop on her April 1 delivery was at Field I. She always looked forward to her largely wordless conversations with Perzanowska there, but today the doctor and the other prisoners receiving the delivery were unusually subdued, and some were crying. A tragedy was unfolding in the compound. Outside one of the barracks, Janina could see that a large group of Belarusian children had been gathered by the SS women overseers. The children were dressed in pretty outfits, the boys with caps and the girls with ribbons in their hair. From inside the barracks, Janina could hear women sobbing and crying out to the children, reminding them of their names and the names of their fathers and villages. Then trucks pulled up to the barrack. As the SS women began lifting the hysterically weeping children into them, the wailing and banging of their mothers locked inside the barrack grew to a deafening din. Janina felt so shattered by the women's anguish that she could barely keep from crying herself. Later, she obtained evidence that the children had been taken to Łódź for Germanization, and she would testify about their abduction after the war.[9]

At Field III, Janina arrived with the usual delivery plus a truck loaded with packages for the prisoners due to depart the next day.[10] She watched with trepidation as the truck with the soup cans and their contraband drove to the kitchen barrack. A prisoner on his way to unload the truck with the packages gave Janina a grin and a salute. As she returned the salute, Janina heard the crack of a whip and saw the prisoner flinch, then flee. Startled, Janina turned and saw Thumann mounted on a horse, his whip in hand. He rode right up to Janina and bent down over her.

"I am very sorry that you are not to be a prisoner here," Thumann snarled, "but someday soon you'll find yourself in a concentration camp, and you won't be any better off than they! The prisoners and kapos might pity you, but if it's my camp, I'll hang you from the nearest pole!"

He bent down farther, his nose nearly touching Janina's, and stared her down with a glare of such intense malice that Janina felt transfixed with fear. She did not show it, however, but kept her gaze evenly on his, willing every muscle to remain still. Time seemed suspended. Then Thumann sneered, straightened, and rode off into the compound.

Hanka began sobbing. She had been sure that Thumann was going to shoot Janina if she answered him. As Hanka urged that they leave Majdanek immediately, she saw Janina suddenly go rigid, as if she were frozen to the ground. Hanka thought the Countess was having a breakdown, but it was terror that had overcome her. She was watching Thumann ride up to the truck from which Zelent was probably at that moment unloading the contraband. Just before he reached it, Thumann veered his horse around and came cantering back toward her.

"What's in that damn truck of yours?" he bellowed.

Janina's nerves immediately snapped back into place. Looking up at Thumann with feigned composure, she replied, "Didn't you see, sir? Soup and bread, plus milk for the sick, as usual."

"You're lying," he shouted, "What else is there?"

Janina straightened up to her full five-foot, one-inch height and answered him again as he bent over her. "Nothing else. If you don't believe me, why don't you have it checked?"

She realized that her tone might spark a new explosion of fury from the SS officer, but hoped that it would at least distract him from the truck. With a grunt of disgust, he yanked the horse's reins and rode off. And the truck returned, relieved of its perilous load. Janina proceeded to complete that day's delivery in her usual, outwardly calm manner, while the prisoners who had witnessed her altercation with Thumann stared in awed relief. A few crossed themselves as they sent up a prayer of thanks for the Countess's escape.

Back at her office, Janina found another report on the upcoming transports in one of the empty soup cans. The second Gross-Rosen transport, scheduled for April 5, would carry eight hundred Polish prisoners, including some of the AK command and many of its members. Every freight car would be assigned a group of resistance fighters, including one who was in on the escape plot.[11] Janina forwarded this information to Elżbieta and Łodzia. On April 3, the final go-ahead for the operation arrived. With the message was a map showing the location in the forest near Kraśnik where armed units would be waiting to attack the train as it passed. Janina was ordered to watch for the departure of the prisoners from Majdanek and then go in person to the railway station to deliver a message confirming that the transport had begun and describing the strength of the SS escort. A liaison would take the message to Colonel Łodzia, who would then get the armed units into place. Maria would radio the time when the train actually departed.

That same day, Majdanek notified Janina that she should bring packages and extra rations on April 4 for all the Polish prisoners being sent to Gross-Rosen on April 4 and 5. When she arrived with the delivery—including maps and instructions for the escape operation—Janina was assigned the Tyrolean guard as her SS escort. He seemed even more jovial than usual, and she could smell alcohol on his breath. "I must bid you farewell, today, Madame," he said in a sentimental tone. "I am leaving with the transport and from there will go home on leave." Then he added with a grin, "With any luck, the war will be over before I report to duty again."

He handed Janina a pack of cigarettes that he hoped she could pass to Zelent, who always received the RGO deliveries to Field III and had developed a sort of friendship with the guard. Janina wished him well, and meant it sincerely. She felt some compassion and even admiration for this SS man who dared to be kind when kindness was punished as treason.

At Field III, the escort guards for that day's transport were already gathering. Some were obviously drunk. The relaxed atmosphere surprised Janina, until she learned that Thumann was not at Majdanek. She was riding on a platform truck with packages for the departing prisoners, and she stayed on it when it drove into the compound. The SS allowed each of the departing prisoners to collect his package from the truck and paid no attention as they spoke to Janina, many to express their thanks for the efforts of the RGO and the Polish Red Cross to help them survive. This allowed Janina to speak relatively freely with her AK contacts who would be on the second transport and knew of the proposal to liberate them, among them Dr. Nowak. She confirmed to them that the operation had been approved and indicated where on the truck they could find maps and instructions. They were all in good spirits, believing that they would soon be free. Their hope strengthened Janina's resolve.[12]

When she saw Zelent, Janina gave him the Tyrolean guard's gift, as well as a letter she had been carrying from Zelent's wife. Although she had stopped doing personal favors for prisoners' relatives, she made an exception for Zelent, whose courage, leadership, and ingenuity in building the camp resistance she deeply admired. She knew he was on the list for the second Gross-Rosen transport, but he informed her that he had managed to have his name removed. He would stay on at Majdanek, which would retain a small number of prisoners for some time longer. Janina questioned his decision, for he had three children, the youngest born after his arrest. "What would you do in my place?" he asked. Janina had to admit that he was right to stay. The Underground needed a contact in Majdanek for as long as it operated, and Zelent was the obvious candidate.[13]

Dr. Ryszard Hanusz approached Janina and furtively handed her his Bible. The brilliant physician had saved many prisoners' lives with a new procedure he developed for treating typhus. But he had been imprisoned in Majdanek since 1941 and in Sachsenhausen before that, and the years of concentration camp life had taken a psychic toll.[14] Tearfully, he begged Janina to find a way to get the Bible to him at Gross-Rosen, for he was absolutely convinced that without it, he would die. Seeing the doctor's desperation, Janina accepted the Bible and assured him that it would be restored to him. She did not admit that she had no idea how to accomplish that.

While she was at Majdanek that day, Janina learned that the camp post office had ceased delivering packages to the compounds after some of its workers shipped out on the first transports. As it happened, Petrak had just been put in charge of the post office, having been transferred away from headquarters after he made critical comments regarding the slaughter of the Jews on November 3. Janina quickly struck a deal with him: she could use her platform trucks to carry packages from the post office to Field III, where the contents of packages for prisoners who had already departed would be distributed. She was able to bring the first batch of packages that same day.[15]

Janina found another report from Majdanek prisoners that evening, and this one had disturbing news. Prisoners in the carpentry workshop were making wooden frames with wire grids the width and height of a freight car. The SS planned to use them to cage prisoners on the Gross-Rosen transports at each end of the train's cars, leaving a space in the middle of each that was the width of the sliding doors. Four SS men would be posted in that space armed with automatic weapons and grenades. There was a rumor that scores of prisoners had escaped from the Natzweiler transport, which might explain why the SS was taking these measures.[16]

The caging of the prisoners would make it much more difficult for them to break out during the attack, Janina realized. On the other hand, the armed units would now know where the SS men were and could shoot into the middle of the freight cars, which would be safer for the prisoners. Although she was happy for the prisoners who escaped the Natzweiler transport, the timing was unfortunate. She wondered whether the escapees used any of the razors and liquor that she smuggled into Field III the day before the transport departed. The tension gripping her was squeezing ever tighter. "Please, let the transport go tomorrow," she thought, "before something else goes wrong."

The next morning, however, Maria notified her that the second Gross-Rosen transport would not leave that day. Perhaps the SS were still outfitting the freight cars, Janina speculated. She received a message from Colonel Łodzia as well, confirming receipt of her latest information and that the plan would go forward. At Majdanek, Janina learned that the transport was scheduled for the next day and that forty-five more SS men had been assigned to guard it. She reported to Colonel Łodzia that fifteen SS men armed with two machine guns would be stationed in each of the forward, middle, and rear freight cars.[17]

Another sleepless night, and then Thursday, April 6, finally dawned in a cold, gray drizzle. The railway timetable indicated that the transport train would leave that afternoon. When Janina and Hanka arrived at Majdanek, the prisoners in Field III were already formed up for the march to the station. Seeing the two women, the members of the committees that had been assigned to distribute the RGO deliveries called out to them. Janina and Hanka went up to the gate and shook hands with the men through the wire. Suddenly, a car horn blasted, a sleek automobile came to a screeching halt behind them, and Thumann and Weiss jumped out.

"What are you doing here?" Thumann shouted in a rage at Janina. "I'm going to shoot you for this!" And he reached for his sidearm.

Weiss put his hand on Thumann's arm. "Do you have a permit?" he demanded of Janina.

"Yes," she replied, and pulled the paper from her pocket. "I am taking official leave of the Polish committees that you approved to distribute the provisions from my organization," she explained, as if the situation were perfectly normal.

"Now you are done and must leave," Weiss informed her. "Even with a permit, you are not allowed at this compound."[18]

Janina and Hanka moved to Field I, from which they would depart for the train station as soon as they saw the prisoners leaving Field III. SS men came marching up to Field III in their shiny black boots, all armed and helmeted, with a skull and crossbones on their collars. Janina's marrow froze at their sight, for with them were packs of dogs, howling like the hounds of hell.[19] Why had she not thought of dogs and provided drugs for them? Hanka began to sob, but Janina urged her to regain self-control.

The prisoners began to march out of Field III, four abreast, filing between the SS. In the front row, Janina saw Dr. Nowak and next to him, holding Nowak's hand, was the renowned pediatrician Dr. Mieczysław Michałowicz. As Janina watched, the frail doctor, nearly seventy, lost one of his wooden clogs in the mud. The SS shouted at him to keep moving, so he went on without it.

The time had come to race to the railway station. But when they got to the road, it was full of prisoners' relatives who had gathered in hope of seeing their loved ones pass by. The horses pulling the truck could not get through. Standing and leaning out of the truck, Janina called out that she was from the RGO and needed to get to the station before the prisoners. Slowly, the crowd gave way and they pushed through to the station. The AK liaison was waiting and immediately departed with Janina's message to Colonel Łodzia.

Janina's part in the plot was done. "It is actually happening!" she thought. And, standing in the station, she broke down in tears, the tension of the past weeks erupting out of her in sobs and gasps. "They will make it," Janina told Hanka. Some would die, Janina knew, but many, perhaps most, would soon be free. "They will make it," she said over and over.

The next day was Good Friday. There were no announcements about an attack on a transport train, and Janina assumed that her comrades would deem it too dangerous to send her a report. She included no contraband in the delivery to Majdanek that day, for her AK contact in Field I had sent a warning about a suspected spy assigned to the labor squad that unloaded the RGO deliveries.

At the gate to Field I, Janina found Dr. Perzanowska standing next to a very pretty young woman with large blue eyes, straight white teeth, and cheeks that looked almost unnaturally pink in a concentration camp. The doctor quickly introduced her.

"This is our Wiśka," she said, using the diminutive form of her name. "Everybody in the compound knows her. She is such a worry-chaser, she can cheer up anybody!" Janina immediately grasped from Perzanowska's tone that Wiśka was the suspected spy. The young woman approached Janina with a charming smile on her red lips and an innocent glow in her blue eyes.

"We shall all be free soon, Countess. One hears that the Russians are already on former Polish territory. They say the Germans in the main administration building are packing. Have you had some more recent news?"

Janina regarded her evenly and replied, "I am not at all interested in these things, only in feeding prisoners, and I am happy to have permission to do that. I hope I can bring in more food for the holidays." And after a pause, she added, "I don't think anyone can complain right now. We must be thankful if it remains as it is. No prisoner need go hungry with the food the RGO brings in. Just looking at you shows it's not so bad at all right now!"

Wiśka tried again, saying wistfully, "If only Thumann weren't here."

"Thumann?" Janina repeated, "I don't deal with him, only with the commandant."

Wiśka gave up and wished Janina a happy Easter. Janina was thankful that the other prisoners had spotted her so quickly and prevented her from seeing the cans with false bottoms.

By the next day, there was still no message about the operation nor any announcement of an attack on a train. Anxiety and doubt were eating at Janina. At Majdanek, she managed to communicate with Zelent. When she heard his news, she wanted to scream: the guards on the transport had just returned, all hale and hearty. There had been no attempt to liberate the train.

After all the planning, work, risk, and sacrifice, nothing had happened. What had gone wrong? The question tortured Janina. When more days passed without any message, she decided that she had to find Elżbieta. All Janina knew about her, however, was that she was a schoolteacher. So, Janina went shopping for lace in the store where her intermediary with Elżbieta worked. Another customer was in the shop when Janina entered. "I'm looking for a doily, blue with lace trim," she told the woman behind the counter. This was the prearranged code. The saleswoman promised to show Janina what she had after she finished with the other customer. But the woman simply could not make up her mind. Finally, the saleswoman said, "I just remembered, Madame, I sold the last blue lace yesterday. But here's the address of my friend's shop. She has exactly what you want." And she handed Janina the address of the school where Elżbieta taught.

Janina found Elżbieta, and learned that her name was Wanda Szupenko. She looked every bit as dejected as Janina felt.

"It was awful," she told Janina. "We didn't find Colonel Łodzia where he was supposed to wait for our message. When we finally found him, he was completely drunk!"

They had begged the colonel to go signal the armed units that were to liberate the transport, but he waved them off and ordered more vodka. At last, he confessed that the operation had never been approved. With no response from the high command to the request for additional forces, the AK District Command had concluded that the plan was too risky to be attempted.[20]

Janina felt overcome with fury and bitterness. The transports provided a unique opportunity to free its imprisoned comrades, but the AK refused to fire a single shot in the attempt. She directed most of her anger at Colonel Łodzia. Why had he misled her into believing that the operation would go forward, causing her to continue risking her life and, even worse, to raise false hopes in the prisoners? She imagined the prisoners who had trusted her riding in the train, whispering to comrades that they would soon be liberated, maintaining readiness for the moment of the attack that never came, and the thought of their hope gradually turning to despair crushed her.

A few days later, Colonel Łodzia appeared in Janina's office after hours. "You have been nominated for the highest military award," he announced.

Janina looked at him coldly. Though she was only a lieutenant and he was her superior officer, she said, "If it comes through your hands, I do not want it. No matter what distinction it is."

Addressing Janina by her AK code name, the Colonel muttered ruefully, "I am sorry, Stefania. You are right, you have a right to tell me whatever you want. I have no excuse."

EIGHTEEN

THE END APPROACHES

April 8, 1944, was Holy Saturday, the day before Easter, when Poles traditionally prepare baskets of food to be blessed by a priest. Commandant Weiss honored his commitment to permit the delivery of special holiday food that day for Majdanek's Polish prisoners, but the camp administration notified Janina that, because the camp was being evacuated, this would be the last time the RGO would be permitted to deliver food to the prisoner compounds. Janina made sure the delivery that day was one that would long be remembered by those who partook of it.[1]

When Janina had put the call out for Easter food for Majdanek prisoners, the people of Lublin responded with their by now customary generosity. Companies that had not donated at Christmas went all out to make up for their earlier negligence. Hams, sausages, honey, candies, chocolate bars, and gingerbread inundated the Lublin Polish Care Committee's storehouse. Janina even persuaded the German authorities to allocate 2,300 kilograms of sugar, 1,200 kilograms of wheat flour, plus marmalade and candies for the Easter meal at Majdanek. Each of the 2,300 Polish prisoners remaining at Majdanek received a parcel containing, in addition to cold cuts, cookies, and sweets, one babka and two eggs. There were flowers and Easter lambs as well. Children in the care committee's shelters decorated the eggs and lambs, which a priest blessed. The hot meal that day consisted of borscht with beans, barley with bacon, and sausage.

When they delivered the Easter food to Majdanek, Janina and Hanka received permission to share an egg with a prisoner in each compound, in accordance with Polish custom. This provided the opportunity for Janina and Perzanowska to make their farewells, for it seemed unlikely that they would see each other again. The doctor had elected to remain with her patients, and they were to leave for Auschwitz in a few days. Perzanowska had come to feel an intimate friendship with Countess Suchodolska, as well as deep admiration for her courage and tireless dedication to helping the prisoners.

Janina held the doctor in the same regard, and as a last favor to her friend had brought with the delivery the mother of Alinka, a young nurse whom Perzanowska had taken under her wing. Both the mother and the daughter had received stern warnings not to speak or signal to each other. When Alinka approached to unload the truck on which her mother sat, the two locked eyes for a moment and began to cry silently. As she handed down items from the truck with hands wet from her tears, Alinka whispered constantly, "Mommy, Mommy, Mommy," while Perzanowska loudly counted each item.

During her deliveries to the compounds that day, many prisoners asked Janina to thank the RGO and the Polish Red Cross on their behalf. Because of the efforts of both organizations, prisoners expressed confidence that they had the strength and health to survive whatever was to come. Their thanks depressed Janina, however. How many of the prisoners she had been providing for really would survive, she wondered, now that none were to be liberated by the AK and all were going far out of the reach of the advancing Red Army? Not all, surely; perhaps not even most. All her effort and risk, it seemed, had been for naught.

The same feeling overcame her later that day, when she went to the train station to watch 2,700 prisoners depart for Auschwitz. After the train left, many of the friends and relatives of the transported prisoners who had come to see their loved ones off crowded around Janina, blessing her for all she had done to help the prisoners survive, until she was finally able to break free and flee back to her office. There she spent the evening thinking of how she could continue to help the former Majdanek prisoners. She had been collecting as much information as she could about who was on the transports, especially her AK colleagues. She forwarded the names of those sent to Auschwitz to Countess Laskowska in Kraków, who was in charge of the Underground's care for prisoners there.

Janina had hoped to send packages to the prisoners consigned to other camps. The SS informed her, however, that the RGO could not provide for Poles who were in camps outside the General Government. At those camps, the SS only permitted packages from family members. As usual, to Janina this refusal simply meant that she had to find another way to achieve her goal. So she recruited women to pose as the wives, mothers, and sisters of former Majdanek prisoners and to send them packages prepared by the Lublin Polish Care Committee. When the parcels reached the former Majdanek prisoners, other Polish prisoners sought to receive them as well, and Janina's volunteers received information about hundreds of other prisoners hoping to acquire relatives who would send them food.[2]

To help the women prisoners leaving Majdanek, Janina planned to hide money in the extra rations that transport prisoners picked up at the food warehouses as they marched out of the camp. The funds were provided by the government in exile delegation in Warsaw. The representative who brought the money marveled as he watched Janina and Hanka insert it into hundreds of little bags of butter.

"Bringing this money to you, I was in constant fear that I would be searched and arrested," he said, "but here you two are, packing money into little bags for the concentration camp as if you were doing nothing more than rolling bandages for a hospital. Your chance of being caught inside the camp is ten times greater than that of a courier traveling on the train from Warsaw to Lublin! Are you really unaware of the risk you are taking, or are you simply resigned to your fate?"

Janina did not know what to make of his question. Did he really have no idea of what they had been doing at Majdanek for the past year?

"Well," she finally replied, "it is neither ignorance nor resignation, but the conviction that what we are doing is right and must be done. Our confidence comes from our knowledge of what this money can do for the prisoners. We've often seen how helpful money can be, even in a camp: to bribe an SS guard or a kapo, or to exchange for food."

In the end, however, the women prisoners did not receive the funds. Janina learned that the kapo in charge of the rations at the warehouse was the prisoner she mistrusted because his offers to help were so insistent and indiscreet. All she could find out about him was that he was not a member of the Underground, and none of her comrades could vouch for him. The risk of betrayal was too great, she concluded, and so she had the bags withdrawn from the rations delivered to the warehouses.

Majdanek was not the only camp in Lublin to receive Easter fare thanks to Janina's efforts. On Easter Sunday, she hosted a holiday dinner at the Krochmalna Street transit camp. It was a major affair, lasting five hours and attended by the head of the district Labor Office, the district medical superintendent, and the commandant of the camp and his deputy. Janina gave formal remarks to all those in attendance, then a representative of the detainees responded, thanking Janina and the RGO for taking them under their protection. They all shared the eggs supplied by the Lublin Polish Care Committee and then dined on borscht and noodles with poppy seeds. Afterward, Janina, Wójcikowa, and three other RGO representatives distributed packages and clothes to the detainees. Although the mood was generally festive, there was some weeping among both the men and the women as they recalled past Easters in homes and with loved ones they would never see again. Some of the detainees asked the RGO representatives to autograph postcards for their families.[3]

The end of the RGO's massive feeding program at Majdanek threatened to put many of the employees involved in it out of work, but Skrzyński managed to obtain funds so that the Lublin Polish Care Committee could retain them. Soon, there was more than enough work to occupy them. In early May, 1,300 new refugees from Volhynia were placed in the Krochmalna camp and under RGO care. Hundreds more refugees followed from both Volhynia and the district, now fleeing the advance of Soviet forces as well as ethnic violence. Krochmalna could not possibly process them all, and so transports arriving at the Lublin station were regularly being sent on to other districts. Janina obtained permission to set up a care center in the station, where the Lublin Polish Care Committee provided hot meals, packages, and medical assistance to the refugees who were passing through. It was even possible to transfer the seriously injured and ill to local hospitals and to keep their families in Lublin while they recovered.[4]

The memory of Dr. Hanusz's tear-stained face begging her to get him his Bible haunted Janina. She could think of no way to smuggle it to him in Gross-Rosen, and it could not be sent in a package without being discovered and removed by the SS. Would it be possible to get the Bible to Hanusz through some official channel? From Zelent, Janina learned that Hanusz had been on good terms with Dr. Heinrich Rindfleisch, who had replaced Blancke as Majdanek's chief doctor. Perzanowska considered Rindfleisch to be the best of the SS doctors, actually capable of being humane. Janina decided to take her chances, and during a visit to Majdanek managed to find Rindfleisch in his office.[5]

She pleaded her case with the doctor, telling him that she was appealing to him not as an SS official but as a physician. "Would you refuse a sick man a harmless medicine he craved, even if you knew scientifically that it could be of no benefit?"

The doctor sprang to his feet before Janina finished. "I am a captain in the SS!"

"And a physician," Janina quickly added.

"How can you expect me to take this to him when you know it is against regulations?"

"What about your doctor's oath?" Janina rejoined. "Haven't you sworn to help the sick with every means in your power? And Hanusz is a sick man, sick unto death, and you are the only physician who can help him!" She wondered whether she had gone too far.

Rindfleisch paced the room, then asked to inspect the Bible. "Are there any markings in it?"

Janina handed it over and he inspected it carefully.

"All right," he finally sighed, "I'll take it to him, provided that I go where they have sent him. But," he added sternly, "if anyone ever finds out about this, be assured that an SS officer will know where to find you, Madame!"

He quickly left the room, and Janina hurried out as well, before anyone could see her and ask what she had been doing there.[6]

On April 19, the women's camp was officially closed when its last remaining prisoners departed on a transport to Ravensbrück. Only 180 male prisoners remained, 90 of them Poles, all housed in Field I. In addition, Field II held about 1,500 wounded Red Army soldiers in a special convalescent hospital that the SS had established for propaganda purposes. Fields III, IV, and V were empty.[7] Thumann and Weiss left in early May.[8]

Majdanek's post office closed as well, so it was no longer possible to bring or mail packages for the prisoners to the camp. However, Janina obtained permission to provide a weekly package for each of the remaining Polish prisoners, which Petrak agreed to pick up from the RGO at Lubartowska Street. In practice, he would arrange for the packages to be picked up whenever Janina called and told him they were ready, so the prisoners received packages almost daily.[9]

This arrangement ended suddenly in mid-May, when Arthur Liebehenschel replaced Weiss as Majdanek's commandant. Just a year earlier, Liebehenschel had been the second highest official in the Inspectorate of Concentration Camps, which oversaw the entire SS camp system. Then he abandoned his wife just before the birth of their fourth child for a secretary in the inspectorate office who was fifteen years his junior. Even worse, it was discovered that the secretary had been arrested years earlier on suspicion of having relations with a Jew. Himmler was scandalized. Liebehenschel was dismissed from his post and transferred to Auschwitz in November 1943, where he served as commandant of the main camp, with supervisory authority over the killing center at Birkenau. His mistress soon joined him and became pregnant. When Liebehenschel refused orders to separate from her and applied to marry her in April 1944, he was punished with the assignment to Majdanek.[10]

Liebehenschel was outraged when he learned that Polish charitable organizations had regularly provided food and medicines for Majdanek prisoners. There were to be no more such arrangements, he ordered, and that applied to the provision of packages as well. He even threatened to arrest anyone from the RGO or the Polish Red Cross who attempted to enter the camp.

Once again, Petrak came to Janina's aid. Disobeying Liebehenschel's order, he regularly came to Lubartowska Street in the evening to pick up packages that he personally delivered to the prisoners. Janina recognized that this was not a sustainable arrangement, however. Petrak could only carry a few packages at a time, and it seemed probable that he would be discovered, which would end all chances of getting permission for any kind of assistance to Majdanek prisoners. After repeated efforts, she finally obtained an appointment to meet with Liebehenschel.

Father Michalski accompanied Janina to the meeting. When they entered the commandant's office, all they could see of him was his back as he stood looking out a window. He neither turned nor spoke, even when Janina greeted him. Hostility seemed to radiate out of the man. Acting as if the situation were perfectly natural, Janina began explaining the purpose of her visit. Suddenly, the commandant erupted.

"What do you think you're doing here?" he screamed, still facing the window. "Do you imagine this is a sanatorium for bandits and enemies of our country? Is that why you keep coming here as if it were a drawing room or something? Feeding these criminals, as if they were the most precious people on earth! This is sheer Polish insolence. Don't you know that this is a concentration camp? Do you think it's a mess hall for gentlemen? You and your committee," he spat, "we should look into your activities. We should investigate all of you, including your precious charges! Those darlings that you are feeding with such dedication—why, they look much better off than our soldiers! They're healthy and strong, don't do a stitch of work all day long and are being fed like princes!"

Janina was all too familiar with such tantrums from German officials. After Liebehenschel's tirade ended, she moved to the other window in the office and, with her back to him, calmly continued. "We are an institution approved by the German authorities to care for the needy among the Polish population, and whatever we have done in Majdanek has been with the agreement of the camp administration."

 1

Janina Mehlberg, ca. 1930s.

 2

Photo ca. 1925–1926 of the students of Kazimierz Twardowski at Jan Kazimierz University in Lwów. Janina Mehlberg is in the bottom row, far right; Henry Mehlberg is in the top row, far left.

3

Henry (then Henryk) Mehlberg, ca. 1936. The photo was included in an album created by Kazimierz Twardowski's students in honor of their professor.

4

Wedding photo of Andrzej Skrzyński with his fourth wife, Zofia Mycielska Skrzyńska, in Wrocław, 1964.

5

A warning sign in German and Polish at Majdanek.

6

Aerial view of Majdanek showing workshops and warehouses in the center and, just above, Field I on the right and the bathing and disinfection facility with the gas chambers on the left. The "Black Road" runs from above the upper left corner of Field I to the Chełm Road.

7

Prisoners' barracks in one of Majdanek's compounds.

8

View of guard towers, fence, and crematorium chimney at Majdanek.

9

“Pacification” of a Polish village, either Biłgoraj or Zamość County (*Kreis*), Lublin District, June–July 1943.

10

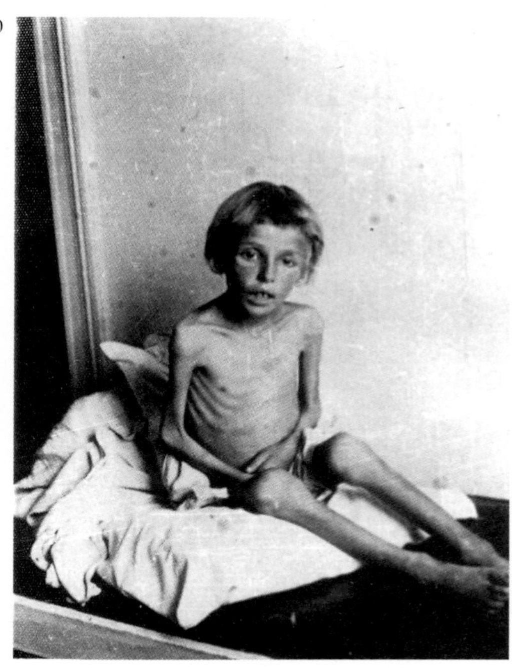

Ania Rempa, a Polish girl from Zamość, released from Majdanek in August 1943. She did not survive.

11

View from the village of Dziesiąta of smoke from the burning of corpses at Majdanek.

12

View of the Zamek prison after the German retreat from Lublin in 1944.

13

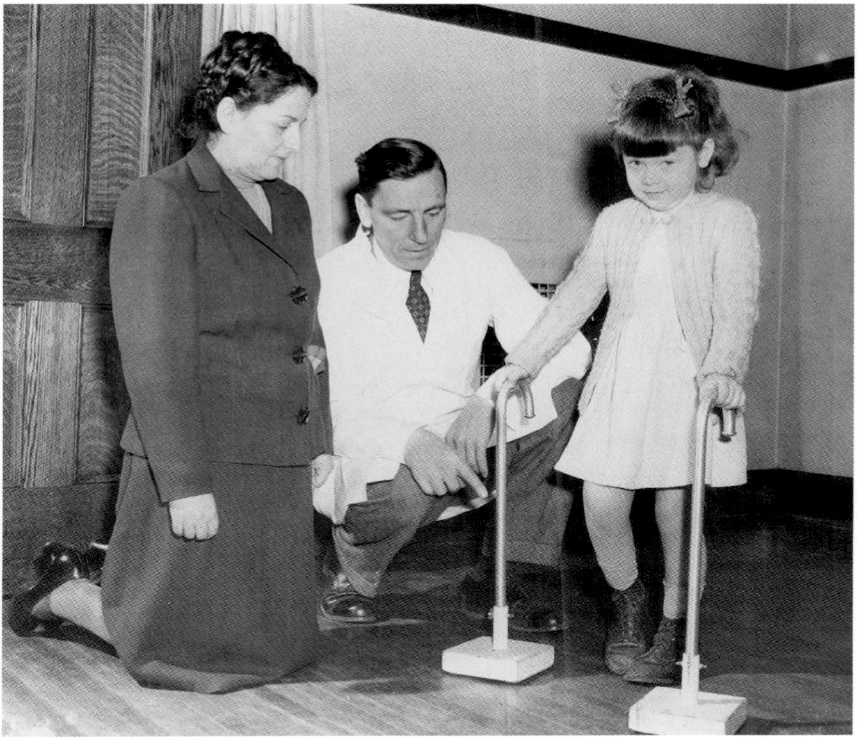

Janina Mehlberg (then known as Suchodolska) tours a Minneapolis school for children with disabilities in 1948. Janina's visit was part of her United Nations fellowship.

14

Photo of Janina and Henry Mehlberg, ca. 1950s.

15

Janina and Henry Mehlberg (middle) with their prewar friend Joseph Klinghofer and his son, Irvin, in Canada, 1961. Joseph was also a Holocaust survivor and assisted the Mehlbergs' emigration to Canada.

16

Photograph of Professor Josephine Mehlberg teaching a mathematics class at Illinois Institute of Technology, ca. 1960.

"Not anymore!" Liebehenschel barked.

Janina was not about to back down. "Perhaps, if there's no need for soup now, we could just send some packages," she suggested reasonably.

"You Polacks!" he shrieked, expressing all his scorn and loathing with the pejorative term. "We throw you out one door and presto, you come in by another!" Then, nonplussed by Janina's cool persistence, he shouted. "I can't hear what you're mumbling there. You're talking to the window!"

Janina turned. "And I don't hear you too well either, Herr *Kommandant*, and perhaps that is why we can't seem to come to an understanding."

At that, Liebehenschel turned to face her for the first time, and, after studying her for a moment, gestured for her to sit down. Uninvited, Father Michalski also took a seat. Janina proceeded to explain to the commandant how the RGO's help would be to his advantage as well. "You have said yourself," she pointed out, "that the people still here were kept to maintain order in the camp. You surely realize that well-fed workers are more efficient than underfed ones. If you consider soup superfluous, I won't insist on it. I could provide packages instead."

He gave up and said gruffly, "Packages, all right, but no luxuries. Only what prisoners in other camps get, nothing extra!"

Janina stood up as tall as she could and replied with dignity, "Then I shall inquire what others are getting, although I can assure you, sir, that I have quite a few years' experience in feeding prisoners." She was glad to have won this much. "May I please have a list of the prisoners to whom we may send the packages?" She already knew who they were, but the list would provide a legitimate basis for her knowledge.

The delivery of food packages for Majdanek's Polish prisoners resumed. On his own initiative, Petrak even allowed the RGO to bring the packages to the camp post office. Since one of the prisoners assigned to carry them to Field I was Janina's AK comrade Czesław Kulesza, Janina was back in occasional contact with the prisoners.

But now there were hundreds more Poles at Majdanek who were not counted in the official rolls of the concentration camp. The Wehrmacht had set up a forced labor camp in Field V to hold the workers it was drafting to build fortifications around Lublin. Most of them were peasants from nearby villages, seized at a moment's notice and interned in the camp with no way to communicate with their families. As soon as she learned of the camp, Janina went to see the German general in charge of the fortifications program to request permission to feed the prisoners. The general insisted that the prisoners' food was adequate and offered Janina the opportunity to interview some of them at a worksite, but only if she spoke to them in German. Janina refused, for the prisoners would not understand her and would view her as collaborating with the Germans. The general relented and allowed Janina to interview the forced laborers in Polish regarding their food and work. The men confirmed that they were receiving sufficient food, but some were obviously too old or weak to perform heavy labor and many had suffered injuries, especially to their feet, because their shoes had worn to tatters. All of them were desperate to get in touch with their families. Janina took down the addresses of the men she spoke to so that she could inform their families that they were in Majdanek.[11]

Janina returned to the Wehrmacht command, this time to a major with authority over the camp in Field V. She proposed that the RGO supply shoes and clothes for the prisoners, postcards that they could send to their families, and a physician to examine their fitness for labor. The last proposal was a concession that she had won for the Krochmalna Street camp, but it was too much for the major, and he refused all three of her requests. In the meantime, as a result of the letters she had written, the relatives of prisoners in the Wehrmacht camp were besieging Janina's office with pleas for help in getting their loved ones released. Local authorities applied to her as well, complaining that the Wehrmacht had left almost no one to tend the fields and so the county would face starvation in the fall.

Undeterred by the major's rejection of her proposals, Janina succeeded in getting another interview with the general. She won his permission to supply shoes and postcards for the prisoners in the Field V camp, and for the prisoners to receive packages from their families. The RGO would be responsible for delivering and distributing the packages and for retrieving and mailing the postcards. The general even ordered that a Wehrmacht physician be assigned to attend to the prisoners in the camp, stipulating that all the medicines and supplies he ordered be provided by the RGO.

The general's approval of all her requests only encouraged Janina to ask for more. She presented one additional proposal: instead of keeping the same contingent of forced laborers in the camp, the Wehrmacht could allow local authorities to assign rotating contingents of laborers who would work on the fortifications for a few days at a time and return to work their fields when the next contingent replaced them. This the general refused out of hand, probably assuming that the matter was now closed. Janina, of course, had no intention of letting it drop.

With the general's permission to distribute shoes, postcards, and packages, Janina once again had access to Majdanek, though only to Field V and via a different road than the one that ran alongside the other compounds. When the Wehrmacht doctor first arrived at Field V, Janina was already there with several assistants, handing out postcards to the prisoners and writing down their addresses and physical complaints. She encouraged prisoners who were sick or injured to go speak with the German doctor, who quickly found himself surrounded by people clamoring to him in a language he did not understand. Janina then introduced herself to the doctor and offered to supply him with an interpreter. His grateful acceptance of her offer led her to conclude that he had some decency. From that point on, the doctor was never at Majdanek without an RGO employee by his side.

By June, there were at least 1,500 forced laborers in Field V, including women and girls. Unsurprisingly, illnesses were spreading rapidly among them, requiring an infirmary to be established. The Wehrmacht could supply no extra doctors, however, or even any nurses. The overwhelmed Wehrmacht physician accepted Janina's proposal that the RGO provide nurses for the infirmary as well as a doctor to be his assistant. The RGO had no trouble finding nurses willing to work shifts at Majdanek.

These arrangements provided new opportunities for rescuing prisoners. The RGO's physician made rounds prior to the arrival of the German doctor and used the time to instruct patients about the symptoms of certain diseases. The Wehrmacht doctor treated the Polish physician as his colleague and agreed with his diagnoses. When Janina pointed out that it made little sense for the Wehrmacht to feed and house people who couldn't work, the doctor agreed and signed forms certifying that patients were unfit for labor. With these in hand, Janina succeeded in persuading the authorities to release the patients into the RGO's care.

Over two weeks, Janina arranged for four hundred prisoners to be released in this way, including all the minors. Then the major visited and found that the camp was missing over one quarter of its prisoners. "This is sabotage!" he said accusingly to Janina.

"We have nothing to do with it," Janina replied. "Your own doctor certified that all those released were unfit."

Then she broached the proposal for local authorities to supply laborers who would work on the fortifications for a few days each week in exchange for the forced laborers in the camp. The major finally agreed to the assignment of temporary workers, but would only permit the release from the camp of prisoners certified by the Wehrmacht physician as unable to work.

That evening, Janina was in Field V, distributing packages and postcards to the prisoners returning from work, when she heard a German officer make an announcement via an interpreter: "All prisoners willing to stay in the camp and work should come forward and be registered. All others will be deported." This was a bluff, Janina knew, intended to deter the prisoners from reporting sick, for they all feared being sent far away from their families. She was standing near the rear of the assembled prisoners and proceeded to squeeze her way between them from row to row, warning them in a staccato whisper not to fall for the trap. She could hear her message being passed farther on. Then she waited in suspense for the result. No one stepped forward to be registered.

"All right then," the officer announced, "tomorrow your names will be taken for the deportation transports." This sham order was withdrawn two days later.

To the prisoners remaining in Field V, Countess Suchodolska was their comforter and protector. They found out her first name and on her name day they gathered to greet her when she arrived. They had taken up a collection from the meager wages that prisoners received and pressed it on her, asking that she use it to buy packages for the neediest outside the camp. The desire of these people, enduring captivity and forced labor, to be of help to others so touched Janina that she wept. Some of the prisoners gave her letters expressing their thanks. The wording of one, written in an awkward scrawl, stayed with her for decades:

> May each smile that you brought to a child's face, may each tear that you helped wipe from a wife's or a mother's eyes, be counted in your favor before the throne of the Almighty. May each of your wishes, you who are an example for Polish womanhood, be granted. May you be spared and saved. Throughout the ages, Amen.
>
> Wojciech Sobol

In mid-June, Janina received a message from Kulesza, her AK comrade in Field I. Several hundred women and children were imprisoned in the compound, in barracks surrounded by barbed wire. They were peasants seized in pacification operations. Some of their men were in the compound as well, held separate from their families and subjected to regular interrogations by the Gestapo. They were not being fed by the Majdanek SS, because they were not classified as concentration camp prisoners, and they were beginning to starve. Kulesza and the other Polish prisoners were providing them with the contents of the packages they were receiving from the RGO, but he begged Janina to find some way to help the pacification prisoners.[12]

Liebehenschel refused to see Janina, claiming he had no responsibility for the peasants. After inquiring at various offices, Janina concluded that she would have to apply to the Gestapo. This meant she would have to go "under the clock," to the Gestapo headquarters in Lublin.

On the day of her appointment there, Janina took Wójcikowa with her, but left her to wait on a bench outside. From the reception desk, Janina was escorted under armed guard through heavy iron doors to an office where a Gestapo officer awaited her. He asked her to state her business.

"To feed the civilians being held in Majdanek—" she began, but he immediately interrupted her.

"Majdanek is not under our jurisdiction. You're wasting your time."

"But the commandant of Majdanek himself directed me to you because these inmates are under Gestapo jurisdiction," she lied.

"You know very well," he answered, "that we keep our prisoners in

Zamek. Only after they're found guilty do they go to Majdanek." With increasing anger, he added, "And there are so many of your bandits that even your prisons can't hold them all and we've had to make camps for them. German soldiers die in battle, German civilians die from bombings, and here we keep your criminals in camps and feed them!"

As usual, Janina waited patiently for this harangue to end. Assuming an air of quiet authority, she continued, "There are prisoners in Majdanek, including women and children, who are under Gestapo jurisdiction. I represent the Polish organization authorized by the Security Police to care for prisoners in the General Government. I therefore request permission to provide food for these prisoners."

The official called around on the office intercom but could find no one who knew anything about what was happening in Majdanek. Another official arrived, and the two interrogated Janina about her identity and activities. She showed no emotion as she answered them. Finally, from the various conversations she overheard, she concluded that she would need to consult a Gestapo officer named Rohlfing, who was not in the building. So she left and retrieved Wójcikowa from the pretty little park that the Germans had created across from the building. "Just like the Germans," she thought, "to plant flowers before the gates of Hell."

On her return visit "under the clock," Janina left Father Michalski on the park bench. Her surmise that SS Second Lieutenant Rohlfing was the official she needed to speak with turned out to be correct. He was in charge of disposing of the people seized in pacification operations who were not shot for supporting the partisans. Only the able-bodied interested him, since he was charged with sending as many as possible to the Reich. Prior to this assignment, Hermann Rohlfing had charge of creating a camp in the woods outside Chełm, about forty-five miles east of Lublin, that served as both a cremation and an execution site. Jewish prisoners whom he personally selected during the Operation Harvest Festival massacre at Majdanek were forced to dig up mass graves and burn the corpses they contained, as well as the bodies of fresh victims brought to the site to be shot or murdered on the way there in gas vans. Rohlfing eradicated the evidence of tens of thousands of murders committed by the Germans of Soviet and Italian POWs as well as Jews and Poles.[13]

When Janina presented her proposal to Rohlfing, he reacted in typical German fashion. "What! You want to feed these bandits? You could be arrested yourself for asking such a thing. How dare you!"

"We have been taking care of prisoners for years," Janina explained calmly. "And besides, they're not all bandits. I saw some who were only this high," she added, holding her hand to indicate a child's height.

"How do you know that?" Rohlfing roared. "Who's your spy in there?"

"I have often visited Field V, and in the distance I noticed children and was surprised, because I didn't think they could have been convicted of any crimes."

At that moment, the air was split by a heart-stopping scream that died out in a gurgle. Janina knew that interrogations occurred on the same floor, but suspected that the sound might have been staged to frighten her. But then a nasty-looking SS man entered, juggling his gun from one hand to the other. "I put him to sleep," he reported with a smirk.

Rohlfing told the man of Janina's inquiry about some children at Majdanek. He smiled, then said he would go check. After a moment, he returned and confirmed Janina's report. Rohlfing acted surprised, claiming this was the first he had heard of the situation and promising to contact Majdanek's commandant about permitting help for the children. Janina did not believe his claim of ignorance but was satisfied. If she could get permission to feed the children, she would find a way to feed the adults as well.

In fact, after he heard from Rohlfing, Liebehenschel permitted the RGO to deliver packages for all the victims of pacification operations being held in Field I. As she had the summer before with the Zamość civilians in Majdanek, Janina persuaded the Security Police to release some of the women and children to the RGO on the grounds that they were not guilty of any crimes and were unfit for labor.[14]

Meanwhile, thanks to the arrangements Janina had set up at Krochmalna, Polish refugees were being routinely released, either because the RGO physicians found them in need of hospitalization or unfit for labor, or because they were family members of the sick or unfit, or because Lublin employers had claimed them as workers. The RGO was winning the release of as many as 95 percent of the Polish refugees. It was unable to do anything for the Ukrainian and Belarusian refugees, however, who were transported to the Reich for forced labor. It was also difficult to gain the release of young, able-bodied people who lacked labor cards and had been seized for work in the Reich. Janina sought to identify members of the AK among them and rescue them. Her contact in the Labor Office, an ethnic German woman, provided false labor cards and sent alerts about impending raids.[15]

In mid-July, Janina received notice from Rohlfing that she was to pick up a group of the pacification prisoners from Field I who were being released to the RGO. On her way to Majdanek, however, she spotted Father Michalski rushing down the street and frantically trying to flag her down. He had just been at Krochmalna and reported that Rohlfing was there and in a rage after finding that he could pack off only a tiny percentage of the Polish detainees to the Reich. He was yelling that "the goddamn bandits" were feigning sickness to be released and then rejoining their units.

"He's now screaming threats against you," Michalski warned Janina. "He blames you for everything. He kept shouting that he would have you arrested and that he was coming for you after he finished with the bandits."

The priest tearfully begged Janina not to go to Majdanek, fearing that Rohlfing would have her seized there. Janina was frightened, but saw no alternative. She could not leave those people in the camp, and only she was authorized to take custody of them.

When she arrived at Majdanek, Janina found the prisoners to be released already waiting at the guardhouse. She asked the guard whether someone would come to release them to her, but all he knew was that they no longer belonged in the camp and she was supposed to take them. So she had them board the truck and drove off.

Knowing that the Gestapo made arrests at night, Janina stopped sleeping at home, although she still went to the office during the day. No one showed up at her residence to arrest her, however. The Soviets were on the offensive again, and the Germans had other things to worry about.

NINETEEN

BLOOD ON THE STAIRS

On July 18, 1944, there was a giant traffic jam in Lublin's streets. Military convoys and tanks were heading in one direction to take up positions against the advancing Red Army. Heading in the other direction were German civilians in cars, trucks, and wagons piled high with the loot they had seized in Poland. Germans filled the city's main rail station, pushing and shoving to board the last trains departing for the Reich. The German occupation of Lublin was disintegrating.

Janina no longer lived at 22 Narutowicza Street, for the Germans had confiscated the building, giving the residents forty-eight hours to move out. Thanks to her position in the RGO, she had been allotted quarters in the German district, in a building just off Hitler-Platz. She had arranged for her "aunties," Countess Władysława and Madame Maria, to obtain housing there as well. When Janina walked out of the building that morning and saw the commotion in the streets, she decided to investigate what was happening with the German administration, using business with the BuF office as a pretext.

In the courtyard of the district administration building, Janina found the BuF secretary, Frau Stiefler, surrounded by files whose pages she was hurriedly feeding to a fire. Janina asked to see her boss.

"He isn't here today, come back tomorrow," Stiefler snapped. The woman had always treated Janina with icy disdain. But then she turned, and Janina saw that her face was etched with anxiety, her lips trembling, and her eyes filling with tears.

"Whatever is the matter, Frau Stiefler?" Janina asked in a sympathetic tone.

"Don't you know that the Bolsheviks are quite near?" Stiefler answered. "Tomorrow we'll all be leaving. The bosses have already left, but I still have some things to do before I go." Then, sobbing, she warned Janina of the horrors committed by Soviet soldiers and urged her to fill out a travel permit for herself, which the office manager could authorize.

Taking leave of Frau Stiefler, Janina went into the building, which seemed eerily quiet. The office manager was not there. Janina wandered about, knocking on various doors, and peeking inside when no one answered. Empty file drawers hung open, trash and sheets of paper were strewn about, but Janina could find no German officials. It appeared that they had all fled, leaving Frau Stiefler behind to destroy the records of their activities.

Janina hurried on to her office. Her workload had expanded in early June, when the RGO received an order to take over all of the prisoner care activities of the Polish Red Cross. The Germans decided that only an organization under their direct control should have access to their prisons, not one that answered to an international body. Skrzyński had pleaded for the transfer to be postponed. He argued that the Lublin RGO could not afford to buy all the materials and medicines that the Polish Red Cross had been supplying or to pay the extra employees needed to acquire and distribute them. The Germans refused. Nevertheless, Christians blamed Skrzyński for what he viewed as a usurpation of his authority.[1]

As a result of the change, Janina was now overseeing the provision of all packages, medicines, and medical equipment for Polish prisoners in Zamek, the nineteenth-century neo-Gothic castle built as a prison. Although it was designed to hold 700 prisoners, there were generally 2,000 to 3,000 there, held in conditions of starvation, disease, and utter squalor. Hundreds of new prisoners had been flowing into the castle in the past two months, mostly captured Polish partisans or Poles accused of resistance activities.

The overall number of prisoners did not change, however, for prisoners had been flowing out of the prison just as quickly, in buses and vans that took them to Majdanek. Not to the camp, though, but straight to the crematorium. At least one of the transports was a gas van that asphyxiated its passengers en route. The other prisoners were shot in the crematorium or in nearby trenches.[2]

Between July 19 and 21, the transports traveled constantly back and forth between Zamek and the Majdanek crematorium, whose five ovens were insufficient to dispose of all the bodies. The order had gone out to the Security Police that no prisoners should fall into the hands of the enemy. Any prisoners who could not be evacuated were to be "liquidated," and the bodies of those shot should be destroyed, whether through burning or by blowing up the prisons where they were murdered. The liquidation order particularly applied to all the Jewish tailors, cobblers, and carpenters being held in Zamek. They had been spared from Operation Harvest Festival in order to produce clothing and furniture for the Security Police.

On the morning of July 22, the people of Lublin could hear artillery fire, which steadily grew louder. Many of them took to basements and shelters, preparing for the battle that was about to engulf the city. Janina went to the office, however, for she had a vital task to complete. A courier was leaving that day for the Underground delegation in Warsaw, probably the last one to travel out of Lublin. She wanted him to take the lists she had been preparing that contained the names, addresses, and precise prisoner numbers of all the concentration camp prisoners to whom Janina and her committee of volunteers had been sending packages.

It was shortly after noon when the courier set off with the lists. Janina allowed herself to relax for a moment and savor the thought that the Germans would soon be gone, if not that day, then in the next few days. And she and Henry were still alive. They had defied the odds, after all.

Dąbrowski entered to relate to Janina what had just happened in his office. A man in Wehrmacht uniform had rushed in, claiming that he had been imprisoned in Zamek and that there had been a massacre there that morning. Dąbrowski was saying that he didn't believe the man, probably he was an *agent provocateur*. . . . But Janina was already out the door and flying down the stairs. She ran around the corner and started down Kowalska Street. The buildings at the top gave way to piles of debris and then fields of rubble, all that was left of the four-hundred-year-old Jewish quarter. Above this desolate landscape loomed Zamek.

Relatives of prisoners were milling about outside the outer wall. Although the entry next to the gatehouse stood open, they feared to enter. Seeing Janina running toward them, some called to her, "The Germans have left time bombs inside!"

Janina continued running up to the gate, and the cries from the crowd became louder and more urgent. "Don't go in there, don't go in, Countess! You'll die in there! They're all dead inside. That's what they want, to finish you off in there." Some dropped to their knees to pray.

Janina saw them but could not stop. She ran through the gate and toward the great arch that led to the castle's interior courtyard. The doors were open, and the Polish custodian was standing inside, holding a ring of keys. He motioned her to the left, "Straight ahead here, Countess, there might be wounded in the hospital hall."

Janina charged ahead but only saw empty beds. Her youngest assistant appeared at her side, having followed Janina from the office. Janina was surprised, for she had always thought the girl rather timid. Seeing a movement in the corner of a cell, they turned over a mattress and found a woman lying under it, still alive but too injured to move on her own. With a shock, Janina recognized her: she was a teacher at a public school in the city. Janina and her assistant half dragged, half carried the woman outside the gates. Then Janina sent her assistant back to the RGO building to fetch help and went searching for a working phone. She found one and called the Polish Red Cross to send ambulances.

She did not wait but ran back into the castle, noticing a wisp of smoke rising from the right side of the building. In the interior courtyard, she ran toward the far left corner, where she knew there were cells with political prisoners. She passed a few bodies lying in pools of blood as she sprinted to the entrance to the ward. Then she stopped. A rippling pool of blood was spreading before her, fed by rivulets of blood that were flowing down the stairs. The air was thick with the stench of a slaughterhouse.

Now she knew where she had to go. Stepping into the pool, she began to climb the stairs, clutching the railing so as not to slip. At the top, she followed the blood to her right and came upon a cell whose door was standing open. Inside were piles of twisted bodies, at least a hundred it seemed, some with skulls shattered from bullet wounds. Janina heard moans and cries and realized that the quick and the dead were mixed together. Others now joined her, and they began trying to extricate the victims who still lived. Janina followed the blood, now ankle-deep, to the end of the corridor. In a large chamber, bodies were stacked in piles more than six feet high. She estimated at least 150. Strewn between the bodies were overturned sewing machines. Some of the corpses, Janina realized, wore armbands marking them as Jews. These were the Jewish tailors, who had so long evaded the fate visited upon their families, only to be murdered at the last moment.

More victims showing signs of life were being pulled out of the piles of bodies. "How many more were still alive but being crushed to death by the weight of the corpses?" Janina wondered. "And which of those being pulled out stood a chance of surviving and should be tended to first?" The castle was shaking from the impact of shells falling nearby. There was no time to waste, she decided; a doctor needed to come immediately to conduct triage. She ran back to the working telephone to call the Lublin Polish Care Committee's physician, but she could not reach him. What doctor could she find who would risk the growing danger in the city to come to this hell?

Janina went out to search the nearby streets. A couple was hurrying by, and the man bore the insignia of a medical officer. Janina stopped him and asked him to go with her. They looked at her in horror. Janina did not understand how frightening she must appear, her clothes splattered with blood and her squelching shoes leaving bloody footprints behind her.

"Don't go, darling," the woman urged, "you'll get killed there. What's the use of having survived the occupation only to perish now?"

Janina fixed the man with a steady gaze. He knew he had a duty to go, as a physician and as a Pole, and that others would know and judge him if he neglected his duty. He went with Janina.

Back in the castle, people were laying the victims out in the courtyard, and relatives were searching among them for their loved ones. Janina saw a mother embracing the wounded head of her son, softly moaning as she wiped blood from his pale face. Nearby, an old man stood over the body of a young boy, screaming "Save my grandson! Save my grandson!" But no one came to his aid, for they were all tending to their own wounded and murdered, and the grandson was obviously dead.

Looking back toward the entrance, Janina saw that the wisp of smoke she had spotted earlier had become a billowing cloud, and she could detect a burning smell. "This place must not burn and take with it the evidence of the crimes committed here!" she thought. She dashed back to the telephone to call the fire department. It took some persuading to get the fire chief to send his crews, but Janina succeeded and the fire was extinguished.

But now the battle had reached the outskirts of Lublin and it had become too dangerous to continue searching for the living. About fifteen of those who had been found were carried on stretchers to the RGO building on Lubartowska Street to await transfer to hospitals. Relatives who found the corpses of their loved ones quickly carted them away. The rest of the victims, some three hundred, had to be left in the castle while the battle of Lublin raged. Only three days later would it be possible to retrieve them.

TWENTY

THE END

When Janina arrived home on July 22, 1944, the residents of her building were already sheltering in the basement, along with a Wehrmacht detachment led by a sergeant. He ordered the tenants to leave their apartments unlocked so that his troops could use them as observation posts. The tenants were only allowed to enter them to prepare meals. As Janina and her neighbors listened to bombs and shells exploding around them, their mood was cheerful. Soon, after nearly five years of terror, their German occupiers would be gone.

By dawn the next morning, tanks were rumbling in Lublin's streets. The soldiers in Janina's building would run out, fire their antitank weapons, and return, their faces dripping with sweat, their eyes wide with fear. A truck parked outside the building, then the sergeant appeared and ordered all the tenants to move to a different part of the basement. Rumors flew. One man claimed that the Germans had thrown grenades into a nearby basement where people were sheltering, another that the Germans were going to push women, children, and the elderly into the streets to block the Soviet tanks. A third reported that the Germans were seizing men and taking them away for forced labor. Panic spread; the tenants were arguing and shouting. Except for Countess Władysława and her sister, who quietly knelt on the damp floor and began one of their special prayers, as if they were at morning Mass.

Janina discounted the first two rumors, but the report that men were being seized for labor sounded all too plausible. Her household now consisted of Henry; Count Skrzyński's eighteen-year-old son, Ryś; and a Volhynian teenager whom Janina had rescued from Krochmalna. She was not about to lose them at this last moment. For Henry, being taken would lead to his exposure as a Jew and certain death.

All four of them went up to their apartment to prepare breakfast. Henry proposed that the three men hide in a windowless dressing room off the bedroom, against which Janina would push a chest of drawers. Janina vetoed this proposal, for their absence would be noticed, and if the Germans found the men, they would be shot. What they needed was a way to convince the Germans not to enter the apartment or seek out the men. Once again, Janina's ability to think like the Germans inspired her with a plan. Leaving the others in the apartment, she went to the basement and reported to the sergeant that Ryś Skrzyński was running a high fever and showing signs of typhoid. The sergeant immediately ordered her to return to the apartment and stay there, along with the three men, so as not to spread the disease. He also gifted her half a bottle of brandy for the patient.

They placed Ryś on a mattress in the apartment's entry, while the two men stayed in the windowless dressing room with the door open so that they would not be accused of signaling out the windows to the Soviets. Meanwhile, Janina "nursed" Ryś by giving him a thermometer, teaching him how to make it register a fever, and schooling him on the symptoms of typhoid.

That night, the wife of the building janitor knocked on the apartment door. There were some escaped Majdanek prisoners in the basement, she reported, and they were begging for men's clothes. Janina mistrusted the woman. She had claimed ethnic German status during the occupation and had snubbed Janina when she first came to the building, but in recent days had transformed into a fervently patriotic Pole. So Janina turned her away, warning that the apartment was not safe because of the presence of infectious disease.

At dawn the next morning, there was more knocking at the door. Janina opened it wide, which she had found was safest. Her blood ran cold. At the door stood the orderly of Dr. Blancke from Majdanek. Seeing him in his SS uniform, armed and helmeted, Janina's first panicked thought was that he had come to seize her. Then she remembered that the SS always came in twos to make arrests. Perhaps he wouldn't even recognize her, since her hair was hanging long rather than as he had always seen it, arranged in braids around her head and under a kerchief. But if he had come to investigate the report of typhoid, how could they fool him? He was well acquainted with the disease from his service at Majdanek. Had they survived so long, only to be taken at the last moment before freedom?

"Well, Madame, so this is where you live!" he began. "I had no idea at whose door I knocked. Nor did I expect to see you again, during this time of retreat. But this is only temporary. Assistance is coming. Then we'll get rid of these wild beasts and they'll be eating potato peels again. You should see them fighting—like animals! They come at us in a tank, we attack it, and they go right on fighting, even when the tank is on fire, even when they're wounded, right until they're all dead. But that's not what I came about. Someone is sick here?"

This bluster in an almost friendly tone gave Janina time to collect her wits. Turning to Ryś, she asked, all sweet concern, "What is your temperature this morning, dear? I haven't taken the thermometer from you yet." Ryś had popped the thermometer into his mouth just before Janina opened the door and now removed it. He reported a high fever. The SS orderly avoided coming too near the mattress, but asked questions about the symptoms. Janina answered some and referred others to Ryś. As the orderly heard their answers, a look of alarm came into his face and he backed away. He expressed surprise to hear of typhoid in this part of the city, where the water was unpolluted, but accepted the diagnosis. Withdrawing into the hallway, he wrote up a sign and fixed it to the apartment door, ordering Janina to stay inside with the others. The sign read, "Entrance Forbidden. Typhoid suspected." A while later, there was another knock, but Janina only found some bottles of medicine when she opened the door. Her plan had succeeded.

Later that day, a neighbor came up from the basement to tell them that the Germans were leaving, and shortly afterward they heard their truck roar off. But German soldiers had set the building next door on fire when they left it, so Janina and her neighbors had some tense moments, wondering whether some disaster was about to befall them. Finally, during the night, Red Army soldiers arrived with fixed bayonets and announced that they were free. Except for the escaped Majdanek prisoners who had arrived the night before. The soldiers decided they seemed suspicious and took them to Zamek.

In the early morning hours of July 25, 1944, the residents of Lublin emerged from their basements and shelters to the heartbreaking sight of their city in ruins. For block after block they saw the roofless, windowless shells of buildings, some still burning. Piles of debris, bomb craters, and burnt-out trucks and tanks rendered the streets impassible. Strewn about were body parts of humans and animals blown to pieces by explosions. Now rotting in the summer heat, the remains sent up a gagging stench and posed the threat of epidemics.[1]

Majdanek had been taken by Soviet forces three days earlier. They found 480 prisoners there, consisting of Soviet POW invalids in Field II and the victims of pacification operations in Field I. The SS had abandoned the camp just hours earlier, force-marching more than 1,000 prisoners over sixty miles and then herding them onto a train to Auschwitz. Along the way, the guards shot hundreds of prisoners who failed to keep pace.[2]

The Majdanek SS managed to destroy most of the camp's records but did not succeed in removing all the physical evidence of the crimes committed at the camp. The gas chambers were not destroyed, and although the crematorium was set on fire, much of it still stood, including all its ovens and a pile of charred human remains. Corpses of victims from Zamek still lay in the nearby trenches. Hills of human ashes and heaps of hundreds of thousands of shoes indicated that murder had been committed there on a massive scale. Majdanek was the first major German concentration camp to be liberated and the first place where physical evidence was found confirming that the Germans had committed mass murder using poison gas in stationary facilities. The Soviets brought in foreign journalists to tour the camp and distributed films showing what the Red Army had found there.[3] The reports and films met with skepticism in the West, however. The *New York Herald Tribune* counseled against crediting "the horror story that comes out of Lublin. Even on top of all that we have been taught about the maniacal Nazi ruthlessness, this example seems inconceivable."[4]

The people of Lublin quickly discovered that their liberation from the German occupier did not, in fact, mean that they were free. As soon as the Germans departed, the Lublin representative of the Underground began to form an administration that answered to the Polish government in exile in London. On July 25, however, the Soviets installed the Polish Committee of National Liberation, or PKWN (*Polski Komitet Wyzwolenia Narodowego*), in power in Lublin. Polish communists had formed it in Moscow at the behest of Stalin, who intended it to administer the Polish territories that the Red Army was liberating.

The next day, the troops of the Polish First Army marched through Lublin's streets. This force, commanded by former Polish Army officer Zygmunt Berling, was created by the Soviets and subordinate to the Red Army, which provided most of its senior officers. Although the AK had fought alongside the Red Army in liberating Lublin, the Soviet military commander of the city gave the AK a choice: join the Polish First Army or give up their weapons and disband. The AK categorically refused the former, and many of its units refused the latter. The Soviet NKVD was prepared for this response. Within days of the Germans' departure, the cells of Zamek and the compounds of Majdanek were being repopulated by members of the AK and the Underground.[5]

As soon as the fighting ceased in Lublin, Janina returned to the RGO office. There, she received an unexpected visitor: the PKWN's deputy minister of labor, social work, and health, Dr. Jerzy Morzycki.

"I am here to express the gratitude and admiration of our Government to you for your deeds of heroic and sacrificial courage during the occupation. I am here to ask you to take part in the celebration of the liberation and the rites for the dead in the Zamek prison, and to talk to us about your struggle."

But Janina had no desire to lend legitimacy to Lublin's new rulers through her participation, particularly as she had just learned that some of her comrades were imprisoned and being interrogated in Zamek. She was so upset by this news that diplomacy failed her. Struggling to keep her voice steady and to hide her distress, she looked into the middle distance and replied, "I am unable, *Monsieur le Ministre,* to accede to this request. I have fought, prayed, and suffered for the day of liberation to come—and so did most of the young people who are now in Zamek."

On August 1, 1944, the AK staged an uprising in Warsaw, believing that Soviet forces were massing just across the Vistula River from the city and would participate in the fight. It was a fatal miscalculation. The Red Army was not across the river in force, and although the Soviets could have provided various kinds of assistance to the Polish soldiers and civilians who were bravely fighting the Germans in the city, Stalin did not want to help the AK score a major victory and install the government in exile in power in Poland's capital.

The uprising took the Germans by surprise. The people of Warsaw rallied to the AK, and its forces seized significant sectors of the city. News of the uprising so enraged Hitler that he ordered not only that it be mercilessly crushed but also that the city be razed and all its inhabitants killed. The Germans began bombing and shelling the city incessantly and sent in reinforcements. Making no distinction between the AK fighters wearing identifying armbands and civilians, SS forces went house to house, pulling out all inside and shooting them. On August 5 alone, the SS shot an estimated 40,000 victims. The AK were hopelessly outmanned and outgunned. By the time the Allies tried to airlift supplies into the city in September, they proved to be too little and too late.

After sixty-three days of heroic fighting, the AK surrendered on October 2, 1944. The Polish death toll in the city was 150,000 to 200,000, more than 85 percent of the victims civilians. The Germans forced the remaining 280,000 Poles in the city to evacuate to a massive camp in Pruszków, from which 100,000 were sent to the Reich for forced labor and thousands more to concentration camps. Then the Germans methodically looted the city and burned it to the ground. When the Red Army finally entered Warsaw in January 1945, more than 80 percent of the city had been reduced to rubble.[6]

Nazi Germany surrendered unconditionally on May 8–9, 1945. While the Allies were celebrating victory, many Poles, including Janina, felt more like mourning. Throughout the long years of terror, suffering, courageous resistance, and horrific death, they had refused to relinquish their hope of seeing their nation restored to full sovereignty. Now, they felt that they had merely exchanged one occupier for another. It appeared that the destiny of what remained of Poland was to be the servile satellite of the Soviet Union under the yoke of a brutal regime. And for Janina, destiny promised still more danger.

TWENTY-ONE

FLIGHT

Janina and Henry had a crucial decision to make in August 1944. Now that the Germans were gone, it was at least theoretically safe for them to revert to their true identities. The temptation to do so was strong. Polish Jews who had survived in hiding were flocking to Lublin, soon joined by those who had survived in the Soviet Union. Janina and Henry yearned to connect with people who shared their trauma and grief. Among them there might be some of Janina's and Henry's family members or friends, or at least someone who could provide information about their loved ones' fate.

Janina realized that she was not out of danger, however. She was liable to arrest, perhaps even execution, should the Soviet NKVD discover her service in the AK. As an RGO official, moreover, she was automatically suspect in the eyes of the new occupier. The Soviets considered the RGO a collaborationist organization, since it was largely led by Polish aristocrats who had acted in obedience to German orders. The NKVD also suspected that the RGO was closely allied to the Polish government in exile and the AK. When NKVD agents arrested two RGO officials in early August 1944 after discovering their AK activities, the scrutiny and harassment of other RGO officials intensified.[1]

Ludwik Christians encouraged Lublin's new rulers in their negative view of the RGO. He did not share Janina's concerns about appearing to legitimize the Soviet-imposed regime. Instead, he curried its favor. The Lublin communist officials, aware of their unpopularity with most Poles, welcomed the opportunity Christians offered them to be seen as working with a highly esteemed international organization. They even gave Christians a seat on the Extraordinary Commission for the Investigation of German Crimes at the Majdanek Camp, established by the Soviets to collect and publicize the evidence of German mass murder. Even though Skrzyński was more than happy to return to the Polish Red Cross the duties that the Germans had forced the RGO to take over, Christians accused the RGO generally and Skrzyński personally of requesting their German masters to invest them with control over the affairs of the Red Cross.

Outraged by Christians's accusation, Skrzyński demanded a hearing before an honor court. There was no longer any place he could go in Poland to get his reputation back, however. His position became untenable, and he was replaced as the RGO advisor. As soon as it was safe to do so, he left Lublin altogether. In 1946, Christians would publish a book about the aid program for Majdanek prisoners in which he gave all the credit to the Polish Red Cross and made no mention of the RGO or any of its officials.[2]

In the summer of 1944, however, Janina was still popular among the people of Lublin because of her work at Majdanek and Krochmalna, and this provided some protection from the suspicion and harassment of the communist authorities. If she revealed now that she was not the countess she had pretended to be but a Jew, it might tarnish her reputation, at least with some Poles. Even with the Germans gone, it was still not safe to be a Jew in Lublin, for some of those who were coming out of hiding and attempting to return to their homes were being attacked, even murdered, by Polish bandits, partisans, and former neighbors.[3] Revealing her true identity would certainly invite questions as to how she obtained her identity papers and RGO position, with the potential result that both she and Skrzyński would be exposed as AK operatives.

Despite its mistrust of the RGO, the new regime could not dispense with the Polish Care Committees' vital work, for even with the Germans gone, the desperate needs of the Poles were undiminished. Many of the committees' workers were resigning, however. Janina was asked to stay on and given the official title of deputy to the Lublin director. Retaining her false identity would ensure that Janina could go on being of service to her compatriots, and now not only to ethnic Poles but also to Polish Jews. There were practical considerations as well: she and Henry would have an income and housing. Her position also enabled her to provide jobs for Wendrucha's wife and for Skrzyński's daughter.[4]

So Janina and Henry decided to retain their false identities, at least for the time being. Together with Countess Władysława and Madame Maria, they were allowed to move back into the Countess's building on Narutowicza Street.[5] When the new administration replaced the RGO with the Central Committee of Social Welfare (*Centralny Komitet Opieki Społecznej* or CKOS) at the end of 1944, Janina was named to its governing board.[6]

In 1945, the Soviets transferred the Polish administration from Lublin to Warsaw. Janina had no choice but to say farewell to her "aunties" and go. As Dr. Janina Suchodolska, social worker, she became the head of the Organization and Inspection Department of CKOS. Traveling throughout her country, Janina saw firsthand the grief and desperation of its people. Some six million Polish citizens died during the war, 18 percent of prewar Poland's population. Half were Jews. The war had orphaned 1.5 million Polish children. Hunger and homelessness were everywhere, accompanied inevitably by epidemics and crime.[7]

Like the RGO, CKOS was a voluntary welfare organization and operated through care committees and branches working at the provincial, county, and local levels. It was able to take over the RGO's facilities and some of the staff in the part of postwar Poland that had been under the General Government, but had to start from scratch in other Polish regions. Janina quickly helped to organize 2,690 committees and branches throughout the country. Her work particularly focused on children and youth, including caring for 169,000 orphans under age three and providing vocational training for the hundreds of thousands of young adults who had been denied an education under the German occupation.[8]

Much of the funding for CKOS came from abroad, from international organizations like the United Nations Relief and Rehabilitation

Administration, and from numerous aid charities and Polish diaspora organizations. Thanks to her linguistic skills, Janina was given charge of CKOS's dealings with foreign funders, and she became CKOS deputy director in April 1946. This aspect of her work brought opportunities to attend international conferences in the West, including in Geneva in 1946 and Paris in September 1947.[9]

Henry was not content to live in Warsaw as Piotr Suchodolski. He longed to resume his work on the philosophy of physics and to pursue an academic career, something he could only do as Henry Mehlberg. Other members of the Lwów-Warsaw School who survived the war also hoped to continue its work in postwar Poland. Henry was able to get a teaching position under his true name at the newly created University of Łódź, whose rector was a former Twardowski student.[10] His new job required that Henry and Janina live apart and conceal their marriage.[11]

In Łódź, Henry succeeded in reconnecting with his brothers Izydor and Juliusz through the Central Committee of Jews in Poland. They informed Henry that their parents had been gassed in Bełżec and that their two married sisters had also been murdered. Izydor had survived the war by passing as Jerzy Markiewicz and was still using that name. Juliusz had survived in the Soviet Union and was planning to immigrate to Palestine.[12]

With the exception of its surviving Jewish citizens, postwar Poland was almost entirely a mono-ethnic state. The Soviet Union annexed prewar Poland's multiethnic eastern regions, while Poland's communist regime drove the ethnic Germans out of its western lands. Even more than before the war, Jewish Poles found themselves treated as undesirable outsiders by their non-Jewish compatriots. Although they supposedly enjoyed the same rights as all Polish citizens, Jews faced rampant discrimination and harassment. Violent attacks were not infrequent, especially against survivors who returned to find their homes and businesses occupied by Poles who had no intention of relinquishing them to their rightful owners. Estimates of the number of Polish Jews killed in the first year following the end of the war range from 500 to 1,500. Local officials tended to turn a blind eye to the violence, if they didn't actively participate in it. The provisional government had no interest in alienating the vast majority of Poles by cracking down on antisemitic discrimination and attacks. Like Henry's brother Izydor, many Jews who had survived on "Aryan" papers chose to retain their wartime identities to avoid falling victim to antisemitism.[13]

The fears of Jews in Poland were crystallized on July 4, 1946. In the city of Kielce, a mob of residents together with Polish soldiers and police brutally stripped and bludgeoned Holocaust survivors who had been living in the Jewish community building. The pogrom took the lives of forty-two Jews and left perhaps eighty seriously injured.[14] After the pogrom, 70,000 Polish Jews fled the country in just a few months, preferring to live in a displaced persons camp or to journey illegally to Palestine than to continue enduring the constant fear of violence in Poland.[15]

Henry was thinking of joining them. He achieved an important career goal in June 1946, when he obtained the habilitation in philosophy that qualified him to be a full professor. If he could get to the United States, he would have far greater opportunity to attract the notice and acclaim that he believed his work deserved. He also saw little prospect that he and Janina would ever be able to live together as themselves and free from fear in Poland.

Henry and Janina managed to establish contact with Henry's uncle Joseph Mehlberg and Janina's cousin Sigmund Pines, both in New York. Pines was the grandson of Janina's grandfather Berl Spinner, who immigrated to the United States before World War I with his wife and six of their children.[16] Since both relatives were willing to sponsor the Mehlbergs' immigration to the United States, Henry applied for a visa for himself and "wife" at the U.S. consulate in Warsaw in August 1946. To complete the immigration process, however, Janina would have to produce a passport showing that she was Henry's wife, and she could not apply for one without revealing to Polish authorities that she had lied to them about her identity.[17]

Henry registered with the Central Committee of Jews in Poland, listing his wife as Pepi Mehlberg née Spinner, a teacher, and stating only that they had survived the war on false papers. As a registered Jewish survivor, he then applied to the Emigration Service Office of the American Jewish Joint Distribution Committee (JDC), which assisted Jews seeking to leave Poland. He hoped that the JDC would be able to get travel papers and an exit permit for Pepi Mehlberg without her alternate identity coming to the attention of Polish authorities.[18]

In 1947, Henry received an appointment as associate professor of philosophy at the University of Wrocław, a significant advancement in his career. Soon after he began teaching there in the autumn, however, he received a warning: communist officials had placed spies in his seminar who were reporting on his teaching.[19] Henry could not afford to take the warning lightly. Poland's communist regime had commenced a Stalinist crackdown, and tens of thousands of Poles suspected of dissent or of spreading unorthodox ideas were being arrested and given lengthy prison sentences.

Once again, the possibility that Henry was in danger jolted Janina into full rescue mode. She had to get Henry out of the country, even if it required her to stay behind in Poland. An idea occurred to her: if she could manage to go on an official trip to the United States, she would make valuable contacts that would pave the way for Henry to go there. As a result of her participation in an international child welfare conference in Paris in September 1947, she had received an invitation to represent Poland on the Council of Foreign Social Institutions. Government rules prevented Janina from accepting, but her growing international reputation as a child welfare expert was something she could leverage. She had a dear friend in New York, the zoologist Maria Anna Rudzińska, who was married to the counselor to Poland's delegation at the U.N., Aleksander Witold Rudziński. With his help, Janina obtained an offer of a U.N. fellowship to study child welfare institutions and practices in the United States. CKOS approved the fellowship on condition that Janina commit to another two years of employment with it after her return. She agreed.[20]

By December 1947, Janina was in Washington, D.C., undergoing training at the Children's Bureau of the Federal Security Agency. Then she was taken on a tour of the eastern United States and the Midwest. She visited orphanages and child care centers, observed extension services, 4-H youth clubs, and school-based extracurricular and recreational activities, and studied the work of local child welfare offices. She also met with CKOS funders and reported how their donations had been put to use.[21]

Local papers took note of the visit by U.N. fellow Dr. Suchodolska. In an interview in Raleigh, North Carolina, Janina, with her usual diplomacy, heaped praise on all that she had heard and seen. Her interviewer expressed her admiration for this "intelligent and interesting representative of the Polish people," described as "small, dark, and bright eyed with massive braids of black hair wound round her head." Although disappointed by Janina's refusal to discuss political issues, the journalist concluded that Dr. Suchodolska was "someone who puts the immediate welfare of all Polish children above politics" and was working only "for the children, the orphans of Poland, with whatever government, with whatever and all and any help that comes to hand." Janina worried that the article might get her in trouble with Polish authorities because she failed to praise Poland's regime.

Throughout her six-month stay in the United States, Janina pursued her goal of getting Henry out of Poland. She contacted philosophers at American universities, hoping to interest them in Henry's work and to arrange a fellowship or appointment for him. Impressed by her presentation, two philosophers at the University of Chicago, Rudolf Carnap and Charles W. Morris, agreed to write to other scholars on Henry's behalf. Janina did not reveal to them that she was Henry's wife but claimed that she was his friend.[22]

Janina took advantage of the lack of censorship in the United States to write freely to her friend Maria Anna Rudzińska in New York about her concerns and her efforts to get Henry out of Poland. With the help of Rudzińska and her husband, Janina was able to get money to her sister Chaja, now Clara, who was living in destitution in Argentina. Janina's other sister, Bluma, was living in Uruguay as Antonina Altmann.

In her letters to Rudzińska, Janina confided her impressions of Americans. Generally, she admired their friendliness and eagerness to help, but she thought them naïve. She also witnessed disturbing evidence of antisemitism in the United States, especially in her meetings with members of the Polish immigrant community. The spewings of one Polish American were so vile that they gave Janina a flashback to the war.

Besides contacting American philosophers about Henry, Janina was consulting his uncle Joseph and her cousin Sigmund Pines about how to get Henry out of Poland as soon as possible. They proposed that Henry go to Sweden, which Janina would transit after the end of her fellowship. She would then remain with him instead of returning to Poland and they could wait there in safety until it became possible to immigrate to the United States.

While in New York City in the spring of 1948, Janina visited the National Council of Jewish Women and spoke with Evelyn Abelson of its Service for Foreign Born. It would prove to be a fateful meeting. Janina explained Henry's situation and even confided that she was Henry's wife but living under a false identity as a Polish official. She asked Abelson for help in getting Henry to Sweden. Abelson was sympathetic, but explained that it would not be possible to obtain a Swedish visa for Henry before Janina had to leave for Poland.

Janina returned to Poland at the end of May 1948 no closer to rescuing Henry than when she had left, and her fear and stress were exacting a toll. As she confided to Rudzińska in the United States, she had not had a moment's peace in the seven years since the Germans occupied Lwów. She became sick during the journey home and arrived in Warsaw in such ill health that she was ordered to go on a rest cure for several weeks, which she spent in the resort town of Cieplice in southwestern Poland. She happened to have acquaintances there: Count Skrzyński and his family.

Meanwhile, back in New York, Abelson had not forgotten the "most involved and delicate" situation of the intriguing Polish woman who had confided in her. She forwarded Henry's biographical statement and the references Janina had gathered to the American Committee for Émigré Scholars, Writers and Artists. In July 1948, the committee arranged for Henry to receive a fellowship offer to teach in Canada from the Lady Davis Foundation, named for its funder, the Canadian Jewish philanthropist Lady Davis. The fellowship awarded an annual salary as well as travel expenses for Henry and his wife.

In order to accept the fellowship, however, Henry had first to obtain an exit permit and authorization from the Polish Ministry of Education to take a sabbatical. After some tense months, he finally set sail to New York on the flagship Polish liner MS *Batory*. Sigmund Pines pulled some strings to get permission for Henry to stay a few days in New York, during which he met with Abelson. Then he traveled on to Toronto. Following his arrival there in March 1949, he was assigned a position in the Department of Applied Mathematics at the University of Toronto.

At last, Henry was safe, and he expected Janina to join him soon. She had been elected to the executive committee of the International Union for Child Welfare (the predecessor of today's Save the Children) in August 1948 and had applied for an exit permit to attend its planning meeting in Brussels in late March. If she did not receive the permit in time, she would certainly attend the annual convention there in May. Once in Brussels, she planned to defect. Abelson alerted the JDC office there to expect her and referred Henry to the Canadian Jewish Congress for assistance in getting Janina from Brussels to Canada. Through contacts at the U.S. State Department, Henry's uncle Joseph Mehlberg ensured that U.S. consulates were informed that Janina, despite being a Polish official, was a not a member of the Communist Party. This information would be passed on to the Canadian consulate in Brussels when Janina applied there for a Canadian visa. Everything was in place for Janina to join Henry in Canada once she got to Brussels.[23]

But she never arrived there. In late February 1949, the Polish government dissolved CKOS and Janina lost her job. Her requests to attend the March meeting and the May conference in Brussels were both denied. Janina was stuck in Poland.[24]

As spring turned to summer, Henry became increasingly desperate. He was supposed to return to Poland in October. Although he had assurances that Canada would accept him as a permanent resident, he did not wish to apply as long as Janina was in Poland. In addition to appealing to Abelson and the National Council of Jewish Women, Henry turned to other agencies for help. The United Service for New Americans, the United Jewish Appeal, the United Jewish Relief Agencies of Canada, the Canadian Jewish Congress, and the Jewish Immigrant Aid Society in Canada all got involved. Henry proposed that Janina apply to immigrate to Israel through the Central Committee of Jews in Poland, where she was registered as Pepi Mehlberg. Janina realized that doing so would inevitably draw the attention of the Ministry for Public Security to her double identity, especially after she was assigned to a position in the Ministry of Labor and Welfare in

August 1949.[25] All the agencies involved in the Mehlbergs' case concluded that they could do nothing as long as Janina was in Poland. She would have to figure out how to escape on her own.

Henry obtained an extension of his sabbatical until the end of March 1950 from the Polish Ministry of Education. As the end date approached, Henry applied for a further extension. The ministry grudgingly agreed but made clear that Henry was to be back at his post in Wrocław by November 1, 1950. If Janina did not get out by then, Henry would go back, despite the danger.

Janina was not about to let that happen. In the summer of 1950, she got word to Henry that she had found a way to leave Poland for East Germany and, once there, would somehow get to the British sector of Berlin. The Canadian Military Mission in Berlin was alerted and had a visa application waiting for her. On August 16, 1950, she walked into the mission's office. It took her nine days to get there after crossing the Polish border.[26] How she managed to do that remains a mystery.

Within two weeks, Janina had permission to immigrate to Canada. It took a while longer to obtain travel papers and funds, however. As a political refugee, she turned to the International Refugee Organization for help with both, only to learn that she had missed the registration deadline of September 1, 1949. In the end, the Allied High Commission in Berlin issued her travel papers, and Henry obtained assistance from the Jewish Immigrant Aid Society in Canada.

Janina finally arrived in Toronto on October 6, 1950. Henry then wrote to the University of Wrocław that he was "pleased to announce" that he would not be returning to his post.

Henry and Janina were together again, and they were free.

TWENTY-TWO

A NEW BEGINNING

Once out of Poland, Janina constructed a new identity for her life in Canada. Using an amalgamation of her previous names, she became Dr. Josephine Janina Bednarski Spinner Mehlberg, mathematician. "Josephine" is the English equivalent of Józefa, which she had long preferred to Pepi. She may have added "Janina Bednarski" to her name in part to reconcile her Polish paperwork as Janina Bednarska Suchodolska with Henry's visa application for her as his wife. But retaining "Janina" in her name was more than a matter of bureaucratic convenience. It also acknowledged that "Janina" was the name of the woman she had actually become over the previous nine years, the identity of a version of herself—perhaps the best version—that she neither could nor wanted to relinquish entirely. Although the friends she made in her new life knew her as Josephine, Henry continued to call her Jeanine, which is Janina in French, his favorite language.[1]

Janina's aspiration to pursue her original career explains the change in her birth date from 1905 to 1915: as a woman, the odds of her getting an academic appointment in mathematics were automatically slim, and they were much worse for a forty-five-year-old than for one who was thirty-five. In listing her credentials, Janina did not specify the subject of her doctorate, correctly expecting that prospective employers would assume she had earned a PhD in math rather than philosophy.

Through Henry, Janina established contacts with mathematicians at the University of Toronto, leading to a one-year appointment as a research assistant in the university's Computation Centre. She joined Canadian mathematics organizations and was invited to give occasional lectures.[2]

Henry was finding much more professional success. His position at the University of Toronto gave him access to philosophers in the United States, where his work was attracting interest. New York University's Sidney Hook invited Henry to join the American delegation to the 1952 Conference for Science and Freedom in Hamburg. Henry's keynote address was so well received that he was one of just four conference attendees invited to speak on German radio. Unlike the others, however, Henry could not bring himself to speak in German while his memories of what he had suffered during the Holocaust were still so fresh. He spoke in English instead.[3]

Janina and Henry quickly developed a supportive social circle in Toronto, thanks to good friends from their days in Lwów, Joseph and Gisela Klinghofer. Joseph was an official of the Canadian Jewish Congress and had supported Henry's efforts to get Janina to Canada. Henry and Janina joined the CJC's education committee and participated in secular activities of Toronto's Jewish community. They also belonged to a tight circle of émigré scholars. People admired Henry's intelligence and wit and found Janina's outgoing cheerfulness utterly charming. For Janina and Henry, the ability to mix openly as themselves and as a married couple after so many years of secrecy and fear filled them with astonished relief. In 1956, they became Canadian citizens.[4]

Their professional ambitions still called them to the United States, however. Henry got his foot inside a very wide door when he received a one-year appointment as a visiting professor at Princeton University in 1955. The University of Chicago came calling and offered Henry Rudolf Carnap's old position in the philosophy department starting in 1956. On September 18, Henry and Janina immigrated to the United States by driving their car across Ambassador Bridge to Detroit. In 1961, they became U.S. citizens.[5]

In Chicago, Henry started a discussion group of local scholars that met at his and Janina's apartment. It was modeled on the philosophical school known as the Vienna Circle. In 1958, he published his first major work written in English, *The Reach of Science,* in which he elaborated upon the theories he presented in Hamburg. But the trajectory of his career stalled when illness struck, possibly as a result of a serious car crash in which both he and Janina suffered injuries. He experienced frequent bouts of aphasia in which he would speak excitedly without realizing that his words sounded like gibberish. Although his mind was as brilliant as ever, most of the scholars in the discussion group lost interest in attending. Students in his logic course would gradually slip out of the classroom as Henry wrote on the blackboard and babbled excitedly.[6]

Janina, on the other hand, experienced far more success in her career than she could have expected in Poland or Canada. In 1957, the University of Chicago hired her as a senior mathematician in its Institute for System Research, a descendant of the United States' wartime Manhattan Project that produced the first atomic bomb. Recruited for her fluency in nonlinear equations, functional analysis, and Russian, she worked on a top secret U.S. Air Force weapons project. The institute's young staff of graduate students and newly minted PhDs regarded Janina as both a respected colleague and "a beloved mother hen."[7]

Her combination of exceptional expertise with a warm and spirited personality enabled Janina to make many connections in the U.S. not only in the field of mathematics but also in engineering, for which her work had important implications. In addition to joining math and engineering societies, she served as secretary of the Chicago chapter of the American Institute of Aeronautics and Astronautics. Well versed in Henry's field of philosophy of physics, she published a paper in the journal *Current Issues in the Philosophy of Science* with the title "Is a Unitary Approach to Foundations of Probability Possible?"

In 1960, Janina joined the mathematics department at Illinois Institute of Technology as an assistant professor. She was a popular professor, scholar, and colleague there, teaching probability theory and engaging in theoretical discourse through papers and lectures. She published "A Classification of Mathematical Concepts" in 1962 as a response to renowned mathematician and department colleague Karl Menger. Within a few years, she rose to full professor at IIT. Two male students obtained their doctorates with Janina as their advisor, whereas Henry had just one.[8]

As a mathematician in the United States, Janina had to become accustomed to being the only woman in the room. She was the first woman appointed to the math department at IIT and the only one for her entire time there. At a conference organized by Dr. Edward Teller, the "father of the hydrogen bomb," she discovered that she was the only woman invited to participate. Feeling out of place, she held herself aloof at the opening reception. When one of the attendees asked why, she explained that she was nervous about giving her talk, because she had not yet acquired an American accent. Her colleague laughed and answered, "Don't you know that many American scientists spend long hours trying to acquire a foreign accent?" His joke helped her relax, and her presentation at the conference was a success. Soon afterward, she was one of the few women invited to the founding conference of the Society for Engineering Science, an interdisciplinary organization with the goal of bridging the fields of engineering, mathematics, and science.[9]

At IIT, Janina made a point of encouraging the few women engineering students who attended her classes. When the math department finally accepted its first woman graduate student, Janina took her under her wing. She was not Janina's student, but Janina agreed to serve on her defense committee. When one of the other professors on the committee began to hector the student on what he perceived as her weak spot, Janina came to her rescue:

"VY you ask her zis kvestion? She *knows* it, she *knows* it!"

The professor nodded obediently and ceased his questioning. Janina had lost none of her formidability.[10]

By the 1960s, Janina and Henry were living in financial security and considerable comfort in a large apartment overlooking a park next to Lake Michigan. The suffering and strain of their past continued to shadow their lives, however. Henry especially felt deeply bitter about all that he had lost, not only most of his family and many friends and colleagues but also time. How much more might he have achieved if Germany's murderous aggression had not interrupted the work and career that were on the brink of success in 1939? He complained that his age should not be figured chronologically from his birth date, because the lost years of the war ought to be subtracted.[11]

Henry and Janina believed that their suffering and loss entitled them to the reparations that West Germany had agreed to provide to Holocaust survivors. Under the reparations agreement then in force, however, they did not qualify: they had lived in the part of Poland occupied by the Soviet Union in 1939, and they were never held in a ghetto, forced labor camp, or concentration camp. These limitations seemed patently unfair to them, so they submitted claims with an alternate history: they had been in Kraków at the start of the war and escaped from the ghetto there in 1943, then paid a farmer to hide them in miserable conditions until the end of the war. The Klinghofers and Rudzińskis submitted affidavits supporting these claims. After more than a decade of bureaucratic nitpicking, West Germany finally decided to grant Janina a pension—two years after her death.[12]

Janina and Henry's friends knew very little about the couple's past. Henry sometimes spoke of living under a false identity as an egg farmer during the war, claiming that he had become an expert on the composition of soils and fertilizers to maintain his cover. He also occasionally boasted that Janina was a hero of the Underground and had saved him, from which some of their friends concluded that Janina was not a Jew.[13]

Janina did not speak about her past. How could she begin to explain what she had experienced without resurfacing the feelings of horror and terror that still visited her in her nightmares? She tried to stay focused on her new life as an American. But still, the ache of sorrow never left her. She longed for the city that she and Henry had loved and would never see again; she grieved for all the loved ones she had lost and for the people whose suffering she had tried and too often failed to relieve; she missed the courageous friends who had risked their lives for her yet never really knew her; and she mourned for the country that had inspired her loyalty and service and that no longer had any place for her.

Janina's health had never been robust, and the extreme stress she lived under as Janina Suchodolska only made it worse. She suffered from hypertension, frequent migraines, and chronic gastric distress. By the late 1960s, her heart began to fail. A heart attack in the spring of 1969 convinced her that her days were numbered, and so she sent for her sister Antonina, now widowed in Uruguay. Someone, Janina reasoned, would have to take care of Henry after she was gone. Antonina arrived on May 21. Five days later, on May 26, Janina died.[14]

Per Janina's plan, Henry applied to obtain permanent residency for his sister-in-law. As he explained in his application, he needed a housekeeper for his "huge" apartment and was confident that Antonina would be "a pleasant companion." When Henry learned that he could not obtain permanent residency for an in-law, he married Antonina on August 8, 1969, less than three months after Janina died. No doubt, she would have approved.[15]

After Henry reached retirement at the University of Chicago, his former colleague there, Charles Morris, arranged a post-retirement position for him at the University of Florida in Gainesville.[16] Antonina died there in October 1973. Less than two years later, Henry, now in failing health, married his nurse, Susie Blackman Clark. It was a marriage of convenience for both, and yet a companionable one. Henry especially enjoyed the company of Susie's children and grandchild, and she even got him to attend her church a few times.[17]

Henry spent his last years in Gainesville working on a major project. At the urging of two American leaders in the field of the philosophy of physics, Robert S. Cohen and Adolf Grünbaum, he collected and synthesized for publication in English his life's work on quantum physics and the nature of time. Henry did not live to see the result, the two-volume *Time, Causality, and the Quantum Theory: Studies in the Philosophy of Science*, but he died knowing that it would see print. After Henry's death on December 10, 1979, Grünbaum and Cohen each added an introductory essay to the first volume that paid tribute to Henry's brilliance and "astonishing erudition" and lamented that persecution and illness had prevented his work from receiving the acclaim it deserved. In his summation, Cohen wrote: "Ever creative, but a troubled victim of his times, Henry Mehlberg disciplined himself with astonishing success, for he overcame political horrors and their attendant private maelstroms. These books are a memorial to a splendid philosopher of science."[18]

There was one project Henry could not see through: the publication of Janina's memoir. Shortly before he died, Henry brought his English translation of the memoir to Dr. Arthur Layton Funk, then chair of the University of Florida's history department. Henry asked the historian to help him polish and annotate the English text to make it suitable for publication.[19] Funk was a specialist in American history, however, with no expertise on the Holocaust or wartime Poland. After Henry's death, Funk might understandably have filed the memoir away in his records. As it turned out, Henry made the right choice. Thanks to Funk's considerable efforts, Janina's story did not go with Henry to his grave.

EPILOGUE

"JANINA'S STORY"

Sometime in the last eight years of her life, Janina decided to reveal, at least on paper, the secret she had kept for more than two decades: that she was the Countess Janina Suchodolska who, as a member of the Polish resistance and an RGO official, had provided lifesaving aid to Polish victims of Nazi persecution during World War II.[1] The result was the account that is the basis for this biography.

For a memoir, Janina's account is remarkably unforthcoming. All the reader can glean about the author's identity is that at the start of the war people called her Janina (which was not actually true), she was a math teacher and the daughter of a wealthy landowner, and she was married to Henry Mehlberg, who taught philosophy. She did not even provide a title for her text. In the collections catalogue of the United States Holocaust Memorial Museum, the memoir is listed simply as "Janina's Story."

The "Janina" of the story is less the author than her alter ego, Countess Janina Suchodolska. The first twenty-seven months of the war take up just fourteen of the memoir's 155 typed pages; the rest are devoted to Janina's life as the Countess. Henry added information about her life before and after World War II in a preface that he wrote after her death and included with the text he presented to Funk. It is a moving and revealing document that deserves to be quoted here in its entirety:

This is a story by Janina Spinner Mehlberg, born in the province of Galicia, Poland, on May 1, 1915. The youngest daughter of a well-to-do Jewish landowner, she grew up happily, an academically promising young woman, gifted in mathematics, living in a comfortable environment where a traditional Polish anti-Semitism was scarcely felt in her cozy setting. She played with the neighboring children of the Polish nobility, having the same nannies as they, her home physically comfortable, the atmosphere polite and well bred.

At 18, Janina married a serious young Jewish scholar, a student of Romance philology and later of philosophy, with the modest ambition "to know everything," and they lived well in Lwow, pursuing their intense intellectual interests. Until the world impinged with gradually increasing violence on their private absorptions and turned the young mathematics teacher into an imposter, a social worker of an unusual cast, and the heroine of Majdanek. She was 24 in 1939, when it began, barely more than 5 feet tall, more than ordinarily pretty, very feminine in her style, and having no test yet in her sheltered and cultivated life of the heroic courage she was to demonstrate in the coming years. Courage not rough-hewn, but operating with an analytic intelligence, as well as passion, and in a perspective that started with a prime value—the saving of as many lives as possible, and proceeding to weigh as impersonally as possible the value of her own life against the number at stake. She based her action on the higher probability—one life was worth less than many. Against this probability rate she operated for years, under Nazi rule and under Soviet, repeatedly risking death, and the worse that might prelude it, because the help she could give to others demanded the chance—indeed, she could see no meaning in her life unless she risked. Personal safety was only the agent to secure further service to those who knew no safety; if it were only for its own sake, for nothing but personal comfort and survival, how ephemeral it was, how worthless in even the short run. She would not survive, if she would survive, having watched out for herself and her own only. It would not have been worth it. She might die, and many times knew this *might be the moment, but not for nothing. Not to live uselessly, nor to die pointlessly.*

This petite Jewish girl passed as a Polish countess in Lublin in the

Second World War, and for her exceptional pains knew she had the love of many ordinary people. Many the breast that was crossed for her, the candle lit for her, and the lives risked to save hers. That this was so she knew, and the knowledge was good, but the main and unforgettable goal was—"how can we save them," and "how many more *can we save," and "it is* still *not enough—we must do* more*!"*

The heroine of Majdanek continued her struggle for help to the people after the liberation from the Nazis. And found herself again in danger from the "liberators" who, toward a presumably different end, used some of the same means. Until she escaped. In early middle age she lived in Chicago, teaching mathematics at the Illinois Institute of Technology, while her husband taught and wrote philosophy at the University of Chicago. They lived modestly and for their work, but were plagued by a couple of automobile accidents and ill health. Until finally, worn and weakened, no doubt, by years of strain and struggle, Janina died of heart failure on May 26, 1969.

She felt it necessary to give testimony, and she is a rare witness indeed. The following is her story.

This preface provides valuable information about Janina's background and motives, as well as testifying to Henry's love and respect for her. As a starting point for verifying Janina's memoir, however, it has two distinct flaws: it misidentifies her first name, and the information it provides about her birth date and her age at subsequent events is off by ten years. Consequently, Barry began the effort to confirm that Janina was Countess Suchodolska by assuming that she was born Janina Spinner on May 1, 1915. Janina's and Henry's U.S. immigration records, obtained through Freedom of Information Act requests, and various directories of prominent American women[2] confirmed this information and noted that she obtained a PhD from the Johannes Casimirus (Jan Kazimierz) University in Lwów in 1938.

Barry discovered that her assumptions were incorrect thanks to the help of three philosophers in Poland. Dr. Jan Hertrich-Woleński and Dr. Stepan Ivanyk, both experts on the Lwów-Warsaw School, each provided her a different photo of Twardowski's students dating from 1925–1926. Henry Mehlberg appears in each, as does a woman identified in one as Pepi

Spinner and in the other as Józefina Mehlberg. Barry concluded that, based on how she was identified in the photos, the woman must be Janina, but she is clearly not age ten or eleven in the photos, as Janina would have been if she were born in 1915. Ivanyk also informed Barry that Pepi Spinner obtained a doctorate in philosophy in February 1928 as one of Twardowski's students in Lwów. She would have been precocious indeed if she had obtained a PhD at age twelve.

Dr. Anna Smywińska-Pohl finally solved the mystery of Janina's identity by obtaining her dissertation records, which show that she submitted her dissertation in 1927 as Pepi Spinner, born May 1, 1905, in Żurawno. This proved that Henry and Janina lied about her background to Canadian and U.S. immigration authorities, a lie that Henry continued to perpetuate after her death. Barry wondered whether this was cause for doubting the veracity of Janina's memoir. On the other hand, she recognized that it was not uncommon for women to conceal or change their true age when they emigrated—Barry's own grandmother had done so.

In 2018, Joanna joined the quest to solve the mystery of Janina Suchodolska's identity. And in short order, she found the definitive evidence that Janina Mehlberg was Janina Suchodolska. It was in the records of the Jewish organizations that helped Henry get to Canada. Normally, such records are not open to researchers, but Joanna won access to them by impressing the archivist with the importance of Janina's story. The records include the correspondence of Evelyn Abelson, Henry's caseworker for the National Council of Jewish Women. Generally, Abelson carefully avoided naming Henry's wife in her communications, mentioning only that she was living under a pseudonym in Poland. But in one internal memo she let the information slip: Henry's wife was Janina "Sukoldosky." In a passionate letter he wrote to Abelson from Canada seeking help in extricating his wife from Poland, Henry also revealed that she was living as Mrs. Suchodolska.

Having proved that Janina Mehlberg was Countess Suchodolska, we set out to confirm the details of her memoir and to trace her life before and after World War II. This book is the product of more than four years of research into sources held by archives and libraries in Argentina, Poland, Ukraine, Germany, Canada, and the United States; in genealogical databases and oral history collections; through contacts with scholars and genealogists in numerous countries, and with Jewish organizations in Argentina, Canada, and Uruguay; and through oral and written interviews. Much of the research was performed during the worldwide Covid pandemic, when archives and libraries were closed and traveling to conduct research was impossible. Fortunately, we reaped the benefit of the redoubled effort of many research centers to digitize their resources and make them available online. We also borrowed secondary sources from colleagues and scoured used book websites to purchase works long out of print. As archives began to reopen in Poland and Ukraine, we hired researchers and enlisted the assistance of archivists. Finally, in the spring of 2022, we were able to take part of the trip we had planned two years earlier to conduct archival research as well as to visit the sites of Janina's life and to retrace her steps during the events recounted in her memoir. Unfortunately, by that time, Russia's invasion of Ukraine precluded our going to the places where Janina and Henry lived before 1941.

Our research took us down unexpected paths to surprising sources but also to numerous dead ends. At times, it seemed as though even beyond the grave Janina wanted to retain her secrets. The only surviving vital records from Żurawno date from 1877–1885, so we could find no birth records for Janina or her siblings. We also failed to find any vital records for her parents and so we are not even sure how many siblings she had. Among the RGO records in the Lublin State Archives, a folder marked "Janina Suchodolska" turned out to be empty. Although she worked for the postwar Polish government and traveled for her official duties, the Institute of National Remembrance (IPN) could not locate any passport file on Janina Suchodolska or any of Janina's other identities. Nor could we find any record of her in the files at the IPN of the communist regime's secret service, which surely investigated her suitability for a government position and monitored her foreign contacts and travel. Janina and her sisters never had children, and we searched in vain for other relatives. It was only as we were reviewing the proofs for this book that we finally located a niece of Henry who had known both the Mehlbergs in the late 1960s.

Some valuable sources turned up in unexpected places, however. The New York Public Library digitized the letters that Maria Anna Rudzińska received from Janina during her tour of the United States as Janina Suchodolska.

Photos of Janina during this U.S. tour published in the Minneapolis *Star Tribune*, the Raleigh *News & Observer*, and the *South Bend Tribune* provide visual proof that Janina Mehlberg was Janina Suchodolska. In the application that Janina filed for compensation from West Germany, we found information about her parents and childhood. After we first drafted the final chapter of this book, a contact in Canada found the information about Janina's defection to the West in Berlin. As we were reviewing the copyedited manuscript, a genealogist extraordinaire from the Jewish Historical Institute in Warsaw provided us new information about the Spinner and Mehlberg families.

Most important, wartime records together with the postwar recollections of Majdanek prisoners, Janina's colleagues, and people she aided corroborate even the most astonishing claims in the memoir and reveal other accomplishments that it does not mention. The wealth and variety of the sources we found presented us with the challenge of how to synthesize them into a chronological narrative of Janina's life as Countess Suchodolska. Her memoir enabled us to tell her story from her perspective, but it is not a strictly chronological account and therefore was much less helpful for determining the timing and sequence of the events it relates. As is common with recollections of events that are years—or in this case decades—in the past, Janina's memoir contains some errors with respect to names and dates, and it conflates some events or confuses their chronology. For example, Dr. Blancke appears as Dr. Blaschke, and the date of "Bloody Wednesday," the Operation Harvest Festival massacre at Majdanek, is given as Wednesday, November 17, rather than Wednesday, November 3, 1943. Similarly, the recollections of Majdanek prisoners and of people who interacted with Janina are either silent about the date of events or provide conflicting timing for them. By triangulating the memoir with personal accounts, wartime records, and postwar scholarship on Majdanek and Lublin, we were able to map out the sequence of events in this book on a timeline. We then composed the narrative to connect the events. In some instances, this has required educated guesswork. Following Janina's example, we reached our conclusions through logical analysis of the sources along with judicious applications of imagination and intuition.

Two questions that have confronted us since we began this project are:

Why did Janina write her memoir, and for whom did she write it? That she waited until the 1960s to write it is not surprising. This is when many of those who had experienced the traumas and tragedies of World War II first found the ability and the will to recount what they had endured. The 1960s also saw a rise in public awareness of the Holocaust, thanks to the international sensation surrounding the trial of Adolf Eichmann in Israel in 1961. Unlike the 1946 trial of German leaders at Nuremberg, the Eichmann trial focused exclusively on Nazi Germany's effort to murder all the Jews in Europe, and the prosecutors called scores of Jewish survivors to testify. The trial was internationally televised, and trial sessions were regularly summarized on the nightly news in the United States. The trial's revelations and the testimony of the witnesses electrified non-Jews in Europe and North America and inspired other Jewish survivors to break their long-held silence about the horrors they had suffered. There was a surge of publications and films about the Holocaust as a result. In fact, the 1960s is when the word "Holocaust" became a widely recognized term for Nazi Germany's genocide of the Jews.

In Poland, the increasing willingness of Holocaust survivors to write and speak about their experiences sparked a "memory war." The narrative that emerged from the accounts of Polish Jewish survivors acknowledged both that some non-Jewish Poles had rescued Jews and that others had watched in indifference, cheered, or even participated in the persecution and murder of their Jewish neighbors by Poland's German occupiers. Wartime and postwar accounts of non-Jewish Poles fully corroborate all these varieties of Polish responses to the Holocaust. Some Poles, however, believed that survivors' recollections of antisemitic collaboration besmirched the national honor. Some also complained that the narrative of Jewish suffering during the Holocaust erased the suffering of non-Jewish Poles as victims of Nazi Germany's murderous racist policies.[3]

Poland's communist government recognized the suffering of Polish Jews under the German occupation and erected memorials at important Holocaust sites in the early 1960s. The official narrative mostly ignored the topic of Polish collaboration in persecuting Jews, however, and tended to equate the suffering of Jewish and non-Jewish Poles. The narrative focused on the heroism of those Poles who fought the occupier and rescued Jews, contrasting the Poles' actions with the supposed passivity of Polish Jews in response to their victimization.

The "memory war" in Poland intensified in 1967 with the outbreak of the Six Day War. Poland followed the Soviet Union's lead in backing Israel's Arab opponents. The Polish government launched an antisemitic campaign that depicted Polish Jews as Zionists who were in league with the West and trying to undermine Poland. In 1968, the government blamed "Zionists" for the demonstrations by Polish university students protesting government censorship and repression. Discrimination and harassment became the order of the day for the 30,000 Poles who lived openly as Jews. In addition, a special government unit ferreted out Polish Jews in official positions who had survived the Holocaust by passing as Aryans and had not reverted to their original identity. They were forced out of their jobs and pressured to emigrate. In this atmosphere, the government's Holocaust narrative preached that the Polish people had *all* collectively and heroically fought to save Polish Jews, only to be repaid by the Jews they had rescued with ingratitude and slander.[4]

Janina was certainly aware of the dueling narratives of the Holocaust and World War II in Poland. For all Polish Jews who had survived the Holocaust, including Janina, the increasingly open and virulent antisemitism in Poland in the 1960s evoked a visceral fear that Jews could once again be subjected to genocide there. According to Funk, Janina wrote her memoir in Polish, and Henry translated it into English after her death. Since Janina's written English was at least as good as Henry's, this may indicate that she did not have time to translate it into English before her death. The memoir's narrative, however, suggests that she intended it for a Polish audience. This would explain why the memoir makes so few references to Jewish suffering and only two oblique references to antisemitism among the Poles. With its emphasis on Polish suffering and heroism, Janina's memoir fits well within the official Polish narrative of the 1960s. Her account counters the exclusion of Jews from the narrative of heroism, however. She was a Polish patriot who risked her life to resist the German occupier, and she was a Jew. As a Jew, she honored Polish culture and traditions, even enabled Majdanek prisoners to celebrate Christmas and Easter. She was grateful to Count Skrzyński, the non-Jewish Pole who saved her, and, as a Jew, she aided and rescued Poles.

Janina's memoir also restores the RGO to its rightful place in the narrative of Polish resilience and self-sacrifice during World War II. Ludwik Christians erased the RGO entirely from his 1946 account of the aid program at Majdanek. His version was adopted by communist officials at that time who sought to discredit the RGO as an organization that collaborated with the Nazis in the service of the "fascist" government in exile. Many Majdanek prisoners who received RGO aid did not know who provided it. In their postwar statements about the food deliveries that saved them from starvation, they either assumed that the food had all come from the Polish Red Cross or they chose not to challenge the official narrative that the Polish Red Cross was the only organization that aided them. Janina's memoir sets the record straight, showing that it was the RGO, not the Polish Red Cross, that led the aid program at Majdanek and provided the lion's share of the food it supplied.

Janina's memoir also pays homage to the deeds of the many individuals in the RGO, the AK, and the Underground who worked with her to resist the Germans and rescue their victims. Many of their names have otherwise been lost to history. She acknowledged the heroism of Count Skrzyński, whose service to his nation during World War II was unknown even to his descendants, and she memorialized the martyrdom of Józef Wendrucha. She especially wrote about her women RGO coworkers who supported both her official and her clandestine activities. It is clear that she forged strong bonds of affection with these women who were willing to give their lives for their country and for one another. The necessity of deceiving them about her true identity must have forced her to behave with a certain reserve that deepened the loneliness of her life as an imposter.

The memoir conveys Janina's wit, courage, ingenuity, and passion, but carries an undertone of sorrow throughout. If Janina did intend her account for a Polish audience, this would explain why it is almost completely silent as to the emotions she felt as a Jew witnessing the suffering and slaughter of her people from the comparative safety of the "Aryan" side. It is almost impossible to fathom how Janina, conscious of being a Jew, dared to enter Majdanek over and over and to deal with the SS officials there, especially after the Operation Harvest Festival massacre. We suspect the answer is that she so fully suppressed the consciousness of her true identity that she essentially became Countess Suchodolska.

One enduring mystery about Janina's memoir is why it omits what was arguably her greatest service to her fellow Poles: winning the release from Majdanek of 2,106 children, women, and elderly civilian expellees in August 1943. This event is amply documented in the wartime records of the RGO, including reports that Janina filed, and she testified to Polish authorities about it in 1946. Janina's omission of this episode from her memoir may indicate that she saw it not as a successful rescue but as a failure, that her memory of the event was not of the many she saved but of the many who died in Majdanek before she could win their release, and of the many who died afterward because their release came too late. Writing the memoir required Janina to call forth many memories of terror, horror, trauma, and anguish, but there may have been some memories that, even decades later, she still could not bear to revisit. In this respect, her memoir may be seen as Janina's last courageous act.

Janina was an exceptionally intelligent and brave woman, but those attributes do not explain why and how she managed to accomplish such remarkable feats. Part of the answer lies in the patriotism that drove her actions, a patriotism not based on the lowest common denominator of ethnicity, creed, or language but on what she perceived to be her nation's highest principles. Another part of the answer lies in her compassion and empathy. They are what drove her continual quest to provide ever greater quantities and types of food, medicines, and other goods for the prisoners at Majdanek. Her compassion and empathy also contributed to her success in obtaining the goodwill and even assistance of Nazi officials and Majdanek's SS personnel. Her empathy inspired her understanding that what Majdanek prisoners needed to survive that unspeakable hell was not just food, but hope; her compassion impelled her to provide hope especially to the prisoners who had been broken and turned traitor.

Janina herself was neither fearless nor flawless, which makes her story all the more inspiring. She displayed no heroic tendencies before the war, and if world events had allowed, she would have gone on living the sheltered life of a rather pampered intellectual. Instead, she found herself in the power of people who rated some human lives as worthless, including her own. In response, she decided to measure the value of her own life by the number of lives she could help save. She pursued her mission with all her intelligence, imagination, and intuition, and with truly stubborn persistence—she simply refused to accept what others told her was impossible. As long as there were lives that needed saving, she was certain that there must be a way to save them.

In his preface to the memoir, Henry explained that Janina wrote it as her testimony. It testifies not only to the events she saw but also to what she learned about human nature by observing it within the terrible crucible that was occupied Poland. She reported the variety of responses she witnessed and analyzed what they revealed about human nature. While the memoir testifies to the heroic efforts of Poles to resist the German occupier and to help one another survive, it also cites instances of infighting and self-serving behavior that detracted from those efforts. It describes how the Germans' brutal persecution elicited responses from their Polish victims not only of courage and patriotic self-sacrifice but also of greed and cruel indifference. She wrote movingly of the agonizing choices that the occupation forced its victims to make, as in the following passage:

> *What would a mother do in the face of the impossible choices put to her? There was one who, with her daughter, hid in the wardrobes of her apartment during a raid. They found her daughter, but not her. The child sobbed and screamed for her mother to save her. The mother kept silent, and survived. I know this from the mother herself who, sobbing out her story, wished herself dead instead of condemned to live with this memory.*
>
> *Another mother hid with her son in a bunker. . . . Her son ventured out at the wrong time; he was seized and shot right there. The mother heard and remained silent. . . .*
>
> *A young Jewish woman was offered the privilege of choosing whether her mother or her husband would be executed the next day. A father was offered his life on condition he stand and watch his son being hanged and smiled all the while. If the smile left his face, he would be hanged, too. He kept smiling. . . .*
>
> *And who is to judge the impulse to survive? Now, years later, I try not to judge but simply to report, since we who continue as members of the*

human race are obliged to know its capacities, however grim and unbearable the knowledge may be. But knowledge is not the same as enduring, and I am not sure that knowledge alone gives us the right to judge. The mystery is too great, how we respond to unbearable demands. Because while physical and psychic tortures broke many, some reacted with what one can only call moral grandeur. I know some and heard of many others who helped their fellow-sufferers at the cost of their own lives, who confessed to others' "crimes," who willingly chose death over a degrading life. So the murder of goodness was not thorough, and this fact, too, must be reported.

Janina's memoir is a call to tolerance. The "grim and unbearable" knowledge of human capacities that her wartime experiences taught her only strengthened her belief in the fundamental value and dignity of every human life. The memoir provides examples of individual Ukrainians, Poles, and Germans who demonstrated both the capacity for what Janina termed goodness—for kindness, courage, and self-sacrifice—and the capacity for evil—to be dishonest, vicious, even murderous. She recognized that both capacities are inherent elements of human nature, and her memoir shows that the probability of a person acting on one or the other of those capacities in any given situation cannot be predicted based on ideology, nationality, ethnicity, or belief.

Janina's memoir is also a call to mercy. She realized that, in an atmosphere of extreme violence and suffering, people may act in ways that would have been utterly out of character had they been allowed to live in peace. She did not wish to excuse or justify the harm caused by people's choices. She thought that people should answer for their deeds, but she also believed that people are not fully defined by either the best or the worst of their actions. This belief provides grounds for both cynicism and hope: while heroes are by nature flawed, villains may have the capacity to prove heroic.

In her relief and resistance work, Janina did not ask or care whether the people who sought her aid were deserving. They were humans and they suffered, and so it was her human duty to help them, to show them mercy, to give them hope.

Janina's story is a call to tolerance, to mercy, and to hope.

CODA

Janina ended her memoir with a two-page chapter titled "Return to Majdanek." It describes a tour she took with a Swedish delegation soon after the camp was liberated. We quote from the end of the chapter here, so that Janina may have the final say regarding her story.

> *I walked with the delegation. I talked, pointed things out, objective and quiet. And I saw how they looked at me, wondering how I had seen all that, and survived. There wasn't much to me physically. I suppose it would be easy to imagine that dealing with this sort of matter every day for years would have crushed me. I considered their wonder inside myself, asking myself the questions that were obvious in their eyes—how had I managed, and what had made me go on? It would have been natural to give up, to stop going to Majdanek, to go to pieces, even. But then there would have been no reason to live. When so many were in such terrible need, I had to live to answer that need. I was one individual only in the vast suffering human family. If I thought only of the dangers to myself or to those I loved, I was worth nothing. But if surviving meant being useful to many, I had to find the strength to survive, which made it possible for me to feel some sense of achievement, even of pride. This, at least, was left me. I had achieved less than I had hoped, but I tried, and my efforts had made a difference, so my life had made some difference, and for that reason I had to go on.*
>
> *Then I thought of those who had been broken, physically and morally, who had betrayed other lives in the hope of saving their own. Of them I*

spoke to these men: "None of us has the right to sit in judgment on them. No one who hasn't been in their shoes—their terrible shoes, often filled with blood. However we risked our necks, it was of our own will. But they were in bondage, and all human pride was beaten out of them. They didn't ask to be martyrs. Most of them no doubt wanted nothing more than to live out their days in an average, humdrum existence, without great impact and without glory. They were forced into martyrdom, and this is perhaps harder than willingly risking your life for an ideal."

There is nothing left to do for them but to remember. And in the way of my ancestors, intone "Yisgadal, v'yiskadash," the Kaddish for the dead, and like the real Countess Suchodolska, "Kyrie Eleison, Christe Eleison."

We will remember. . . .

ACKNOWLEDGMENTS

In the course of verifying Janina's memoir and uncovering her full story, we have benefited from the assistance, advice, and encouragement of many people in a number of countries. That Janina's memoir was preserved and came to light is thanks first of all to Henry Mehlberg, who entrusted his English translation of Janina's account to Arthur Layton Funk of the University of Florida. Funk went to remarkable lengths to make Janina's story known. In addition to giving a copy of Henry Mehlberg's translation to Barry, he created a separate version of the memoir by polishing the English and adding annotations. With the permission of Bobbie Curtis and Jeri Hough, the daughters of Henry's third wife, Susie Blackman Clark, Funk donated his annotated and edited version of the memoir to the United States Holocaust Memorial Museum (USHMM), along with photos of Janina and Henry Mehlberg.

In her early research on Janina, Barry was assisted by Katarzyna Pietrzak-Kret, then at the USHMM. Henry's former student Arthur Fine (University of Washington) shared his memories of the Mehlbergs. Fine also connected Barry with Jan Hertrich-Woleński (Jagiellonian University, Kraków), who in turn put her in touch with Stepan Ivanyk (University of Warsaw) and Anna Smywińska-Pohl (Jagiellonian University). All three shared their knowledge of the Lwów-Warsaw School, provided valuable sources, and helped Barry discover Janina's actual name and date of birth.

In 2018, when Debórah Dwork was a Senior Fellow-in-Residence at the USHMM Mandel Center for Advanced Holocaust Studies, Barry (then a

Mandel Center historian) sought her advice about authenticating Janina's memoir. Dwork recommended her former doctoral student, Joanna Sliwa, as a consultant, and thus began our partnership. We are both enduringly grateful to Dwork for the connection.

Throughout this project, we have benefited from the assistance of Alina Skibińska (Polish Center for Holocaust Research and the USHMM), who located and copied records in Poland for us and provided valuable suggestions and contacts. We are also indebted to Gunnar Berg (YIVO), who helped Joanna find and access the records that definitively confirmed for us that Janina was Countess Suchodolska.

As we were planning our research trip to Poland and Ukraine for spring 2020, the Covid-19 pandemic erupted. For the next two years, we benefited immensely from the generous assistance of individuals—archivists, scholars, activists, experts, and colleagues—in North America, South America, and Europe. We are indebted to everyone who showed solidarity, interest, and dedication despite the difficult circumstances they were facing. We could not have written this book at this time without their assistance.

We owe thanks to many colleagues at the USHMM. Throughout the pandemic, when the museum as well as its library and archive were closed, the library reference staff helped Barry access indispensable books and resources. Suzy Goldstein Snyder provided us the accession records for "Janina's Story" and put us in touch with Jeri Hough, Henry's stepdaughter. Natalya Lazar clarified details of Ukrainian history. Jacek Nowakowski introduced Barry to the story of Countess Karolina Lanckorońska. Diane Saltzman and Elizabeth (Betsy) Anthony arranged for us to present our project remotely to the museum's group of Holocaust survivor volunteers and to the Mandel Center, respectively. The support and enthusiasm of both groups were wonderfully encouraging.

Also in the United States, Jeffrey Cymbler of Jewish Records Indexing (JRI)–Poland offered genealogical advice. Sarah Coates (University of Florida), Jenifer Petrescu (Congregation B'nai Israel, Gainesville), and Carl Schramm (Montefiore Jewish Cemetery) searched their archives. Adara Goldberg (Holocaust Resource Center of Kean University) made key introductions and acquainted us with Canadian archives. We appreciated the willingness of Marjorie Senechal (Smith College) and Eugene Allgower (Colorado State University) to share with us their memories of Janina from their student days at IIT. Senechal also provided us scans of Janina's letters at the New York Public Library, shared information she uncovered about Janina's work as a mathematician, and helped us obtain information about women mathematicians in prewar Poland. Joshua Pines gave us information about Janina's cousin Sigmund Pines who supported the Mehlbergs' efforts to emigrate from Poland. We are very grateful to Henry's stepdaughter Jeri Hough for endorsing our project and sharing her memories of Henry. An invitation from the organizers of the "Heroines of the Holocaust" symposium at the Wagner College Holocaust Center allowed us to share Janina's story with international academic colleagues.

In Canada, we received archival and historical assistance from: Patti Auld Johnson (University of New Brunswick); Jocelyn Bourque (Canadian Museum of Immigration at Pier 21); Valerie Casbourn (Library and Archives Canada); Paula Draper; Sarah Fogg, Andréa Shaulis, and Eszter Andor (Montreal Holocaust Museum); Tys Klumpenhouwer (University of Toronto); Carson Phillips (UJAFED Toronto); and Janice Rosen (Canadian Jewish Archives). Donna Bernardo-Ceriz (UJA Ontario Jewish Archives) provided documentation about Janina's escape from Poland. Irvin Klinghofer shared his memories and photographs of the Mehlbergs. Hernan Tesler-Mabé (University of Ottawa) connected us with individuals in South America.

In Argentina, we are indebted to Eliana Hamra (Holocaust Museum, Buenos Aires) who obtained information about Janina's sister Clara. Emmanuel Kahan (CONICET and National University of La Plata) sought records from the country's Foreign Affairs archive. Malena Chinski connected us with Diana Wang (Generations of the Shoah in Argentina), on whose suggestion we reached out to the Argentine Israelite Mutual Association (AMIA). Grupo Reunir-Amia volunteers Clara, Elda, and Tomás uncovered information about Clara for us.

In Uruguay, Rita Vinocur (Uruguay Holocaust Remembrance Center) enthusiastically agreed to help with tracing information about Janina's sister Antonina. Jana Beris Jerozolimski (Semanario Hebreo) placed an ad in the local Jewish paper seeking information about Antonina.

In Israel, Idan Bierman, the grandson of Henry's brother Izydor, connected us with his aunt Eva Tene. Speaking from England, Tene shared with us her memories of living with the Mehlbergs in Chicago from 1965 to 1968.

In Germany, we received archival help from Wolfgang Grimm and Martin Kalibe (Bezirksregierung Düsseldorf) and guidance from Jens Hoppe (Conference on Jewish Material Claims Against Germany).

In Poland, we owe thanks to many archivists, scholars, researchers, and museum professionals. Teresa Klimowicz (Grodzka Gate–NN Theater) researched collections at the Lublin State Archive for us and later gave us an enlightening tour of her institution. Joanna Fabijańczuk (Kraków JCC) reached out to Izabela Olejnik, who copied documents at the University of Łódź. Renata Grzegórska and Barbara Krzyżanowska (University of Warsaw); Anna Jaśkiewicz (Przemyśl State Archive); Piotr Józefiak (Adam Mickiewicz University in Poznań); Karolina Anna Kołodziejczyk (Metropolitan Catholic Archives in Lublin); Grzegorz Przybysz and Magdalena Wątorska (University of Wrocław); Anna Radoń (Jagiellonian University); Agnieszka Reszka (Jewish Historical Institute); and Agnieszka Ziomek (University of Łódź) conducted archival searches in their institutions. Michał Bojanowski (Chidusz Jewish Foundation in Wrocław) put us in touch with Agnieszka Michalik, who in turn showed us sources about Janina's prewar life. Danuta Ciesielska and Krzysztof Ciesielski (Jagiellonian University) offered invaluable information about the circle of mathematicians in Lwów and pointed us to important digital sources. Tomasz Dietl (Polish Academy of Sciences) shared his recollections of Andrzej Skrzyński. Sylwia Mazurek-Męcfel connected us with Elżbieta Romiszowska-Mazurek, Skrzyński's granddaughter, who, in turn, shared information about and photographs of Skrzyński. Anna Ożyńska-Zborowska and Wojciech Rostworowski (relatives of Skrzyński's fourth wife, Zofia Mycielska Skrzyńska) responded instantly with a key postwar photograph of Skrzyński. Justyna Janiszewska (Polish-U.S. Fulbright Commission); Magdalena Kozłowska and Łukasz Krzyżanowski (University of Warsaw); and Kazimierz Rędziński (Jan Długosz University of Humanities and Sciences) made connections to researchers. Adam Kopciowski (Maria Curie-Skłodowska University) explained details about postwar Jewish life in Lublin. Noam Silberberg (Genealogy Department, Jewish Historical Institute) replied immediately with records pertaining to Janina, Henry, and their families that had eluded us and the other experts we consulted.

The staff of the State Museum at Majdanek deserve special mention for their outstanding assistance. Marta Grudzińska obtained extremely valuable sources for us and provided fascinating information about Dr. Perzanowska and the women's hospital at Majdanek. In addition to advising us on our research, Łukasz Myszała spent many more hours than he had planned giving us tours of Majdanek and Lublin and sharing his encyclopedic knowledge of both places during World War II. Wojciech Lenarczyk shared his expertise in the camp's history and helped with archival research. Dariusz Libionka provided expert historical guidance.

Also in Lublin, we thank Łukasz Krzysiak (National Museum in Lublin) for arranging a tour of the Under the Clock Museum, for the gift bags with books, and for archival advice.

Unfortunately, the Russian aggression on Ukraine in February 2022 and the ongoing war made it impossible for us to travel there. We are grateful to Volodymyr Zilinskyi (Ivan Franko National University of Lviv) and Slav Tsarynnyk (Lviv Ecotour) for their readiness to conduct research in Lviv archives. We hope for peace in Ukraine and look forward to visiting the places connected to Janina's life.

We are grateful beyond words to our literary agent, Joëlle Delbourgo. Joëlle instantly recognized the remarkable story that we wanted to tell and indefatigably advocated for us and our work. We are grateful to Debbie Cenziper for making the connection and for her advice on how to tell Janina's story to a general readership.

At Simon & Schuster, we had the good fortune to work with Bob Bender, our editor, and with Johanna Li, associate editor. Both shared our excitement in bringing Janina's story to a broader audience. Bob helped us craft a narrative for a general readership, particularly by curbing our proclivity as historians to provide more contextual detail than was strictly necessary to tell the story. We benefited from the amazing attention to detail of our copy editor, Fred Chase.

We each express our gratitude to those in our circles who have supported us in this process. Joanna thanks her supervisor at the Claims Conference, Wesley Fisher, for his broad support. Joanna's friends—Dara Bramson, Rachel Rothstein, and Magda Wróbel—understood that she often had to decline rather than accept, and yet they continued to cheer her on. Lukasz Sliwa offered his gourmet meals and signature coffee to sustain his sister over long work hours. Joanna credits her parents with inspiring her interest in history and cultivating languages that enabled her to do this research. Joanna's husband, Karol Maźnicki, an enthusiastic ally, fostered an environment that allowed her to pursue this project.

Barry is grateful to her supervisor, Patricia Heberer-Rice, director of the USHMM's Division of the Senior Historian, and to Lisa Leff and Robert Ehrenreich of the Mandel Center at the USHMM for their understanding and support as Barry reduced her hours, then took a leave of absence to work on this book. She thanks her brother, Forrest "Hap" White, for suggesting the title *Counterfeit Countess*. Throughout the long and often challenging process of producing this book, she was cheered on by her children, Lydia and Frank Blackmore, their spouses Jackson Kimbrell and Julia Lisowski, and her siblings and siblings-in-law. Her friends Lesly Berger, Trudy Clark, and Kristin Stone made sure she occasionally came up for air and human contact. Mike Meyerson provided expert legal advice as well as friendship. Finally, Barry wishes to acknowledge her mother, Edith Reynolds White, artist, poet, librarian, civic leader, World War II codebreaker, and civil rights activist. She was the first to show Barry what an intelligent and determined woman can accomplish when she refuses to accept "No" for an answer.

NOTES

The principal source for this book is Henry Mehlberg's unpublished and untitled translation from Polish of Josephine Janina Mehlberg's account of her life during World War II, which includes a preface by Henry Mehlberg. We worked from the carbon copy of the translation manuscript that Arthur Funk gave to Elizabeth "Barry" White in 1989. The specific information drawn from the manuscript is not cited in the notes. Funk also created an edited and annotated version of the memoir that is available at the United States Holocaust Memorial Museum (USHMM): Accession number 2003.333, "Janina's Story."

INTRODUCTION

1. This figure is based upon the most recent and thorough analysis of Jewish victims at Majdanek to date: Chmielewski, "Żydzi w KL Lublin," in *Więźniowie KL Lublin 1941–1944*, ed. Kranz and Lenarczyk, 264–65.
2. Krzyżanowski and Soroka, "The Polish Underground Resistance in the Lublin Area," 145–56.
3. Like Janina and Henry Mehlberg, Lemkin studied at Jan Kazimierz University in Lwów.

ONE: BEFORE

1. Much of the information in this chapter about Janina's life before World War II, her character, and her relationship with her husband, Henry Mehlberg, is drawn from the following sources: Henry's preface to Janina's memoir; photographs included in "Janina's Story," USHMM; restitution and pension applications submitted to the West German government by the Mehlbergs, "Henry Mehlberg," VA 278344, and "Janina Mehlberg," VA 278345, State Finance Office, Compensation Payments / Landesamt für Finanzen, Amt für Wiedergutmachung—Saarburg (BEG); interview with Dr. Arthur Fine by Elizabeth White; interviews with Dr. Marjorie Senechal and Eva Tene by authors.
2. "Pepi Mehlberg," CKŻP, Wydział ewidencji i statystyki 1945–1950, 303/V/425

/M 4762/174027, Archive of the Jewish Historical Institute (AŻIH). In the late nineteenth century, only 5 percent of agricultural land in Eastern Galicia was owned by Jews. Pohl, *Nationalsozialistische Judenverfolgung in Ostgalizien, 1941–1944*, 126.

3. Under Austrian rule, Galicia was divided into western and eastern parts. Eastern Galicia encompassed the borderlands, which today is Western Ukraine. The area has been known to Ukrainians as "Halychyna."
4. Snyder, *Black Earth*, 23; Veidlinger, *In the Midst of Civilized Europe*, 37–39.
5. Böhler, "Post-war Military Action and Violence (East Central Europe)," *1914–1918 Online: International Encyclopedia of the First World War*, https://encyclopedia.1914-1918-online.net/article/post-war_military_action_and_violence_east_central_europe, accessed September 27, 2021; Budnitsky, "Jews, Pogroms, and the White Movement," 1–23; Veidlinger, *In the Midst of Civilized Europe*, 1–5, 288–303.
6. We are grateful to Dr. Danuta Ciesielska, Institute for the History of Science, Polish Academy of Sciences, for this information.
7. For the history of the Lwów-Warsaw School, see: Woleński, *Logic and Philosophy in the Lvov-Warsaw School*; *Tradition of the Lvov-Warsaw School: Ideas and Continuations*, ed. Brożek, Chybińska, Jadacki, and Woleński. For the role of women in the movement, see Pakszys, "Kobiety w filozofii polskiej. Dwa pokolenia Szkoły Lwowsko-Warszawskiej."
8. "Z Uniwersytetu Jana Kazimierza we Lwowie," *Chwila*, March 9, 1928, p. 13, accessed January 6, 2021, https://libraria.ua/en/numbers/6/26480/?PageNumber=12&ArticleId=983777&Search=pepi%20spinner.
9. Henry was born on October 7, 1904, in Kopyczyńce to Nuchim Mehlberg and Sara Chane née Jamenfeld. Information about his family derives from Księgi metrykalne gmin wyznania mojżeszowego z terenów tzw. zabużańskich, 1789–1943, sygn. 2268, 2419, 2858, 3460, Main Archive of Old Records (AGAD).
10. Information about Henry's academic career derives from the following records: "Mehlberg Henryk," 1946–1951, Ministerstwo Edukacji Narodowej Departament Kadr, sygn. 3586, Archive of New Records (AAN); "Mehlberg Henryk," Archives of the University of Łódź (AUŁ); "Mehlberg Henryk," Tom I: AUW.6/2.180, p. 101, Archives of the University of Wrocław (AUW); and "Henryk Mehlberg," 387b-14, Archives of the University of Adam Mickiewicz (AUAM).
11. Archiwum Kazimierza Twardowskiego, Korespondencja Naukowa, Tom 23. Ły–Meh, pp. 96–144, Digital Archive of Combined Libraries.
12. Ibid.
13. "Letter from Kazimierz Twardowski," February 26, 1934, Roman Ingarden Digital Archive; "Odczyty," *Chwila*, January 9, 1935, p. 10.
14. "Spis prac D-ra Henryka Mehlberga," 3586, p. 9, AAN; "Letter to Kazimierz Twardowski," July 29, 1935, and "Letter to Kazimierz Twardowski," July 11, 1937, Roman Ingarden Digital Archive.
15. Archiwum Kazimierza Twardowskiego, "Księga Pamiątkowa," October 20, 1936, Digital Archive of Combined Libraries.

16. "Henry Mehlberg," VA 278344, BEG. *The 1930 Poland Industry, Business, and Finance Directory*; *The 1930 Poland Industry Directory*, vol. 4: *Food*; *The 1930 Poland and Danzig Business Directory (Trade, Industry, Handicraft, and Agriculture)*; and *The 1932/1933 Poland Telephone Directory* (excluding city of Warsaw), Genealogy Indexer, https://genealogyindexer.org/, accessed August 10, 2022.
17. Kochanski, *The Eagle Unbowed*, 7, 22–25; Gross, *Polish Society Under German Occupation*, 9–28.
18. Pohl, *Nationalsozialistische Judenverfolgung in Ostgalizien*, 27.
19. Rędziński, "Studenci żydowscy we Lwowie w latach 1918–1939."
20. Bartov, *Anatomy of a Genocide*; Heller, *On the Edge of Destruction*; Kochanski, *The Eagle Unbowed*, 26–32.
21. Evans, *The Third Reich in Power*, 678–99; Weinberg, *A World at Arms*, 31–35.
22. In September 1939, Janina, then known as Józefa Mehlberg, published a review of *Sur la Nation de Collectif* by Jan Herzberg in *The Journal of Symbolic Logic*.
23. Announcements for Henry's talks can be found in the Jewish newspaper *Chwila*. One of them announced the Mehlbergs' joint radio program: "Słuchajmy dziś Radia," *Chwila*, 3 November 1937, p. 12.

TWO: THE BEGINNING OF THE END

1. In addition to Janina's memoir, the description of Polish attitudes and experiences during the German attack are drawn from Klukowski, *Tagebuch aus den Jahren der Okkupation 1939–1944*; Shatyn, *A Private War*, 113–19; Jolanta Jaworska, interview with Janina Wiener, Centropa, https://www.centropa.org/biography/janina-wiener, accessed November 3, 2021.
2. Kochanski, *The Eagle Unbowed*, 121; Snyder, *Black Earth*, 120, 127; Burleigh, *Moral Combat*, 152–55; Mazower, *Hitler's Empire*, 98; Beorn, *The Holocaust in Eastern Europe*, 76–77.
3. Amar, *The Paradox of Ukrainian Lviv*, 44, 50.
4. Janina Wiener oral history; Joseph Klinghofer oral history, Interview 4059, USHMM, USC Shoah Foundation Visual History Archive; Lanckorońska, *Those Who Trespass Against Us*, 1–22; Gross, *Revolution from Abroad*, 126–43.
5. Kochanski, *The Eagle Unbowed*, 125–26.
6. Ibid., 123; Gross, *Revolution from Abroad*, 106.
7. Gross, *Revolution from Abroad*, 193–97; Snyder, *Black Earth*, 57; 120–32; Asher, "The Soviet Union, the Holocaust, and Auschwitz," 898.
8. Snyder, *Black Earth*, 122.
9. Ibid., 120–23; Beorn, *The Holocaust in Eastern Europe*, 87; Pohl, *Nationalsozialistische Judenverfolgung in Ostgalizien*, 55.

THREE: TERROR COMES TO LWÓW

1. Himka, "The Lviv Pogrom of 1941," 209–43; Pohl, *Nationalsozialistische Judenverfolgung in Ostgalizien*, 54–62.

2. Pohl, *Nationalsozialistische Judenverfolgung in Ostgalizien*, 53–54; Arad, Krakowski, and Spector, eds., *The Einsatzgruppen Reports*, i–ix; Krausnick and Wilhelm, *Die Truppe des Weltanschauungskrieges*, 3–37, 150–72.
3. Zygmunt Albert, translation from *Kaźń Profesorów Lwowskich*, https://www.lwow.home.pl/lwow_profs.html, accessed November 1, 2021.
4. Pohl, *Nationalsozialistische Judenverfolgung in Ostgalizien*, 68–69; Amar, *The Paradox of Ukrainian Lviv*, 120–37.
5. Pohl, *Nationalsozialistische Judenverfolgung in Ostgalizien*, 55–58; Winstone, *The Dark Heart of Hitler's Europe*, 103–4; Berkhoff and Carynnyk, "The Organization of Ukrainian Nationalists and Its Attitude toward Germans and Jews," 150.
6. Pohl, *Nationalsozialistische Judenverfolgung in Ostgalizien*, 45–52.
7. Ibid., 64–66.
8. Ibid., 64–66; 123–25.
9. Ibid., 75–77; Winstone, *The Dark Heart of Hitler's Europe*, 106, 153.
10. Winstone, *The Dark Heart of Hitler's Europe*, 114–15; Pohl, *Nationalsozialistische Judenverfolgung in Ostgalizien*, 123–35.
11. Pohl, *Nationalsozialistische Judenverfolgung in Ostgalizien*, 119–41.

FOUR: TRANSFORMATION

1. Pohl, *Nationalsozialistische Judenverfolgung in Ostgalizien, 1941–1944*, 158–60; Document #23: diary entries of Tadeusz Tomaszewski, in *Polen*, ed. Friedrich; Redner, *A Jewish Policeman in Lwów*; Golczewski, "Polen," in *Dimension des Voelkermords*, ed. Benz, 445–46.
2. Pohl, *Von der "Judenpolitik" zum Judenmord*, 87–90.

FIVE: THE DYSTOPIAN UTOPIA

1. Akta Miasta Lublina, zespół 22, 2145/22, State Archive in Lublin (APL).
2. Kershaw, *Hitler*, 146–55; Majer, *"Non-Germans" Under the Third Reich*, 63, 625n224.
3. Aly, *Final Solution*, 34; Friedländer, *The Years of Extermination*, 11–12.
4. Koehl, *RKFDV*, 56.
5. Mallmann, Böhler, and Matthäus, *Einsatzgruppen in Polen*, 62–63; Mędykowski, *Macht Arbeit Frei?*, 7–8.
6. Gross, *Polish Society Under German Occupation*, 73–75; Burleigh, *Moral Combat*, 142.
7. Winstone, *The Dark Heart of Hitler's Europe*, 96–98.
8. Memo from Heinrich Himmler re: "Some Thoughts on the Treatment of Aliens in the East," 15 May 1940, in *Europa unterm Hakenkreuz*, ed. Heckert and Röhr, 171–72.
9. Longerich, *Politik der Vernichtung*, 273–78; 289–92; Hayes, *Why?*, 73–113.
10. Winstone, *The Dark Heart of Hitler's Europe*, 38; Majer, *"Non-Germans" Under the Third Reich*, 261–64; Burleigh, *Moral Combat*, 135–36.
11. Aly, *Final Solution*, 34–35; Madajczyk, *Die Okkupationspolitik Nazideutschlands in*

Polen 1939–1945, 405–13, Table 15; *Europa unterm Hakenkreuz*, ed. Heckert and Röhr, 56–59.

12. Gross, *Polish Society Under German Occupation*, 62–63.
13. Majer, *"Non-Germans" Under the Third Reich*, 276–82, quotation on 281; Pohl, *Von der "Judenpolitik" zum Judenmord*, 90; Winstone, *The Dark Heart of Hitler's Europe*, 43–44, 49–52.
14. Gross, *Polish Society Under German Occupation*, 148–59; Winstone, *The Dark Heart of Hitler's Europe*, 67–75, quotation on 50.
15. Akta Miasta Lublina, zespół 22, 2145⁄22, APL.
16. Shatyn, *A Private War*, 156–57; Madajczyk, *Die Okkupationspolitik Nazideutschlands in Polen 1939–1945*, 279.
17. Majer, *"Non-Germans" Under the Third Reich*, 290, 290f; Burleigh, *Moral Combat*, 142; Madajczyk, *Die Okkupationspolitik Nazideutschlands in Polen 1939–1945*, 347–48; Mazower, *Hitler's Empire*, 127.
18. Rations varied by district in the General Government. In the fall of 1941, the caloric value of the basic daily rations for Poles in Warsaw was 418, while in Radom, special workers could receive as much as 613 calories. Madajczyk, *Die Okkupationspolitik Nazideutschlands in Polen 1939–1945*, 283–84, 285: Table 10. According to the World Health Organization, 2,100 calories per person/per day is the minimum amount needed to sustain a population: World Health Organization, "Food and Nutrition Needs in Emergencies," 1, https://www.who.int/i/item/food-and-nutrition-needs-in-emergencies.
19. Musial, *Deutsche Zivilverwaltung und Judenverfolgung im Generalgouvernement*, 160–63.
20. Majer, *"Non-Germans" Under the Third Reich*, 272.
21. Ibid., 149–53; Pohl, *Von der "Judenpolitik" zum Judenmord*, 80; Madajczyk, *Die Okkupationspolitik Nazideutschlands in Polen 1939–1945*, 220–24, 245: Table 7; Winstone, *The Dark Heart of Hitler's Europe*, 171.
22. Gross, *Polish Society Under German Occupation*, 110.
23. The information about the Lublin Ghetto is drawn from: Photos, testimonies, and articles on the website of the Grodzka Gate–NN Theatre, especially Jakub Chmielewski, "The Ghetto in Podzamcze—boundaries and area," trans. Monika Metlerska-Colerick, https://teatrnn.pl/lexicon/articles/the-ghetto-in-podzamcze-boundaries-and-area/, accessed January 30, 2022; Martin Dean, "Lublin," *The United States Holocaust Memorial Museum Encyclopedia of Camps and Ghettos*, ed. Martin Dean, 675–78; Pohl, *Von der "Judenpolitik" zum Judenmord*, 90–95; Silberklang, *Gates of Tears*, 157–219.
24. Schwindt, *Das Konzentrations- und Vernichtungslager Majdanek*, 79.
25. Madajczyk, *Die Okkupationspolitik Nazideutschlands in Polen 1939–1945*, 454–78; Gross, *Polish Society Under German Occupation*, 186–89; Musial, *Deutsche Zivilverwaltung und Judenverfolgung im Generalgouvernement*, 145–46; Winstone, *The Dark Heart of Hitler's Europe*, 69, 104.

SIX: ANNIHILATION

1. Poprzeczny, *Odilo Globocnik*, 27–34; 61–78; Bartrop and Grimm, *Perpetrating the Holocaust*, 102–4.
2. Black, "Rehearsal for 'Reinhard'?," 220; Madajczyk, *Die Okkupationspolitik Nazideutschlands in Polen 1939–1945*, 188–89.
3. White, "Majdanek," 3; Pohl, "Die Stellung des Distrikts Lublin in der 'Endlösung der Judenfrage,'" in "*Aktion Reinhardt*," ed. Musial, 91.
4. The information in this chapter on the Lublin *Selbstschutz*, Globocnik's early forced labor camps for Jews, and plans for the reservation are drawn from: Black, "Rehearsal for 'Reinhard'?," 211–22; Mędykowski, *Macht Arbeit Frei?*, 138–77; Silberklang, *Gates of Tears*, 114–28; Winstone, *The Dark Heart of Hitler's Europe*, 77–80; Pohl, *Von der "Judenpolitik" zum Judenmord*, 49–51, 79–85; Musial, *Deutsche Zivilverwaltung und Judenverfolgung im Generalgouvernement*, 110–22; and Gruner, *Jewish Forced Labor Under the Nazis*, 244–46. Musial argues that the 50,000 to 70,000 figure, supported by Pohl and Gruner, is much too high: *Deutsche Zivilverwaltung und Judenverfolgung im Generalgouvernement*, 167.
5. Dziadosz and Marszałek, "Więzienia i obozy w dystrykcie lubelskim w latach 1939–1944," 59.
6. Musial, *Deutsche Zivilverwaltung und Judenverfolgung im Generalgouvernement*, 201–3, quotation on 203; Pohl, "Die Stellung des Distrikts Lublin in der 'Endlösung der Judenfrage,'" 91.
7. Quoted in White, "Majdanek," 4.
8. Aly, *Final Solution*, 185–86; Evans, *The Third Reich at War*, 172–75; Gerlach, *The Extermination of the European Jews*, 67–68.
9. White, "Majdanek," 3–5; Musial, *Deutsche Zivilverwaltung und Judenverfolgung im Generalgouvernement*, 202.
10. Musial, *Deutsche Zivilverwaltung und Judenverfolgung im Generalgouvernement*, 201–4.
11. For the "euthanasia" program and its connection to the "final solution," see: Friedlander, *The Origins of Nazi Genocide*.
12. Pohl, "Massentötungen durch Giftgas im Rahmen der 'Aktion Reinhardt,'" in *Neue Studien zu Nationalsozilististischen Massentötungen durch Giftgas*, ed. Morsch and Perz, 191–92; White, "Majdanek," 9; Black, "Die Trawniki-Männer und die 'Aktion Reinhard,'" in *"Aktion Reinhard,"* Musial, ed., 309–52.
13. Longerich, *Politik der Vernichtung*, 441–44; Czech, *Auschwitz Chronicle, 1939–1945*, 84–87; Pohl, "Massentötungen durch Giftgas im Rahmen der 'Aktion Reinhardt,'"191.
14. Longerich, *Politik der Vernichtung*, 466–67.
15. Friedländer, *The Years of Extermination*, 272–81; Roseman, *The Wannsee Conference and the Final Solution*, passim.
16. For a brief history of *Aktion* Reinhard and a tally of its victims, see: "Operation Reinhard (Einsatz Reinhard)," *Encyclopedia of the Holocaust*, United States Holocaust

Memorial Museum, https://encyclopedia.ushmm.org/content/en/article/operation-reinhard-einsatz-reinhard, accessed January 21, 2022. For the tally of Jewish deaths at Auschwitz, see "Auschwitz," *Encyclopedia of the Holocaust*, https://encyclopedia.ushmm.org/content/en/article/auschwitz, accessed January 21, 2022.

17. For the changes in the ghetto in the run-up to its liquidation, see: Pohl, *Von der "Judenpolitik" zum Judenmord,* 110–11; Dean, "Lublin," *The United States Holocaust Memorial Museum Encyclopedia of Camps and Ghettos,* ed. Martin Dean, 676; Chmielewski, "The Ghetto in Podzamcze—boundaries and area," https://teatrnn.pl/lexicon/articles/the-ghetto-in-podzamcze-boundaries-and-area, accessed January 22, 2022.
18. Pohl, *Von der "Judenpolitik" zum Judenmord,* 113–17; Dean, "Lublin," 676; time-coded English notes to July 9, 2003, oral history interview of Jacek Ossowski, RG-50.488.0177, USHMM. The website of the Grodzka Gate–NN Theatre in Lublin provides photos of the Lublin Ghetto and detailed descriptions of its history and of the destruction of Lublin's Jews: https://teatrnn.pl/zydzi/en/holocaust-19391944, accessed January 22, 2022.
19. Klukowski, *Tagebuch aus den Jahren der Okkupation 1939–1944*, 337; "The camp in Bełżec," attachment to April 1942 report of the Polish Home Army Lublin detachment, Document 66, in *Polen*, ed. Friedrich, 260–62.
20. Anna Wylegała, "Entangled Bystanders," in *Trauma, Experience and Narrative in Europe after World War II,* ed. Kivimäki and Leese, 132; Madajczyk, *Die Okkupationspolitik Nazideutschlands in Polen 1939–1945,* 189–90; Kłapeć, *Rada Główna Opiekuńcza w dystrykcie lubelskim w latach 1940–1944*, 34.
21. Klukowski, *Tagebuch aus den Jahren der Okkupation 1939–1944*, 332.

SEVEN: "BETTER TO DIE A SOLDIER"

1. Zimmerman, *The Polish Underground and the Jews, 1939–1945*, 149–58; Golczewski, "Die Heimatarmee und die Juden," in *Die polnische Heimatarmee*, ed. Chiari, with Kochanowski, 643–45, 664–65.
2. Zimmerman, *The Polish Underground and the Jews, 1939–1945*, 57; Lanckorońska, *Those Who Trespass Against Us*, 20.
3. Komorowski, "Facetten des polnischen militärischen Widerstandes und seine Aktualität," in *Die polnische Heimatarmee*, ed. Chiari, with Kochanowski, 683.
4. Peploński, "Die Aufklärung der Heimatarmee," in *Die polnische Heimatarmee,* ed. Chiari, with Kochanowski, 180–81; Biskupska, *Survivors*, 150–56. For the role of women in the AK, see Höger, "Frauen als Kombattanten," in *Die polnische Heimatarmee*, ed. Chiari, with Kochanowski, 387–410.
5. Majer, *"Non-Germans" Under the Third Reich*, 318–19.
6. Kłapeć, *Rada Główna Opiekuńcza w dystrykcie lubelskim w latach 1940–1944*, 173–200; Winstone, *The Dark Heart of Hitler's Europe*, 134.
7. Kłapeć, *Rada Główna Opiekuńcza w dystrykcie lubelskim w latach 1940–1944*, 120–21; Musial, *Deutsche Zivilverwaltung und Judenverfolgung im Generalgouvernement*, 96–98.

8. Kłapeć, *Rada Główna Opiekuńcza w dystrykcie lubelskim w latach 1940–1944*, 117–21, 156–61.
9. Series of memos to the Polish Care Committees in Lublin District from Janina Suchodolska, Secretary to the RGO Advisor for Lublin District, June 1942, RGO-Lublin, sygn. 8, pp. 104–12, APL; Kłapeć, *Rada Główna Opiekuńcza w dystrykcie lubelskim w latach 1940–1944*, 156.
10. Kłapeć, *Rada Główna Opiekuńcza w dystrykcie lubelskim w latach 1940–1944*, 168–69; "Należności za podróże służbowe rowerami," June 20, 1942. APL RGO-Lublin, sygn. 8, p. 109; Majer, *"Non-Germans" Under the Third Reich*, 318–19.
11. Kłapeć, *Rada Główna Opiekuńcza w dystrykcie lubelskim w latach 1940–1944*, 150, 168–69.
12. Ibid., 117; Winstone, *The Dark Heart of Hitler's Europe*, 143–45; Kochanski, *The Eagle Unbowed*, 275; Majewski, "Konzept und Organization des 'zivilen Kampfes,'" in *Die polnische Heimatarmee*, ed. Chiari, with Kochanowski, 305.
13. Wachsmann, *KL*, 286.
14. Ibid., 261, 283; Streit, "Soviet Prisoners of War in the Hands of the Wehrmacht," in *War of Extermination*, ed. Heer and Naumann, 81, 86. British radio intercepts of Majdanek daily status reports show that 112 Soviet POWs remained at the camp on January 16, 1942; by February 19, 1942, the number dropped to 58: Kuwałek, Kranz, and Ciwek-Siupa, "Odszyfrowane radiotelegramy (. . .)," 210–32.
15. Testimony of Stanisław Goljan, October 29, 1947, GK 196/153.cz.1, pp. 73–78, Institute of National Remembrance (IPN), Chronicles of Terror, https://www.zapisyterroru.pl/dlibra/publication/3683/edition/3664/content?navq=aHR0cDovL3d3dy56YXBpc3l0ZXJyb3J1LnBsL2RsaWJyYS9sYXRlc3Q_YWN0aW9uPVNpbXBsZVNlYXJjaEFjdGlvbiZ0eXBlPS02JnA9MA&navref=NG9tOzRucCAydWI7MnRzIDJlbDsyZTI, accessed August 25, 2023.
16. Kranz, *The Extermination of Jews at Majdanek Concentration Camp*, 20–21; Vrba and Bestic, *Escape from Auschwitz*, 53–69. Descriptions of the suffering and death of Jews on deportation trains also available in: Klukowski, *Tagebuch aus den Jahren der Okkupation 1939–1944*, 337; "31.8.1942. 'Judenumsiedlung' in Rawa-Ruska," National-Socialism Archive, Dokumente zum Nationalsozialismus, https://www.ns-archiv.de/verfolgung/polen/rawaruska/umsiedlung.php, accessed March 28, 2020.
17. Vrba and Bestic, *Escape from Auschwitz*, 77; Ambach and Köhler, eds., *Lublin-Majdanek*, 72.
18. Marszałek, *Majdanek*, 143; Kranz, *The Extermination of Jews at Majdanek Concentration Camp*, 23; Schwindt, *Das Konzentrations- und Vernichtungslager Majdanek*, 168–70; Smorczewski, *Bridging the Gap*, 126–27.
19. The information in this chapter about Countess Lanckorońska is drawn from: Lanckorońska, *Those Who Trespass Against Us*, xvi–xxii, 53–144.
20. Kłapeć, *Rada Główna Opiekuńcza w dystrykcie lubelskim w latach 1940–1944*, 241–46.
21. Orth, *Die Konzentrationslager-SS*, 189; Wachsmann, *KL*, 117–18, 198.

22. Malm, "Przed i za drutami," in *Braterska Pomoc,* ed. Machuła and Wiśniewska, 84–109; State Museum at Majdanek, "Saturnina Malm—A 'Quiet Heroine,'" August 17, 2018, https://www.majdanek.eu/en/pow/saturnina_malm_-_a__quiet_heroine/50, accessed April 9, 2022.
23. Malm, "Przed i za drutami," 84–109; Ambach and Köhler, *Lublin-Majdanek,* 171–79; Wachsmann, *KL,* 385; Kuwałek, Kranz, and Ciwek-Siupa, "Odszyfrowane radiotelegramy (. . .)," 210–32.
24. Wachsmann, *KL,* 385–87; Marszałek, *Majdanek,* 40; Pauer-Studer and Velleman, *Konrad Morgen,* 51.

EIGHT: FROZEN CARGO

1. Madajczyk, *Die Okkupationspolitik Nazideutschlands in Polen 1939–1945,* 422–25; Kozaczyńska, "When There Were No More Tears Left to Cry," in *Crime Without Punishment,* ed. Kostkiewicz, 101–7. In addition to other sources cited in this chapter, much of the information provided regarding the Zamość resettlement operation in the winter of 1942–1943 and the RGO's response is drawn from records of the RGO, sygn. 46, pp. 1–6, 10–15, 19, 21, 41–42, AAN, and accessible at RG-15.550, 2_125_0_1.2_46. pp. 10–34, USHMM.
2. Madajczyk, *Die Okkupationspolitik Nazideutschlands in Polen 1939–1945,* 422–25; Laura Crago, "Szczebrzeszyn," *Encyclopedia of Camps and Ghettos,* ed. Dean, 713–15; Adam Kopciowski and Laura Crago, "Zamość," *Encyclopedia of Camps and Ghettos,* ed. Dean, 735–38; entries from October 21 through November 26, 1942, Klukowski, *Tagebuch aus den Jahren der Okkupation 1939–1944,* 376–87.
3. Kochanski, *The Eagle Unbowed,* 269.
4. Schwindt, *Das Konzentrations- und Vernichtungslager Majdanek,* 122–29.
5. Quotation, ibid., 123; Kranz, "Das Konzentrationslager Majdanek 1941–1944," in *Bildungsarbeit und historisches Lernen in der Gedenkstätte Majdanek,* ed. Kranz, 281–83; Minutes of October 30, 1942, Polish Care Committee meeting, RG -15.550, 2_125_0_2.1468/382, USHMM; "Tätigkeitsbericht des Polnischen Hilfskomitees für Stadt und Land Lublin für November 1942," December 18, 1942, Distrikt Lublin, sygn. 238, pp. 1–5, APL.
6. Madajczyk, *Die Okkupationspolitik Nazideutschlands in Polen 1939–1945,* 422–25; Document 123, *Europa unterm Hakenkreuz,* ed. Heckert and Röhr, 238–39.
7. Document 123, *Europa unterm Hakenkreuz,* ed. Heckert and Röhr, 238–39.
8. Kozaczyńska, "When There Were No More Tears Left to Cry," 101–4; Jaczyńska, *Sonderlaboratorium SS,* 187–97.
9. Document 123, *Europa unterm Hakenkreuz,* ed. Heckert and Röhr, 238–39.
10. Kozaczyńska, "When There Were No More Tears Left to Cry," 105–7.
11. "Protokół przesłuchania świadka: Janina Suchodolska," December 2, 1946, IPN 108/272, GK 281/272; SO Rd 272, Archive of the State Museum at Majdanek (APMM).
12. Kłapeć, *Rada Główna Opiekuńcza w dystrykcie lubelskim w latach 1940–1944,* 253–59.

13. Wnuk, *Dzieci polskie oskarżaja*, 189–90, quoting the testimony of Janina Suchodolska.

NINE: THE POLISH QUESTION

1. Madajczyk, *Die Okkupationspolitik Nazideutschlands in Polen 1939–1945*, 218–19.
2. Wachsmann, *KL*, 627, 409–24.
3. Ibid., 421–27; Wiśniewska, "Pomoc więźniom Majdanka," 235–36.
4. Kuwałek, Kranz, and Ciwek-Siupa, "Odszyfrowane radiotelegramy (. . .)," 210–32; Kranz, "Konzentrationslager Lublin," 37; Grudzińska, "Polacy na Majdanku," in *Więźniowie KL Lublin 1941–1944*, ed. Kranz and Lenarczyk, 272–82.
5. Wachsmann, *KL*, 419; Document 126, *Europa unterm Hakenkreuz*, ed. Heckert and Röhr, 244; entries for January 11 and January 25, 1943, in Leszczyńska, *Kronika obozu na Majdanku*, 116, 122.
6. Wachsmann, *KL*, 421–24; Grudzińska "Polacy na Majdanku," 284–87; White, "Majdanek," 7.
7. February 17, 1943, cover letter and February 11, 1943, memo from Türk, Abteilung BuF, Hauptabteilung Innere Verwaltung, Generalgouvernment, Lublin District Office, sygn. 209, pp. 138–39, APL; Wiśniewska, "Pomoc więźniom Majdanka," 235–42. In addition to Janina's memoir, the information in the rest of this chapter, except where otherwise noted, is drawn from: "Sprawozdania Pol. K.O. Lublin z akcji dożywiania więźniów, 1943–1944," RGO sygn. 1487, AAN, in Fot. 19, APMM; Kłapeć, *Rada Główna Opiekuńcza w dystrykcie lubelskim w latach 1940–1944*, 246–47.
8. Monthly activity reports of the Polish Care Committee for Lublin city and county, August and October 1942, sygn. 209, pp. 12, 38, APL; Madajczyk, *Die Okkupationspolitik Nazideutschlands in Polen 1939–1945*, 111–13.
9. Krzymowska, *Lubelska Chorągiew Harcerek w latach 1939–44. Pomoc dla więźniów Majdanka*, VII/0-72, 193–94, APMM.

TEN: MAJDANEK

1. Hermann Florstedt SS Officer personnel file, Microfilm Publication A 3343, SSO-044B, National Archives and Records Administration (NARA).
2. Wachsmann, *KL*, 99; information provided by Łukasz Myszała, State Museum at Majdanek, May 2022.
3. The descriptions and information about Majdanek in this chapter are drawn from a wide variety of sources, as well as the authors' observations at Majdanek, consultation with Łukasz Myszała of the State Museum at Majdanek in May 2022, and review of historical photos in the museum's archive. The main primary sources, secondary studies, and accounts of former prisoners and SS personnel relied upon in this chapter include: Lenarczyk, ed., *Majdanek w Dokumentach*, particularly Documents 1.12, 1.20 through 1.25, and 4.1 through 4.5; Kuwałek, Kranz, and Ciwek-Siupa, "Odszyfrowane radiotelegramy (. . .)," 210–32; Judgment in the criminal

proceedings against Lothar Hoffmann et al., Staatsanwaltschaft beim Landgericht Wiesbaden, 8 Ks 1/70; Kranz, *The Extermination of Jews at Majdanek Concentration Camp*; Kranz and Lenarczyk, eds., *Więźniowie KL Lublin 1941–1944*; Marszałek, *Majdanek*; Marszałek, "Budowa Obozu Koncentracyjnego na Majdanku w latach 1942–1944," 21–90; Murawska, "System strzeżenia i sposoby izolacji więźniów w obozie koncentracyjnym na Majdanku," 76–132; Kwiatkowski, *485 Days at Majdanek*; statement of former administration officer at Majdanek Hans Behrstein, RG-06 War Crimes Investigation and Prosecution, .025 Central Archives of the Federal Security Services (former KGB) of the Russian Federation, 19 K-99809 006.025*19, USHMM; accounts of former Majdanek prisoners, especially Julian Gregorowicz, 148–51, and Dr. Jan Nowak, 171–79, in *Lublin-Majdanek*, ed. Ambach and Köhler; Jerzy Korcz, "15 Months in Majdanek," RG-15.271M, Zbiór pamiętników, relacji i ankiet byłych więźniów (Sygn. VII), roll 1/5-167, USHMM; Dionyz Lenard letter fragment #88, *Polen*, ed. Friedrich, 309–22; Perzanowska, *Gdy myśli do Majdanka wracają*.

4. Witte and Tyas, "A New Document on the Deportation and Murder of Jews During 'Einsatz Reinhardt' 1942," 470.
5. Elizabeth White interviews in the Federal Republic of Germany of former Majdanek guards Andreas E., January 12, 1988, Munich; Michael F., January 13, 1988, Stuttgart; Anton K., January 18, 1988, Hanau.
6. Black, "Foot Soldiers of the Final Solution," 22, 34.
7. In addition to the memoir, the information about the relief efforts at Majdanek of the RGO, Polish Red Cross, and the Underground is drawn from a variety of studies and firsthand accounts, including: Wiśniewska, "Pomoc więźniom Majdanka," 239; Malm, "Przed i za drutami," in *Braterska Pomoc*, ed. Machuła and Wiśniewska, 84–109; Brzosko-Mędryk, *Niebo bez ptaków*, 440–56; Mańkowski, ed., *Hitlerowskie więzienie na Zamku w Lublinie 1939–1944*; Kwiatkowski, *485 Days in Majdanek*; account of Antonina Łopatyńska in Anna Krzymowska, "Lubelska Chorągiew Harcerek w latach 1939–44, Pomoc dla więźniów Majdanka," VII/0-72, APMM; Perzanowska, *Gdy myśli do Majdanka wracają*; account of Zofia Orska, sygn. 129, APMM; account of Adam Panasiewicz, VII/M-234, APMM; account of Romuald Sztaba, XXII-9, APMM.
8. Document 8.3, *Majdanek w Dokumentach*, ed. Lenarczyk.
9. Grudzińska, "The Fate of Children at the Majdanek Concentration Camp," in *The Young Victims of the Nazi Regime*, ed. Gigliotti and Tempian, 171–200.
10. Grudzińska, "The Women's Medical Ward in *Frauenkonzentrationslager* Lublin (Majdanek), Presentation for Conference," *Medical Review Auschwitz: Medicine Behind the Barbed Wire*, September 12–21, 2021, https://www.mp.pl/auschwitz/conference/edition2021/session1/show.html?id=280502, accessed May 24, 2022.
11. Skrzyński June 1, 1943, memo; Kwiatkowski, *485 Days in Majdanek*, 173.
12. Stefania Perzanowska, "The Women's Camp Hospital at Majdanek," trans. M. Kapera, *Medical Review—Auschwitz* (January 7, 2020), https://www.mp.pl/aus

chwitz/journal/english/223573,majdanek-womens-camp-hospital#1, accessed June 3, 2022. Muhsfeldt's name is sometimes spelled Mussfeld or Mussfeldt.

ELEVEN: JANINA'S LISTS

1. Kwiatkowski, *485 Days in Majdanek*, 214.
2. Document 2.19, *Majdanek w Dokumentach*, ed. Lenarczyk; Kranz, "'Generalplan Ost' und 'Endlösung' im Distrikt Lublin," 253–54; Winstone, *The Dark Heart of Hitler's Europe*, 198–202.
3. Jaczyńska, *Sonderlaboratorium SS*, 136; Skrzyński's July 1, 1943, report on his meeting that day with Müller, 2_125_0_2.1_469/78, USHMM.
4. December 2, 1946, statement of Janina Suchodolska, VII-135-104, APMM; Markiewicz, *Nie dali ziemi skąd ich ród*, 222.
5. Documents 2.19, 15.10, *Majdanek w Dokumentach*, ed. Lenarczyk; Grudzińska, "The Fate of Children at the Majdanek Concentration Camp," in *The Young Victims of the Nazi Regime*, ed. Gigliotti and Tempian; Gajderowicz and Skrzyniarz, "Children of the Zamość Region in the Majdanek Camp (in Selected Archive Files and Personal Accounts)," in *Crime Without Punishment*, ed. Kostkiewicz, 115–30; "Transit Camp at ul. Krochmalna 6 and 31," accessed May 26, 2022.
6. Kiriszczenko, "Mother's Death," *Majdanek Concentration Camp*, ed. Rajca and Wiśniewska, 65–57; Urszula Tochman-Welc account in *Majdanek*, ed. Grudzińska, 131–36; Kwiatkowski, *485 Days in Majdanek*, 215–18; Document 4.6, *Majdanek w Dokumentach*, ed. Lenarczyk; Wnuk, *Dzieci polskie oskarżają*, 116–21.
7. Entries for July 1943, in Leszczyńska, *Kronika obozu na Majdanku*; Wiśniewska, "Pomoc więźniom Majdanka," in *Majdanek 1941–1944*, ed. Mencel, 238; Kwiatkowski, *485 Days in Majdanek*, 215–18.
8. September 18, 1943, note re: action to help in camps at 6 and 31 Krochmalna Street, RGO 50, AAN, in Fot. 5, pp. 49–50, APMM; Markiewicz, *Nie dali ziemi skąd ich ród*, 222–25; Woroniak, "Ocalić od zapomnienia," 36–39.
9. Madajczyk, *Die Okkupationspolitik Nazideutschlands in Polen 1939–1945*, 119–21, 135; Winstone, *The Dark Heart of Hitler's Europe*, 115 (quotation), 201–3.
10. Madajczyk, *Die Okkupationspolitik Nazideutschlands in Polen 1939–1945*, 111–17, 120–21; Winstone, *The Dark Heart of Hitler's Europe*, 202; Wendler letter in SS officer personnel file of Odilo Globocnik, Berlin Document Center, also available in Microfilm Publication A3343, Series SSO, NARA.
11. Madajczyk, *Die Okkupationspolitik Nazideutschlands in Polen 1939–1945*, 122; Document 15.9, *Majdanek w Dokumentach*.
12. Poprzeczny, *Odilo Globocnik*, 342–51.
13. Skrzyński August 3, 1943, report on his August 2 meetings with Wendler and Höfle, RGO-Lublin, sygn. 19, pp. 6–9, APL.
14. Pohl, *Von der "Judenpolitik" zum Judenmord*, 115, 118, 146, 183–84.
15. Skrzyński August 3, 1943, report.

16. Skrzyński activity report for August 1943, sygn. 685, pp. 64–66, AAN; Skrzyński August 20, 1943, report to RGO Kraków on releases from transit camps, RGO 29 "Korespondencja z Doradcą Okręgu Lubelskiego" cz. 3, 1943, pp. 119–20, APL.
17. Except where otherwise noted, the narrative of Janina's efforts to obtain the release from Majdanek of expellees is based on: Suchodolska September 7, 1943, memo on taking over people from the Majdanek camp, RGO-Lublin, sygn. 19, pp. 12–13, APL; Skrzyński August 20, 1943, report; December 2, 1946, testimony of Janina Suchodolska, VII-135-104, APMM; Kłapeć, *Rada Główna Opiekuńcza w dystrykcie lubelskim w latach 1940–1944*, 252–53; Wnuk, *Dzieci polskie oskarżaja*, 118; the authors' observations at Majdanek.
18. Globocnik September 10, 1943, letter of recommendation in Florstedt's SS Officer personnel file, A 3343, SSO-044B, NARA.
19. Entries for August 9, 10, 11, 12, 13, 1943, in Leszczyńska, *Kronika obozu na Majdanku*.
20. Document 15.10, *Majdanek w Dokumentach*, ed. Lenarczyk.
21. September 18, 1943, note re: action to help in camps at 6 and 31 Krochmalna Street, RGO 50, AAN, in Fot. 5, pp. 49–50, APMM; Skrzyński activity report for August 1943; Suchodolska September 8, 1943, memo.
22. Document 2.19, *Majdanek w Dokumentach*, ed. Lenarczyk; Kranz, "'Generalplan Ost' und 'Endlösung' im Distrikt Lublin," 253–54.
23. Statement of Janina Suchodolska; Wnuk, *Dzieci polskie oskarżaja*, 189, 200–201.

TWELVE: RESCUE

1. Wnuk, *Dzieci polskie oskarżają*, 116–21.
2. Mańkowski, ed. *Hitlerowskie więzienie na Zamku w Lublinie 1939–1944*, 293; Wiśniewska, "Pomoc więźniom Majdanka," in *Majdanek 1941–1944*, ed. Mencel, 242–44; recap of July 1943, in Leszczyńska, *Kronika obozu na Majdanku*; Kiełboń and Leszczyńska, *Kobiety Lubelszczyzny represjonowane w latach 1944–1956*, 33–35.
3. Adam Panasiewicz, VII/M-234, pp. 7–10, APMM.
4. Quotation in Majdanek Museum, "Saturnina Malm—A 'Quiet Heroine'"; Malm, "Przed i za drutami," in *Braterska Pomoc*, ed. Machuła and Wisńiewska, 109–11.
5. Suchodolska September 11, 1943, memo on September 8 meeting with the Chief of the Governor's Office, RGO-Lublin, sygn. 19, pp. 10–11, APL.
6. Document 2.1, *Majdanek w Dokumentach*, ed. Lenarczyk; Skrzyński activity report September through November 1943, RG 15.550, 685/72-80, USHMM; Grudzińska, *Polacy na Majdanku*, 276–78; Kranz, "Konzentrationslager Lublin," 54; recap for August 1943, in Leszczyńska, *Kronika obozu na Majdanku*; Madej, "Erste Opfer," in *Unser Schicksal*, ed. Kranz, 17–27; Marszałek, *Majdanek*, 61.
7. Skrzyński activity report September through November 1943, RG 15.550, 685/72-80, USHMM; Skrzyński August 12, 1943, letter to Wendler, RGO-Lublin, sygn. 19, pp. 4–5, APL.

8. Suchodolska September 11, 1943, memo.
9. Lublin Care Committee minutes of September 29, 1943, meeting and monthly report for September 1943, RG 15.550, 469/117-1120, USHMM.
10. Rudling, "Historical Representation of the Wartime Accounts of the Activities of the OUN-UPA (Organization of Ukrainian Nationalists–Ukrainian Insurgent Army)," 163–89; Snyder, *The Reconstruction of Nations*, 154–77.
11. Social Report No. 38 (Oct. 9, 1943), Polish Government-in-Exile, RG-15.046M, 3/372–75, USHMM; Kłapeć, *Rada Główna Opiekuńcza w dystrykcie lubelskim w latach 1940–1944*, 260–67.
12. December 2, 1946, statement of Janina Suchodolska, VII-135-104, APMM.
13. Markiewicz, *Nie dali ziemi skąd ich ród*, 223–25.
14. Woroniak, "Ocalić od zapomnienia," 36–39; Szlachetka, "Zapomniany obóz przy ul. Krochmalnej."
15. Suchodolska October 30, 1943, memo on October 29 meeting at the BuF district office, RGO-Lublin, sygn. 46, pp. 41–43, APL.

THIRTEEN: SOUP WITH A SIDE OF HOPE

1. Globocnik September 10, 1943, note, Hermann Florstedt SS Officer personnel file, NARA; Marszałek, "Budowa obozu koncentracyjnego na Majdanku w latach 1942–1944," 39–53; Wiśniewska, "Praca więźniów Majdanka," in *Majdanek*, ed. Mencel, 177–82.
2. Oswald Pohl September 7, 1943, note on conference, Nuremberg Document NO-599, Trials of War Criminals before the Nuernberg Military Tribunals under Control Council Law no. 10 (hereafter: Green Series), 5: 377–79; Florstedt SS Officer personnel file; White, "Majdanek," 13.
3. Pohl September 30, 1943, report to Himmler, Nuremberg Document 1469-PS, Green Series, 5: 379–82; Wachsmann, *KL*, 426. The mortality figures were for registered prisoners only and did not include Jews sent to Auschwitz or Majdanek to be murdered on arrival.
4. Weingartner, "Law and Justice in the Nazi SS," 289; Kranz, "Konzentrationslager Lublin," 49; Kwiatkowski, *485 Days in Majdanek*, 202–3.
5. It was long assumed that Florstedt was executed with Koch, but no document has been found to confirm this, and there are indications that he may have survived the war and lived under an assumed name. Kranz, "Konzentrationslager Lublin" 57n; Wachsmann, *KL*, 387; Pauer-Studer, Velleman, and Cohn-Sherbok, *Konrad Morgen*, 47–53.
6. Janina Siwińska, VII/M-234, APMM; Adam Panasiewicz, VII/M-234, APMM; Marszałek, *Majdanek*, 156–61; Perzanowska, "Pomoc lubelskich organizacji społecznych więźniom Majdanka," 1–13; Zakrzewski, *A my żyjemy dalej*, 105.
7. Testimonies regarding Bajerke by Mirosława Odi and Halina Wencka in Chronicles of Terror, https://www.zapisyterroru.pl/dlibra/publication/3495/edition/3476

/content?navq, accessed June 9, 2022; testimony of Wilhelm Karl Petrak, 1383/1-8, APMM; June 27, 1969, statement of Alfred Hoffmann, Kserok. 1846, APMM.

8. Perzanowska, *Gdy myśli do Majdanka wracaja*, 28, 148; Kwiatkowski, *485 Days in Majdanek*, 114–15; Józef Korcz, VII/M-1, APMM; "15 miesięcy na Majdanku—wspomnienia," 69; Marszałek, *Majdanek*, 44–45.
9. XII-12, k. 19, k. 25, APMM.
10. In addition to the memoir, the narrative about the permission for soup deliveries is based on the following: reports of Suchodolska's October 15, 1943, meeting with the Majdanek commandant, RGO sygn. 1487, in Fot. 19, pp. 178–99 and sygn. 108, in Fot. 8, k. 32, AAN, APMM; Kłapeć, *Rada Główna Opiekuńcza w dystrykcie lubelskim w latach 1940–1944*, 247–48; Wiśniewska, "Pomoc więźniom Majdanka," in *Majdanek 1941–1944*, ed. Mencel, 239–40.
11. Pohl, *Von der "Judenpolitik" zum Judenmord*, 185.
12. In addition to the memoir, the narrative of the soup deliveries is based on: Hanna Kuskowska [*sic*: Huskowska] later Młynarska, VII/M-234, APMM; Kwiatkowski, *485 Days in Majdanek*, 249–55; Wiśniewska, "Pomoc więźniom Majdanka," 239–40. The first meeting between Janina and Perzanowska and their subsequent relationship have been described by both Janina in her memoir and by Perzanowska in several sources, including: *Gdy myśli do Majdanka wracają*, 99–102; "Pomoc lubelskich organizacji społecznych więźniom Majdanka," 6–11.
13. Mailänder, *Female SS Guards and Workaday Violence*, 163–64, 241–44; Schwindt, *Das Konzentrations- und Vernichtungslager Majdanek*, 233, 238, 260; Perzanowska, *Gdy myśli do Majdanka wracają*, 29–30.
14. Kwiatkowski, *485 Days in Majdanek*, 341–42.
15. Sahara 57/C 13. XI.43, APMM; XII-10, k.177-178, APMM.

FOURTEEN: HARVEST OF DEATH

1. Hanna Huskowska, VII/M-234, APMM; Kwiatkowski, *485 Days in Majdanek*, 341–42.
2. In addition to Janina's account of the letter from Majdanek prisoners, the information about *Aktion Erntefest* in this chapter is based on: Kranz, *Extermination of Jews at Majdanek*, 63–69; Pohl, *Von der "Judenpolitik" zum Judenmord*, 170–74; Schwindt, *Das Konzentrations- und Vernichtungslager Majdanek*, 266–80.
3. SS and Police Leader Warsaw Jürgen Stroop May 16, 1943, report on the destruction of the Warsaw Ghetto, Nuremberg Document PS-1061, Harvard Law School Library Nuremberg Trials Project, http://nuremberg.law.harvard.edu/documents/4432-report-to-ss-officials?q=stroop+report#p.8, accessed June 17, 2022; Arad, *Bełżec, Sobibor, Treblinka*, 286–98, 322–41; "Sobibor Uprising," USHMM Holocaust Encyclopedia, https://encyclopedia.ushmm.org/content/en/article/sobibor-uprising, accessed June 17, 2022.

FIFTEEN: CHRISTMAS AT MAJDANEK

1. XII-10, k. 277–78, APMM; Kwiatkowski, *485 Days in Majdanek*, 267–68, 276; Jerzy Korcz, "15 Months in Majdanek," VII/M-1, 116–17, APMM; Kranz, "Konzentrationslager Lublin," 94.
2. Martin Gottfried Weiss SS Officer personnel file, NARA; Orth, *Das Konzentrationslager-SS*, 233–40; Schwindt, *Das Konzentrations- und Vernichtungslager Majdanek*, 271, n 386.
3. RGO Lublin report for September 1 to November 30, 1943, RG 15.550\125 Rada Główna Opiekuńcza 2_125_2.4 sygn. 685, 72–80, USHMM; XII-10, k. 271–72, APMM.
4. Christians, *Piekło XX wieku*, 187–230; Romuald Sztaba, XXII-9, APMM.
5. Marszałek, *Majdanek*, 156–161; Kłapeć, *Rada Główna Opiekuńcza w dystrykcie lubelskim w latach 1940–1944*, 248–49; November 16, 1943, meeting memo, RGO-Lublin, syg. 19, p. 1, APL; Suchodolska October 26, 1943, note, RGO 30 "Korespondencja z Doradcą Okręgu Lubelskiego" cz. 4, 1943, p. 390, APL; XII-10, k. 529, APMM; Kwiatkowski, *485 Days in Majdanek*, 281–82.
6. Christians, *Piekło XX wieku*, 263–66; XII-10, k. 415–16, APMM; Saturnina Malm, VII/M-260, 18–20, APMM.
7. Maria Gancarz, XXII-1, APMM; Ossowska, *Przeżyłam*, 302; Kwiatkowski, *485 Days in Majdanek*, 281–82.
8. Skrzyński December 15, 1943, memo, "Pełnomocnik RGO, Doradca na Okręg Lubelski. Okólniki i pisma," 1940–1941-194, RGO 24, p. 45, APL; RGO report for the period December 1, 1943, to January 31, 1944, RG 15.550\125, 2_125_2.4 sygn. 685, pp. 82–87, USHMM.
9. Perzanowska, *Gdy myśli do Majdanka wracają*, 126–27; Brzosko-Mędryk, *Niebo bez ptaków*, 545; Rebecca Voisich, "Majdanek: Revisitng Resistance," Museum of Jewish Heritage, July 23, 2020, accessed August 12, 2022, https://mjhnyc.org/blog/majdanek-revisiting-resistance/.
10. The information in this chapter about Christmas at Majdanek and Krochmalna and New Year's Eve at Majdanek is based, in addition to the memoir, on: February 2, 1944, note on Christmas and New Year's action at Majdanek, RGO 31, cz. 1, p. 101, APL; Perzanowska, *Gdy myśli do Majdanka wracają*, 126–27; Brzosko-Mędryk, *Niebo bez ptaków*, 492–95; Kwiatkowski, *485 Days in Majdanek*, 290–93, 312; Ossowska, *Przeżyłam*, 304; Stanisławski, *Pole śmierci*, 220.
11. "Mensch—bei uns in Deutschland kommt das nie in Frage," quoted in Stanisławski, *Pole śmierci*, 220.

SIXTEEN: CAT AND MOUSE

1. Rogerie, "Transporty chorych," in *Majdanek*, ed. Grudzińska, 210–14; Kwiatkowski, *485 Days in Majdanek*, 297–98; Leszczyńska, "Transporty i stany liczbowe obozu," in *Majdanek*, ed. Mencel, 9–128; Kranz, "Das Konzentrationslager Majdanek 1941–1944," 290; Kranz, "Konzentrationslager Lublin," 64–65.

2. XII-10, k. 495–96, APMM.
3. Madajczyk, *Die Okkupationspolitik Nazideutschlands in Polen 1939–1945,* 190–92; Gross, *Polish Society Under German Occupation,* 163f, 207–9; Winstone, *The Dark Heart of Hitler's Europe,* 203.
4. Marszałek, *Majdanek,* 134–35; Kwiatkowski, *485 Days in Majdanek,* 299–301, 310–11.
5. Kwiatkowski, *485 Days in Majdanek,* 114–15.
6. Marszałek, "Konspiracja w obozie," *Majdanek,* ed. Mencel, 360; Voisich, "Majdanek: Revisiting Resistance."
7. Marszałek, *Majdanek,* 165–57; Wanda Szupenko, XXI-162–65, APMM.
8. XII-10, k. 529, APMM.
9. Kłapeć, *Rada Główna Opiekuńcza w dystrykcie lubelskim w latach 1940–1944,* 152.
10. Perzanowska, "Pomoc lubelskich organizacji społecznych więźniom Majdanka," 9–13; Maria Gancarz, XX-1, APMM; Brzosko-Mędryk, *Niebo bez ptaków,* 450–56. The Polish writers whose works Janina smuggled into Majdanek included Sienkiewicz, Słowacki, Mickiewicz, Prus, and Żeromski.
11. XII-10, k. 521, APMM; Kwiatkowski, *485 Days in Majdanek,* 300; Perzanowska, *Gdy myśli do Majdanka wracają,* chapters 24 and 25.
12. XII-10, k. 495-496, APMM; Kwiatkowski, *485 Days in Majdanek,* 297–98; Rogerie, "Transporty chorych," 210–14.
13. RGO report for period February 1 to March 14, 1944, RG 15.550, 685/91-97, USHMM; XII-10, k. 521, APMM; Wiśniewska, "Pomoc więźniom Majdanka," 239–40.
14. RGO report for period February 1 to March 14, 1944; report from the camp on Krochmalna, February 1 to March 17, 1944, RGO 31 cz. 1, 304, APL; Kłapeć, *Rada Główna Opiekuńcza w dystrykcie lubelskim w latach 1940–1944,* 240–45.
15. Wiśniewska, "Pomoc więźniom Majdanka," 244–45; Kłapeć, *Rada Główna Opiekuńcza w dystrykcie lubelskim w latach 1940–1944,* 141–42.
16. November 15, 1944 staff listing, RGO 142, APL.

SEVENTEEN: THE PLOT

1. RGO Lublin report for March 15 to May 1, 1944, RGO 32 "Korespondencja ogólna Doradcy" 1944, pp. 267–71, APL.
2. Marszałek, *Majdanek,* 168–69.
3. RGO Lublin report for March 15 to May 1, 1944; Skrzyński May 5, 1944 note re: help for prisoners departing Majdanek, RGO 50, AAN, in Fot. 5, APMM; April 4, 1944, message from "Stefania" (Janina Suchodolska), XII-10, k. 663-664, APMM.
4. Wanda Szupenko ("Elżbieta"), XXI-162–65, APMM; Marszałek, *Majdanek,* 165, 168–69.
5. Marszałek, *Majdanek,* 175; entries for March 28 and 29, 1944, in Leszczyńska, *Kronika obozu na Majdanku.*

6. RGO Lublin report for March 15 to May 1, 1944; entry for March 30, 1944, in Leszczyńska, *Kronika obozu na Majdanku.*
7. Entry for March 31, 1944, in Leszczyńska, *Kronika obozu na Majdanku;* Mencel, "Konzentrationslager Lublin. General Characteristics," in *Majdanek,* ed. Mencel, 515.
8. Skrzyński May 5, 1944, note re: help for prisoners departing Majdanek; Hanna Huskowska, VII/M-234, APMM.
9. December 2, 1946, testimony of Janina Suchodolska, VII-135-104, APMM; Marszałek, *Majdanek,* 181–83.
10. Entry for April 2, 1944, in Leszczyńska, *Kronika obozu na Majdanka.*
11. April 4, 1944, message from "Stefania" (Janina Suchodolska), XII-10, k. 663-664, APMM.
12. Ibid.; Kwiatkowski, *485 Days in Majdanek,* 363–68.
13. Undated message fragment, probably from "Stefania" (Janina Suchodolska), XII-10, k. 584, APMM; Kwiatkowski, *485 Days in Majdanek,* 363–68.
14. Gajowniczek, "Choroby i epidemie. Rewir," in *Majdanek 1941–1944,* ed. Mencel, 226; Kwiatkowski, *485 Days in Majdanek,* 278.
15. Skrzyński May 5, 1944, note re: help for prisoners departing Majdanek; February 26, 196? interrogation of Wilhelm Karl Petrak in the (West German) case against Benden et al., XIX 1383/1-8, APMM; Adam Panasiewicz, "Poststelle," in *Braterska Pomoc,* ed. Machuła and Wiśniewska, 112–27.
16. Document 18.6, *Majdanek w dokumentach,* ed. Lenarczyk; Marszałek, *Majdanek,* 176; Kwiatkowski, *485 Days in Majdanek,* 361.
17. April 5, 1944, message from "Stefania" (Janina Suchodolska), XII-10, k. 663–64, APMM.
18. Skrzyński May 5, 1944, note re: help for prisoners departing Majdanek; Hanna Huskowska, VII/M-234, APMM.
19. Kwiatkowski, *485 Days in Majdanek,* 363–68.
20. Marszałek, *Majdanek,* 168–69.

EIGHTEEN: THE END APPROACHES

1. In addition to the memoir, the description of Easter at Majdanek in 1944 is based on the following: Skrzyński May 5, 1944, note about Easter food for Majdanek, RGO 32, p. 320, APL; RGO Lublin report for March 15 to May 1, 1944, RGO 32, pp. 267–71, APL; Perzanowska, "Pomoc lubelskich organizacji społecznych więźniom Majdanka," 11–12; Jadwiga Lipska-Węgrzecka, XII-49, APMM; Kwiatkowski, *485 Days in Majdanek,* 369; Marszałek, *Majdanek,* 181–83.
2. Note re: help for prisoners departing Majdanek, RGO 50, AAN, in Fot. 5, APMM; Kłapeć, *Rada Główna Opiekuńcza w dystrykcie lubelskim w latach 1940–1944,* 249.
3. Skrzyński undated note, RGO 32, p. 273, APL.
4. Protocol No. 40 of Lublin Care Committee, April 27, 1944, RGO Documents, Wydział II Organizacyjno-Inspekcyjny Dział Organizacyjny II.0.4, p. 296, APMM;

Skrzyński May 13, 1944, note on refugees from Kowel at Krochmalna, RGO 32, 274; undated report on the evacuation, RGO 31, pp. 99–100, AAN.

5. Perzanowska, "O niektórych hitlerowskich lekarzach w Majdanku," 6–7; Kwiatkowski, *485 Days in Majdanek*, 278.
6. Some months later, Rindfleisch was assigned to Gross-Rosen. Dr. Hanusz survived the war.
7. Wiśniewska, "Pomoc więźniom Majdanka," 240; Marszałek, *Majdanek*, 183.
8. Thumann transferred to Neuengamme. After the war, he was tried and executed by the British for crimes he committed there. Weiss was tried and executed by the Americans for his crimes at Dachau. Marszałek, *Majdanek*, 45, 189; Kranz, "Das Konzentrationslager Majdanek 1941–1944," 29.
9. Note re: help for prisoners departing Majdanek, RGO 50, AAN, in Fot. 5, APMM; Kwiatkowski, *485 Days in Majdanek*, 399.
10. Orth, *Die Konzentrationslager-SS*, 242–46; Kranz, "Das Konzentrationslager Majdanek 1941–1944," 291. After the war, Poland's Supreme National Tribunal sentenced Liebehenschel to death for his crimes at Auschwitz and Majdanek and he was executed. Marszałek, *Majdanek*, 45, 188.
11. In addition to the memoir, the information about the Wehrmacht forced labor camp in Field V is based on the following: June 1944 report of the Lublin Care Committee, RGO Documents Wydział II Organizacyjno-Inspekcyjny Dział Organizacyjny II.0.4, p. 325, APMM; Protocol 42 of the Lublin Care Committee, June 30, 1944, RGO documents, Wydział II Organizacyjno-Inspekcyjny Dział Organizacyjny II.0.4, p. 334, APMM; Skrzyński July 13, 1944, report, RGO 108, AAN, in Fot. 8, APMM; Grudzińska "Polacy na Majdanku," 298; Marszałek, *Majdanek*, 183; Kranz, "Das Konzentrationslager Majdanek 1941–1944," 291; Kwiatkowski, *485 Days in Majdanek*, 412.
12. December 2, 1946, statement of Janina Suchodolska, VII-135-104, APMM; Wiśniewska, "Pomoc więźniom Majdanka," in *Majdanek 1941–1944*, ed. Mencel, 240; Wnuk, *Dzieci polskie oskarżają*, 116–21; Kwiatkowski, *485 Days in Majdanek*, 416–19.
13. Angrick, *"Aktion 1005,"* 822–40.
14. Release certificates for women and children held at Majdanek, signed Suchodolska, July 14, 1944, VI, 18/1-8, APMM.
15. Undated report on the evacuation, RGO 31, pp. 99–100, AAN.

NINETEEN: BLOOD ON THE STAIRS

1. Polish translation of June 5, 1944, letter from Schreiter, BuF, to Skrzyński, RGO-Lublin 7, pp. 64–65, APL; Lublin Care Committee Report for June 1944, RGO Documents, p. 327, APMM; Skrzyński July 13, 1944, report, RGO 108, AAN, in Fot. 8, APMM; Mańkowski, *Hitlerowskie więzienie na Zamku w Lublinie, 1939–1944*, 287; Kłapeć, *Rada Główna Opiekuńcza w dystrykcie lubelskim w latach 1940–1944*, 274–89.

2. In addition to the memoir, this paragraph and the following information in this chapter are based on the following sources: Mańkowski, *Hitlerowskie więzienie na Zamku w Lublinie, 1939–1944*, 355–56; Barbara Oratowska, Łukasz Krzysiak, and Marcin Michniowski, eds., "75 rocznica likwidacji niemieckiego więzienia na Zamku lubelskim / 75th Anniversary of the Liquidation of the German Prison in the Lublin Castle" (Lublin: The Lublin State Museum, 2019); Protocol 206 Piotr Malesza, January 25, 1946, Protocols of the Municipal Commission for the Investigation of German Crimes in Lublin, APMM; Marian Wiess, XXI-162–76, APMM; Zofia Orska, sygn. 169, APMM.

TWENTY: THE END

1. Oral histories of Janusz Andrzej Winiarski, April 19, 2004, and Łukasz Kijek, "Walki o Lublin w lipcu 1944 roku," Grodzka Gate–NN Theatre, https://teatrnn.pl/leksykon/artykuly/walki-o-lublin-w-lipcu-1944-roku, accessed August 12, 2022.
2. Marszałek, *Majdanek*, 184–85.
3. See, for example, the 1944 Soviet-produced film *Das Blut der Opfer Schreit zum Himmel!* (The Blood of the Victims Cries to the Heavens!), RG Number: RG-60.0028 | Film ID: 5, USHMM.
4. Kochanski, *The Eagle Unbowed*, 396.
5. Ibid., 377–96; Reynolds, "'Lublin' Versus 'London,'" 622–24; Harald Moldenhauer, "Der Sowjetische NKVD und die Heimatarmee im 'Lubliner Polen' 1944–1945," in *Die polnische Heimatarmee*, ed. Chiari with Kochanowski, 275–99.
6. Kochanski, *The Eagle Unbowed*, 400–425.

TWENTY-ONE: FLIGHT

1. Kłapeć, *Rada Główna Opiekuńcza w dystrykcie lubelskim w latach 1940–1944*, 274–89.
2. Ibid.; Finder and Prusin, *Justice Behind the Iron Curtain*, 32; Christians, *Piekło XX wieku*.
3. Kopciowski, "Zajścia antyżydowskie na Lubelszczyźnie w pierwszych latach po drugiej wojnie światowej," 178–79.
4. Kłapeć, *Rada Główna Opiekuńcza w dystrykcie lubelskim w latach 1940–1944*, 274–89; Suchodolska correspondence, RGO 7, pp. 1–5, APL; November 15, 1944, staff listing, RGO 142, APL.
5. Akta Miasta Lublina, zespół 22, 2145/22, State Archive in Lublin (APL).
6. Note to Piotr Suchodolski, January 14, 1946, "Henryk Mehlberg," p. 5, AUŁ; Note to Janina Suchodolska, October 24, 1945, "Janina Suchodolska" personnel file, CKOS 43, AAN; Protocol from the first meeting of CKOS, 13 December 1944, sygn. 243, AAN; Memo re: the creation of CKOS, March 3, 1947, sygn. 242, AAN.
7. Gross, *Polish Society Under German Occupation*, 85; International Conference

of Social Work, "Public Health and Welfare Technical Bulletin" (August 1948); Kornbluth, *The August Trials*, 5; "Janina Suchodolska" personnel file, CKOS 43, AAN.

8. Memo re: the creation of CKOS, March 3, 1947, sygn. 242, AAN; "Note," March 3, 1947, CKOS 242, pp. 46–47, AAN; Margarette Smethurst, "Polish Social Worker Observes Home Demonstration Activities," *News & Observer* (Raleigh, NC) January 17, 1948, 5.
9. "Janina Suchodolska" personnel file, CKOS 43, AAN; Protocol 22 of CKOS Board meeting, July 8, 1946 and Protocol 39 from CKOS meeting, September 29, 1947, sygn. 243, AAN; "Tells How UNRRA Aided Polish Child Agencies," *Daily Herald* (Chicago, IL), February 13, 1948, 14.
10. Information about Henry's academic trajectory here and later in this chapter derives from: "Henryk Mehlberg," AUŁ; "Mehlberg Henryk," sygn. 3856, AAN; "Henryk Mehlberg," 387b-14, AUAM; "Mehlberg Henryk," Tom I: AUW.6/2.180, AUW.
11. In her December 2, 1946, testimony to Polish authorities, Janina indicated that she was single, the daughter of Wojciech and Franciszka Suchodolski, and born in 1909. VII-135-104, APMM.
12. Jewish Immigrant Aid Society of Canada application submitted by Henry August 21, 1950, "Pepi Mehlberg," Ontario Jewish Archives; "Personal file of Mehlberg, Isidor, born in the year 1906 and of further persons," Reference Code 1718000_038.080, Arolsen Archives. Juliusz was a dentist and Izydor was a physician. Izydor and his wife, Helena (née Szwermer), had two daughters, Ewa and Anita. Juliusz was married to Tola (Antonina) née Mandelkorn. Information about Henry's relatives derives i.a. from the postwar registration cards of Polish Jews, Collection 303/V/425 /CKŻP, Wydział ewidencji i statystyki 1945–1950, AŻIH.
13. Kornbluth, *The August Trials*, 82–88; Gross, *Fear*, 39–72.
14. Gross, *Fear*, 78–90.
15. Historian Dariusz Stola's estimate quoted in Węgrzyn, *Wyjeżdżamy! Wyjeżdżamy?!*, 58–59.
16. In addition to Pinkas (Janina's father), Berel and Czarna (née Falik) Spinner had six children: Jonas, Aron, Pessie, Lena (Lea), Malka, and Pauline. We are grateful to Noam Silberberg, Genealogy Department of the Jewish Historical Institute in Warsaw, for providing this information.
17. Information about Janina's and Henry's emigration efforts derives from: "Henryk Mehlberg," USNA RG 246 File J-5613, YIVO Institute for Jewish Research (YIVO); "Pepi Mehlberg," Ontario Jewish Archives; "Henry Mehlberg," JDC Archives.
18. "Henry Mehlberg," JDC Archives; "Pepi Mehlberg," CKŻP, Wydział ewidencji i statystyki 1945–1950, 303/V/425/M 4762/174027, AŻIH; Warsaw Office 1945–1948, JDC Archives.
19. Interview with Dr. Arthur Fine by Elizabeth White, March 1, 2018.
20. Protocol 39 from CKOS meeting, September 29, 1947, sygn. 243, AAN; Memo,

October 24, 1947, sygn. 242, AAN. A philosopher as well as a legal scholar, Rudziński did not revert to his original name of Steinberg after the war. "Aleksander Witold Rudzinski," https://www.geni.com/people/Aleksander-Rudzinski/6000000023840977953, accessed August 3, 2022; Eric Pace, "Dr. Aleksander W. Rudzinski, 89, Polish Diplomat Who Defected," *New York Times*, April 8, 1989, 1:10.

21. The information about Janina's activities in the United States during her stay as Janina Suchodolska and about Henry's immigration to Canada comes from the following: Janina's letters to Anna Rudzińska, The Aleksander and Anna Rudzinski Collection, 1919–1995, General Research Division, New York Public Library (NYPL) (we thank Dr. Marjorie Senechal for sharing with us information about this source); "Henryk Mehlberg," YIVO; Smethurst, "Polish Social Worker," *News & Observer*; "Tells How UNRRA Aided Polish Child Agencies," *Daily Herald*; "UN Guest Visits Aid Home," *South Bend Tribune* (South Bend, IN), February 28, 1948, 21; "Welfare Program Studied by Pole," *Indianapolis Star* (Indianapolis, IN), February 23, 1948, 32; "Praises New Hampshire's Welfare Department," *Newport Daily Express* (Newport, VT), March 18, 1948, 9.
22. Other scholars Janina contacted included Ernest Nagel, Carl Gustav Hempel, and Alfred Tarski. Hempel and Tarski, both educated in prewar Europe and Henry's peers, had been part of the Vienna Circle of philosophers. Tarski, a philosopher and a mathematician, was connected to the Lwów-Warsaw School.
23. "Henryk Mehlberg," YIVO.
24. "Janina Suchodolska" personnel file, CKOS 43, AAN; CKOS protocol, March 2, 1949, CKOS 287, AAN; Brenk, "Działalność Powiatowego Komitetu Opieki Społecznej w Koninie w latach 1945–1949," 120.
25. Janina's letter to Anna Rudzińska, July 24 [1949], NYPL; October 4, 1949, letter to JDC from Janina Suchodolska, Department Head [Naczelnik Wydziału], Ministerstwo Pracy i Opieki Społecznej, JDC Archives, item 2460216.
26. The information in this chapter about Janina's escape from Poland and immigration to Canada comes from: "Pepi Mehlberg," Ontario Jewish Archives.

TWENTY-TWO: A NEW BEGINNING

1. Josephine Janina Mehlberg U.S. immigration file A10 678 524, U.S. Citizenship and Immigration Services (USCIS); "Josephine Janina Bednarski Spinner Mehlberg," https://prabook.com/web/josephine_janina_bednarski_spinner.mehlberg/1103449, accessed August 2, 2022; interview of Dr. Fine.
2. Staff Cards: Mehlberg, University of Toronto Archives.
3. Robert S. Cohen, "Editorial Note," Mehlberg, *Time, Causality, and the Quantum Theory*, xv–xvii.
4. Communication between Joanna Sliwa and Dr. Irvin Klinghofer, August 13, 2021; Josephine Janina Mehlberg U.S. Immigration File A10 678 524.
5. Josephine Janina Mehlberg U.S. immigration file A10 678 524; Henry Mehlberg Immigration File, A10 678 676, USCIS.

6. Adolf Grünbaum, "Preface," Mehlberg, *Time, Causality, and the Quantum Theory*, xiii–xiv; interview with Dr. Fine; interview with Dr. Marjorie Senechal by authors, August 18, 2020.
7. Much of the information about Janina's work as a mathematician in the United States was provided by Dr. Marjorie Senechal, including the notes and slides for her February 21, 2023, HOM SIGMAA online lecture, "Josephine Mehlberg (1905–1969)."
8. Ibid.; Josephine Janina Mehlberg U.S. Immigration File A10 678 524; "Josephine Janina Bednarski Spinner Mehlberg," prabook.com; interview with Dr. Fine.
9. Janina's talk at the University of California, Davis conference was on "Laplace Transforms in Solving Differential Equations with Complex Coefficients." "Janina Mehlberg" VA 278345, BEG; "Josephine Janina Bednarski Spinner Mehlberg,"https://prabook.com/web/josephine_janina_bednarski_spinner.mehlberg/1103449, accessed August 2, 2022.
10. Interview of Dr. Fine; Senechal, "Josephine Mehlberg (1905–1969)."
11. "Janina Mehlberg," VA 278345, BEG; "Henryk Mehlberg," YIVO.
12. "Janina Mehlberg," VA 278345; "Henry Mehlberg," VA 278344, BEG.
13. Cohen, "Editorial Note"; interviews with Dr. Fine and Dr. Senechal.
14. Josephine Janina Mehlberg U.S. Immigration File A10 678 524; "Janina Mehlberg," VA 278345, BEG; Antonina Mehlberg U.S. Immigration file A18371852, RG 566, Records of the U.S. Immigration and Naturalization Service, NARA (Kansas City, MO).
15. Antonina Mehlberg U.S. Immigration File A18371852.
16. Grünbaum, "Preface."
17. Social Security Death Index entry for Antonina Mehlberg; Florida Marriage Index entry for Henry's marriage to Susie Clark (listed as Edna Benefield) on August 16, 1975; Elizabeth White phone interview with Jeri Hough, Susie Clark's daughter, September 15, 2022.
18. Grünbaum, "Preface"; Cohen, "Editorial Note," quotation on xvii; Mehlberg, *Time, Causality, and the Quantum Theory*.
19. Arthur L. Funk, "Editor's Foreword," "Janina's Story."

EPILOGUE: "JANINA'S STORY"

1. We base our dating of the memoir on two of its references: 1) Janina was unaware that Anton Thumann had been tried and executed after World War II for crimes he committed at Neuengamme, and she speculated that he was living in Argentina. Awareness that some Nazi criminals fled to Argentina after the war arose following the abduction of Adolf Eichmann in Argentina by Israeli agents in 1960 and his subsequent trial in 1961. 2) Commenting on the value of bacon as currency on the black market, Janina wrote that no one was concerned then about cholesterol levels. The first general warning about the possible connection between dietary cholesterol and heart disease was put out by the American Heart

Association in 1961. David Kritchevsky, "History of Recommendations to the Public about Dietary Fat," *The Journal of Nutrition* 128, no. 2 (February 1998): 449S–452S.

2. See, for example, *Who's Who of American Women*, 5th ed. (1968–1969).
3. Plocker, *The Expulsion of Jews from Communist Poland*, passim.
4. Ibid.; Podbielska, "'The Righteous' and March '68," 363–87.

BIBLIOGRAPHY

ARCHIVAL COLLECTIONS

Argentina

Argentine Israelite Mutual Association, Buenos Aires (AMIA)
Foreign Affairs Archive, Buenos Aires
Israelite Association of Coronel Suárez, Coronel Suárez

Canada

Canadian Jewish Archives, Montreal (CJA)
Immigration, Refugees and Citizenship Canada (IRCC)
Library and Archives Canada, Ottawa (LAC)
Ontario Jewish Archives, Toronto (OJA)
Montreal Holocaust Museum, Montreal
University of New Brunswick Libraries and Archives, New Brunswick
University of Toronto Archives, Toronto

Germany

Arolsen Archives
State Finance Office, Compensation Payments, Saarburg (BEG)

Poland

Archives of Jagiellonian University, Medical Department, Kraków
Archive of Emanuel Ringelblum Jewish Historical Institute, Warsaw (AŻIH)
Archive of New Records, Warsaw (AAN)
Archive of the State Museum at Majdanek, Lublin (APMM)
Archives of the University of Adam Mickiewicz, Poznań (AUAM)
Archives of the University of Łódź, Łódź (AUŁ)
Archives of the University of Wrocław, Wrocław (AUW)

Association of Jewish Veterans and Persecutees in World War II, Warsaw
Institute of National Remembrance, Warsaw (IPN)
KARTA Center, Warsaw
Lublin Archdiocese Archive, Lublin
Main Archive of Old Records, Warsaw (AGAD)
State Archive in Lublin (APL)
State Archive in Przemyśl (APP)

Ukraine

State Archive of Lviv Oblast, Lviv, Ukraine (DALO)

United States

Archives of the American Jewish Joint Distribution Committee, New York (JDC)
Montefiore Cemetery, New York
Mount Sinai Memorial Chapels, East Brunswick, NJ
National Archives and Records Administration, College Park, MD (NARA)
The New York Public Library, New York (NYPL)
United States Holocaust Memorial Museum, Washington, D.C. (USHMM)
University Archives and Special Collections, Illinois Institute of Technology, Chicago (IIT)
University of Florida Archives, Gainesville
YIVO Institute for Jewish Research, New York (YIVO)

OTHER RESOURCES

Ancestry, https://www.ancestry.com/
Auschwitz Memorial and Museum, http://www.auschwitz.org/
Center for Urban History, https://www.lvivcenter.org/
Centropa, https://www.centropa.org/
Chronicles of Terror, https://www.zapisyterroru.pl/
Digital Archive of Combined Libraries, https://archiwum.polaczonebiblioteki.uw.edu.pl/
Digital Libraries Federation, https://fbc.pionier.net.pl/
Genealogy Indexer, www.genealogyindexer.org/
Geni, https://www.geni.com/
Gesher Galicia, https://www.geshergalicia.org/
Greater Poland Digital Library, https://www.wbc.poznan.pl/dlibra
Grodzka Gate–NN Theatre, https://teatrnn.pl/
Harvard Law School Library Nuremberg Trials Project, http://nuremberg.law.harvard.edu/
JewishGen, https://www.jewishgen.org/databases/
Jewish Records Indexing–Poland, https://jri-poland.org/
"Josephine Janina Bednarski Spinner Mehlberg," https://prabook.com/web/josephine_janina_bednarski_spinner.mehlberg/1103449

Libraria: Ukrainian Online Periodicals Archive, https://libraria.ua/en/
Museum of Jewish Heritage, https://mjhnyc.org/
Premeditated Murder of 25 Polish Professors, https://www.lwow.com.pl/Lwow_profs.html
National-Socialism Archive, https://www.ns-archiv.de/
Ohistorie, https://ohistorie.eu/o-nas/
Polona, https://polona.pl/
The Roman Ingarden Digital Archive, http://ingarden.archive.uj.edu.pl/en/home/
Stanford Encyclopedia of Philosophy, https://plato.stanford.edu/
State Museum at Majdanek, https://www.majdanek.eu/
United States Holocaust Memorial Museum, https://encyclopedia.ushmm.org/
Virtual Shtetl, https://sztetl.org.pl/
World Health Organization, https://www.who.int/

NEWSPAPERS

Chwila (Lwów)
Daily Herald (Chicago)
The Indianapolis Star
The Newport Daily Express (Vermont)
News & Observer (Raleigh)
The New York Times
South Bend Tribune (Indiana)

INTERVIEWS (ORAL AND WRITTEN)

Dr. Eugene Allgower, email with authors, July 18, 2022.
Dr. Arthur Fine, interview by Elizabeth White, phone, March 1, 2018.
Jeri Hough, interview by Elizabeth White, phone, September 15, 2022.
Dr. Irvin Klinghofer, email with Joanna Sliwa, August 13, 2021.
Joshua Pines, interview by authors, online, August 27, 2020.
Dr. Marjorie Senechal, interview by authors, online, August 18, 2021.
Eva Tene, interview by authors, online, June 20, 2023.
Elizabeth White interviews in the Federal Republic of Germany of former Majdanek guards Andreas E., January 12, 1988, Munich; Michael F., January 13, 1988, Stuttgart; Anton K., January 18, 1988, Hanau.

BOOKS

Aly, Götz. *Final Solution: Nazi Population Policy and the Murder of the European Jews.* Translated by Belinda Cooper and Allison Brown. New York: Arnold and Oxford University Press, 1999.

Amar, Tarik Cyril. *The Paradox of Ukrainian Lviv: A Borderland City Between Stalinists, Nazis, and Nationalists.* Ithaca: Cornell University Press, 2015.

Ambach, Dieter, and Thomas Köhler, eds. *Lublin-Majdanek: Das Konzentrations- und*

Vernichtungslager im Spiegel von Zeugenaussagen. Vol. 12, *Juristische Zeitgeschichte NRW*. Düsseldorf: Justizministerium des Landes NRW, 2003.

Angrick, Andrej. *"Aktion 1005"—Spurenbeseitigung von NS-Massenverbrechen 1942–1945: Eine "geheime Reichssache" im Spannungsfeld von Kriegswende und Propaganda*. Göttingen: Wallstein Verlag, 2018.

Arad, Yitzhak. *Bełżec, Sobibor, Treblinka: The Operation Reinhard Death Camps*. Bloomington: Indiana University Press, 1999 (first published in 1987).

Arad, Yitzhak, Shmuel Krakowski, and Shmuel Spector, eds. *The Einsatzgruppen Reports: Selections from the Dispatches of the Nazi Death Squads' Campaign Against the Jews, July 1941–January 1943*. New York: Holocaust Library in cooperation with Yad Vashem, 1989.

Bartov, Omer. *Anatomy of a Genocide: The Life and Death of a Town Called Buczacz*. New York: Simon & Schuster, 2018.

Bartrop, Paul R., and Eve E. Grimm. *Perpetrating the Holocaust: Leaders, Enablers, and Collaborators*. Santa Barbara, CA: ABC-CLIO, 2019.

Beorn, Waitman Wade. *The Holocaust in Eastern Europe: At the Epicenter of the Final Solution*. London: Bloomsbury, 2018.

Biskupska, Jadwiga. *Survivors: Warsaw Under Nazi Occupation*. Cambridge: Cambridge University Press, 2022.

Black, Peter. "Die Trawniki-Männer und die 'Aktion Reinhard.'" In *"Aktion Reinhard,": der Völkermord an den Juden im Generalgouvernement 1941–1944*. Edited by Bogdan Musial. Osnabrück: Fibre, 2004, 309–52.

Brożek, Anna, Alicja Chybińska, Jacek Jadacki, and Jan Woleński, eds. *Tradition of the Lvov-Warsaw School: Ideas and Continuations*. Leiden: Brill, 2016.

Brzosko-Mędryk, Danuta. *Niebo bez ptaków*. Warsaw: Prószyński i S-ka, 2021.

Burleigh, Michael. *Moral Combat: Good and Evil in World War II*. New York: HarperCollins, 2011.

Caban, Ireneusz, and Zygmunt Mańkowski. *Związek Walki Zbrojnej i Armia Krajowa w Okręgu Lubelskim 1939–1944*. Lublin: Wydawnictwo Lubelskie, 1971.

Chiari, Bernhard, ed., in collaboration with Jerzy Kochanowski. *Die polnische Heimatarmee. Geschichte und Mythos der Armia Krajowa seit dem zweiten Weltkrieg*. Munich: R. Oldenbourg Verlag, 2003.

Chmielewski, Jakub. "Żydzi w KL Lublin." In *Więźniowie KL Lublin 1941–1944*. Edited by Tomasz Kranz and Wojciech Lenarczyk. Lublin: Państwowe Muzeum na Majdanku, 2022, 264–65.

Christians, Ludwik. *Piekło XX wieku. Zbrodnia, hart ducha i miłosierdzie*. Warsaw: Katolickie Towarzystwo Wydawnicze "Rodzina Polska," 1946.

Cichopek Gajraj, Anna. *Beyond Violence: Jewish Survivors in Poland and Slovakia, 1944–1948*. Cambridge: Cambridge University Press, 2014.

Czech, Danuta. *Auschwitz Chronicle, 1939–1945*. New York: Henry Holt, 1990.

Dean, Martin, ed. *The United States Holocaust Memorial Museum Encyclopedia of Camps and Ghettos*. Vol. 2, *Ghettos in German-Occupied Eastern Europe*, s.v. "Lublin," 675–78.

Bloomington: Indiana University Press in association with the United States Holocaust Memorial Museum, 2012.

Draus, Jan. *Uniwersytet Jana Kazimierza we Lwowie 1918–1946. Portret kresowej uczelni.* Kraków: Księgarnia Akademicka, 2007.

Evans, Richard J. *The Third Reich at War*. New York: Penguin, 2010.

———. *The Third Reich in Power*. New York: Penguin, 2005.

Finder, Gabriel N., and Alexander Victor Prusin. *Justice Behind the Iron Curtain: Nazis on Trial in Communist Poland*. Toronto: University of Toronto Press, 2018.

Friedlander, Henry. *The Origins of Nazi Genocide: From Euthanasia to the Final Solution.* Chapel Hill: North Carolina University Press, 1995.

Friedländer, Saul. *The Years of Extermination: Nazi Germany and the Jews, 1939–1945.* New York: HarperCollins, 2007.

Friedrich, Klaus-Peter, ed. *Polen: Generalgouvernement August 1941–1945*. Munich: Oldenbourg Verlag, 2014.

Gajderowicz, Magdalena, and Ryszard Skrzyniarz. "Children of the Zamość Region in the Majdanek Camp (in Selected Archive Files and Personal Accounts)." In *Crime Without Punishment: The Extermination and Suffering of Polish Children During the German Occupation, 1939–1945*. Edited by Janina Kostkiewicz. Kraków: Jagiellonian University Press, 2021, 115–30.

Gajowniczek, Jolanta. "Choroby i epidemie. Rewir." In *Majdanek 1941–1944*. Edited by Tadeusz Mencel. Lublin: Wydawnictwo Lubelskie, 1991, 194–231.

Gerlach, Christian. *The Extermination of the European Jews*. Cambridge: Cambridge University Press, 2016.

Golczewski, Frank. "Die Heimatarmee und die Juden." In *Die polnische Heimatarmee. Geschichte und Mythos der Armia Krajowa seit dem zweiten Weltkrieg*. Edited by Bernhard Chiari, in collaboration with Jerzy Kochanowski. Munich: R. Oldenbourg Verlag, 2003, 635–78.

———. "Polen." In *Dimension des Völkermords: Die Zahl der jüdischen Opfer des Nationalsozialismus*. Edited by Wolfgang Benz. Munich: Oldenbourg Verlag, 1991, 411–97.

Goldberg, Adara. *Holocaust Survivors in Canada: Exclusion, Inclusion, Transformation, 1947–1955*. Winnipeg: University of Manitoba Press, 2015.

Gross, Jan Tomasz. *Fear: Anti-Semitism in Poland After Auschwitz*. New York: Random House, 2007.

———. *Polish Society Under German Occupation: The Generalgouvernement, 1939–1944.* Princeton: Princeton University Press, 1979.

———. *Revolution from Abroad: The Soviet Conquest of Poland's Western Ukraine and Western Belorussia*. Princeton: Princeton University Press, 2002.

Gross, Jan Tomasz, and Irena Grudzińska Gross, eds. *War Through Children's Eyes: The Soviet Occupation of Poland and the Deportations, 1939–1941*. Translated by Ronald Strom and Dan Rivers. Stanford: Hoover Institution Press, 1985.

Grudzińska, Marta. "The Fate of Children at the Majdanek Concentration Camp." In *The Young Victims of the Nazi Regime: Migration, the Holocaust and Postwar Displacement.*

Edited by Simone Gigliotti and Monica Tempian. London/New York: Bloomsbury, 2016, 171–200.

———."Polacy na Majdanku." In *Więźniowie KL Lublin 1941–1944*. Edited by Tomasz Kranz and Wojciech Lenarczyk. Lublin: Państwowe Muzeum na Majdanku, 2020, 267–86.

Grudzińska, Marta, ed. *Majdanek. Oboz koncentracyjny w relacjach więźniów i świadków*. Lublin: Państwowe Muzeum na Majdanku, 2011.

Gruner, Wolf. *Jewish Forced Labor Under the Nazis: Economic Needs and Racial Aims, 1938–1944*. Translated by Kathleen Dell'Orto. New York: Cambridge University Press with the United States Holocaust Memorial Museum, 2006.

Hayes, Peter. *Why? Explaining the Holocaust*. New York: W. W. Norton, 2017.

Heckert, Elke, and Werner Röhr, ed. *Europa unterm Hakenkreuz: die faschistische Okkupationspolitik in Polen (1939–1945)*. Berlin: VEB Deutscher Verlag der Wissenschaften, 1989.

Heller, Celia S. *On the Edge of Destruction: Jews of Poland Between the Two World Wars*. Detroit: Wayne State University Press, 1994.

Himka, John-Paul. *Ukrainian Nationalists and the Holocaust. OUN and UPA's Participation in the Destruction of Ukrainian Jewry, 1941–1944*. Stuttgart: ibidem, 2021.

Höger, Katja. "Frauen als Kombattanten." In *Die polnische Heimatarmee. Geschichte und Mythos der Armia Krajowa seit dem zweiten Weltkrieg*. Edited by Bernhard Chiari, in collaboration with Jerzy Kochanowski. Munich: R. Oldenbourg Verlag, 2003, 387–410.

International Military Tribunal, *Trials of War Criminals before the Nuernberg Military Tribunals under Control Council Law no. 10, October 1946–April 1949*. Nuremberg, 1949.

Jaczyńska, Agnieszka. *Sonderlaboratorium SS. Zamojszczyzna „pierwszy obszar osiedleńczy w Generalnym Gubernatorstwie."* Lublin: Instytut Pamięci Narodowej, 2012.

Kershaw, Ian. *Hitler: A Biography*. New York: W. W. Norton, 2008.

Kiełboń, Janina. *Migracje ludności w dystrykcie lubelskim w latach 1939–1944*. Lublin: Państwowe Muzeum na Majdanku, 1995.

Kiełboń, Janina, and Zofia Leszczyńska. *Kobiety Lubelszczyzny represjonowane w latach 1944–1956*. Lublin: Wydawnictwo Test, 2002.

Kiriszczenko, Piotr. "Mother's Death." In *Majdanek Concentration Camp*. Edited by Czesław Rajca and Anna Wiśniewska. Translated by Anna Zagorska. Lublin: Państwowe Muzeum na Majdanku, 1983, 65–57.

Kłapeć, Janusz. *Rada Główna Opiekuńcza w dystrykcie lubelskim w latach 1940–1944*. Lublin: Wydawnictwo UMCS, 2011.

Klukowski, Zygmunt. *Tagebuch aus den Jahren der Okkupation 1939–1944*. Edited by Christine Glauning and Ewelina Wanke. Translated by Karsten Wanke. Berlin: Metropol Verlag, 2017.

Kochanski, Halik. *The Eagle Unbowed: Poland and the Poles in the Second World War*. Cambridge: Harvard University Press, 2012.

Koehl, Robert L. *RKFDV: German Resettlement and Population Policy, 1939–1945: A*

History of the Reich Commission for the Strengthening of Germandom. Cambridge: Harvard University Press, 1957.

Komorowski, Krzysztof. "Facetten des polnischen militärischen Widerstandes und seine Aktualität." In *Die polnische Heimatarmee. Geschichte und Mythos der Armia Krajowa seit dem zweiten Weltkrieg.* Edited by Bernhard Chiari, in collaboration with Jerzy Kochanowski. Munich: R. Oldenbourg Verlag, 2003, 679–90.

Kornbluth, Andrew. *The August Trials: The Holocaust and Postwar Justice in Poland.* Cambridge: Harvard University Press, 2021.

Kozaczyńska, Beata. "When There Were No More Tears Left to Cry: The Tragic Fate of the Polish Children Displaced from the Zamość Region in 1942–1943." In *Crime Without Punishment: The Extermination and Suffering of Polish Children During the German Occupation, 1939–1945.* Edited by Janina Kostkiewicz. Kraków: Jagiellonian University Press, 2021, 99–114.

Kranz, Tomasz. "Das KL Lublin—zwischen Planung und Realisierung." In *Die Nationalsozialistichen Konzentrationslager—Entwicklung und Struktur,* vol. 1. Edited by Ulrich Herbert, Karin Orth, and Christoph Dieckmann. Göttingen: Wallstein Verlag, 1998, 363–89.

———. "Das Konzentrationslager Majdanek 1941–1944. Zeittafel." In *Bildungsarbeit und historisches Lernen in der Gedenkstätte Majdanek.* Edited by Tomasz Kranz. Lublin: Państwowe Muzeum na Majdanku, 2000.

———. *The Extermination of Jews at Majdanek Concentration Camp.* Lublin: Państwowe Muzeum na Majdanku, 2010.

———."'Generalplan Ost' und 'Endlösung' im Distrikt Lublin." In *Bildungsarbeit und historisches Lernen in der Gedenkstätte Majdanek.* Edited by Tomasz Kranz. Lublin: Państwowe Muzeum na Majdanku, 2000.

———. "Konzentrationslager Lublin. Powstanie, organizacja, działalność." In *Więźniowie KL Lublin 1941–1944.* Edited by Tomasz Kranz and Wojciech Lenarczyk. Lublin: Państwowe Muzeum na Majdanku, 2020, 17–132.

Kranz, Tomasz, ed. *Unser Schicksal—eine Mahnung für Euch* (. . .) *Berichte und Erinnerungen der Häftlinge von Majdanek.* Lublin: Państwowe Muzeum na Majdanku, 1994.

Kranz, Tomasz, and Wojciech Lenarczyk, eds. *Więźniowie KL Lublin 1941–1944.* Lublin: Państwowe Muzeum na Majdanku, 2020.

Krausnick, Helmut, and Hans-Heinrich Wilhelm. *Die Truppe des Weltanschauungskrieges. Die Einsatzgruppen der Sicherheitspolizei und des SD, 1938–1942.* Stuttgart: Deutsche Verlagsanstalt, 1981.

Kroll, Bogdan. *Rada Główna Opiekuńcza, 1939–1945.* Warsaw: Książka i Wiedza, 1985.

Kwiatkowski, Jerzy. *485 Days at Majdanek.* Stanford: Hoover Institution, 2021.

Lanckorońska, Karolina. *Those Who Trespass Against Us: One Woman's War Against the Nazis.* Toronto: Pimlico, 2006.

Langnas, Saul. *Żydzi a studja akademickie w Polsce w latach 1921–1931 (studjum statystyczne).* Lwów: Żydowskie Akademickie Stowarzyszenie Samopomocy Środowiska Lwowskiego, 1933.

Lenarczyk, Wojciech, ed. *Majdanek w Dokumentach*. Lublin: Państwowe Muzeum na Majdanku, 2016.

Lenarczyk, Wojciech, and Dariusz Libionka, eds. *Erntefest: Zapomniany epizod Zagłady, 3–4 listopada 1943*. Lublin: Państwowe Muzeum na Majdanku, 2009.

Leszczyńska, Zofia. *Kronika obozu na Majdanku*. Lublin: Wydawnictwo Lubelskie, 1980.

———. "Transporty i stany liczbowe obozu." In *Majdanek 1941–1944*. Edited by Tadeusz Mencel. Lublin: Wydawnictwo Lubelskie, 1991, 93–128.

Libionka, Dariusz, ed. *Akcja Reinhardt. Zagłada Żydów w Generalnym Gubernatorstwie*. Warsaw: Instytut Pamięci Narodowej, 2004.

Longerich, Peter. *Politik der Vernichtung. Eine Gesamtdarstellung der nazionalsozialistischen Judenverfolgung*. Munich: Piper Verlag, 1998.

Machuła, Ryszard, and Anna Wiśniewska, ed. *Braterska Pomoc. Wspomnienia dotyczące pomocy społeczeństwa Lubelszczyzny ofiarom hitlerowskiego terroru*. Lublin: Państwowe Muzeum na Majdanku, 1978.

Madajczyk, Czesław. *Die Okkupationspolitik Nazideutschlands in Polen 1939–1945*. Translated by Bertold Puchert. Berlin: Akademie Verlag Berlin, 1987.

Madej, Jósef. "Erste Opfer." In *Unser Schicksal—eine Mahnung für Euch* (. . .) *Berichte und Erinnerungen der Häftlinge von Majdanek*. Edited by Tomasz Kranz. Lublin: Państwowe Muzeum na Majdanku, 1994, 17–27.

Mailänder, Elissa. *Female SS Guards and Workaday Violence: The Majdanek Concentration Camp, 1942–1944*. Translated by Patricia Szobar. Lansing: Michigan State University Press, 2015.

Majer, Diemut. *"Non-Germans" Under the Third Reich: The Nazi Judicial and Administrative System in Germany and Occupied Eastern Europe, With Special Regard to Occupied Poland, 1939–1945*. Translated by Peter Thomas Hill, Edward Vance Humphrey, and Brian Levin. Baltimore: Johns Hopkins University Press, 2003.

Majewski, Piotr. "Konzept und Organisation des 'zivilen Kampfes.'" In *Die polnische Heimatarmee. Geschichte und Mythos der Armia Krajowa seit dem zweiten Weltkrieg*. Edited by Bernhard Chiari, in collaboration with Jerzy Kochanowski. Munich: R. Oldenbourg Verlag, 2003, 303–24.

Mallmann, Klaus-Michael, Jochen Böhler, and Jürgen Matthäus. *Einsatzgruppen in Polen, Darstellung und Dokumentation*. Darmstadt: Wissenschaftliche Buchgesellschaft, 2008.

Malm, Saturnina. "Przed i za drutami." In *Braterska Pomoc. Wspomnienia dotyczące pomocy społeczeństwa Lubelszczyzny ofiarom hitlerowskiego terroru*. Edited by Ryszard Machuła and Anna Wiśniewska. Lublin: Państwowe Muzeum na Majdanku, 1978, 84–109.

Mańkowski, Zygmunt, ed. *Hitlerowskie więzienie na Zamku w Lublinie, 1939–1944*. Lublin: Wydawnictwo Lubelskie, 1988.

Marczak-Bukowska, Ewa. *Przyjaciele, koledzy, wrogowie? Relacje pomiędzy polskimi, żydowskimi i ukraińskimi studentami Uniwersytetu Jana Kazimierza we Lwowie w okresie międzywojennym (1918–1939)*. Warsaw: Neriton, 2019.

Markiewicz, Jerzy. *Nie dali ziemi skąd ich ród. Zamojszczyzna 27 XI 1942-31 XII 1943*. Lublin: Wydawnictwo Lubelskie, 1967.

Marszałek, Józef. *Majdanek: The Concentration Camp in Lublin*. Warsaw: Interpress, 1986.

Mazower, Mark. *Hitler's Empire: How the Nazis Ruled Europe*. New York: Penguin, 2009.

Mazur, Grzegorz. *Życie polityczne polskiego Lwowa, 1918–1939*. Kraków: Księgarnia Akademicka, 2007.

Mędykowski, Witold Wojciech. *Macht Arbeit Frei? German Economic Policy and Forced Labor of Jews in the General Government, 1939–1943*. Boston: Academic Studies Press, 2018.

Mehlberg, Henry. *Time, Causality, and the Quantum Theory: Studies in the Philosophy of Science*. Vol. 1, *Essay on the Causal Theory of Time*. Edited by Robert S. Cohen. Holland: D. Reidel Publishing Company, 1980.

Melchior, Małgorzata. *Zagłada a tożsamość. Polscy Żydzi na "aryjskich papierach." Analiza doświadczenia biograficznego*. Warsaw: IFiS PAN, 2004.

Mencel, Tadeusz. "Konzentrationslager Lublin. General Characteristics." In *Majdanek 1941–1944*. Edited by Tadeusz Mencel. Lublin: Wydawnictwo Lubelskie, 1991, 509–19.

Mencel, Tadeusz, ed. *Majdanek 1941–1944*. Lublin: Wydawnictwo Lubelskie, 1991.

Moldenhauer, Harald. "Der Sowjetische NKVD und die Heimatarmee im 'Lubliner Polen' 1944–1945." In *Die polnische Heimatarmee. Geschichte und Mythos der Armia Krajowa seit dem zweiten Weltkrieg*. Edited by Bernhard Chiari, in collaboration with Jerzy Kochanowski. Munich: R. Oldenbourg Verlag, 2003, 275–99.

Motyka, Grzegorz. *Wołyń '43*. Warsaw: Wydawnictwo Literackie, 2016.

Murawski, Roman. *The Philosophy of Mathematics and Logic in the 1920s and 1930s in Poland*. Basel: Birkhäuser, 2014.

Musial, Bogdan. *Deutsche Zivilverwaltung und Judenverfolgung im Generalgouvernement. Eine Fallstudie zum Distrikt Lublin 1939–1944*. Vol. 10, Deutsches Historisches Institut Warschau, *Quellen und Studien*. Wiesbaden: Harrassowitz Verlag, 1999.

Orth, Karin. *Die Konzentrationslager-SS: Sozialstrukturelle Analysen und biographische Studien*. Göttingen: Wallstein Verlag, 2013.

Ossowska, Wanda. *Przeżyłam. Lwów-Warszawa 1939–1946*. 2nd ed. Warsaw: Towarzystwo Opieki nad Majdankiem Oddział Warszawski, 1995.

Pakszys, Elżbieta. "Kobiety w filozofii polskiej. Dwa pokolenia Szkoły Lwowsko-Warszawskiej," Humanistyka i Płeć. Vol. 2, *Kobiety w poznaniu naukowym wczoraj i dziś*. Edited by Elżbieta Pakszys and Danuta Sobczyńska. Poznań: Wydawnictwo Naukowe UAM, 1997, 263–82.

Panasiewicz, Adam. "Poststelle." In *Braterska Pomoc. Wspomnienia dotyczące pomocy społeczeństwa Lubelszczyzny ofiarom hitlerowskiego terroru*. Edited by Ryszard Machuła and Anna Wiśniewska. Lublin: Państwowe Muzeum na Majdanku, 1978, 112–27.

Pauer-Studer, Herlinde, and J. David Velleman. *Konrad Morgen: The Conscience of a Nazi Judge*. London: Palgrave Macmillan, 2015.

Peploński, Andrzej. "Die Aufklärung der Heimatarmee." In *Die polnische Heimatarmee. Geschichte und Mythos der Armia Krajowa seit dem zweiten Weltkrieg*. Edited by Bernhard Chiari, in collaboration with Jerzy Kochanowski. Munich: R. Oldenbourg Verlag, 2003, 169–86.

Perzanowska, Stefania. *Gdy myśli do Majdanka wracają. Wspomnienia lekarki z obozu koncentracyjnego w Lublinie.* Warsaw: Prószyński i S-ka in cooperation with Państwowe Muzeum na Majdanku, 2022 (first published in 1970).

Plocker, Anat. *The Expulsion of Jews from Communist Poland: Memory Wars and Homeland Anxieties.* Bloomington: Indiana University Press, 2022.

Pohl, Dieter. "Die Stellung des Distrikts Lublin in der 'Endlösung der Judenfrage.'" In *"Aktion Reinhardt": Der Völkermord an den Juden im Generalgouvernement 1941–1944.* Edited by Bogdan Musial. Osnabrück: fibre Verlag, 2004.

———. "Massentötungen durch Giftgas im Rahmen der 'Aktion Reinhardt.'" In *Neue Studien zu Nationalsozilististischen Massentötungen durch Giftgas. Historische Bedeutung, technische Entwicklung, revisionistische Leugnung.* Edited by Gunter Morsch and Bertrand Perz. Berlin: Metropol Verlag, 2011, 185–95.

———. *Nationalsozialistische Judenverfolgung in Ostgalizien, 1941–1944. Organisation und Durchführung eines staatlichen Massenverbrechens.* Munich: R. Oldenbourg Verlag, 1996.

———. *Von der "Judenpolitik" zum Judenmord. Der Distrikt Lublin des Generalgouvernements 1939–1944.* Frankfurt: Peter Lang, 1993.

Poprzeczny, Joseph. *Odilo Globocnik: Hitler's Man in the East.* Jefferson, NC: McFarland, 2004.

Redner, Ben Z. *A Jewish Policeman in Lwów: An Early Account, 1941–1943.* Translated by Jerzy Michalowicz. Jerusalem: Yad Vashem, 2015.

Rogerie, André. "Transporty chorych." In *Majdanek: Obóz koncentracyjny w relacjach więźniów i świadków.* Edited by Marta Grudzińska. Lublin: Państwowe Muzeum na Majdanku, 2011, 210–14.

Roseman, Mark. *The Wannsee Conference and the Final Solution: A Reconsideration.* Rev. ed. London: Folio Society, 2012.

Schwindt, Barbara. *Das Konzentrations- und Vernichtungslager Majdanek. Funktionswandel im Kontext der "Endlösung."* Würzburg: Königshausen und Neumann, 2005.

Shatyn, Bruno. *A Private War: Surviving in Poland on False Papers, 1941–1945.* Translated by Oscar E. Swan. Detroit: Wayne State University Press, 1985.

Silberklang, David. *Gates of Tears: The Holocaust in the Lublin District.* Jerusalem: Yad Vashem, 2013.

Smorczewski, Ralph. *Bridging the Gap: Reminiscences.* Leicester: Matador, 2007.

Snyder, Timothy. *Black Earth: The Holocaust as History and Warning.* New York: Tim Duggan Books, 2015.

———. *The Reconstruction of Nations: Poland, Ukraine, Lithuania, Belarus, 1569–1999.* New Haven: Yale University Press, 2003.

Sommer Schneider, Anna. "Behind the Iron Curtain: The Communist Government in Poland and Its Attitude Toward the Joint's Activities, 1944–1989." In *The JDC at 100: A Century of Humanitarianism.* Edited by Avinoam Patt, Atina Grossmann, Linda G. Levi, and Maud S. Mandel. Detroit: Wayne State University Press, 2019, 315–60.

———. *Sze'erit hapleta. Ocaleni z Zagłady. Działalność American Jewish Joint Distribution Committee w Polsce w latach 1945–1989.* Kraków: Księgarnia Akademicka, 2014.

Stanisławski, Andrzej. *Pole śmierci*. Lublin: Wydawnictwo Lubelskie, 1969.

Streit, Christian. "Soviet Prisoners of War in the Hands of the Wehrmacht." In *War of Extermination: The German Military in World War II, 1941–1944*. Edited by Hannes Heer and Klaus Naumann. New York: Berghahn Books, 2000, 80–91.

Suchmiel, Jadwiga. *Działalność naukowa kobiet w Uniwersytecie we Lwowie do roku 1939*. Częstochowa: Wydawnictwo WSP, 2000.

Twardowski, Kazimierz. *Dzienniki*, 2 vols. Warsaw: Adam Marszałek, 1997.

Veidlinger, Jeffrey. *In the Midst of Civilized Europe: The Pogroms of 1918–1921 and the Onset of the Holocaust*. New York: Metropolitan Books, 2021.

Viola, Lynne. *Peasant Rebels Under Stalin: Collectivization and the Culture of Peasant Resistance*. New York: Oxford University Press, 1996.

Vrba, Rudolf, and Alan Bestic. *Escape from Auschwitz: I Cannot Forgive*. New York: Grove Press, 1964; New York: Black Cat, 1986.

Wachsmann, Nikolaus. *KL: A History of the Nazi Concentration Camps*. New York: Farrar, Straus & Giroux, 2015.

Węgrzyn, Ewa. *Wyjeżdżamy! Wyjeżdżamy?! Alija gomułkowska 1956–1960*. Kraków: Austeria, 2016.

Weinberg, Gerhard. *A World at Arms: A Global History of World War II*. Cambridge: Cambridge University Press, 1994.

Winstone, Martin. *The Dark Heart of Hitler's Europe: Nazi Rule in Poland Under the General Government*. London: I. B. Taurus, 2015.

Wiśniewska, Anna. "Pomoc więźniom Majdanka." In *Majdanek 1941–1944*. Edited by Tadeusz Mencel. Lublin: Wydawnictwo Lubelskie, 1991, 233–52.

Wnuk, Józef. *Dzieci polskie oskarżaja*. Lublin: Wydawnictwo Lubelskie, 1975.

Wójcik, Wiesław. "Budowanie środowiska matematycznego w Polsce w dwudziestoleciu międzywojennym." In *Stosunki Polsko-Żydowskie. Kultura, literatura, sztuka i nauka w XX wieku*. Edited by Zofia Trębacz. Warsaw: Żydowski Instytut Historyczny im. Emanuela Ringelbluma, 2020, 341–58.

Woleński, Jan. *Logic and Philosophy in the Lvov-Warsaw School*. Dordrecht: Kluwer Academic Publishers, 1989.

Wylegała, Anna. "Entangled Bystanders: Multidimensional Trauma of Ethnic Cleansing and Mass Violence in Eastern Galicia." In *Trauma, Experience and Narrative in Europe after World War II*. Edited by Ville Kivimäki and Peter Leese. Cham, Switzerland: Palgrave Macmillan, 2021, 119–48.

Zakrzewski, Jan. *A my żyjemy dalej (. . .) Wspomnienia więźnia Majdanka*. Lublin: Wydawnictwo Lubelskie, 1977.

Zaremba, Marcin. *Wielka trwoga: Polska 1944–1947. Ludowa reakcja na kryzys*. Kraków: Znak and Instytut Studiów Politycznych Polskiej Akademii Nauk, 2012.

Zimmerman, Joshua D. *The Polish Underground and the Jews, 1939–1945*. New York: Cambridge University Press, 2015.

ARTICLES

Asher, Harvey. "The Soviet Union, the Holocaust, and Auschwitz." *Kritika: Explorations in Russian and Eurasian History* 4, no. 4 (Fall 2003): 886–912.

Berkhoff, Karel C., and Marco Carynnyk. "The Organization of Ukrainian Nationalists and Its Attitude toward Germans and Jews: Iaroslav Stets'ko's 1941 Zhyttiepys." *Harvard Ukrainian Studies* 23, no. 3–4 (December 1999): 149–83.

Black, Peter. "Foot Soldiers of the Final Solution: The Trawniki Training Camp and Operation Reinhard." *Holocaust and Genocide Studies* 25, no. 1 (Spring 2011): 1–99.

———. "Rehearsal for 'Reinhard'? Odilo Globocnik and the Lublin Selbstschutz." *Central European History* 25, no. 2 (1992): 204–26.

Böhler, Jochen. "Post-war Military Action and Violence (East Central Europe)." *1914–1918 Online: International Encyclopedia of the First World War*, https://encyclopedia.1914-1918-online.net/article/post-war_military_action_and_violence_east_central_europe.

Brenk, Mikołaj. "Działalność Powiatowego Komitetu Opieki Społecznej w Koninie w latach 1945–1949." *Polonia Maior Orientalis* 3 (2016): 113–22.

Budnitsky, Oleg. "Jews, Pogroms, and the White Movement: A Historiographical Critique." *Kritika: Explorations in Russian and Eurasian History* 2, no. 4 (Fall 2001): 1–23.

Dziadosz, Edward, and Józef Marszałek. "Więzienia i obozy w dystrykcie lubelskim w latach 1939–1944." *Zeszyty Majdanka* 3 (1969): 54–122.

Grudzińska, Marta. "The Women's Medical Ward in *Frauenkonzentrationslager* Lublin (Majdanek)," presented at the 3rd international conference Medical Review Auschwitz: Medicine Behind the Barbed Wire, September 12–21, 2021, Kraków, https://www.mp.pl/auschwitz/conference/edition2021/session1/show.html?id=280502.

Grudzińska, Marta, and Marta Kubiszyn. "'To was tutaj tak strasznie biją? (. . .) Nie, nas nie. Tylko Żydów': Żydzi w obozie na Majdanku w świetle relacji polskich więźniów." *Studia Judaica* 21: 2: 42 (2018): 333–71.

Himka, John-Paul. "The Lviv Pogrom of 1941: The Germans, Ukrainian Nationalists, and the Carnival Crowd." *Canadian Slavonic Papers* 54: 2–4 (June-September-December 2011): 209–43.

Kopciowski, Adam. "Zajścia antyżydowskie na Lubelszczyźnie w pierwszych latach po drugiej wojnie światowej." *Zagłada Żydów Studia i Materiały* 3 (2007): 178–207.

Kritchevsky, David. "History of Recommendations to the Public about Dietary Fat." *The Journal of Nutrition* 128, no. 2 (February 1998): 449S–452S.

Krzyżanowski, Jerzy R., and Wacław W. Soroka. "The Polish Underground Resistance in the Lublin Area: A Duologue." *The Polish Review* 20, no. 4 (1975): 145–56.

Kuwałek, Robert, Tomasz Kranz, and Beata Ciwek-Siupa. "Odszyfrowane radiotelegramy ze stanami dziennymi z obozu koncentracyjnego na Majdanku (styczeń 1942–styczeń 1943 r.)." *Zeszyty Majdanka* 24 (2008): 210–32.

Łapot, Mirosław. "Incydenty antysemickie w szkołach lwowskich (1867–1939)." *Przegląd Nauk Stosowanych* 6 (2015): 107–19.

———. "Uczniowie żydowscy w szkołach średnich we Lwowie w dobie autonomii galicyjskiej." *Prace Naukowe Akademii im. Jana Długosza w Częstochowie* 26, no. 1 (2017): 309–21.

Marszałek, Józef. "Budowa obozu koncentracyjnego na Majdanku w latach 1942–1944." *Zeszyty Majdanka* 4 (1969): 21–90.

Mehlberg, Josephine J. "A Classification of Mathematical Concepts." *Synthese* 14, no. 1 (March 1962): 78–86.

Mehlberg, Józefa. Review of "Sur la Nation de Collectif" by Jan Herzberg. *The Journal of Symbolic Logic* 4, no. 3 (September 1939): 121.

Murawska, Zofia. "System strzeżenia i sposoby izolacji więźniów w obozie koncentracyjnym na Majdanku." *Zeszyty Majdanka* 1 (1965): 76–132.

Perzanowska, Stefania. "O niektórych hitlerowskich lekarzach w Majdanku." *Przegląd Lekarski—Oświęcim* (1966): 209–11.

———. "Pomoc lubelskich organizacji społecznych więźniom Majdanka." *Przegląd Lekarski—Oświęcim* (1965): 140–44.

———. "Szpital obozu kobiecego w Majdanku" ("The Women's Camp Hospital at Majdanek.") Translated by M. Kapera. *Przegląd Lekarski—Oświęcim* (1968): 169–80, https://www.mp.pl/auschwitz/journal/english/223573,majdanek-womens-camp-hospital#1.

Podbielska, Alicja. "'The Righteous' and March '68." *Kwartalnik Historii Żydów* 2, no. 270 (June 2019): 363–87.

Rędziński, Kazimierz. "Studenci żydowscy we Lwowie w latach 1918–1939." *Prace Naukowe Akademii im. Jana Długosza w Częstochowie* 25 (2016): 581–601.

———. "Towarzystwo Żydowskich Studentów Filozofii Uniwersytetu Jana Kazimierza we Lwowie (1922–1939)." *Rocznik Polsko-Ukraiński* 20 (2018): 11–35.

Reynolds, Jaime. "'Lublin' versus 'London'—The Party and the Underground Movement in Poland, 1944–1945." *Journal of Contemporary History* 16, no. 4 (October 1981): 617–48.

Rudling, Anders. "Historical Representation of the Wartime Accounts of the Activities of the OUN-UPA (Organization of Ukrainian Nationalists–Ukrainian Insurgent Army)." *East European Jewish Affairs* 36, no. 2 (2006): 163–89.

Szlachetka, Małgorzata. "Zapomniany obóz przy ul. Krochmalnej." *Gazeta Wyborcza*, November 16, 2007.

Weingartner, James J. "Law and Justice in the Nazi SS: The Case of Konrad Morgen." *Central European History* 16, no. 3 (September 1983): 276–94.

White, Elizabeth B. "Majdanek: Cornerstone of Himmler's SS Empire in the East." *Simon Wiesenthal Center Annual* (1990): 3–21.

Wiśniewska, Anna. "Organizacyjny i materialny wkład lubelskiej Rady Głównej Opiekuńczej w dzieło pomocy dla Polaków osadzonych na Majdanku." *Zeszyty Majdanka* 8 (1975): 5–33.

Witte, Peter, and Stephen Tyas. "A New Document on the Deportation and Murder of Jews During 'Einsatz Reinhardt' 1942." *Holocaust and Genocide Studies* 15, no. 3 (Winter 2001): 468–86.

Wójcik, Wiesław. "Fenomen polskiej szkoły matematycznej a emigracja matematyków polskich w okresie II wojny światowej." *Zagadnienia Filozoficzne w Nauce* 53 (2013): 11–52.

Woroniak, Anna. "Ocalić od zapomnienia. Nieznane hitlerowskie obozy przejściowe w Lublinie w latach 1940–1944." *Odkrywca*, December 2008: 36–39.

Wylegała, Anna. "About 'Jewish Things': Jewish Property in Eastern Galicia during World War II." *Yad Vashem Studies* 44 (2016): 83–119.

PHOTO CREDITS

1. "Janina's Story," Accession Number: 2003.333. Courtesy of the U.S. Holocaust Memorial Museum.
2. Photo courtesy of Jan Woleński (a gift from his teacher Izydora Dąmbska) and reproduced with permission.
3. P-OM-15_AKT-KP_058_karta-034. Commemorative Book in Honor of Kazimierz Twardowski. Courtesy of Digital Archive of Combined Libraries.
4. Courtesy of Anna Ożyńska-Zborowska and Wojciech Rostworowski.
5. CAF/PAP L-314-12.jpg. Archive of the Central Photographic Agency/Polish Press Agency.
6. Courtesy of the State Museum at Majdanek.
7. Photograph 73996. Courtesy of the U.S. Holocaust Memorial Museum.
8. Photograph 65975. U.S. Holocaust Memorial Museum, courtesy of Michel Reynders.
9. Photograph 06043. U.S. Holocaust Memorial Museum, courtesy of Jerzy Tomaszewski.
10. Courtesy of the State Museum at Majdanek.
11. Photograph 83854. Courtesy of the U.S. Holocaust Memorial Museum.
12. Photograph MHMLA_007aa. Courtesy of the National Museum in Lublin.
13. *Minneapolis Tribune* photo by Roy Swan.
14. "Janina's Story," USHMM Accession Number: 2003.333. Courtesy of the U.S. Holocaust Memorial Museum.
15. Courtesy of Irvin Klinghofer.
16. 036.04.07, Dan Ryan collection, 1954–1980, Section 27, University Archives and Special Collection. Courtesy of the Paul V. Gavin Library, Illinois Institute of Technology.

INDEX

Page numbers xi to xv refer to maps.